When Minds Converse

When Minds Converse

A Social Genealogy of the Human Soul

PHILIP PETTIT

OXFORD
UNIVERSITY PRESS

Great Clarendon Street, Oxford, OX2 6DP,
United Kingdom

Oxford University Press is a department of the University of Oxford.
It furthers the University's objective of excellence in research, scholarship,
and education by publishing worldwide. Oxford is a registered trade mark of
Oxford University Press in the UK and in certain other countries

© Philip Pettit 2025

The moral rights of the author have been asserted

All rights reserved. No part of this publication may be reproduced, stored in a retrieval system, transmitted, used for text and data mining, or used for training artificial intelligence, in any form or by any means, without the prior permission in writing of Oxford University Press, or as expressly permitted by law, by licence or under terms agreed with the appropriate reprographics rights organization. Enquiries concerning reproduction outside the scope of the above should be sent to the Rights Department, Oxford University Press, at the address above.

You must not circulate this work in any other form
and you must impose this same condition on any acquirer

Published in the United States of America by Oxford University Press
198 Madison Avenue, New York, NY 10016, United States of America

British Library Cataloguing in Publication Data
Data available

Library of Congress Control Number: 2024946875

ISBN 9780198863113

DOI: 10.1093/9780192608208.001.0001

Printed and bound by
CPI Group (UK) Ltd, Croydon, CR0 4YY

The manufacturer's authorised representative in the EU for product safety is
Oxford University Press España S.A. of El Parque Empresarial San Fernando de Henares, Avenida
de Castilla, 2 – 28830 Madrid (www.oup.es/en or
product.safety@oup.com). OUP España S.A. also acts as importer into Spain
of products made by the manufacturer.

For Tori

Contents

Acknowledgments	ix
Introduction: the hypothesis and the project	xi
1. Preliminaries to the argument	1
1.1 Human-specific capacities	1
1.2 The genealogical project	4
1.3 Introducing the humanoids	18
1.4 Signaling and speech	26
1.5 Interlude: following rules	34
2. Agency with judgment	49
2.1 Agency, basic and human	50
2.2 Signaling and asserting	57
2.3 Assertion and judgment	67
2.4 Judging and thinking	72
2.5 Interlude: degrees of belief	81
3. Rationality with reasoning	93
3.1 Rationality and reasoning	94
3.2 Reinforcing judgments	104
3.3 Reasoning, social and mental	114
3.4 Varieties of reasoning	120
3.5 Interlude: the role of rules	125
4. Perception with percipience	131
4.1 Perception in general	133
4.2 The advent of percipience	142
4.3 Percipient consciousness	155
5. Normativity and value	167
5.1 Injunctive social norms	169
5.2 Norms and commitments	183
5.3 Commitment and value	197
6. Responsibility and free will	207
6.1 The notion of holding responsible	208
6.2 Responsibility in the humanoids	218
6.3 From responsibility to free will	241

7. Personhood and self-identity	257
7.1 The idea of person and self	258
7.2 Personation and personhood	270
7.3 Persons and their selves	286
Conclusion: toward ethics and politics	301
In summary: a philosophical anthropology	317
Bibliography	341
Index	353

Acknowledgments

The topics addressed in this work are signaled by the titles of Chapters 2–7, which were presented in earlier versions as the 2019 John Locke lectures at Oxford University. Some material in the lectures was also tried out in various other forums, particularly in the Charles Taylor Lectures in Montreal, Sept. 2019; the Rotelli Lectures, presented virtually in Milan, June 2020; the Einstein Lectures in Berne in Oct. 2021; and the Brentano lectures in Vienna in Oct. 2022. The material was also tested in some individual lectures: notably, the Clair Miller Lecture in 2022 at the University of North Carolina, Chapel Hill; the Merlan Lecture in 2022 at the Claremont Colleges; and the Condorcet Lecture in 2023 at the Sorbonne. The discussion at these events was of great importance in shaping the ideas in the book—particularly discussion over the six weeks of the Locke Lectures—as were the sets of referee comments commissioned by my ever-supportive editors at Oxford University Press.

The text was shaped over a period of six years and perhaps the most important influence on its shaping was the extended discussion of the material in graduate seminars that I presented at the Australian National University in 2019 and early 2023, and at Princeton in an undergraduate seminar in 2018 and two graduate seminars: a virtual event in 2020, and an in-person event in 2022. I am deeply indebted to the participants in those seminars, since their contributions helped to shape and reshape my ideas, guarding me against a range of errors and oversights, though surely not against all. I taught the 2020 seminar jointly with Sam Berstler, then a colleague in Philosophy at Princeton, and I learned in particular from her contributions; I was greatly helped too by the detailed reports she sent from an MIT reading group that looked at an earlier version of the text.

In late 2023 I worked on preparing the book for publication as a Fellow at the Center for the Advanced Study of the Humanities, Humboldt University, Berlin, and I benefited from many discussions, especially with Barbara Vetter and David Boylan, within the project conducted on Human Abilities. While there, I was also able to consider and reply to commentaries, published in *Inquiry* in 2024, on my 2018 book *The Birth of Ethics*, learning from the criticisms provided by the commentators, Adam Lerner, Tristram McPherson, David Plunkett, and Manuel Vargas. Finally, I learned enormously from ongoing discussion with colleagues at the ANU and Princeton and I register my debts at various points in the book. But I should single out some with whom I spent many enlightening and enjoyable hours, exploring issues at the center of their expertise and often only at the margins of mine: Christopher Bottomley, Alan Hajek, Brian Hedden, Victoria McGeer, and Daniel Stoljar. I dedicate the book to Victoria who has a special place in my personal as well as my philosophical life.

Introduction: the hypothesis and the project

The achievements of our species are obvious but remarkable. They include our development of technologies of agriculture, manufacture, communication, and travel; our creation of different cultures, traditions, and communities; the economic, political, and international organization of our lives together; and the celebration of our universe in religion and art, as well as its exploration in history, philosophy, and science. Some of these achievements have worked for ill, endangering peace among our kind and even, wittingly or not, the prospect of continued, thriving life on earth. But they are still striking enough for it to make sense that an extra-terrestrial visitor might see us—in a way, unfortunately, that we often see ourselves—as masters of our world, not just one species sharing the planet with others.

One of the most significant intellectual challenges for us as a species is to make sense of why we are so different from other animals, even from those who are genetically close.[1] Seeking a response to the challenge, this book identifies six capacities that distinguish us from other species, and then seeks to explore their source. The line defended is that these capacities do not reflect a special faculty or set of faculties with which our forebears were born but rather skills that emerged with participation in language-based, conversive practices.

Although informed by findings in the natural and social sciences, the argument pursued in support of this idea is philosophical. The claim is that language and converse provide a means for the appearance of the relevant practices and a motive for individuals to participate in those practices, thereby developing the associated skills. The upshot is that the human mind or soul, which is distinguished by those skills or capacities, is a social creation. It is a precipitate—a spectacular, unplanned byproduct—of the conversive life that we and our forebears have evolved and enjoyed from the earliest days of our kind.

This general idea is not original, of course. Many contemporary and classical figures have argued that what entitles us to name our species *homo sapiens* is that we are in the first place *homo loquens*: a hominin that speaks and converses. Aristotle emphasized the theme when he cast the human being as *zōon logon echōn*, the animal that has *logos*: that is, speech or, by extension, reason. Perhaps one of the best-known recent advocates has been Stephen Hawking, who in a famous quote once said: 'mankind lived just like the animals. Then something happened which

---

[1] For a range of contributions on the different aspects of recent work on animal minds, see (Andrews and Beck 2018).

When Minds Converse. Philip Pettit, Oxford University Press. © Philip Pettit 2025.
DOI: 10.1093/9780192608208.001.0001

unleashed the power of our imagination. We learned to talk and we learned to listen.'[2]

The book defends a specific form of this general idea, arguing that distinctive human capacities like those of judgment and reasoning, making evaluations, and ascribing responsibility are dependent for their existence on the emergence of conversive practices; they are constituted by skills in exercising those practices socially and in interiorizing them psychologically. And the defense of that claim assumes the specific form of an as-if narrative or genealogy: an account of how those practices and skills would be robustly likely to emerge among creatures of our general character—I call them humanoids—as a result of developing communication in language. In this Introduction I provide an initial overview of the specific hypothesis defended and of the project undertaken in its defense.

Before looking at what is explored in the book, however, it may be worth mentioning something that is neglected: artificial intelligence. The hypothesis defended naturally raises a question about the prospects for artificially intelligent agents. But while I say something on the contrast between humans and simple robots, and of course on the contrast with other animals, I say nothing about the development of the artificial intelligence associated with large language models, as they are called.

This is because the remarkable capacity of a system like ChatGPT in assembling the answers to certain questions on the basis of statistical patterns in its inputs does not yet make it into an agent. Such a system does not engage agentially with the environment in a way that would enable it to pursue certain goals successfully across varying scenarios. No doubt there will soon be robots that do engage with the environment and embody a similar capacity, and they will count as agents by the line supported here. But will they enjoy the distinctive capacities of human or human agents? Will they be able to develop capacities for judgment and reasoning, for example, distinguish between what they value and what they want, and hold themselves responsible to those values? The lesson supported by our discussion is that short of achieving a conversive life with one another, or indeed with us, they will be unable to do so.

The hypothesis

An introductory analogy

The claim that language makes certain practices accessible is analogous to the claim that a zero-based arithmetical notation like our decimal system makes a

---

[2] https://www.youtube.com/watch?v=du_iG7Veupc.

series of operations possible that would have been effectively inaccessible without it: say, within the counting system of the Romans. Those operations include the addition of arbitrarily large numbers to one another, which becomes child's play with the help of the formula taught in elementary classrooms. And they naturally extend, with the further notational rules—if you like, the further algorithms—that are deployed in multiplication and division. Try adding or multiplying or dividing in Roman numerals and the point will be obvious.

The capacity that arithmetical practice elicits constitutes a skill, since it emerges only with experience in the moves that the practice makes possible. Nature does not provide children with the innate ability to add or multiply or divide, only with the innate ability, given a suitable notation, to play the adding or multiplying or dividing game. And however late and however slowly the decimal system emerged among our kind, every child can be inducted readily into the notation and the practice, benefiting from the insights of those who went before.

As operating under the rules of a zero-based notation makes arithmetical practice and skill accessible, so the hypothesis of this book is that converse in a natural, human language—canonically but not exclusively a verbal language—gives rise to the practices and capacities addressed. Like the ability to add or multiply or divide, those capacities have the status of skills that depend on induction in conversive habits.

The analogy with the zero-based notation is only of limited significance, however. Where that notation was purely a cultural invention, natural language presumably emerged, making converse possible, under the pressures of natural selection. And where the arithmetical practices that the mathematical notation made possible only appeared in historical time, the conversive practices enabled by language, on the hypothesis adopted here, have almost certainly been part of cultural, human capital for more than a hundred thousand years.

If language is the notation that allows conversive practices, as the decimal notation allows arithmetical, what might have led our forebears to have evolved those practices in the presence of language? Perhaps they appeared as cultural innovations like the skills of multiplying and dividing. Perhaps they emerged under the pressures of natural evolution, being selectively advantageous in the wake of language for those who developed them. Or perhaps they emerged under a mix of those mechanisms: perhaps, for example, they first appeared as cultural innovations, and natural evolution then played a role in selecting for higher levels of competence in their exercise. The hypothesis defended here does not force us to choose between those or other alternative stories of origin.

We return in the first chapter to the consistency of the hypothesis with such different stories of origin. The important point is that, however they emerged in the wake of language, the relevant conversive practices play a crucial role in grounding or constituting certain distinctive human capacities. Those capacities are dependent on access to language, and on the conversive practices that language enables, in the way that the skills of adding, multiplying, and dividing are dependent on access to a suitable mathematical notation and on the operations that it makes possible.

The targeted capacities

We target six capacities for how, on the face of it, they mark off our kind from other species; they may not be the only abilities that distinguish us, but they are prominent candidates for that role. Three are capacities of a broadly processing character: making judgments, reasoning to conclusions, and exercising what I call percipience. And another three are relational capacities that we display in interaction with one another: enjoining certain norms and values, holding ourselves and one another responsible to those values, and connecting with one another in the manner of persons. In virtue of their processing and relational span, the account given of those six capacities constitutes a philosophical anthropology, to rework a term from Kant, rather than a philosophical psychology. The book aspires, as in the subtitle, to provide an account of the human soul, not just of the human mind.

Taking up the processing abilities of human beings, the capacity for judgment, in the sense I give the word, enables us to make intentional efforts in researching and considering certain questions and, assuming we decide the evidence is sufficient, in forming beliefs about the answers. All animals routinely update their beliefs in more or less automatic reaction to changes in their environment: this may involve revising, contracting, or expanding the range of beliefs on which they act. But we human beings can also ask ourselves questions and when we decide that the evidence allows, make up our minds in response; we can act intentionally with a view to updating or confirming our beliefs, depending on what is required.

Turning to the second processing capacity, all animals are disposed within one or another set of limits, to move in automatic adjustment from forming certain beliefs to forming other beliefs that the new beliefs support. But we human beings do not depend on automatic adjustment alone. We can also ask ourselves about how far our existing beliefs support other beliefs—how far they present evidence in support of those further attitudes—and we can intentionally prompt ourselves, even in the absence of automatic adjustment, to adopt the supported beliefs as well; in the sense intended here, we can reason.

Finally, all animals depend on perception for the beliefs they form about their world. But other animals appear to be captives of perception, unable to interrogate it for how far it supports one or another judgment or for whether it is a reliable indication of how things are. We human beings, by contrast, can stand back from what we perceive and probe it actively on such issues. We recruit perception to the service of judgment and reasoning and assume a degree of control over the issues we want perception to address, over the extent to which it should determine what we come to believe, and over whether or not to take a perception to be reliable: to reflect reality rather than mere appearance. The capacity for such control constitutes percipience, in our sense of the term. While it is derivative from the more basic capacities for judgment and reasoning, it is very distinctive and worthy of notice in its own right.

The claim in the book is that these three processing capacities, paradigms of human competence, depend on language, that we develop them in conversive, interpersonal exchange, and that while we may exercise them in an intrapersonal, mental form, say in judging or reasoning for ourselves, we do that by virtue of interiorizing the social counterparts.

The three other capacities targeted are explicitly relational in character, being manifested in how we commit to commonly valued norms, hold ourselves and one another responsible for compliance with our commitments, and assume the status of persons in how as a consequence we interact with one another. As the capacity of percipience derives from the more basic capacities for judgment and reasoning, so the capacity for interacting as persons derives from the more basic capacities for committing to values and assuming and ascribing responsibility for living up to them. But like percipience, it is distinctive enough to be noteworthy in its own right.

The relational capacities are more immediately recognizable than their processing counterparts. We form and commit to certain common norms—as we also do to more personal projects—and enjoin conformity for all parties, representing it as categorically binding and impartially valuable. We hold ourselves and one another responsible for how far we live up to such norms and other commitments insofar as we take ourselves to be in control of how we perform and fit to be blamed or praised for that performance. And we assume the status of persons insofar as we assume responsibility in such a wide range of commitments that we effectively invite others, and indeed ourselves, to rely on the *persona* we thereby present; we authorize that self-representation in the sense of conveying the message: this is who I am, this is who you can rely on me to be.

These relational capacities mark off our kind from other animal species in the same way that our processing capacities do. The claim defended in their case is that we depend on language and converse for the interpersonal or relational exercise of those capacities, which is scarcely surprising, and that we also depend on language and converse for how we exercise them within ourselves in an intrapersonal, psychological mode.

The project

The genealogical methodology

Philosophy lacks the resources to explore the origins of these capacities in human prehistory or their current grounding in our neural and psychological make-up.

But it can resort to an exercise of disciplined conjecture—an extended thought experiment—in exploring a parallel thesis, and that is what is attempted here. I imagine certain creatures—the humanoids—who lack anything like human language but resemble human beings in other independent respects. And then I look at the effects that the appearance of language would have, under suitably realistic conditions, on humanoid capacities.

The question at issue in the exercise is whether the exposure to language and converse would elicit—presumptively for the first time—the capacities associated with judgment, reasoning and percipience, normativity, responsibility and personhood. Would the encounter with conversive language be robustly likely to have such an effect on humanoids: that is, robustly over a range of salient variations in their circumstances? Would it be likely to have that effect, independently of fortuitous contingencies like those invoked in just-so stories?

The book offers a positive response, maintaining that the humanoids would be robustly likely to evolve those capacities in response to the opportunities and pressures that a linguistically structured world would provide. In the conversive environment that language opens up, the humanoids would be motivated to take steps leading to the emergence of suitable processing and relational practices. And by virtue of the conversive equipment that language provides, they would have the means of taking those steps and developing the targeted capacities: these would emerge as skills in the exercise of the corresponding practices.

In the first of the following chapters, I look in greater depth at the range of capacities on which the book focuses, at the genealogical methodology invoked in explaining their emergence among the humanoids, and at how the humanoids might plausibly develop language and begin to move along the track charted in the genealogy. This chapter lays down important preliminaries but might be omitted in a quick reading of the book. In the six chapters that then follow I look in turn at how the relevant practices would be likely to emerge. I argue in each case that the humanoids would have the motives and the means to bring them into existence, developing the corresponding skills: that is, the capacities targeted here.

I present these developments as if each capacity must emerge earlier than the next. This temporal sequencing is useful for the flow of the narrative and is justified by the fact, underlined in the text, that while earlier practices might emerge in advance of later, none of the later practices could appear in advance of earlier. Despite that asymmetry, however, there is nothing to rule out the possibility that certain practices and skills might co-evolve among the humanoids at more or less the same time. Thus, for all that the temporal order of the chapters suggests, some of the processing practices of judgment, reasoning, and percipience, and some of the relational practices associated with normativity, responsibility, and personhood, might develop among the humanoids in a mutually reinforcing manner.

Some chapter sections of the text deal with topics that are not essential for following the genealogy offered and are often of a more technical cast. I describe these as interludes. They include a section on the problem of rule-following in the first chapter, a section on beliefs and degrees of credence in the second, and a section on rule-following and reasoning in the third chapter. There is also a sub-section in Chapter 1 on demystification and metaphysics that I cast as an interlude. Like the sections mentioned, it can be skipped without serious loss to an understanding of the project.

From humanoid to human

While this counterfactual genealogy looks at how relevant practices and the corresponding skills would likely emerge among the humanoids, the point is to explore the nature and the role of those skills or capacities among us. If the humanoids would be robustly likely to evolve those practices in the wake of language and converse, eliciting the corresponding skills, that suggests that in our case too the practices may depend on language, and that the capacities that mark us off as a species are constituted by associated practice-dependent skills. The suggestion is that, however such conversive practices appeared among our human forebears—as we shall see, they need not have emerged on the pattern described in the genealogy— our distinctive capacities may amount like those of the humanoids to skills in the exercise of such practices.

The genealogy will support our hypothesis about human capacities insofar as it achieves two effects in each case. First, it tells a plausible story about how the humanoids would be prompted by language, in suitably realistic conditions, to develop suitable social practices. And second, it gives a plausible account of how those practices would be likely to elicit the corresponding capacities in an interiorized, mental version. To the extent that the humanoids are modeled on our human kind, a genealogy of the relevant capacities will suggest that the capacities may have the same socially sourced, practice-dependent character in our case too. It will offer some support for a view that Michael Dummett (1973, 362) defends in the case of one of those capacities when he says that judgment is 'the interiorization of the external act of assertion'.[3]

If it is accepted, that suggestion argues for rejecting any view that takes the relevant capacities to be faculties that are born with us—or to be aspects of a single general faculty—ready to be activated by suitable triggers in the course of maturation.[4] It supports the idea that like the humanoid protagonists in the genealogy, our human forebears were enabled by conversing in language to develop suitable social practices, to interiorize those practices mentally, and to develop the

---

[3] For a similar view, see (Brandom 2000, Ch. 1).
[4] On that view, the capacities would have the status of cognitive instincts carried in our genes. For a discussion of that and other approaches, see (Heyes 2018, 9–11).

corresponding skills. And it thereby supports the claim that we in later generations come into possession of those capacities by virtue of being inducted into social practices and learning to interiorize them. It projects a society-first image of the human mind.

A historical precedent

In the history of philosophy, the view sketched here is a relative of a view maintained in the unduly neglected work of Thomas Hobbes on the nature of human beings (Pettit 2008a).[5] According to Hobbes, language makes it possible for human beings to engage with one another socially in forming shared, abstract conceptions of things; to debate and reason with one another about what is or is not the case; to make individual commitments to one another; and to operate as persons in their relationships. And in making those external activities possible, on his view, language also makes their mental analogues possible: thinking and reasoning with oneself, for example, committing to act in a certain manner, and assuming the identity of a stable persona.[6]

Hobbes (1994a) first sketched this view in a manuscript he circulated when he moved to Paris in 1640. In 1637, Descartes (1985, 139–40) had argued that what makes human beings special is the inner reality of a thinking mind, a *res cogitans*, and that however impressive our external, linguistic performance, it is merely the sign of that special reality within. Descartes himself thought that the reality within is non-physical, but the contrast with the Hobbesian view would survive even on a physicalist account of what it involves.[7] Whatever we do externally in the use of words, for example in conversive practices of reasoning with one another, the Cartesian idea is that we do it by exercising the pre-existing faculties associated with forming *pensées* and *volontés*, internal acts of thought and will. Hobbes maintained, to the contrary, that the social, language-dependent practices come first and that it is only by virtue of participating in those practices that human beings are able to display counterpart activities in the privacy of the mind. The social use of language, by this account, is not a sign of the special character of the human mind, but rather the source.

---

[5] This aspect of his thought is likely to have had an important, if unacknowledged influence on Jean-Jacques Rousseau and, via Rousseau, on the romantic tradition of the late eighteenth century.

[6] While this reading is defended at length in my book on Hobbes, *Made with Words* (2008a), it has not been much emphasized in other interpretations. Yves Charles Zarka (1995, 20) paraphrases the Hobbesian position nicely, however, when he writes: '*l'homme n'est pas simplement un etre qui parle, c'est un etre qui devient ce qu'il est par la parole*'; 'the human being is not simply an entity that speaks, it is an entity that becomes what it is by speech'.

[7] The contrast would also survive if the reality within was taken to be linguistic in a purely mental way: if it was taken to involve a language of thought, for example (Fodor 1975).

If the genealogy is successful, then that will argue in some measure against anything like the Cartesian view of the human mind or soul and in favor of a broadly Hobbesian picture. At the least it will provide an intelligible and plausible alternative to Descartes' faculty-based view, underwriting a story about how the targeted capacities are constituted and about what role they play: a story, in other words, about their nature and function. Thus, the genealogy will suggest, as in the humanoid case, that each of the capacities is primarily a social, practice-dependent skill, on a par with the ability to add or multiply or divide, and that the purely mental exercise of that skill comes about, like mental arithmetic, by way of interiorization. And, given that account of its nature, the genealogy will imply that the function of the supporting practice in human life is to generate the sort of benefits, social and mental, for which it would emerge and stabilize among the humanoids.

Recasting the philosophical payoff

In supporting this neo-Hobbesian view, then, the genealogy will not only purport to explain why human beings might have the targeted capacities, but also provide candidate accounts of the nature and function of those abilities, explaining how they are constituted among human beings. More specifically, it will direct us to candidates for the role of conceptual and theoretical deservers of the terms in which we ascribe the six targeted capacities to ourselves (Pettit 2020). The skills that the genealogy identifies as referents will ideally satisfy enough connotations of the terms that we use or might use to describe the capacities—'judgment', 'reasoning', and so on—to count as conceptual deservers of those names. And, ideally, the referents will make sufficient sense of the importance we assign to those capacities in human life to count as theoretical deservers as well.

The capacities associated with judgment, reasoning, and percipience, normativity, responsibility, and personhood have long been staples of inquiry in philosophy and in fields as disparate as theology and anthropology, psychology, and neuroscience. If it is true that conceptually and theoretically deserving counterparts would emerge among the humanoids by virtue of exposure to language and converse, then that suggests that as the counterfactual capacities are constituted, so too may be the actual. There is no guarantee that the correspondence is perfect, of course, but there is ground for posing what Sidney Morgenbesser used to call the Yiddish *modus tollens*. If not this, what? If the human capacities are not constituted like the humanoid, how on earth are they constituted?

Insofar as the genealogy bears in this way on human as well as humanoid nature, it should also have implications for the ideals that are central to human life. If we come into our own, like the humanoids, by virtue of conversive interaction, developing our distinctive processing and relational capacities within the practices it makes available, then that is bound to suggest ideals for the form that interaction and organization should assume. I take up that suggestion in the Conclusion, arguing that the conversive character we and the humanoids enjoy provides us with a ground for construing the ideals of equality, respect, and freedom in a distinctive manner, and for taking those universal ideals—subject, no doubt, to different cultural specifications—to be central in our relationships and societies. This discussion indicates the way in which the philosophical anthropology defended here connects with central issues of ethics and politics.

In the chapters that address the six targeted capacities, I look primarily at how access to language would lead the humanoids to evolve corresponding practices—first in an interpersonal form, then in an intrapersonal—and at how the practices would elicit skills that answer to the capacities. But I do not argue in any of these specific cases that as it is with the humanoids, so it is with our own kind; I take that overall claim to be plausible in light of the genealogy, but I do not take pains to defend it capacity by capacity.

I go some way toward redressing this lack, however, by providing at the end of the book an account of how human capacities must look if they are modeled on those of the humanoids. This account sketches the philosophical anthropology that the book aims to support. To the extent that it is plausible, it will vindicate our reliance on the genealogy, and serve at the same time as a reminder or summary of how the genealogical argument goes.

A coda and a caution

The project undertaken here takes me toward the limits of my competence, and it is reasonable to wonder, as I wonder myself, about why I have embraced it. The motives that have spurred me on include the following, I think, which I list in no particular order: a wish, perhaps somewhat grandiose, to find a grounding for ethical and political ideals in a unified view of human nature; intellectual excitement at the challenge of exploring and conducting a long-haul thought experiment; the pleasure of doing philosophy in a way that engages the imagination as much as the intellect; a belief that a good way of learning about anything is by making the familiar look strange—in this case, by viewing human nature from the perspective of the humanoid; and, of course, the ambition, constitutive of philosophy, to speak to larger themes.

I was first awakened to that ambition when as a student in Ireland I discovered the work of Jean-Paul Sartre. For reasons good or bad, I was not persuaded by the Sartrean vision in which an unconstrained human will imposes a rich cultural veneer on a bare meaningless world. But I was swept away by the range of that vision and, of course, by the style with which he developed it in his early philosophical and literary work. I became a convert to the idea that even those of us incapable of the imaginative leaps in which he excelled should not despair of finding a pedestrian path to a standpoint of comparable range.

I believe I have learned a great deal in working through the thought experiment both in exchange with others and on my own. But of course, I may be wrong about that. Perhaps I ought already to have known much of what I learned; or perhaps the lessons it seemed to support are actually false. Still, I remain optimistic and look forward to seeing how others respond. I recognize that I must have gotten a range of things wrong, but I hope at least that my attempt will motivate others to do better.

While I have found the project appealing, I fear that the documentary of human capacities that it attempts may sometimes look like a one-sided celebration. As we noted earlier, painting a picture of the capacities that the humanoids would be robustly likely to evolve—and that we human beings certainly display—runs the risk of highlighting the positive features of our species and downplaying its negative bugs. For that reason, it is important to stress that for all the wonder that those capacities may evoke, their exercise in the human case has been responsible for ill as well as good.

As it happens, Thomas Hobbes took the same cautious attitude when he defended a social, practice-dependent view of human capacities. He argued in general that the very capacities that mark us off from other animals, by grace of our access to language, have disabling as well as enabling effects. Thus, he held that our ability to make assertions and judgments, assuming related attitudes, often leads us to do this carelessly, without attention to the evidence; that our capacity to reason makes it too easy to lead others, or indeed ourselves, into fallacy and fancy; and that both combine to make us worry excessively about what is to come: this, to the point that we are 'famished even by future hunger' (Hobbes 1998a, 10.3, 39–40). Again, he argued that our capacity to relate to others and compare ourselves to them often corrupts our desires, leading us to seek pre-eminence among our fellows; the fact that something seems good to us, he says, 'is nothing if everybody has it, since it consists in comparison and pre-eminence' (Hobbes 1998b, 1.2).

Thus, while Hobbes (1998a, 10.3, 39–40) insists that language enables human beings to lead a life that has 'far surpassed the condition of other animals', he was extremely cautious—and we would be right to display a similar caution—about embracing an excessive optimism about our kind. This book ought strictly to be accompanied by a study that would plumb the nether dimension of the space that language has opened up for our species. The Hobbesian lesson that we should keep in mind is cast by him in a terse but elegant Latin observation: *oratione homo non melior fit sed potentior*. Translating somewhat freely, we might keep the refrain as a *basso continuo* to accompany the following discussions: 'Language makes human beings more powerful, but it does not make them better.'[8]

---

[8] This is translated in (Hobbes 1998a, 10.3, 41) thus: 'by speech man is not made better, but only given greater possibilities'.

1
Preliminaries to the argument

Before beginning our narrative of humanoid development, we need to do a little more by way of explaining its target, its character, and its significance. In the following five sections we look first at the practices and capacities that are targeted here; characterize the genealogical project undertaken and the illumination it promises; defend the assumptions that the genealogy makes about the humanoids and their situation; explain what it would be for them to develop a simple language; and, in an interlude section that goes further afield, sketch an account of how they might master the rule-following that competence in such a language presupposes. The chapter may be harder going that the later chapters and can perhaps be omitted on a quick reading.

1.1 Human-specific capacities

1.1.1 Six activities and capacities

Apart from the mastery of natural language, there are at least six major activities and capacities that are significant and distinctive of human beings. We reviewed these briefly in the Introduction: first, intentionally making judgments, when the evidence allows, about what is or is not the case; second, intentionally reasoning about how far certain evidence warrants a conclusion on such a factual or related matter; and third, the derivative activity of exercising judgment and reasoning in probing perceptions for what they involve and support: for short, the exercise of percipience.

These three activities and capacities have a cognitively processing character and are lacking, so far as we can see, in other species. Other animals certainly form beliefs and desires, automatically updating their attitudes in light of incoming data, but they show no evidence of seeking to make judgments and determining what attitudes to form. Equally, other animals naturally move from certain beliefs and desires to other attitudes that these rationally require, but they do not display a capacity to do this in active reasoning. Finally, other animals attend to the perceptual data before them in one or another case, adjusting attitudes appropriately in response to those inputs, but they do not interrogate and appreciate the data for what they are and what they entail; they do not exercise the capacity of percipience. The contrast on all three fronts is captured nicely in the observation that despite the many glorious capacities of non-human species, no other animal ever seems to act in the manner epitomized in Rodin's famous sculpture, *Le Penseur*; none ever demonstrates the capacity to rack their brains about what to believe or what to seek: none ever seems to reflect and think.

While these first three capacities serve us in cognitive processing, the other three have a socially relational character. First, establishing shared social norms, making commitments in which we bet on ourselves to conform to those norms, and evolving evaluative practices that reflect those developments. Second, holding one another—and ourselves—responsible for living up to such values, censuring failure and commending success. And third, the capacity that appears when we make such a wide range of commitments—and acknowledge our responsibility for discharging them—that we authorize a corresponding self-representation and assume the status of a person: we invite others, and indeed ourselves, to rely on our living up to that persona.

These relational capacities also lack any parallels in the case of other species. Thus, other animals sometimes display extraordinary fidelity to their groups or mates or young, but they give no evidence of valuing such behavior in the sense of backing themselves to display it. Again, other animals often respond negatively to the uncongenial behavior of conspecifics, as in tit-for-tat responses within a sequence of interactions, but this is very different from the way in which we human beings hold ourselves and one another responsible. Finally, other animals are rarely wayward in the attitudes they display across time and place, but they do not put themselves forward as reliable interlocutors in the fashion of human beings, assuming and authorizing a certain persona: a model of who they are.

1.1.2 Public and private spheres of exercise

The striking thing about these six capacities is that they manifest themselves in two quite different spheres. One is in the realm of external, social activities, the other in the realm of internal or mental acts. They are exercised both in interpersonal activities that we conduct in public and in intrapersonal activities that we pursue privately within ourselves.

Thus, to illustrate the public aspect, we certainly exercise judgment when we consider questions on which others seek our opinions, and deliver a sincere response. Equally, we reason about the answer that such a question deserves when we defend it to others, offering considerations that we take to support it. And of course, we often conduct such public activities when we appeal to what we take to be commonly available and appreciated in perception. Indeed, not only do we act socially when we make a case for one or another claim to others, we also act socially by putting our heads together, as in comparing our judgments on questions with which we are both concerned, in reasoning with one another about what judgments we should uphold together, or in exercising those capacities when we attend jointly with others to the data available in perception.

Interpersonal and social though these activities are, they also have an intrapersonal, mental dimension. The activities envisaged will only serve our shared purposes insofar as they are sincere, and sincerity already imposes some psychological constraints. To be sincere, what we publicly judge to be the case must be what we judge to be the case, period; how we publicly reason in defense of a judgment must be how we reason, period; and how we publicly claim to perceive things must be how we perceive them, period. On our ordinary way of thinking, doing these things, period, means giving them a presence, not just in the social, linguistic world—even insincere overtures would have such a presence—but in mental space as well.

Given the mental aspect of these processing activities in their social role, it is not surprising that they can also figure, in our ordinary conception of them, as activities that may play a purely intrapersonal or psychological part. As an act in one of these domains can retain its social aspect without the mental—that is the lesson of insincerity—so an act can retain its mental aspect without its social. This happens when we think silently about whether to go along with another on some issue. But it happens even more saliently when we assume the part of the other in raising questions for ourselves and play the role of interlocutor in the effort to resolve them. We do this in making judgments on questions that we pose for ourselves, in reasoning with ourselves about how to answer such questions, and in conducting such private judgment and reasoning in interrogating how things present in perception.

The same public–private pattern appears in the case of the relational as well as the processing activities. We may publicly commit to certain norms and values, hold one another responsible to them, and invite one another to rely on us as a person. But if we do so sincerely, then we will do these things privately as well as publicly; if we do them insincerely, we will do them publicly alone. And if we do them in our hearts without any public expression, we will do them only in a private space.

When we do these things intrapersonally, as in the case of the processing capacities, we may even take ourselves as the addressees. Thus, as we back ourselves with others to live up to certain norms and values, so we may commit ourselves to ourselves in that same respect; we may make resolutions to live up to them, as distinct from just forming intentions to do so, or predicting that we will. As we hold others to account for their failure to live up to their commitments, so we may hold ourselves to account for failing to uphold our own. And as we hold up a persona on which we invite others to rely, so we hold up such a persona to ourselves, seeing it as a model of who we are or aspire to be: casting it as the self we authorize or identify with.

1.1.3 A priority issue

The fact that our six activities and capacities figure in both the external and the internal forums raises a question as to which aspect of our performance is primary. It is this priority issue that lies at the source of the division, already mentioned in the Introduction, between René Descartes and Thomas Hobbes in the early 1640s (Pettit 2008a). Let us assume with them that the social and mental forms of the capacities are not explained by a common factor; it is not clear, after all, what that might be. The question, then, is whether the competence in social performance that language makes possible explains our competence in the mental version, or whether things are the other way around. Does our life in the outer exercise of these capacities make our inner life possible? Or is the independent appearance of the inner life a prerequisite of the outer?

The hypothesis that this book supports is that the capacities are primarily social: they materialize in each of us as we are inducted into certain social practices that language makes accessible and appealing; and once established, they are co-opted into a psychological role as we interiorize them and exercise them for our own private benefit. It defends a society-first view of the human mind and soul. The book provides support for that view by developing a narrative about how the capacities would emerge among our humanoid counterparts: in other words, by resorting to the method of conceptual or pragmatic genealogy (Queloz 2021).

1.2 The genealogical project

1.2.1 The idea

Take any phenomenon that calls for philosophical explanation, such as the nature of law or the function of conventions.[1] The genealogical method consists, first, in considering a situation in which creatures like us in a world that is like ours in relevant ways live in the absence of such an institution: law or convention in these examples; and then, in exploring how far there is reason to think that without any planning or contract, those counterparts of ours would be robustly likely to adjust to their world—likely regardless of a salient range of contingencies—in a way that brings something like that institution into existence.

---

[1] The method has been used in philosophy in many other areas too. It is used explicitly by Wilfred Sellars (1997) in his attempt to explain the way we ascribe and conceptualize psychological states; by Edward Craig (1990) in an account of the service provided by the ascription of knowledge; and by Bernard Williams (2002) to explain the role of sincere and scrupulous truth-telling and associated concepts. I have also used it myself in an attempt to explain the nature and role of ethics (Pettit 2018a). For an excellent account of this methodology—better, perhaps this family of methodologies—see (Queloz 2021).

The reference to robust likelihood is important, distinguishing the method from two salient alternatives: on the one side, the weaker approach that would seek just to show that the targeted institution could have appeared without any miracle among creatures like us; and, on the other, the stronger approach that would explain how the institution could plausibly have appeared in the actual history of our own kind. It is distinct on the one side from how-possibly explanations, as they might be called, and on the other from how-plausibly accounts. While how-possibly and how-plausibly explanations can be of great importance in other contexts, they are distinct from the sort of genealogical explanation pursued here.[2]

There is more to say, however. The genealogy presented seeks to show how the appearance of language and converse among the humanoids would be robustly likely to lead to their development of the six capacities targeted. But it presupposes that language itself could have appeared without the prior existence of those capacities; otherwise, the genealogy would serve no useful purpose. And so, in the final two sections of this chapter we will be looking at how language could appear without such capacities, since that is a preliminary claim that needs defending. But in arguing for the view that it can, we shall only be providing a how-possibly account of its emergence. The weak claim about language is that it could appear among the humanoids without any sort of miracle, not that it was robustly likely to appear; for all we need assume, it may have depended on a fortuitous development in their evolutionary history. The strong claim about the targeted capacities is that once language and converse are present among them, it is robustly likely that the humanoids will develop those abilities.

To the extent that a genealogy argues that the phenomenon it addresses would be robustly likely to materialize under conditions that are relevantly like those that prevail among us, it promises to deliver three potential benefits. First, it shows that there is nothing inherently mysterious about the nature of the phenomenon at issue; second, it suggests that its role is to play a benefit in the actual world corresponding to the benefit that supports its emergence in the counterfactual; and third, it directs us to a way in which the phenomenon could have come into existence in the actual world, without implying that that is the way in which it actually or even probably emerged. Standard examples of the sort of genealogy envisaged bear out these claims.

---

[2] Cailin O'Connor (2019, 6–8) contrasts how-potentially explanations in a similar fashion with how-possibly explanations. How-possibly explanations are offered, plausibly, by those who follow the creature-construction methodology that H. P. Grice (1975b) championed. Foreshadowed by Jonathan Bennett (1964) in his study of rationality, it is invoked by Michael Bratman (2014) in analysis of shared agency, for example, and by Peter Railton (2014) in analysis of belief. Arguably, it was also employed in Donald Davidson's (1984) attempt, beginning in the 1960s, to render our semantic mastery of a natural language intelligible by showing that it could be generated by learning a Tarski-like truth theory for the language. How-plausibly explanations have not been so common, but a good example is Barbara Vetter's (2022) attempt to make sense of how we come to think in modal terms.

1.2.2 Illustrating the idea

Herbert Hart (1961; 2012) offered a classic explanation of positive law on these genealogical lines. He maintained that in a pre-legal, relatively egalitarian world, people like us would organize society around informal, beneficial norms; that these would raise problems as a result of being indeterminate and inflexible in themselves and contested in their application; that people would be robustly likely to develop one or another solution to each issue, giving rise to secondary rules for determining and applying the primary; and, intuitively, that such a system of primary and secondary rules or norms would constitute a legal system.

David Lewis (1969) took a similar, genealogical approach to the explanation of convention. He pointed out that a counterfactual world without conventions would give rise to coordination predicaments: situations where everyone wants to do the same as others, as in driving on the same side of the road or using the same code of politesse, but no one is sure of what others will do. And then he argued that the inhabitants of that world would adjust spontaneously, in light of salient or preceding solutions, so as to resolve such predicaments; and that the resolutions would give rise to practices answering intuitively to our notion of a convention, or at least a regimented version of that notion.[3]

Both Hart and Lewis take their genealogies to reveal the mundane nature and function of laws and conventions; to that extent the stories have a demystifying effect. Both present the institutions they address as byproducts of intelligible responses on the part of human beings, as they are byproducts of that kind among the protagonists in the narratives. And both argue that that those institutions serve a useful role or function, akin to the role that explains their emergence in the counterfactual world. Hart suggests that it is in the nature of a legal system to regiment and regulate the operation of the informal norms needed to govern any community, and Lewis that it is in the nature of conventions to make it manifest to people how to resolve the coordination predicaments likely to arise in any social interactions.

Apart from explaining the nature and function of such institutions, the genealogies have the incidental effect of indicating that it is at least possible that laws and conventions emerged in actual societies on the same lines, or partly on the same lines, as in the counterfactual model. They show that it need not have taken a god or a genius, or indeed a contract between relevant parties, to establish them. But neither Hart nor Lewis attaches much importance to that third implication of the genealogies they provide.

The genealogies presented by Hart and Lewis contrast with the genealogy of morals associated with the work of Friedrich Nietzsche (1997) in the nineteenth

---

[3] For a detailed account and development of genealogies that build on Lewis's in the case of convention, Hart's in the case of law, see (Pettit 2023b, Ch. 1).

century. They vindicate the institutions they target in the sense of purportedly revealing a nature and a function that explains their appeal. By contrast, a Nietzschean genealogy would debunk the claim of an institution to be of utility for people overall; it would suggest, as Nietzsche suggests about morality, that it is an institution designed only to serve the interests of a section of the community. And where Hart and Lewis do not offer their genealogies as an account of how laws and conventions actually evolved, Nietzsche often treats his genealogy as an account of the actual history of morality.

It is important to see that the accounts that Hart and Lewis offer of the nature and function of the institutions they address will retain their plausibility, even if it is granted that, historically, laws and conventions actually evolved, in most or all countries, in quite a different manner from that envisaged in the genealogies. The point of the genealogy in each case is to draw a lesson about the nature and function of those institutions from the fact that had they not appeared under any other pressure, still, as the genealogy supposes, they would have been robustly likely to emerge in an unplanned way—at least under suitably egalitarian conditions—as a result of people's spontaneous responses to the problems and opportunities that they would have faced.[4]

That counterfactual observation is important, not because it indicates a possible way in which the institutions might have actually emerged, but because it teaches an important lesson about the actual nature and function of law and convention. If those institutions would have been robustly likely to appear in the counterfactual scenario, where there was no intelligent designer to give them life and no contract among relevant parties to sustain them, then the reasons why they would still have appeared may direct us to something significant about their actual nature and the function they actually serve: the utility they have.

1.2.3 The idea extended to the targeted capacities

The project undertaken in this book is an exploration of the six human-specific capacities targeted, in the genealogical spirit of Hart and Lewis rather than Nietzsche. It explores those capacities by arguing that the appearance of language would prompt the humanoids under suitably egalitarian conditions to generate certain conversive practices and, in the exercise of such practices, to develop those capacities, first as social skills and then as skills that can be put to a purely psychological use. Insofar as humanoids are reliable models for human beings, and their

---

[4] The qualification about the egalitarian conditions is not explicit in Hart or Lewis but is taken for granted, as I read them; after all, deep inequalities would undermine the possibility of common laws or symmetrical conventions. Is the qualification realistic enough to make the genealogies suitable? The considerations I offer in the next section when I look at the equality presupposed in the genealogy presented here would suggest that it may be.

world is suitably similar to ours, the genealogy supports a practice-dependent view of the capacities.

The genealogy begins with a world in which our humanoid counterparts lack the capacities targeted but still gain access to language. Whether by virtue of natural selection for a special capacity for language—say, a recursive ability—or the effect of a range of existing capacities combining appropriately, or of the two at once, they come to use language to a communicative end; for simplicity we shall assume that the language is oral and verbal in character. According to the argument developed in the genealogy, then, the opportunities and pressures activated in this novel linguistic environment would be robustly likely to bring certain practices into existence among the humanoids, first in a social form and then in a psychological, and that the skills elicited by the exercise of those practices would constitute capacities like those linked to judgment, reasoning, and percipience, normativity, responsibility, and personhood. If we can tell a plausible narrative that supports this counterfactual genealogy of such practices and skills, then that will suggest that Hobbes was correct in taking the social to be explanatorily prior to the mental: this, among the humanoids and, by plausible extension, among humans.

If successful, this genealogy will deliver general benefits akin to those illustrated in the other cases. It will demystify the nature and function of the relevant practices and thereby the nature and function of the associated capacities, presenting these as skills in the interpersonal and, by extension, the intrapersonal exercise of the practices. And in the course of doing so, it will provide an indication, however incidental to the purpose of the genealogy, of how at least in principle the practices and capacities may have evolved among our kind.

The point of the genealogy, by this account, is to address the priority issue that divided Descartes from Hobbes, and to supply reason to think that the six capacities targeted are practice-bound: that they consist in skills of conforming to interpersonal practices and, with interiorization of those practices, to their intrapersonal counterparts. This claim is starkly opposed to the Cartesian view that the capacities exist independently as upstream realities and that conformity to the corresponding practices is a downstream effect of their exercise. For Descartes, those capacities are realized in a non-material mind, but a similar, broadly Cartesian view might maintain that they are physical configurations in the brain. For Descartes too, the capacities realized in the mind are not linguistic in character—they do not require anything like a language of thought, for example (Fodor 1975)—but a broadly Cartesian view might still hold that they are linguistic in some pre-social way. The genealogy would argue against the Cartesian capacity-first claim, regardless of which of these forms it assumes, supporting a practice-first alternative, in particular an alternative in which interpersonal practices are primary, intrapersonal are derived.

How does the genealogy provide a reason for maintaining the practice-first view? Well, it shows that even if the humanoids lacked the capacities to begin with, the presence of language and converse would more or less ensure the emergence in suitable conditions of suitable practices, interpersonal and intrapersonal, and that skills in abiding by those practices would constitute the capacities targeted. If we take the humanoids as models of human beings, and their world as a model of ours, that suggests that in our case too, the capacities exist as skills in the exercise of independently intelligible practices: specifically, practices that are enabled by language. And since that neo-Hobbesian view of our capacities is more parsimonious than the broadly Cartesian alternatives, it ought to have greater appeal: it demystifies the nature and function of those capacities among human beings.

There is more to be said, first, about the relevance of the genealogy to the question of origin and, second, about the demystification that the genealogy promises to provide. We address those topics in the following two sections. The discussion of demystification raises tricky issues of metaphysics, as we shall see, and we address those in a third, interlude section that takes us away from the main business of the genealogy; this may be skipped without serious loss to the understanding of the genealogy..

1.2.4 The genealogy and history

We have already mentioned that the genealogy does not commit us to a particular view of how the humanoids gain access to language and converse; we allowed that their access may depend on a special recursive capacity that emerges at a particular moment, on the effect of combining existing capacities in a certain manner, or on the two at once.[5] That means that regardless of how in that regard our forebears came to language, the genealogy can shed light on the nature and function of those capacities among human beings, representing them as skills in the exercise of linguistically elicited practices: in the first place, interpersonal practices, in the second intrapersonal. All it requires is that their access to language enabled them to interact in a way that gave rise without any planning to the appearance of those practices.

The genealogy may help to explain the nature and function of the capacities targeted, even if the actual use of language, unlike its use in the genealogy, developed and spread slowly among our kind (Heyes 2018, Ch. 8; Planer and Sterelny 2021). However gradual its emergence, language could still have prompted the development of the relevant practices and skills, if only their development in fits and starts. And it would still have prompted that development, if the emergence of language

---

[5] For a defense of the first possibility, see (Hauser, Chomsky, and Fitch 2002; Berwick and Chomsky 2016). All that the genealogy rules out is that having emerged on the basis of a singular evolutionary development, language then elicited the intrapersonal capacities first and the interpersonal second. As mentioned already, that is to rule out a Cartesian view.

involved a mix of cultural and natural stages (Deacon 1997; Crispo 2007). On that picture, cultural innovation gave rise initially to a simple language, and natural selection for competence led in stages to the appearance of ever more enhanced languages.

Thus, the genealogy can cast light on the nature and function of the six targeted capacities among human beings, regardless of how exactly language and converse emerged; it can still provide support for the idea that those capacities are skills in the exercise of linguistically elicited practices, primarily interpersonal practices and, derivatively, intrapersonal counterparts. And, unsurprisingly, it may also support that idea, regardless of how those practices themselves emerged in the wake of language. Consistently with being ushered in by the social use of language, the practices may have emerged among our forebears, and elicited corresponding skills, in any of a range of ways. Among the plausible stories about how the practices could have appeared, two are pure in character, one mixed. But each is consistent with the view of the nature and function of the practices, and the associated skills, that the genealogy supports.[6]

According to a first pure story, which would prioritize cultural selection, individual initiative gave rise among our forebears to social practices beneficial to relevant agents, and these spread and stabilized in cultural transmission across the ages, down to our own day. According to a mixed story, such culturally nurtured practices were supported and progressively enhanced by genetic selection for dispositions that reinforced them; the enhancement achieved under any round of genetic intervention would have prompted genetic support and enhancement in the following round, leading to a progressive sequence of cultural development and genetic assimilation (Crispo 2007). Finally, according to a second pure story, which would prioritize natural selection, random mutations led in the presence of social language to behavioral dispositions and social practices that were advantageous to their bearers, and that were naturally selected for the advantage they conferred.

The counterfactual genealogy does not rule for or against any such story about the origin of the human practices that it takes to ground the capacities targeted here. But, to venture for a moment beyond the remit of the project we have undertaken, two observations suggest that the mixed story may be the most plausible. First, the practices do not automatically come onstream with the maturation of children, as the pure natural theory would suggest: they require induction and training. And second, children seem to be naturally primed to exercise and enjoy those practices, contrary to what the pure cultural theory would predict.

---

[6] I focus only on standard evolutionary changes that benefit individuals and that may be expected to stabilize for that reason. I ignore the possible relevance of group selection: a process in which the advantage that a change confers on a group in a presumptive pattern of intergroup conflict leads to its survival and stabilization.

To expand on this observation, we human beings get to be inducted with remarkable ease into the relevant sorts of practices, so that even if our forebears were culturally innovative in developing the practices, we do not have to replicate their achievement in every generation. It seems more likely that the slow forces of natural selection embedded culturally evolved practices in our genetic make-up. Nature may have done this by providing us as children with a disposition to take up the practices, for example, a facility in learning them, or a rewarding degree of pleasure in their exercise.[7]

1.2.5 The genealogy and demystification

As the genealogies offered by Hart and Lewis are meant to remove any mystery or magic that laws and conventions might have been taken to involve, so the genealogy offered here is meant to serve the same role in relation to the practices targeted and the skills or capacities they elicit. It is designed to support a hypothesis that would make naturalistic sense of the capacities, explaining their existence and exercise without necessarily raising doubts about the picture of the world projected in natural science.

The genealogy would not make naturalistic sense if it required the world to be populated by purportedly non-physical or non-natural properties. These would be properties of a kind that natural science does not invoke and that cannot be grounded in properties that it does: their presence is not ensured and explained by the presence of properties recognized in science. Non-natural properties would include those of the kind that Descartes postulated in his image of a non-physical *res cogitans*, a thinking substance, lodged within the space, the *res extensa*, of the human body. The genealogy does not invoke any such properties, however, since it presents the capacities targeted as the precipitate of causally explicable social practices. But while the genealogy does not commit us to non-physicalism on this ground—while in that sense it demystifies the capacities targeted—it does not imply that non-physicalism in something like the Cartesian sense is definitely false. This will become clear in Chapter 4 when we address percipience. We may provide a naturalistic account of the judgment and reasoning exercised in percipience. But percipience presupposes the prior existence of perception and perceptual

---

[7] With one difference, the mixed story sketched resembles the sort of cultural evolutionary psychology espoused by Celia Heyes (2018; 2023). She addresses different capacities from those we target but criticizes analogues of our pure stories in their case too, arguing that the relevant capacities are cognitive mechanisms—skills or, as she calls them, gadgets—that are transmitted across the generations. She rejects the idea that the particular practices she explores were genetically assimilated (Heyes 2018, 206–09). But whether or not her argument on that point is persuasive (Turner and Walmsley 2020), genetic assimilation may well have played a role in stabilizing over time the practices that we address. My thanks to Ross Pain and Rachael Brown for useful discussions of this point.

consciousness, as we shall see, and nothing we say here establishes that this must be purely physical in the relevant sense.

There is a second, more challenging reason, however, why the genealogy may seem to presuppose a world that is populated with non-physical properties. On almost every version of the world that natural science is taken to presuppose, its fundamental, grounding properties are descriptive rather than prescriptive in character. They are properties that can be recognized in common by subjects with different views as to what is good or bad, right or wrong, and so on: properties such that adherents of those rival prescriptive attitudes can agree in principle on where, as a matter of descriptive fact, they are and are not realized. But the capacities targeted in the genealogy make sense only on the assumption that the agents involved, human or humanoid, hold prescriptive beliefs and occupy a world with the prescriptive properties allegedly required to make those beliefs true. So can how the genealogy hope to demystify those capacities? How can it aspire to explain why they would emerge among the humanoids without assuming an essentially prescriptive or value-bound world: a world that cannot be adequately characterized in any descriptive, naturalistic terms?

The engagement of prescriptive properties in the practices and capacities targeted is evident on all sides. Judging implies following a rule in predication, reasoning implies following a rule in deriving conclusions from premises, and percipience a rule in determining the deliverances of perception. And where there is a rule to follow, there are prescriptive requirements in play: conditions that the agent ought to satisfy, or that it is right that they should satisfy, in the exercise of the capacity. Again, normative valuing means determining how it is right to choose, ascribing responsibility how someone ought to have behaved, and displaying personhood how someone ought to be faithful to others or to themselves.

We may assume that prescriptive claims that are linked in these ways with the relevant capacities, are truth-conditional in character and require the world to be fit to make them true. That assumption is independently plausible and is particularly appealing for tactical reasons: it makes it more difficult to defend naturalism than an analysis that would deny that the prescriptive claims are truth-conditional, reducing the point of prescription to expressing a feeling or wish or something of that non-cognitive kind. The genealogy offered here is required to postulate only cause–effect and other empirical sequences in the interaction of the humanoids with one another and with their common world. So how then can it make sense of capacities that have prescriptive presuppositions? How can it claim to demystify them in a naturalistic way?

There are two salient ways in which we might attempt to demystify prescriptive claims in a naturalistic manner, consistently with taking them to be truth-conditional. One would offer a naturalistic account of the application conditions governing the concepts employed in those claims: conditions that guide agents in detecting corresponding properties. The other would offer a naturalistic account of the conditions under which agents might come to master the concepts involved, developing dispositions to characterize things in prescriptive terms.

Naturalists in the first camp would offer a translation in wholly naturalistic terms of what prescriptive claims postulate.[8] They would hold that as an a priori knowable matter, there is reason to make a prescriptive claim about something—that it is good or bad, right or wrong—just in case the option has a certain naturalistic character. According to this line, there are naturalistically salient conditions that make it appropriate, by the prior understanding of anyone able to make a prescriptive claim—and so in a manner that may guide what they say—to ascribe such a property.[9]

Demystification of this kind is unlikely to be available, and it is certainly not provided in the genealogy presented here. For all that the genealogy shows, and for all that is indubitably demonstrable, there may be no a priori knowable, naturalistic character to what agents have in mind whenever they speak of what ought to be the case, how it is right to choose, what there is most reason to do, and the like. Thus, we need not quarrel with Scanlon (1998), for example, when he suggests that nothing more can be said in analysis of the idea that a consideration provides a reason to do something than that it counts in favor of acting in that way, where counting in favor is of course itself a prescriptive notion.

The alternative sort of demystification would not claim to offer any such translation or interpretation of prescriptive claims but only to provide a naturalistic account that, consistently with the truth of the claims, explains how and why agents make them; specifically, to provide such an account without implying that there are naturalistic translations available for the claims. This variety of demystification is best explained by the analogous way in which philosophers standardly demystify indexical utterances—those involving terms like 'I' or 'now' or 'here'—in a non-indexical manner.

It is widely recognized that there is no way of giving a satisfactory translation or interpretation of indexical claims in non-indexical terms (Lewis 1979a; Perry 1979). Take the claim someone might make in saying or thinking, 'I am in danger', and now compare it with its non-indexical counterpart, 'NN is in danger', where 'NN' may be a proper name of the speaker or a non-indexical co-referring expression. The sentences may refer to the same person but only the claim corresponding to the first will necessarily play the role of putting that person on alert; the other

---

[8] For reasons of simplicity, I ignore attempts to give naturalistic reduction an alternative, non-analytical form.

[9] This approach is very different from the moral functionalism that I have joined Frank Jackson in defending (Jackson and Pettit 1995). Our functionalist theory aims at giving an account of what is true of human beings—ultimately, what is naturalistically true of them—in virtue of which they can be said to think in prescriptive terms. But it does not offer a naturalistic, translational account of what it means to say that something is good or right. Rather, it explains in the manner of the second sort of demystification how people can think in prescriptive terms although, unlike a genealogy, it does not seek to explain why they might be drawn to do so.

claim will not do so unless they are aware of being NN and in a position to judge, 'I am in danger'.[10] This observation shows that that there is more to indexical utterances and thoughts—there is more to the role they play for an agent—than anything that can be expressed in non-indexical terms; there is no possibility of translating or interpreting the claims in non-indexical language.

But despite the fact that non-indexical terms cannot be used to translate or interpret indexical claims, they provide a means of explaining how and why agents can get to make and assent to true indexical claims (Jackson 1998). We can use purely non-indexical resources to explain that by coming to use 'I' to refer to themselves, 'now' to refer to the time of utterance, and so on—by developing those referential practices—people will be enabled to speak and think in indexical terms. And understanding how they can speak and think in that way, we can readily see why, given the economy achieved, they will be motivated to do so.

The how and the why of indexical speech and thought will become clear to us insofar as we can simulate the effect on agents of developing the referential practice supported by the novel terminology. Being familiar with indexical thinking in our own practice—having an insider's understanding of what it involves—we can recognize that the effect of using 'I' to refer to themselves as speaker, for example 'now' to refer to the time of utterance, would be to lead them to think indexically. The simulation will be informed by our prior experience in the use of indexicals and in the practice of referring to things indexically.

The analogy with indexical thought should help explain why, at least in principle, the sort of naturalistic story provided in our genealogy can serve to illuminate the prescriptive thoughts associated with the practices it targets, without offering anything like a translation of those thoughts into naturalistic language. The story might make sense of why in the presence of a practice of assertion and judgment, the humanoids would form beliefs about what they ought to say; in the presence of a practice of explaining and vindicating what they say, why they would draw conclusions about what the evidence supports; and in the presence of a percipient practice, why they would see their perceptions as requiring them to make one or another response. And equally, to go to relational practices, the story might explain why the humanoids would think of certain norms or actions as worthy of being valued; why they would see others or indeed themselves as fit to be held responsible to their values for the actions they take; and why they would see that, constituting persons who are necessarily committed on a range of fronts, they ought to be true to themselves in related domains.

The genealogy sketched here is designed to realize these possibilities, making naturalistic sense of how and why humanoids—and by extension humans—would

---

[10] Of course, sentences like, 'The person speaking now is in danger' or, 'The utterer of this sentence is in danger' might play the same alerting role. But they can do so only insofar as they too employ indexical terms—'here' and 'this'—and enable the speaker to judge, 'I am in danger'.

come to the practices and capacities targeted. The indexical analogy helps to explain how it can do this. Our experience of indexical thinking will help us to simulate the effect of introducing indexical practices of reference, and to recognize how that effect will support indexical thought. And assuming that the genealogy is successful, our experience of prescriptive thought will serve us in a parallel manner. Starting from a naturalistic characterization of their processing and relational practices, the genealogy will invite us to simulate the effect on the humanoids of operating within those practices, and will let us see that they would naturally be led to adopt and follow the prescriptive modes of thinking relevant in each case.

In the indexical case, and in the case with which we are concerned, the claims made and the prescriptive realities addressed will enjoy a certain epistemic autonomy in relation to the truths of natural science. Learning in the familiar way to discern indexical and prescriptive facts will require immersion in the corresponding practices and will not be elicited by a knowledge of the truths of science. But neither the indexical nor the prescriptive realities will be metaphysically autonomous. That a certain indexical or prescriptive claim obtains will be ensured and explained by the fact that corresponding non-indexical and non-prescriptive claims are true of the relevant practice and of the world in which it is exercised. Both the indexical and the prescriptive realities will be metaphysically grounded in how things are in more fundamental, naturalistic terms (Rosen 2010; Fine 2012).

These remarks about how a genealogy can demystify the capacities targeted, prescriptive though they are in character, has merely a promissory status at this point. The claim that the genealogy will achieve this form of demystification can only be justified, case by case, in the development of the narrative. Justification will require the genealogy to elicit a simulation of the perspective that their practices would give the humanoids, and to support the claim that the associated prescriptive properties would become salient from within that perspective and prompt the emergence of the capacities targeted.

1.2.6 Interlude: demystification and metaphysics

If the genealogy achieves this demystifying effect, it will sponsor a view of the world of the humanoids, and perhaps our world, in which regular naturalistic properties are not the only properties around because there are other properties, in particular prescriptive properties, that they ground; properties in this usage may be monadic or relational. But, to raise a last question, incidental to the main purpose of the genealogy, is it reasonable to treat such prescriptive properties as real, if non-fundamental features of the world? Shouldn't we be more parsimonious and take only the fundamental grounding properties to be real? Not, I suggest, if we adopt what is plausibly the most useful and serviceable notion of a property.

By all accounts, every property can be paired with the infinite set of particular items that instantiate or might instantiate it. But not every set of particulars will constitute a property. Some sets may be random collections with nothing in common between the members. What will it be, then, for a set of particulars to constitute a property, with its members displaying a suitable commonality? The fact, plausibly, that it is possible to determine other members of the set from a proper, finite subset of the items involved. The fact, in other words, that there is a more economical way of identifying the set than simply listing all of its members. The fact, as it is sometimes put, that the set is patterned.[11]

When a set is patterned in this sense, constituting a property, it may be possible to find an explicit key or definition to reveal the pattern. Thus, we may explicitly identify the key to the squareness pattern by defining a square as a closed figure formed by four straight lines of equal length, each at a 90-degree angle with its neighbors. But for many patterns and properties that human or humanoid subjects recognize, there won't be an explicit or definitional key available; an example might be, the property of length that is used in the definition of squareness. In such a case, the evidence that the set of instances constitutes a property is just that those subjects, by virtue of genes or training, can be sensitized to it. They can be triggered, presumably in a neuropsychologically intelligible manner, to identify other instances on the basis of exposure to a proper subset. This exposure, so the idea goes, will give them a disposition, they know not how, to extrapolate to other cases, letting those cases count as instances of the same property; thus, the identification of such instances will not presuppose an existing conception or recognition of the property, opening up an explanatory circle.

For animals other than humans and humanoids, there will be no properties that they can unlock with an explicit key. But there will be many sets of items that they are sensitized to in this way, so that those sets constitute properties. Any natural similarity class will count as a property in virtue of an animal's sensitization to it: the class might be a kind of plant on which an animal feeds, a sort of predator that it avoids. And so will any range of items that the animal is conditioned to treat in a certain way: say, the triangular doors that a pigeon may be conditioned to peck on by the reward of a seed. The idea is that because the animal is naturally or artificially disposed to treat them in the same way—to treat them, in our language, as being of a kind—the members of the set are patterned and constitute a property: one that the animal will be able to reidentify across instances in virtue of its disposition.[12]

---

[11] For background, see (Chaitin 1975; 1988); (Dennett 1991); (Jackson, Pettit, and Smith 1999); and (Kipper 2021).

[12] In writing in this way of conditioning, and the associated notion of training, I do not mean to subscribe to any particular account of the process; for example, I do not mean to argue against the perspective in (Gallistel 2002).

As sensitization may be grounded in conditioning as well as nature, so it may be sourced for humans and humanoids in the training they receive within a practice. Someone versed in a background culture will easily distinguish funny from failed jokes, someone familiar with etiquette in a given society will recognize that some overtures to a stranger are cheeky, others polite, and so on. Practices like these can enable insiders to see a pattern where others cannot, and will establish that the set of items at issue does constitute a property.

The property revealed on a biological or cultural base may be of little significance, of course, for those not party to that base; it may just be of species-specific or indeed practice-specific interest. Thus, the color properties that are accessible in virtue of the biological make-up of our human or humanoid kind, or properties like politeness that are discernible from within our cultural practices, may be important for us without being of importance more generally; they may have a narrow as distinct from a wide cosmological role (Wright 1992). But regardless of how idiosyncratic such properties may be, they still contrast with mere, unpatterned sets of items. And for creatures of our kind, it would be a repudiation of how the world presents to us—a rejection of the view from our-where as distinct from the view from nowhere—to deny them importance in our representation of the world.

Thus, if the genealogy provided here is successful, it will support a variety of realism about the capacities targeted and the prescriptive properties they presuppose. This picture suggests that the language of science may be unable to equip a person to identify those properties, and indeed those capacities, in the ordinary manner; immersion in the corresponding practices is likely to be essential for cottoning on to the patterns involved. But that suggestion is consistent with naturalism, for if the genealogy is successful, then a language that posits only scientific or scientifically grounded properties can suffice to explain why those patterns should become salient to anyone operating within the relevant practices.

To return to the analogous case of color properties, for example, such a language will provide the means of explaining how the spectral reflectance allegedly associated with a color like red affects creatures with the visual cortex of neurotypical humans and humanoids, letting the color become available to them in their experience and discrimination. Assuming that the association proves to be scientifically well grounded, it will make it possible to see how surfaces that reflect incident light to a designated specification, will all look red under presumptively normal circumstances to presumptively normal subjects.

That something like this holds is ensured by a naturalistic vision of the world but that lesson does not mean that we should give up on the significance of redness or any other of the colors discernible to our kind, or on the significance of any of the prescriptive and other properties that our practices make salient. On the contrary, the naturalistic lesson should reassure us that those properties are not figments of our imagining but features that we have every reason to take seriously and even, where appropriate, to savor. They are deliverances of our encounter with the world that are not otherwise available for us to track experientially, even if the delivery system that gives them salience is only fully explicable within the terms of natural science.

1.3 Introducing the humanoids

So much for the benefits that the projected genealogy might provide in demystifying the nature and function of the targeted practices and skills among humanoids and humans. In order to make the counterfactual genealogy credible as a source of such lessons, however, we need to work with assumptions about the pre-linguistic capacities and circumstances of humanoids that make them into plausible models of human beings. We need to give an account of the base from which the genealogical project starts.

1.3.1 The character of humanoids as organisms and agents

There are two sets of features that our humanoid counterparts must share with us insofar as they, like us, are organisms and agents. Qua organisms of any kind, they will need food and related resources, they will have to compete for these in a world of moderate scarcity, and they will tend to do so on a relatively self-regarding basis: they may care for others but will care in a special way for themselves and their kin. And qua organisms that are like us in particular, they will depend in many contexts on one another's assistance, relying for their survival and development on the assistance of others and support from the groups to which they belong. But though dependent on one another's assistance, they will also resemble us in occasionally proving insensitive to the needs that this dependency generates; free riding will be a constant temptation.

Qua agents, the humanoids may be expected in general to form beliefs about themselves, about the animals and objects around them, and about the spatial and causal relations that obtain in their world, on the same common, presumptively rational basis that is provided by shared evidence. Equally, qua agents, they may be expected to act reliably in pursuit of familiar, intelligible goals on the basis of those beliefs. And qua agents who have to rely on one another, as we have to rely on one another, they must be disposed, despite their self-regarding instincts and despite occasional bouts of free riding, to be sensitive in good measure to the needs of others in the actions they take.

These are unproblematic features to assume in the character of humanoids since their presence in our own kind is hardly controversial and presumably does not depend on our having language. The characterization makes no mention of emotion or passion, nor will our genealogy depend on ascribing such attitudes to the humanoids. There are two reasons for this. One, there is a relatively stable basis on which to argue about how agents would be likely to think in certain situations and likely to act therefore in pursuit of their goals, but there is no equally firm basis on which to argue about what emotions they would be likely to harbor. Two, the neglect of emotion in the genealogy is not a serious loss since there are few if any points in the narrative where allowing emotions to enter would be likely to undermine the claims made.

On the contrary indeed, there are a number of points where the introduction of emotion would be likely to help rather than hinder the narrative. The economy of esteem invoked at various points would be strengthened if the disesteemed faced the ill feeling as well as the bad opinion of others. The role of commitment in conveying assurance to others, as assumed in discussing relational practices, would be reinforced by emotional signaling of the sort that it is hard to feign (Frank 1988). And the effect of blame in regulating others, which is invoked in the discussion of responsibility, would be boosted by the credible display of feelings of resentment or indignation.

1.3.2 The context of humanoid interaction

Consistently with competing as organic agents in a world of moderate scarcity, however, the humanoids might or might not be relatively equal. As we shall see, the genealogy works only under the assumption that they interact more or less as equals. Yet the genealogy must postulate a context of interaction among humanoids that is more or less realistic, being similar to the context in which we human beings interact. Otherwise we can hardly derive a lesson about the nature and function of our capacities from an account of how they would be robustly likely to appear among the humanoids.

The requirement of relative equality would seem to conflict with the desideratum of realism. Human societies may have been relatively egalitarian in the long period between the first appearance of *homo sapiens*, probably more than one hundred thousand years ago, and the agricultural revolution ten to twelve thousand years ago (Boehm 1999; Boix and Rosenbluth 2014). But they have been undoubtedly inegalitarian since about the time of that revolution and the rise, in its wake, of settled towns and cities (Scott 2017). Societies since that time have been generally hierarchical, with some subgroups of members dominating the members of other subgroups, and at least since the rise of states, with some societies dominating other societies.

We shall assume in the genealogy that the society of humanoids we envisage does display a relative equality of power across the membership, with no subgroup dominating others, and that it is the only society in the world or at least that it is not dominated by other societies. We shall assume, in that sense, that the society is not hierarchical in itself and does not operate within a hierarchical world. This assumption will make the genealogy relatively simple and straightforward and, as we shall see in the Conclusion, make it useful for considering some ideals of ethics and politics. But does it make the conditions of the humanoids so unrealistic, so different from ours, that the genealogy cannot carry many lessons for human practices and capacities?

No, it does not. Even if the humanoid society and the humanoid world are egalitarian, the lessons we derive under that assumption may still apply in our hierarchical circumstances. For while there has been little or no society-level or world-level equality in our world, at least since the time of the agricultural revolution, still there has often been a high degree of equality at lower levels of each society in the internal relationships between the members of one or another subgroup, even a subgroup that is dominated externally. Thus, a subgroup of the oppressed or marginalized, the poor or the powerless, or at least a subgroup within such a subgroup—say, a subgroup of women members—may well be internally egalitarian: each member within the group may be able to relate as an equal with their fellows, if not with those without.

Even a restricted equality of this kind in the actual world should be enough to make the potential lessons of the genealogy relevant to humans. Thus, the discipline of tit-for-tat reciprocity and an economy of esteem that the genealogy identifies, together with the expectations it imposes on assertion and judgment—and by extension on other processing capacities—is only likely to emerge in a community of equals. But even if that community in the actual world is just a subgroup of the society, the lessons of the genealogy will still carry for each individual as a member of such a grouping. And again the same message will hold for the lessons of the genealogy about the relational as well as the processing capacities of humans: individuals may be expected within their subgroup community, if not across the society more widely, to pursue constrained practices like those associated with commitment, holding responsible, and operating as persons. On both the processing and relational fronts, people's experience within relatively egalitarian subgroups should enable them, at least in principle, to develop the practices and related capacities in the sort of development documented by the genealogy.

This being so, we might have opted for a different course within the genealogy itself; we might have assumed only that while humanoid society is hierarchical, and perhaps exists within a hierarchical world, still there is a requisite degree of equality within the subgroups of the society. For reasons of simplicity and convenience, however—and for reasons related to the ideals discussed in the Conclusion—we shall generally assume that there is equality across all the members of the humanoid society we envisage, and that that society is the only one in the world or, if there are others, that it relates as an equal to them. But the argument would go through in general—we later note a few cases where this is not so—even if there were a degree of equality only among the members of one or another humanoid subgroup, with those subgroups relating to one another on a hierarchical pattern.

1.3.3 More on the character of the humanoids

So far, our assumptions about the character of the humanoids are supported by common sense as well as social science, postulating familiar capacities that do not intuitively presuppose access to language. But there are other linguistically independent human capacities that are highlighted by recent research findings and that we should also ascribe to the humanoids, though they do not figure as platitudes of common sense. These involve the ability to perceive agency in others, to share agency with others, to teach agential skills to others, and to exercise agency to a communicative purpose. Such capacities are linguistically independent in the sense that the scientifically available evidence on the history of our forebears suggests that they preceded language, at least in their simpler forms. In some cases, indeed, such forms are present in non-linguistic animals and also in pre-linguistic children.[13]

1.3.4 Perceiving agency

The ability to ascribe agency to another—to identify and interpret their mind — has been a focus of psychological research from the time, some decades ago, when it was documented at different levels in other animals (Premack and Woodruff 1978), as well as in young children at pre-linguistic stages of development (Wimmer and Perner 1983; Perner 1991). Sometimes this ability is taken to involve interpreting agents in light of a presupposed theory of mind, sometimes as an exercise based on simulating the position of the agents interpreted (Carruthers and Smith 1996). And sometimes too it is seen as an ability derived from the more basic ability of human beings to shape and scaffold the attitudes of others and indirectly their own (Zawidzki 2013; McGeer 2015). But we can set aside those differences in the present context. The main point is that, however it is understood, people's ability to read the minds of others, imputing agency to them, is well supported in the empirical literature.

This ability was supported from the mid-century by the discovery that from an early age, children see some things as inanimate objects and other things as agents; this appears in the way in which they generally take geometrical shapes

---

[13] While their presence in pre-linguistic children may be historically due to genetic assimilation of culturally evolved linguistic practice, it still shows that such capacities can in principle be supported by human nature without the presence of language.

moving about on a two-dimensional screen to be pursuing various goals (Heider and Simmel 1944; see too Klin and Jones 2006). The basic idea in postulating such a mind-reading ability among human beings is well cast by Daniel Dennett (1987) as a disposition to take up the intentional stance in seeking to understand other agents. This is a more or less spontaneous, even irrepressible, disposition to assume that whatever a presumptive agent does, at least in otherwise normal conditions, it does as a perceived means of pursuing a desired goal: a means that makes rational sense, given how it perceives its situation. Despite differences in accounts of the process in which this disposition manifests itself, there is little or no doubt that it comes naturally to human beings, and to many other animals, and that we can reasonably ascribe it to our would-be counterparts in the narrative presented here.

1.3.5 Sharing agency

But human beings—and, we may assume, humanoids—do more than just ascribe agency to one another in this way. They also act together, in exercises of shared agency, to achieve ends they take to be commonly appealing. It is well established in the empirical literature that even as toddlers, we have the capacity to act jointly in pursuit of shared ends, expecting and even demanding a share in the spoils of the activity pursued. And this, despite being relatively self-interested in the sense of prioritizing the welfare of ourselves and our kin. The signal work in this area is due to Michael Tomasello and his collaborators over the past few decades.

Their research reveals that children between the ages of 1 and 3 are 'internally motivated', as Tomasello (2016, 47) puts it, 'to help others, with no need for external incentives'. And this motivation goes hand in hand with a disposition to collaborate in the pursuit of joint goals. 'From soon after their first birthdays, and continuing up to their third birthdays', he says, children 'come to engage with others in collaborative activities' and 'to divide the common spoils of a collaboration equally' (Tomasello 2014, 41). This disposition, he adds, has 'a species-unique structure' and does not 'depend on cultural conventions or language'.[14]

According to Tomasello (2016), the capacity for joint activity was selected for among our forebears—not, he surmises, in other great apes—in a period of obligate foraging between about 400k and 100k years ago. In that period our forebears, he argues, would have had to forage together or die alone; they would have had to develop mutual reliance of the kind that joint activity supports (Renfrew 2007). And, presumably because of genetic assimilation, that cultural development would

---

[14] As with the ability to read minds, there are different accounts given in the empirical and philosophical literature of our ability as human beings to act jointly with others, but we need not go into the issue between them here. See (Bratman 2014); (Gilbert 2015); (Tuomela 2007); and (Searle 2010); for an overview of the issues between such writers, see (Ludwig 2016).

have been absorbed by their first nature, making children today spontaneously cooperative. Whether or not Tomasello is right about other great apes, the evidence from very young human children suggests that we may reasonably ascribe a similar, innate capacity for joint action to our humanoid counterparts.

Two features of joint activity, as he emphasizes, are worthy of note. One is that as a preliminary to such activity, the humanoids must also be capable of joint attention. They must be able to attend to their perceived environment, aware that all are attending in that manner, and aware that all are registering whatever they attend to. And the other feature is that they must each be capable of adopting the perspective of others—partners in the activity—and indeed the perspective of the group that they form together with those others. As we shall assume that humanoids are like humans in being capable of acting together for a goal, so we shall assume that they have these related capacities for joint attention and perspective-taking.

If the humanoids are jointly cooperative, they are bound to be able to identify failures on the part of others to play their part in some joint activity and, more important, bound to be disposed to respond negatively to such failures. They may later shun those who let them down on a previous occasion, not wanting to be hurt again. They may be willing to interact on something like a tit-for-tat pattern, as other animals do, cooperating to begin with, and later doing what their partner did before (Axelrod 1984; Nowak 2006).[15] And if Tomasello (2014) is correct, they may even be willing to identify and punish those who fail to cooperate in a joint enterprise. He argues that children are naturally disposed to do this and takes that to indicate—perhaps assuming genetic assimilation—that our forebears did so on an innovative basis, without yet having such a facilitating disposition. As he claims, 'in the small-scale collaborative interactions of early humans, individuals actively chose some collaborative partners and shunned others, and in some cases even rewarded and punished partners' (Tomasello 2014, 87).[16]

1.3.6 Teaching agential skills

But human beings do more than act together for certain goals. They act, more specifically, for the goal of passing on the proven ways of doing things successfully and the received ways of understanding their surrounds.

Kim Sterelny (2012) has drawn on a range of disciplines to make the empirical case for taking human beings, and indeed the wider class that includes other, vanished hominins, to display the pedagogy assumed here (see too Renfrew 2007,

---

[15] Human beings may also have an innate disposition to punish offenders, even offenders who have hurt only others, as some have argued (Fehr and Gächter 2002).
[16] When Tomasello (2009; 2014; 2016) speaks here of sanctions or punishments, he may have in mind reactions that are too sophisticated to be independent of language. For a critique of Tomasello on this point, see (Pettit 2018c).

Chs 6–7; Lalande 2017). He argues that well before the likely appearance of language, our forebears implemented something he describes as apprentice learning. The young would have learned as apprentices from their elders in an environment rich with informational resources like tools, examples, and consultants. At the least, their elders would have intentionally allowed them to play a part in that environment and pick up important skills.

Sterelny (2012, 37–8) holds that 'a full apprentice model of expertise transmission' did not materialize until a few hundred thousand years ago, applying in activities like tool-making, child-minding, and foraging. At that point, teaching-and-learning might have assumed the character of shared agency. But he cites reasons for thinking that it was also relevant for early hominins a couple of million years ago. The young 'learned by doing, in environments that advantageously shaped individual trial-and-error learning' and were 'structured advantageously by adults through the exercise of the adults' own expertise'; in these environments, for example, 'tools, partially completed tools, and raw materials were readily available as objects of play, experiment, and exploration'.

While teaching and learning, and shared agency in general, would have assumed a particularly sophisticated form with the advent of language, we may assume with Tomasello and Sterelny that they would have existed in some shape prior to language. This claim is reinforced by the fact that, as pre-linguistic children display dispositions to act together with others, so they often display specifically pedagogical dispositions, as when a child playing with building blocks indicates where another should place their block.

1.3.7 Communicative agency

But not only do we have good grounds for assuming a pedagogical capacity among our humanoids. It turns out that there is good reason also to take the humanoids to be capable of intentional communication. The crucial consideration here is that at least in certain contexts other great apes display such a capacity without having access to language.

The ability to communicate in a natural language has been subject to a variety of analyses in the philosophical and related literature. But almost all accounts start from the pioneering work of Paul Grice (1957; 1975a; 1989a), which has been elaborated and refined in a long tradition of relatively sympathetic interpretation (Neale 1992). Those accounts direct us to distinctive features of communication among human beings that have only partial analogues in the inherited signaling systems of other animals (Sperber and Wilson 1986; Scott-Phillips 2015).

Simplified and recast somewhat, the Gricean model proposes that any form of communication that is worthy of the name—any form of communication of the kind that is standard in natural language—requires the communicating agent to act with a double intention toward the party addressed. First, the communicator must act with the intention of getting the addressee to respond after a certain fashion. And second, the communicator must act with the intention of getting the addressee to do this by recognizing what they are seeking: by recognizing the response they intend to elicit.[17]

Suppose, for example, that we are camping, that I am putting up the tent and that I find myself in an awkward position: I dare not leave the tent or it will fall down but in order to prop it up I need a pole that lies ten meters away. You are collecting wood nearby, but I cannot ask you for the pole as I have some important pegs held between my teeth. What I do then is to make a grunting sound, attract your attention, and point with my head or a free hand toward the missing pole. This gets you to recognize that I want the pole, that I want you to recognize that that is what I want and to be prompted thereby to respond as I intend you to respond: to come back, pick up the pole and hand it to me.

My response-centered intention in this case identifies the goal I seek: that you should give me the pole. My recognition-centered intention identifies the means on which I rely: that you will see what I seek and be prompted to satisfy my goal. All that I need do to satisfy my intention to get you to give me the pole is to reveal that intention. And being aware of this, that is precisely what I do. By manifesting my wish that something should be so—that you should hand me the pole—I manage, thanks to your perception and cooperation, to make it so.

The nature of communication, as understood on this simple model, shows up nicely in contrast to what might be taken to occur in the courtship interactions among certain species of birds. The male bird dances in a way that promises to attract a mate but, for all the standard account implies, it may not act intentionally for that end; it may be selected to find the dancing attractive for its own sake, at least when its hormone levels rise. And the female bird that responds appropriately to the dance, say by approaching the male, may not intentionally seek to mate; it may be selected to make that response, at least under suitable hormonal conditions, without foreseeing the mating to which it leads.

It seems reasonable to ascribe a properly communicative ability to our humanoids, even in advance of language. This is because of the evidence for such a capacity that chimpanzees display in scenarios of targeted help, as they are often called (Yamamoto, Humle, and Tanaka 2009; 2012; Moore 2016). In one example of this sort of situation, a chimp needs an instrument like a stick to which only a second chimp has access; there is an obstacle between them that blocks the first chimp from grasping it. Simplifying the scenario somewhat, the first chimp attracts the attention of the second and reaches toward the stick, when it must be clear to each

---

[17] I ignore a third requirement recognized in the literature, that it be overt or public that the communicator is seeking a certain end by getting the audience to recognize the end sought (Strawson 1964; Neale 1992). While the requirement is certainly important for other purposes, it is not relevant for ours.

that the stick is beyond their reach. The second chimp, noticing what the first is doing, hands over the stick in response to the attempted reach, sometimes selecting it over other possibilities on the basis of contextual cues as to the first chimp's situation and needs.[18]

The natural interpretation of this sort of exchange is that the first chimp is intentionally getting the second to recognize what it is after by reaching toward the stick and that the second responds on the basis of recognizing that the first chimp is trying to get the stick in a context where it clearly cannot succeed (Moore 2017). It is hard to see how a language of communication could emerge from such interactions, given the limited gestural resources available.[19] But equally, it is hard to deny that the exchange involves something in the vicinity of the communication that natural language mediates among human beings.

As chimpanzees can act with a communicative intention, so we may assume that our humanoids will be able to do so too.[20] And as we human beings have the apparatus required to produce and discriminate a great number of sounds, so we may assume that our humanoids will have that same capacity (Fitch 2010). Thus, they will have an ability to use such sounds, enhanced no doubt by gesture and expression, to direct the attention of another to what they seek in this or that scenario, and to prompt the other thereby to provide them with what they want. And they will be able to act intentionally within this exchange, whether in communicating the message or in responding to it. The initiator will act on the basis of a desire to direct the attention of the other to what they want and the respondent will act on the basis of a desire, however sourced, to give the initiator what they want.

1.4 Signaling and speech

Language in the full, familiar sense is a system for constructing an indefinitely large set of signs or signals—in the paradigmatic, verbal case, declarative sentences—that can be used to communicate information on the basis of the units that it employs: in the paradigmatic case, words. It may be used for interrogative, imperative, and other purposes, to be sure, but those purposes would all seem to presuppose this basic informative function. And as a system designed for that informative role, language generally allows speakers to negate and conjoin sentences, to construct conditional sentences, to innovate along the lines that a transformational syntax allows, and to communicate novel messages in their particular utterances, relying

---

[18] For video, see https://commons.wikimedia.org/wiki/File:Chimpanzees-Help-Each-Other-upon-Request-pone.0007416.s001.ogv.
[19] This may be overly pessimistic, in view of the gestural theories of the origin of language. A classic in the recent literature is (Hewes 1973).
[20] This is particularly plausible, given the selectional history shared between chimpanzees and human beings. See (Tomasello 2022).

on context to enable them to deploy techniques like implicature and insinuation, irony and metaphor.

We must assume in our genealogy that there is nothing naturalistically mysterious about how the humanoids would come to language, as there is presumably nothing mysterious about how it first appeared among our own kind. In this and the next section, we try to justify that assumption by telling a story about how they might evolve a simple language and reach the point from which our genealogy proper begins Chapter 2. More specifically, we tell a story about the emergence of language among the humanoids that does not presuppose the prior presence of any of the capacities the genealogy seeks to explain; if it did, then that would undermine the very point of the genealogy.

As we noted earlier, the genealogy that begins in the next chapter offers a story about how probably—how in a robust sense of probability—the humanoids would be led by the appearance of language to develop the capacities we are targeting here. The discussion in this and the next section of how they might come to speak offers an account of a how-possibly rather than a how-probably character. It is designed to show that there is nothing inherently mysterious in the idea that the humanoids might evolve a simple form of language de novo, and do so without having already enjoyed capacities linked to judgment, reasoning or percipience, normativity, responsibility, or personhood. There is no suggestion that it was robustly likely to appear; for all we assume, its appearance among the humanoids, perhaps even its appearance among our own kind, may be a happy accident.[21]

We begin the discussion in this section with an account of how certain non-human animals use signs that come to them naturally, to carry and convey information. We look afterwards at how the humanoids might begin from such a system of non-intentional signaling to develop an intentional, communicative practice. And then we explore the developments that would transform that practice into a proper linguistic exercise.

In the final section of the chapter, we move into difficult terrain, addressing the puzzle of how the humanoids could come to follow rules, even basic undefined rules, as they must do if they are to pursue intentional signaling. That section is treated as an interlude, since many think that there is no real problem of rule-following and others hold that the problem can be solved in a different manner from that advanced here. The hope is that by not requiring readers to accept the resolution presented in the final section, I can maximize the audience for the genealogy itself.

---

[21] Paul Grice (1989b, Ch. 18) offers a similar account of how a creature like one of our vervets might come in a series of naturalistically intelligible steps to be capable of using its non-intentional signs intentionally and even, assuming an appropriate audience, communicatively.

1.4.1 Non-intentional signaling

Signaling to an informative effect is common among non-human animals. For a salient example, consider the way that vervet monkeys in a particular part of Kenya share a set of signs—specifically, signs that come naturally to them—for various dangers; these take the form of warning calls that the perception of a danger prompts them to emit (Seyfarth and Cheney 1984; Cheney and Seyfarth 1985; 1990).[22] The monkeys in that environment have one call for an eagle, another for a leopard, another for a snake in the grass, and so on through a limited number of examples. They tend as adults to produce those natural signs under appropriate stimuli and to take appropriate cover in response to the calls of others; the young gradually come into line with this pattern, although without any obvious teaching.[23]

These vervet monkeys vary the extent of their signaling, depending on which other monkeys are around—members of their family, for example, or dominant members of the group—and they may not signal at all in certain circumstances. That suggests that their signaling may be intentional under some description: say, in winning the attention of a higher-status monkey or a close relative. But there is no reason to think that it is intentional qua signaling: that it is pursued intentionally or even knowingly as a way of informing others. By the accounts on offer, vervet signaling does not constitute an intentional effort to get others to respond as the signaled danger makes it rational to respond; in that sense it is not an intentional form of signaling.

Despite not being signs that are used intentionally or knowingly in communication, however, the natural calls of the vervets give us an idea of how signs can carry and convey information (McDowell 1980). The eagle call among vervet monkeys will carry the information that an eagle is posing a danger insofar as it reliably correlates with the presence of an eagle. And it will convey that information to others insofar as it reliably elicits in them the same behavior that the perceived presence of the eagle would elicit.

By received accounts, such a call will elicit different behaviors in different hearers, since the action required to take cover will vary, depending on where the hearer is positioned. What it elicits in each is the disposition—specifically, an evidence-responsive disposition—to behave as if an eagle posed a danger: that is, a disposition to behave as its desires would require—in particular, a desire to avoid an attack by the eagle—if an eagle were present. And that is to say, as we shall see in the next chapter, that in a broadly functionalist sense the call elicits a belief that

---

[22] For a book that places their work in historical perspective, see (Radick 2007).
[23] The relatively small repertoire of sounds appears to be fixed across the species, being naturally producible and discriminable by each monkey, but variations in locality may have the effect of somewhat altering the messages they convey in different populations; in another area of Africa where lions pose the same threat as leopards, the leopard call is used by the vervets for lions.

an eagle is present.[24] Thus, as the vervet call will carry information that there is an eagle nearby in virtue of correlating reliably with the presence of an eagle, so it will convey that information in virtue of reliably eliciting in hearers the belief that an eagle is present.

1.4.2 Intentional signaling

Based on the possibility illustrated by the vervet monkeys, it is plausible to assume that the humanoids will be able to use natural signs or signals to the same informative effect: to the same effect in eliciting beliefs in their audience. They will presumably have access to gestures or facial expressions or sounds—the range of available sounds will be particularly large, as it is with us—that may serve the same natural purpose as the warning calls of the vervets. Like those calls, they will carry information about the situations with which they correlate. And like those calls, they will convey that information to others, eliciting beliefs that things are as they indicate.

This access to signs will not take the humanoids, any more than it takes the vervet monkeys, into linguistic space. In order for them to enter this space, they must not just have access to signs that carry information about the environment. They must also be able to use those signs intentionally in order to convey that information to others: in order to elicit in hearers the belief that things are as the signs indicate.

It need not take a miracle for the humanoids, assuming they have the means–end intelligence of human beings—and more generally the intelligence of the great apes—to begin to make intentional use of signs that initially emerge, like those of the vervets, on a natural basis. Assuming that they will often want to get others, such as their kin, to form certain beliefs—say, that a danger is looming—they will likely recognize that they can elicit those beliefs by resort to appropriate signs and will be led in consequence to use the signs intentionally. They will use a sign out of the desire to elicit such a belief, given their own belief that their use of that sign will have the desired effect.

As the humanoids are each led to use certain signs intentionally, they will presumably recognize that others do so too: that they use the signs to elicit suitable beliefs and actions in their hearers. And not only that. They will presumably respond appropriately as hearers to the use of a sign, not in virtue of its having a natural effect like the effect of a warning call on a vervet monkey, but rather in virtue of their

---

[24] To speak of belief rather than knowledge is just to follow the standard tradition in the ethology of other species. Speaking of belief does not spring from a commitment to a picture of knowledge as a complex state that we conceptualize as a state of belief that satisfies further conditions, such as that of being true, for example, and being justified or reliable; the concept of knowledge, for all that is assumed, may be prior to the concept of belief in our own thinking (Williamson 2000; Hyman 2006).

recognizing what the speaker intends. They would presumably repress its natural effect, after all, if they thought that the speaker intended something else: say, just to tease or amuse or distract them.

This being so, the appearance of intentional signaling among the humanoids will lead them, by the account introduced earlier, to communicate with one another in their use of these natural signs. They will each have a response-centered intention in using a sign: that is, an intention to elicit a suitable belief and action in their hearer. And they will each have a corresponding recognition-intention: that is, an intention to get their hearer to respond appropriately in virtue of recognizing the response they seek. At this point they will take their use of natural signs into communicative space.

These remarks are designed to show that there is nothing inherently mysterious in the idea that the humanoids would develop a system of intentional and communicative signaling. If our observations are successful in that regard, then they may also help to make sense of why the humanoids should go further still. There are a number of steps that they would intelligibly take, and we shall assume within the genealogy developed in the following chapters that they have actually taken them.

Before looking at those steps, it may be useful to introduce a comment on the notion of information that we rely on throughout the book. Here, and indeed elsewhere, the word 'information' is sometimes used to mean correct information and sometimes to mean would-be or alleged information. It will imply correctness when we speak of the information that a non-intentional signal like a vervet monkey's warning call carries and conveys. It will imply only alleged correctness when we speak of the information that a speaker communicates intentionally to a hearer. Rather than separate out such differences in the text, we may generally rely on context to make clear which use of the term is in play.

1.4.3 Further developments

Back now to the steps we may expect the humanoids to take once they have learned to use signs intentionally. First, they will presumably evolve the use of conventional as well as natural signs for purposes of conveying information, given that such signs would enhance their capacity to elicit desired effects in one another. They will be able to develop such signs, of course, only if they can give arbitrarily chosen sounds the same meaning for all, enabling those sounds to communicate the same information in each usage. But David Lewis's (1969) genealogy of conventions, which we sketched earlier, explains how they might achieve this convergence in an unplanned, spontaneous manner. The humanoids will naturally be motivated to resolve the coordination predicaments that divergence of usage would create. And, as Lewis suggests, they will presumably be able to rely on a shared sense of salience or analogy or precedent for converging on common patterns of usage and on common meanings for their signs.[25]

A second development we might expect among the humanoids is that they will learn to use signs, not just to convey information about the environment in an assertoric mode, but also for the purposes served among us by interrogative, imperatival, or optative utterances. Suppose that they have a certain sign for water. It will be natural for anyone thirsty to use the water sign, not to convey information about the environment, but rather about themselves: for example, that they need water. This will be intelligible insofar as the humanoids are equipped to ascribe beliefs and desires, by our earlier assumptions, and will presumably have the capacity to interpret the utterance of the word for water in light of their understanding of what a speaker seeks.

A third development that we should certainly expect in the communicative exchanges among humanoids is the appearance of deception and the recognition on all sides that an individual may purport to convey misleading information about the environment or about themselves. It will occasionally be in the interest of an individual to deceive others in this way, say in hiding the existence of a food source, and that will surely be manifest to all. Thus, the appearance of intentional, communicative signaling has a dark as well as a bright side. We will return to this aspect of communication in the next chapter, looking at the pressures that may lead the humanoids to be reliable and cooperative in their signaling.

Taking up a fourth possibility, will the humanoids learn to combine signs as we combine words in complex sentences? Well, one development we should certainly expect, is that they will learn to negate a sign, so that the negated utterance communicates that things are not the way the original sign would convey. If the humanoids use their signs to an informative purpose, they will presumably find themselves in occasional disagreement. And that will make it more or less essential for them to register such divergence in a way that requires something like a negation operator.

Are the humanoids likely to go further in combining their signs and, to that extent, in constructing sentences? We may assume that they will find it useful to be able to connect signs conjunctively or disjunctively since that would not seem to be difficult and might be useful for them in keeping tabs on what they or others hold. But will they be able to combine sentences in more complex ways? Will they have access to conditionals, for example, communicating that if something is the case, then something else must hold as well? Perhaps not. That capacity may only come on stream, as we shall see in Chapter 3, after they have learned the practice of reasoning.[26]

---

[25] For a more sophisticated account of why signaling systems of this kind would emerge, see (Skyrms 2010).
[26] A mastery of negation and connectives would enable the humanoids to define the material conditional, holding in familiar notation that p—>q if and only if it is not the case that p and not-q.

Turning to another possibility, will the humanoids be able to combine words into sentences on the complex patterns of a systematic, transformational syntax? The humanoids need not be able to do so for our genealogy to take off. But such a development, perhaps one requiring a genetic mutation, would certainly enhance their linguistic and conversive capacity and there is nothing about our genealogical assumptions that prohibits us from envisaging its appearance at some stage, earlier or later, in the narrative.

Finally, to take up a fifth possibility: will the humanoids be able to use their sentences to convey one message in one context, a different message in a second, and so on? They may plausibly have a use for simple indexical sentences where words like 'I' and 'here' and 'now' have referents that vary across context. But will they be able to innovate more deeply, letting context interact with convention to shape novel messages?

In ordinary human languages, context may help to give specific content, not just to an indexical ('I', 'here', 'now'), but to an attributive ('tall', 'strong'), or a quantifier ('all'), or even to the similitude posited in a simile ('like a red rose'). Or it may fix the reading of an ambiguous sentence ('Flying planes can be dangerous'), or determine the content conveyed by a metaphor ('Richard is a lion'). In such cases the effect is to transform the conventional meaning or truth-condition of the sentence itself, as shown by the fact that negating the sentence means negating the transformed message, not the literal one: denying that Richard is a lion means raising a question about his bravery rather than insisting prosaically that he is a human being, not a feline animal.[27]

In other cases, however, context does not transform the conventional truth-condition of a sentence in ordinary language but indicates that while a speaker is using a sentence in its literal sense, and in an assertoric mode, the intention is to convey something other than its literal message. The ironical remark is one example, as when Shakespeare's Marc Antony says of Caesar's assassins: 'Brutus is an honorable man; so are they all, all honorable men'. Insinuation is another, as when a teacher writing a letter of reference comments that the student has very nice handwriting. And implicature is a third, as when someone conveys a hidden message in remarking that while someone is a politician, they are perfectly honest. Where the literal content of a sentence is replaced in the first set of cases by the transformed content, it is hijacked rather than replaced in this second set of cases and is made to carry a special speaker meaning.

But even if that is enough to make sense of certain conditional transitions, short of an independent ability to reason, it will be enough only if we allow them access to the devices exploited in implicatures (Jackson 1987).

[27] Testing in this way for whether a truth-condition is transformed means applying a relative of what is often known as the Frege-Geach test. See (Geach 1972).

Will the language we have been envisaging with the humanoids enable them to use their signs to such novel, context-dependent effects? Or, with the possible exception of indexical sentences, will it confine them to the strict literal usage and understanding of their conventional signs? We may happily assume that their initial language will have this confining effect, since that is enough to get the genealogy underway. But we shall see in the course of the genealogy that as the humanoids learn to reason—this is the topic of Chapter 3—they will learn to recognize that they may use context to generate novel messages of the kinds illustrated; they will be able to rely on one another to exercise reasoning, however implicitly, in decoding those messages. Thus, as reasoning is likely to enable the humanoids to master complex conditional sentences, so it will enable them to let language transcend the limitations that convention on its own would impose.

1.4.4 Is language necessary as well as sufficient?

These observations on how the humanoids might master a simple language are meant to support the central claim in the genealogy to be developed here, that access to such a language is enough to prompt the development de novo of the capacities targeted; it provides a condition sufficient to make it robustly likely that the humanoids will evolve those capacities. But this sufficiency claim raises a natural question. Does anything in the genealogy, or in our argument more generally, suggest that the mastery of language is necessary as well as sufficient for the emergence of the capacities? Does anything suggest that they could not appear in any creatures that did not have language?

Strictly speaking, the genealogy does not require an answer to the necessity question. But we have already suggested, and will continue to suggest, that non-human animals do not show evidence of the intentional activity involved in judgment, reasoning, or percipience, or associated with normativity, responsibility, and personhood. Thus, it may be useful to say something to explain that suggestion, offering a reason to think that mastery of a language may indeed be necessary as well as sufficient for the appearance of those capacities.

Creatures who lack anything like human language will still be able to act intentionally for various ends in the external world. To anticipate discussion in the next chapter, they will be able to act out of a desire to change aspects of their environment or their relationship to that environment, being guided in the enterprise by beliefs about the concrete items around them: the animals they pursue or avoid, the places where they like to spend time, and so on. But can they form beliefs about more abstract and elusive entities and let such beliefs guide intentional action? Can they form beliefs about the beliefs of another, or indeed their own beliefs, and act with a view to shaping those attitudes, as human beings do in exercising the capacity for judgment? Or can they form beliefs with a view to similar actions about the elements relevant to the capacities associated with reasoning and percipience, normativity, responsibility, and personhood?

In order to act on the concrete objects in their external environment such agents will have to be able to recognize the concrete items relevant to the efforts they make and form beliefs about them; they must have a conception of any food they seek or any predator they try to evade. And in order to act on the environment of the mind, whether in another's case or in their own, they would have to be able to recognize and conceptualize relatively abstract entities like beliefs and desires, evidence and reason, obligation and commitment. We shall see in the following chapters how the concepts required will become accessible to creatures like our humanoids once they have a natural language at their disposal. But it is hard to see how animals without such a language could ever identify and target such elusive items. Thus, it may well be, as we often suggest, that language is necessary as well as sufficient for the appearance of judgment and the other capacities targeted.[28]

1.5 Interlude: following rules

1.5.1 The problem

If the humanoids are to use basic, undefined signs intentionally—say, one- or two-word predications like 'red' or 'stick' or 'left of'—then they must be able to identify the items signified—the classes or kinds or properties predicated—and to track them intentionally in communicating information; they must be able to identify instances reliably, though not infallibly, and try to follow the rule of predicating a term only of such instances. Thus, if expressions like 'red' or 'stick' or 'left of' belong in their basic, undefined repertoire of terms, they must be able to identify instances of the signified class or kind or property—relations count for these purposes as properties—and must be reliably equipped to try, without any guarantee of success, to use the predicate only when that abstract feature is concretely instantiated.

This exercise requires the humanoids to follow the item signified—equivalently, to be guided by the meaning of the sign for that item—as they might follow a rule. The rule they follow may be formulated like this: use the predicate involved, only where the property or kind is instantiated. They must follow that rule intentionally and reliably; they must be guided by the signified item in their use of the sign while not being insured against occasional error.

---

[28] The discussion in the next section suggests that the mastery of signs may also be required for the ability to follow basic rules, which is presupposed by the capacity for judgment and by the other capacities targeted in the genealogy.

That all sounds fine but it gives rise to what has come to be known as the rule-following problem. This was identified most influentially in the work of Ludwig Wittgenstein (1958; 1978), and given further prominence in a constructive interpretation of Wittgenstein's approach by Saul Kripke (1982); see too (Wright 1980). Where Wittgenstein focuses on perceptual cases of basic rule-following, as with a basic, undefined term for a property like 'red' or 'stick', Kripke focuses on the plus-function that presumably guides us, and would guide the humanoids, in calculating sums and in recognizing instances of addition; we assume that this too is basic in the sense that it is not defined for us in other terms.

The core problem with following a rule—specifically, a basic undefined rule—is that the abstract item that the rule-follower is supposed to target has an indefinite number of instances and cannot be made available for targeting and tracking in a way that encompasses all of them. Any finite sample of instances will instantiate many other classes or kinds or properties as well as the intended one. This holds on the same basis as the more familiar claim that any finite set of integers can be extended in an indefinite number of ways; it can be taken as a sample of an indefinite number of larger sets. So how do agents, human or humanoid, get to target the intended property and then track it across novel situations, predicating it only in cases where it is actually instantiated?

Our genealogy will be persuasive only to the extent that the humanoids might plausibly solve this problem, learning in their first forays into intentional signaling to track abstract classes or kinds or properties in their use of basic signs. Rather than assume that there must be some resolution of this difficulty, or that it is not a serious problem, we try in this section to sketch an account of how the humanoids might come to do this. We focus on how they might actively try to apply a basic predicate of their simple language, taking a suitable property as a target to track in how they use a sign like 'red' or 'stick' or 'left of' or indeed 'addition'. If an agent can do this actively, they will also be able to do it as a matter of established habit: they will be guided in a similar fashion, following the rule in a standby or virtual manner, if they can rely on a red flag—this may just consist in something's feeling anomalous—to alert them to any departure from the rule and to prompt a return to active consideration of the case.[29]

The account of rule-following presented here gives a crucial role to social triangulation among the humanoids and offers a society-first view of this basic practice that nicely complements the society-first view of the capacities explained in the genealogy that follows. Like our earlier discussion of the humanoid access to language, it has a how-possibly character, seeking only to show that rule-following is not mysterious or miraculous. That is all that is required to provide a basis on

---

[29] The story told draws many strands from my earlier discussions of the problem, collected in (Pettit 2002). For a similar account, see (Pettit 2023a).

which to pursue the genealogy—itself, as we know, a how-probably story about the humanoids—in later chapters.

1.5.2 The applicational model of rule-following

In raising the rule-following problem, both Wittgenstein and Kripke work with the assumption that trying to conform to a rule means identifying the rule and then looking in case after case to see if it applies. They start from what we might describe as an applicational model of rule-following. Thus, Wittgenstein takes this model as background when he asks how a rule, understood as something like a formula, could guide me or any agent in determining whether it applies in a novel situation, instructing me on what to do: 'how can a rule shew me', he asks, 'what I have to do at *this* point?' (Wittgenstein 1958, para. 198).[30] Kripke (1982, 22) asks in the same style, how it can be that I or any other subject can be guided or directed by a basic rule. How can it be, as he puts it, that 'there is something in my mind ... that instructs me what I ought to do'. After all, as he comments, 'I do not predict what I will do', in such a case, 'but instruct myself what I ought to do to conform'.

This problem will clearly arise for the intentional signaling capacity that humanoids must have if they are to learn language and embark on linguistic communication. They will have to begin with basic signs that they cannot define in other terms, seeking to be guided by the signified property or kind or class as they decide on what sign to use in one or another case. But how can they target an entity that has such an indefinite extension and put themselves in a position to track it across different situations? How can they try to conform to the rule that requires them to use such a sign—such a sentence—only when the signified item is present?

The crux of the problem, as both Wittgenstein and Kripke present it, is that we cannot tell a plausible story about how someone, human or humanoid, might learn a basic rule and be able to apply it—interpret its requirements—without a definition. The alternative to learning a rule by means of a definition would presumably be, learning it by ostension. This would involve examining a finite set of examples—say, examples of addition—and developing an ability to identify a rule there and to apply it across a potentially infinite number of other cases. But what is it about any set of examples that would establish that one way of extrapolating to other cases is correct, another incorrect?

Take $1 + 2 = 3, 2 + 3 = 5, 6 + 5 = 11$. What is it about those examples that might ensure that $11 + 7 = 18$ is an example of the same function but $13 + 3 = 25$ is not? The problem, as Wittgenstein (1958, para. 198) says, is that whatever I choose to do in identifying where the rule leads 'is, on some interpretation, in accord with

---

[30] Thus, Robert Brandom (1994, 64–66) takes rules in Wittgenstein's sense as items to be consulted, as indeed we might consult a formula.

the rule'. Kripke (1982, 8) emphasizes a related point when he asks how I can know that the rule I had in mind in treating the earlier examples as additions implies that 13 + 3 = 16, not 25. Who 'is to say what function this was', he asks, since in the past I can only have given myself 'a finite number of examples instantiating this function?' What is it that I am supposed to recall from those earlier examples, then, that tells me now what function I had in mind?

The rule-following problem looks quite insoluble from within this way of seeing it, as Wittgenstein himself insists. Rejecting the applicational—he would say the interpretational—way of thinking, he maintains that 'there is a way of grasping a rule which is *not* an *interpretation,* but which is exhibited in what we call "obeying the rule" and "going against it" in actual cases' (Wittgenstein 1958, para. 201).[31] In thinking in an interpretational way, he suggests, 'we are like savages, primitive people, who hear the expressions of civilized men, put a false interpretation on them, and then draw the queerest conclusions from it' (para. 294).

Kripke displays no such tendency to reject the applicational way of thinking. Thus, taking the problem as formulated within applicational assumptions, he suggests—or strictly, suggests that Wittgenstein holds—that it is insoluble and that only a skeptical response is defensible. According to the line he sketches, describing someone as following a basic rule is really an honorific. It is a grandiose way of saying that from the point of view of the relevant community the person is an insider: one of us, as others in the society will think. And so, presumably, the aim of an individual in following a rule will be to adjust so as to be in sync with others.[32]

1.5.3 The implementational model of rule-following

What line are we to take on rule-following, if the applicational model is a failure? How are we to explain the capacity we assume in humanoids to learn to use basic signs intentionally, employing them in accordance with rules that relate each sign to an item it signifies?

We might think of turning to Wittgenstein, since he rejects the applicational way of thinking. But the story he offers, alas, is quite obscure. He may be clear about what misleads us, but he is so elusive about his own solution—about what we should think—that his comments have generated an industry of scholarship. Thus, he compares a rule to a signpost, suggesting that the solution is to see rule-following as governed by social convention: 'a person goes by a sign-post only in so far as there exists a regular use of sign-posts, a custom' (Wittgenstein 1958, no 198).

---

[31] For a useful account of Wittgenstein's rejection of the role of interpretation in basic rule-following, see (Miller 2015) and, for a more general overview, (Miller 2024). See also (Swindlehurst 2020).
[32] On the account to be presented here, the humanoids will seek convergence with one another for the sake of determining in an exercise of triangulation what is likely to be the case. On Kripke's account, they will seek convergence, not for any such independent reason, but for its own sake.

Emphasizing the social aspect, he adds that 'obeying a rule is a practice,' so that 'it is not possible to obey a rule "privately"'(Wittgenstein 1958, 202). But what exactly this means remains obscure in his preferred, aphoristic formulations.

The approach to be defended here may pick up some lines of thought that Wittgenstein has in mind when he emphasizes the social character of rule-following. But it is better developed in its own terms, not as a reading of his work. It involves holding that what humanoids can be intelligibly taken to do, on the guiding assumptions behind our genealogy, involves implementing rules as distinct from applying them.

On this implementational model, the humanoids will be able to follow rules in virtue of two dispositions that they must have under our guiding assumptions about their make-up. The first is an extrapolative inclination in each humanoid, given the presentation of some instances of a suitable property, to take some other items as being of a kind with it, and others as not being of that kind. And the second is an inclination to balk at such an extrapolation—in effect, such a classification—in the light of divergence from others.

1.5.4 The extrapolative inclination in rule-following

On the assumption that the humanoids resemble human beings and many non-human animals in linguistically independent features, they will be prompted by exposure to certain sets of samples to extrapolate to wider, open sets, where an open set of that kind will thereby constitute a similarity class that is salient for them. The prompting may be in virtue of nature, as when a simple animal spontaneously treats suitable items as edible foods or useful nesting materials, as predatory enemies or pursuable prey. Or it may be in virtue of training as with a pigeon that is conditioned by the reward of seeds to peck at triangular doors.

This means that the humanoid young may be alerted by their elders to various classes of things, including the class associated with a color or shape property, a relational property, or a certain kind of object. Thus, if they are introduced to prompting examples from a salient class by the use of an associated sound, as in a training regime, that should lead them to treat certain other items as fit to be tagged in that same way. There may be nothing that makes it uniquely rational to extrapolate from such examples in just one direction, of course; that is the lesson on which Wittgenstein and Kripke focus. But it is nonetheless that case that, sharing in our nature, the humanoids will be routinely triggered by a suitable sample set to treat it as a subset, of just one larger, potentially infinite set; and this, regardless of what such treatment involves.[33]

---

[33] In language introduced in the interlude on demystification and metaphysics in the third section, their make-up will embody a key that directs them to the property associated with that set, and not to any other property. Of course, that set or property may not be strictly unique; the key they embody by

When a humanoid agent is alerted to the existence of a class or property or kind in the simple manner envisaged, they will be disposed by nature or training to extrapolate from certain instances to others. But they will not extrapolate to those other instances, because they are instances of the relevant kind: that would require them already to be aware of that kind. They will be disposed to extrapolate appropriately by virtue of the natural, neuropsychological functioning that presumably operates within them in a sub-personal, unconscious fashion. They will not be disposed to extrapolate as they do because of seeing things as instances of the kind; they will see them as instances of that kind because of being disposed to extrapolate to those instances.[34]

Kripke makes much of this extrapolative or classificational inclination in acknowledging that subjects may be expected to have a disposition to continue more or less blindly in identifying other instances of a similarity set—say, to apply the same tag to them—that is presented in some initial examples. But he does so in the course of insisting, plausibly, that just to be moved by such a disposition is not yet to be guided by a rule: say, a rule for how to tag them. Even simple animals give evidence of such an inclination when they are trained or conditioned to respond to instances of a certain kind of stimulus with a certain form of treatment. And it would be absurd to take them in the relevant sense to be following rules.

Consider the pigeon that is conditioned by the reward of a seed to peck at triangular doors, and only triangular doors, within a range of doors to which it is exposed. And suppose, plausibly, that the conditioning enables it to do this regardless of the precise form or color or size of the doors. The pigeon will be sensitized by that conditioning to the property of triangularity—or, allowing for some idiosyncrasy, an approximation of that property—within the relevant domain of doors. Its sensitization will establish that the set of doors in question constitutes a property: that is, as we saw in the interlude on demystification and metaphysics in section 3, a set such that other members can be identified—this, by the key implemented in the pigeon's brain—from a proper subset. But its sensitization will not enable it to follow a rule for picking out triangles; it will presumably respond to each triangular door on the basis of a brute inclination, not out of an intention to respond as triangularity makes it appropriate to respond.

As with the pigeon, a disposition on the part of humanoids to respond to one or another set of items with a tag that they have been primed to use will not mean that they act out of an intention to use the tag only of items displaying the property that

---

nature or training may pick out a small family of sets or properties that overlap in all or most of the cases they will ever confront.

[34] For a sketchy account of how such an inclination, grounded in neuropsychological make-up, might make salient a class of a certain color, see (Pettit 2003). The idea in a case like this is that things look to be of a certain color because of engaging a suitable subject's or tracking inclination in the subject, not the other way around.

the initial examples exemplify. The tagging disposition that humanoids manifest may be no more sophisticated than the pecking disposition of the pigeon. But still, that tagging disposition may serve the humanoids in a manner that takes them closer to intentional tagging and intentional signaling.[35]

The pigeon that responds to triangular doors in a systematic fashion is disposed in response to such a door—broadly, in response to evidence—to act as it would be rational for it to act, given its desire for the reward on offer, if indeed the door were triangular. It displays an evidence-sensitive disposition, as we may say, to treat the door as triangular. Anticipating discussion in the next chapter, this means that in each case it forms a belief that the door is triangular.

By analogy with that achievement, the humanoid subjects who respond to instances of the color red by tagging it with a corresponding sound like 'red' will treat each instance as red: that is, will act as it would be rational for them to act, assuming a desire to tag, if indeed it were red. In other words, they will believe in each instance where the presentation tends to elicit a suitable tagging response that the item presented is red although, lacking the desire to tag in some instances, they may not always display that disposition in action.

This is to say that the tagging practice of the humanoids, like the pigeon's pecking habit, will reveal a belief, now in one case, now in another, that a particular item has a certain character. But the tagging practice will enable the humanoids, at least in principle, to do something more than form beliefs about the particular items in an extrapolatively relevant class. With the same tag given to the range of items in that class, it can also be used to pick out the class itself.

Suppose that one humanoid does not hear how another has tagged something such as an animal that the other alone can see, and that a third party relieves their ignorance of how the speaker tagged the animal by using the tag themselves, as in uttering the appropriate sound: say, 'zebra'. That third party may not themselves believe that the animal is a zebra, so that their use of the tag cannot indicate the presence of a belief that it is a zebra; they will use the tag within quotation marks, so to speak. But what belief in the third party will be associated with this use of the tag? Presumably, that the belief that the speaker assigned the animal to the zebra-class.

In this sort of usage the tag serves not to assign the animal to the zebra class, but to refer to the class—designated by the quotation-marks use of the tag—and to pick it out as the class to which the speaker assigned the animal. The example shows that tags will enable the humanoids to direct attention for themselves or others, not

---

[35] It may be a limitation in biological nature that individuals find it natural to extrapolate in a specific direction from a set of examples. But it is a happy limitation, as Borges (1962) emphasizes in his story of 'Funes the Memorious'. Funes saw only particulars, being 'the solitary and lucid spectator of a multiform, instantaneous and intolerably precise world'. And that made thought impossible. 'To think', as Borges says, 'is to forget differences, generalize, make abstractions. In the teeming world of Funes, there were only details, almost immediate in their presence.'

just to particular items presented to them, but to abstract items like the classes or kinds or properties under which particulars are presented. Let a tag be used in the formation of particularistic beliefs about a range of items, and it will also be available for use in identifying the class to which those particulars are assigned. And insofar as humanoids use the tag in that way, they will be able to form beliefs about the class itself; the domain of their beliefs will include abstract as well as concrete objects.

The observation here picks up an old idea that it is only with words that classes or kinds, properties or universals, get to become objects of attention about which people can form beliefs. Hobbes gives expression to that idea when he argues that a universal property would have no salience for human beings in the absence of a word or appellation for its instances. As he puts it in one context, 'the appellation white bringeth to remembrance the quality of such objects as produce that colour or conception in us' (Hobbes 1994a, 5.2).[36]

This line of thought argues that insofar as the humanoids tag particular things on the basis of extrapolative inclinations elicited by nature or training, they will have a means of identifying the class to which it can be used to assign particulars, making that class or kind or property an object of attention. That observation is sufficient to figure in a how-possibly account of rule-following such as we are seeking here. But, for the record, will the humanoids have any reason or motive to focus on abstract kinds in this way? It turns out that they will, given the assumption, supported in the third section, that like human beings they have the capacity and disposition to act together for shared purposes.

In order for agents to practice jointly intentional activity of this kind, they must not only be sensitized to particular activities or objects in the manner of the pigeon. They must also be sensitive to the kinds of activities, say foraging or hunting, that they may want one another to enact in a certain context. And equally they must be sensitive to the kinds of objects that those activities are designed to target: the animals to be hunted, for example, the plants to be collected. Even in the absence of a tagging practice, they would have to be able to make those kinds salient to one another. How can they do this prior to having tags? Presumably by treating particulars in some contexts, not as particulars, but as exemplars of one or another kind: say, by treating a simulated hunting action as a way of proposing a hunt or a particular animal visible in the distance as a way of designating the prey to be hunted.[37]

But while the humanoids might treat particular instances as exemplars of a kind, their capacity to do so, and to propose and pursue joint actions, would be enormously enhanced by the use of tags to pick out kinds in common. And so we might

---

[36] See also (Hobbes 1994b, 4.6–4.10) and (Pettit 2008a, Ch. 2).
[37] In using instances to exemplify kinds in these ways, the humanoids would be availing themselves of the distinctive mode of signaling that Nelson Goodman (1969) describes as exemplification.

expect the humanoids to embrace the practice whereby tags can come to serve in that role. They will have a motive as well as a means to make abstract classes and kinds into objects to which they can refer and attend. Those items will be epistemically available to them as objects about which to form beliefs and related attitudes like desires.

1.5.5 Extrapolating is not enough for rule-following

But if such *abstracta* are accessible in that way to them, won't this on its own enable the humanoids to follow rules? More specifically, won't it enable them to form the intention to use a basic tag in accordance with the rule of doing so only in the presence of the associated property? Won't it enable them to identify that class or kind or property and to let it guide them on whether to use the tag in this or that instance? The answer to these questions is no.

By our assumptions, their extrapolative dispositions will help the humanoids to act together successfully in the general run of things, leading them to respond in the same way to more or less common properties. But it remains the case, that they will each be prompted to respond in relevant cases by their personal disposition: they could hardly be prompted by someone else's. Those dispositions are bound to come apart in some cases, however, due to differences in the circumstance and competence of individuals. And so, when they come apart, the humanoids are bound to go different ways. They may continue to use the same tagging sound, where this is individuated by its sub-personally registered phonetic character. But they will each use that sound on a somewhat different pattern.

But now we can see the problem with thinking, on the basis of the story so far, that the humanoids will be following rules in their tagging practices. If they are each prompted by their own disposition, then they cannot ever count as applying a tag mistakenly to something that lacks the relevant property or as overlooking the presence of the property and failing to apply the tag. And not being liable to mistake or to overlook the property associated with a tag, they cannot be thought to track that property, trying to use the tag only in its presence. The idea of trying to satisfy a constraint, intentionally seeking to meet it, will apply only if the constraint is one that the agent might fail, despite their best efforts, to satisfy.

The reason for the immunity of the humanoids to this sort of error or oversight is due to the fact that, by the account so far, the property any one of them identifies on the basis of their extrapolative disposition is just the property that is realized in the particular instances that trigger their disposition. If they are led to posit the property in this or that item on the basis of how the disposition prompts them to tag it, the property will be present whenever they apply the tag and will be absent whenever they fail to apply it. The problem is that the extrapolative inclination that serves as a diagnostic in prompting the tagging response will also serve as the determinant of whether the property is present or absent.

The tagging will not constitute an exercise in which they might go wrong, whether because of misunderstanding the property associated with the tag or misreading the item to which it is or is not applied. The tagging cannot count as an intentionally controlled exercise in which they can go astray. It will amount to little more than a sort of baptism on their part: a decision, in view of their personal inclination, to dub or not dub something with the tag.

1.5.6 The balking inclination in rule-following

On the story just elaborated, it will follow that if two or more individuals use a given, phonetically individuated tag in different ways, then they will not count as disagreeing with one another about how to dub things with that tag: about the property associated with the tag. They will each associate a different property with the tag they use, although those properties must approximate one another—their extensions must overlap in good part—if the humanoids are to be generally successful in their joint undertakings. In the end, they will each march to their own private drum, letting their extrapolative inclination prompt them in at least some instances to go in a different direction from others. There will be no drum that they might hope to be prompted by in common and no basis for any one of them to judge that they may have been prompted to go in the wrong direction.

Is there a way of developing our story so as to make room for the idea that the humanoids might target a common property in their use of a tag and might recognize the possibility of disagreement? Yes, there is. The implementational model of rule-following aims to achieve that effect by positing a second, balking inclination to interact with the extrapolative disposition in a way that gives the humanoids a common property to track and occasionally disagree about.

The case for positing this balking inclination derives from the guiding assumption that the humanoids are not just naturally disposed toward joint action, which was important in the previous discussion: they are disposed in particular toward the sort of joint action in which one plays the role of teacher or master and another that of student or apprentice. However tacitly or infrequently they play those roles, the manifest fact that they can do so will ensure that, perhaps in the manner of a working, unarticulated assumption, they will take one another to occupy a common world and to enjoy a shared capacity to learn about that world. And that means that they must be puzzled at any divergence between them in how they use a given tag in response to things; it will not square with their working assumptions.

The puzzle that any discrepancy in their tagging dispositions raises will presumably cause the humanoids to balk, and to assume that one or other of the discrepant parties has not tagged things appropriately; for simplicity, we may take it that not everyone gets it wrong. How, then, will they react? Well, if one is a master, and others are apprentices, the others may defer to the master. Or if it is one against many others, that individual may defer to the majority. Or of course they may go their different ways in the case on hand, especially if it is of no practical import, each assuming that they are in the right.

Will they try to explain why they respond in different ways, looking for a factor that may be treated as a cause of error or oversight on someone's part: a disrupter, as they will come to see it, of the relevant individual's response? If they were to do that, then the explanation would presumably direct them to a failure of functioning on one or another side: a failure to be exposed fully to the world, for example, or a failure to process the inputs from that world in the same way as others. And that being so, they might learn reliably, if not invariably, to identify a disrupter of such a kind in the case of discrepant taggings and, in light of correcting for its effects, they might be able to restore convergence between them.

Presumably, they will be capable of discerning some events as the causes of others, since that is a capacity present at some level in non-human animals and in young children (Sperber, Premack, and Premack 1996). And being able to discern such events—being able, in our terminology, to extrapolate and classify them—they will be in a position to tag the relational property of causation, now in this instance, now in that. That being so, they will presumably look for the causes that lead them, despite their common access to a common world, to respond differently in tagging a given item.[38] The cause they postulate will presumably be a factor like an obtruding object that affects the access of some of the parties to how things are or a factor like distraction or fatigue that affects how they see the things they access. They will have a motive for seeking such a causal explanation, since it will put them in a position to identify factors that put some astray—the novice, those in the minority, or in principle just about anyone—and in recognizing whose response is disrupted, to achieve convergence once again.

Since the humanoids are like human beings, of course, they may never reach convergence even on the basic issues relevant here. In that case, again like our own species, they may adopt any of a variety of stances. They may insulate and ignore the difference in tagging, assuming there is no way to resolve it; or assume on each side that those on the other, being subject to an unrecognized failure, mistag things; or perhaps hold that, like baldness, the property they disagree on is vaguely defined, and that the case on hand is in a borderline area where divergence is acceptable.

The interplay between their extrapolative and balking inclinations will enable or even force the humanoids to see that with any property of the kind associated

---

[38] The line of response depicted here will enable them in principle to resolve discrepancies in tagging the causal relationship itself.

with a basic tag, their spontaneous extrapolative disposition may lead them astray. Under the influence of something affecting their access to inputs or their processing of inputs, they may miss the presence of a certain property, or be mistaken about its presence in a case where it is absent. Their personal inclination to classify things together in a certain way cannot have a special status, as it would if it established the associated class in the authoritative mode of a baptism. It can constitute only a corrigible indication of the class or kind or property at issue: a diagnostic but not a determinant of its presence.

This means that it will now make sense for the humanoids to seek to use a certain tag of this or that item only if the property associated with the tag is present there. They will be prompted spontaneously by their extrapolative disposition to use or not use the tag in a given case. But they will do so only on the assumption, no doubt a default assumption, that there is nothing affecting their access to inputs or their processing of inputs that might be indicted in the explanation of discrepancies among them. The property they seek to track in their use of a tag will be one that they can expect to identify successfully only in the absence of disrupters that are apt to have such an effect: only in the presence of what they can see as normal or ideal conditions (Pettit 1999). Their extrapolative disposition may serve as an indispensable diagnostic of the presence of the property but it cannot count in itself as a determinant of whether or not it is present.

On the picture projected in this story, the humanoids will triangulate on one another's responses in seeking out the properties that their tags identify and that provide the rules to follow in their tagging. They will look for convergence with others in their tagging performance although not for its own sake. Convergence will not matter for them as such—not in the way it seems to matter for Kripke's Wittgenstein—but only as an indication, however defeasible, that they have tagged the items they confront in a manner that is faithful to the nature of the world that they share with one another.

As we envisage the humanoids taking this step, we can see why they can treat their tagging responses to the world as signs of how the world, as it presents to them, is. It will make sense for them to take the tags or words used by another as carrying potentially useful information about the world and equally it will make sense for them to issue their own verbal responses as ways of conveying such information to others. To anticipate the discussion in the next chapter, they will be able to think of their responses and the responses of others as intentionally authored assertions about the nature of the environment.[39]

---

[39] In comments on an earlier version of this approach, Alex Miller (2018, 278–88) suggests that I assume that the parties who come to follow rules must first speak the same language, which itself presupposes rule-following. I hope the presentation here shows that that is not so.

1.5.7 Implementing rather than applying rules

On this account of rule-following, the humanoids will be able to follow basic, undefined terms insofar as the following conditions are satisfied.

- Each will intentionally use a basic sign ('red', 'bulky') in this or that case
- in sensitivity to an extrapolative inclination that comes naturally to them,
- balking at going with that inclination in the case of divergence from others,
- and relying on well-tested triangulation to determine how they ought to go.

Given the fulfilment of such conditions, the humanoids will count as following rules in their use of basic signs. They will intentionally use any such sign to register in case after case the presence or absence of the class or kind or property that answers to how triangulation with others would reliably lead them. This class or kind or property, in other words, is that which would be detected by anyone in the absence of those disrupters that triangulation is designed to uncover in the course of achieving convergence: that is, in the presence of conditions that count by that intersubjective test as normal or ideal.

This model of rule-following is distinguished from the applicational model by the fact that the humanoids will follow rules as an incidental result of seeking to tag things on a certain pattern and not as an independently salient means of doing so. In tagging things in response to how they present, they will seek to provide information on how things are in a world they take to be shared in common between them, and accessible to all. Their extrapolative or classificational inclinations will give them a first take on how things are, with their tags allowing them to track the properties they predicate in different instances. But given the assumption of a commonly accessible world, they will be permanently ready to doubt that response. The appearance of differences with others will be evidence of the presence of potential disrupters, as they will learn to see them, and will give them pause. And, depending on where the disrupters prove to operate, it may lead them to reject the tagging of others or to revise their own.

In pursuing this activity, the humanoids will do something that manifestly constitutes following rules. Alert to the general classes or kinds or properties associated with their tags—these will be fixed in triangulation with others—they will seek to tag or describe things as those intersubjectively determined features make it appropriate to do. They will conduct the intentional activity of recording how things are in accordance with rules that require them to predicate a property of something, or assign it to that class or kind, only when the property is present. But they need not be aware of those rules as such and will not count as applying them with a view to describing things accurately. By virtue of the interaction between their extrapolative and balking dispositions, they will follow rules, but only in the sense of implementing rather than applying them.

Socrates asked Euthyphro whether the gods love the holy because it is holy or whether it is holy because the gods love it. We might have asked a parallel question in opening this discussion of how the humanoids can follow rules in intentionally signaling. Do they manage to signal because they follow rules? Or do they follow rules because they signal? In other words, is their rule-following a means or a byproduct of signaling? On the applicational model, it is presented as a means; on the implementational model, as we can now see, it is counts as a byproduct.

It is worth emphasizing that the implementational model of rule-following does not require any high intellectual ability or aspiration on the part of the humanoids. In presenting the model, we have had to describe stages in its emergence as if they involved a cascade of enlightening insights. But for all that the model requires, we may take the humanoids to have confidence on a default basis in their extrapolative, tagging instincts, to assume without thinking that something is amiss if they tag things differently from others, and to look spontaneously for an explanation of such differences that may restore convergence. Relying on such unarticulated assumptions, the humanoids will find a world in which classes, kinds, and properties are as salient as the particulars that instantiate them, and display a presumptive objectivity that can be tested, if needs be, by resort to triangulation. As they perceive that world, it will lend itself to an exercise of tagging particulars in accordance with their presumptively objective properties, where that will amount to intentionally signaling how things are for the benefit of any audience.[40]

On this account of how the humanoids might come to follow basic rules, and be positioned to use signals intentionally, it is essential that they learn to relate to one another in a triangulating way, though they will hardly recognize the triangulation as such. Presumably, an individual humanoid may have learned to do this in the past and then go on to isolate themselves like a Robinson Crusoe. But by the story told, everyone must have interacted at some point with others and relied on the explanation of divergence to give them a sense of the objective world.

That raises a question that often figures in discussions of rule-following. Would it be inherently impossible for creatures to develop an individual capacity for rule-following without the sort of social interaction that allows the humanoids to follow rules? That possibility is hardly likely among creatures who are social in the way humans and humanoids are social, relating to one another as teachers and learners. But is it a bare, metaphysical possibility?[41]

---

[40] The negotiation of difference is also important, as we shall see, in making sense of reasoning. But even relatively intuitive reasoning involves elements that need not be present in the exercise of rule-following, as that is characterized here. More on this in the last section of Chapter 3.

[41] Thus, it is conceivable in principle that an individual creature like one of our humanoids might recognize that their own responses vary over time; might identify obstructing factors that explain this variation, without relying on triangulation with others, as in the story we develop; and might try to track the property—potentially, an idiosyncratic property—that shows up only in the absence of such obstruction. For defenses of rule-following that is private in this sense, see (Blackburn 1984) and (Azzouni 2017).

Happily, we can leave open that question, and indeed some related metaphysical issues, in this discussion.[42] The goal has simply been to explain how the humanoids might make use of basic signaling materials—the resources of a simple language—in the intentional exercise of exchanging information with one another. Intentional signaling of that kind does assume a capacity on the part of the humanoids to aim to conform in their utterances to the classes or kinds to which they assign things, the properties they predicate of them, and to let those entities guide them like rules in what they choose to say. What we have seen should be sufficient to show how they may be expected to do this. And that takes us to a point where we may turn to the genealogy of the six capacities targeted. We do that in the next chapter when we look at how their access to language might enable the humanoids to develop the capacity for judgment.[43]

---

[42] Thus, I set aside the issue of whether on our model, the referent of a term like 'plus' must be indeterminate beyond the boundary where it becomes impossible for humanoids or humans to make judgments and triangulate. For some discussion, see (Pettit 1993, Postscript; 2002, Pt. 1).

[43] My thanks to Kim Sterelny for a discussion of many of the issues in this chapter. And my thanks to James Willoughby for detailed comments on an early draft.

2
Agency with judgment

The conjecture explored in this book, as the first chapter documents, is that a range of distinctively human capacities appears in two forms, one social, the other mental; that the social capacity involves skill in a corresponding interpersonal practice; and that the intrapersonal counterpart appears with the exercise of that skill in a novel, mental context. Our aim is to defend that conjecture by arguing that suitable counterfactual counterparts—the humanoids—would be robustly likely to respond to the emergence of language by developing the social practices and then adapting them to use within their own minds.

We begin in this chapter with the capacity for making judgments, in particular making judgments about what to believe; we will comment also, but only later and more briefly, on the capacity for making judgments about what to prefer as between various alternatives, and about what in appropriate circumstances to decide and do: what intention or policy to form. The capacity, in ordinary terms, involves making up our mind about the attitudes to have and the actions to perform.

Like other animals, we often have our minds made up for us, as when evidence from perception or memory or imagining prompts us unthinkingly to update our beliefs or preferences or intentions or to undertake certain actions. But we human beings can take intentional charge of this shaping of our minds, at least on certain issues. We can make intentional efforts to form judgments in response to the evidence available to us, to form corresponding attitudes and to take corresponding actions. It is that capacity for judgment that is targeted here.

Judgments appear at a particular moment in time and contrast in that regard with states of belief and the like that endure, however briefly, over time. In one common usage, the term 'judgment' refers to the event constituted by the onset of a belief and in that sense any intentional agent may be said to form judgments. But judgment in the sense intended here is something characteristic of human beings. It is an act that normally ensures the formation of a corresponding belief, as when someone who makes the judgment that p holds the belief that p. And it is an act that is subject to the agent's intentional control. The agent can choose to make a judgment on whether p or not p, they can choose to seek and scrutinize the evidence either way, and in the presence of evidence that p they can even choose to rely on it in making a judgment or, perhaps because of playing safe, to refrain from doing so.

This discussion of the capacity for judgment is in five sections. In the first, we look at how any intentional agent is bound to form and act on attitudes of beliefs and desire, and how human beings go one better in relying on judgment in the course of attitude formation. In the second section, we look at how language would enable the humanoids to communicate information to one another and how, under reputational pressures, it would elicit a practice of doing so reliably: a practice of making reliable assertions about how things are. We then argue in the third section that when they make such assertions, the humanoids will count as making judgments and that, recognizing this, they will be able to make judgments without giving them expression in words. In the fourth section, we look at the benefit to humanoids of being able, evidence presumptively permitting, to make assertions and judgments in response to the questions of others, and argue that the prospect of a similar benefit will lead them to raise and answer questions for themselves: to interiorize the social practice, taking intentional steps to shape their own beliefs and related attitudes. Finally, in the fifth section, we look at how humanoid judgments and associated on–off beliefs can relate to degrees of confidence or credence; we cast this discussion as an interlude since it is not essential to the development of the genealogy.

2.1 Agency, basic and human

2.1.1 A simple model of agency

By all accounts an agent is a system that acts reliably, whether as a result of selection or design, to bring about certain goals or purposes. But agency requires more than the pursuit of purposes. Otherwise, the sunflower plant that tracks the sun—that reliably moves so as to maintain its orientation toward the sun—would count, implausibly, as an agent.

As we think of agency in our ordinary exchanges, the most obvious requirement over and beyond the pursuit of certain purposes is that this pursuit should be maintained over variations in the circumstances of the system: variations that are more significant, intuitively, than those in the angle of the sun that the sunflower has to cope with. A system may count as an agent and be so simple that it has only a single goal, but still, it must be able to pursue that goal across different scenarios, adjusting its behavior so as to realize the goal under the particularities of each situation.

Take the simple robot that is constructed to pursue the goal of putting glasses and bottles on a flat surface into an upright position (List and Pettit 2011, Ch. 1). Suppose the robot has an eye-like receptor that it uses to scan the objects on the surface, looking for whether any glass or bottle is on its side or upright. And suppose that, presented with a bottle on its side, the robot is designed to adjust so as to put the object upright, regardless of its size or shape, its distance from the robot, or the direction in which it lies. The robot will be able to do this, at least when things go well, with the help of wheels for moving, levers for lifting, mechanisms for grasping, and so on.

This robot will constitute an agent in the sense of having a goal that it is organized to pursue across different scenarios—these will differ in the presence of bottles or glasses, for example, in the size of the objects present, and in their distance and direction from the robot—adjusting its behavior as success in realizing its goal requires. In order to achieve that goal, it must be capable of reliably registering the relevant features of any scenario where it operates; this will involve assuming a corresponding state, correlated with the scenario, that prompts it to behave appropriately for realizing its goals in that environment. Insofar as the state is suitably correlated with the environment, and prompts appropriate behavior, it will constitute the robot's representation of the scenario. Prompted by exposure to the situation where it finds itself, the robot will have to enter such a representational state and exit any states that conflict with it. And as it begins to act on that representation, say in moving to raise a bottle into an upright position, it will have to form further representations of how it is doing: of how close it is at any point to the bottle, of whether it is close enough to stop and try to raise it, and so on (Hurley 1998).[1]

That the robot reliably registers and responds to inputs from its situation—or, as we shall also say, to data or evidence on the situation—does not mean that it is aware of what it registers as data or evidence. It will be disposed by its make-up to pay those inputs attention in forming relevant representations, and to adjust its other representations to fit with those it forms. But it will have no representation of why it does so. In order to figure as data or evidence, the inputs must have a suitable, reliable impact on the agent's representations and, in that sense, its representations must be evidence-sensitive. But the robot itself need not have any representation of the role evidence plays in eliciting its representations.

That the robot does not have an ability to represent this role means, in a straightforward sense, that it lacks a concept of evidence (Geach 1957). It would likely have a need of such a concept or representational ability only if it practiced reasoning, as we shall see in the next chapter. The fact that it can represent objects that count as glasses and bottles, however—or, allowing for some idiosyncrasy, things that approximately correspond to glasses and bottles—means that it does have concepts for such kinds or properties, forming representations in which they figure as predicates. Its concepts of those properties will be stimulus-dependent in the sense that

---

[1] We may abstract here from the issue of how representations may be constituted. The robot's representation that there is a glass on its side at such and such a distance in such and such a direction may consist in a distributed set of adjustments across its make-up, for example—in a whole-body configuration—provided that this configuration disposes it to act appropriately in pursuit of its goal. Critiques that deny the role or significance of representations often denigrate, not representations as such, but representations conceived in a specific mode.

they can figure in its representations only when they are registered or presented via its processing system.

It may be useful to comment in passing on stimulus dependence and independence, as the distinction will come up again. The robot's concept of the property of being a glass is stimulus-dependent because it enables the robot to form only representations of currently registered scenarios and only representations in which that property figures as a predicate. The concept would be weakly stimulus-independent, as we may put it, if it also enabled the robot to form representations of possible, unregistered scenarios in which it figured as a predicate: this, as in a representation that what it previously registered, or what it possibly might yet register, is or is not a glass. And it would be strongly stimulus-independent if it enabled the robot to form representations of scenarios—presumably, unregistered scenarios—in which the property conceptualized figures, not as a predicate, but as the subject of predication: this, as in a representation that the property of being a class correlates with the property of being fragile.[2]

Back now to the main narrative. Taking the robot as a model of simple agency, we may say in familiar Humean terms, that an agent is a system that reliably acts to fulfill its goal-seeking states according to reliably formed representational states. Or drawing on more familiar concepts—more on them in a moment—it is a system that acts reliably for the satisfaction of its desires according to its reliably formed beliefs.

The robot's reliability in forming beliefs constitutes cognitive rationality—more on this in the next chapter—its reliability in acting so as to satisfy desires according to its beliefs constitutes executive rationality. The robot may not be unfailingly reliable or rational but, if it is to count properly as an agent, then in general it must fail only when circumstances are abnormal by independent criteria. Thus, the robot may be misled under certain lighting about the position of an object; and it may not manage to put an object at the edge of a table upright: it may knock it to the floor. Given our specification of its goals, the robot would fail cognitively in the first case, executively in the second.[3]

One final observation before we leave the robot. To ascribe reliability or rationality to an agent is to assume that how it represents things to be, and how it uses its representations in pursuing its purposes, is due to its own organizationally structured processing. The ascription will be out of place—indeed the ascription

---

[2] For an excellent treatment of the distinction between stimulus-dependent and stimulus-independent concepts, and some related issues, see (Camp 2009). And for important background, particularly on the generality test that stimulus-independent concepts satisfy, see (Evans 1982).

[3] The disjunction problem raised by Jerry Fodor (1990) bears on how to determine the right specification for a given agent on the basis of behavioral evidence alone. We should certainly acknowledge that it may not be the property that makes something a bottle or a glass, but only a property that approximates that feature, as acknowledged above. We shall assume, however, that something about the design of the robot—or in the case of animals, something about their evolutionary history (Millikan 1984)—will make it possible to identify the precise property targeted.

of agency will also be out of place—if like a remotely controlled drone, the robot performs appropriately but only under the influence of wirelessly communicated instructions. The ascription will also be out of place if the robot is the creation of an ingenious, fantastical planner who, foreseeing every circumstance it is ever likely to face, builds it to make a pre-designed, rational response to each stimulus of that kind, without any need for processing. To perform reliably up to par, as we understand reliability, the agent must do so on the basis of its own organization; in particular, it must do so in a way that does not depend on guidance from a controller remote in space or on planning by a controller remote in time.[4]

2.1.2 A functionalist model

The Humean picture of agency supported by our robot example gestures at a functionalist model of belief, and indeed also of desire (Stalnaker 1984). This model has the general benefit of enabling us to distinguish states of beliefs from states of desire and the more specific benefit of explaining what makes it the case that a belief has a certain content or that a desire is aimed at a certain goal.

Thus, to start with the general point, the belief that something is the case will be distinguished from the desire that it be the case insofar as it is sensitive to evidence or data that that is so. Evidence that p necessarily or robustly—that is, robustly over presumptively contingent factors—elicits the belief that p, and evidence that not p necessarily or robustly eliminates it, whereas this is not so with the desire that p (Anscombe 1957; Smith 1987).

Turning now to the more specific question, what makes the evidence-responsive disposition of an agent into the belief that p, not that q or that r? And what makes a desire into a desire to X rather than a desire to Y?

The belief that p is a disposition robustly to act as it would be rational to act, given the agent's other presumptively consistent beliefs and desires, if it were the case that p: for short, to act as if p.[5] Note that to act robustly as if p is not to do so necessarily, which means that a system can be an agent without being a perfect agent. And what then of the desire to X? Abstracting from the differences between preferences and intentions—more on this later in the chapter—the desire to X will

---

[4] The requirement of organizational structure would deny the status of an agent to the marionette controlled from Mars, which Christopher Peacocke (1983) imagines. And the requirement of organizational processing would rule out Blockhead, so called: the system, imagined by Ned Block (1981), that is fitted by its designer with a table to determine appropriate behaviors—that is, behaviors that seem to give evidence of suitable purpose and representation—in all relevant circumstances. See (Jackson 1992).
[5] The shorthand appeals for convenience but may sometimes be misleading. Thus, for someone to act as if they are amused, in the ordinary sense of that phrase, is not to act as it would be sensible for them to act, given their other beliefs, if it were the case that they were amused. In later uses, the shorthand should be understood in the way it is spelled out here.

consist in the agent's disposition robustly to act as it would be rational to act, given the agent's beliefs and other desires, in order to X.[6]

Our functionalist model of agency is not uncontroversial but it is at least familiar, being supported in somewhat different versions by recent philosophers like David Lewis (1983), Robert Stalnaker (1984), and Daniel Dennett (1987). Some other models may take agency to be less demanding—perhaps even allowing the sunflower to be an agent—and some may make it more demanding: this, perhaps, in a way that would require the sorts of judgmental and reasoning capacities we have yet to introduce (Davidson 1984, Ch. 11). But the model presented is at least an intelligible reconstruction of our common-sense assumptions, and it gives us a natural starting point for the genealogy.

Our account of the functionalist model is over-simplified, however, in three important respects. The first simplification is implied in the way we have been presenting it rather than being required by the model itself. The presentation suggests, in a common phrase, that beliefs and desires are propositional attitudes: attitudes toward a proposition that is believed—say, that p—or toward a proposition that the agent desires to realize: say, that q. But insofar as such attitudes are characterized in a dispositional or functional way, they need not require an agent to be aware of propositions as items to which they are related in a believing or desiring way. The agent may not be able to hold beliefs about propositions and pick out this or that belief by citing the proposition that serves as its content. The functionally characterized beliefs and desires ascribed may only be propositional attitudes in the sense in which magnitudes or forces are numerical quantities (Loar 1981).[7]

The second simplification in our account, to focus on the case of belief, is that it abstracts from the fact that among the variations with which most agents will have to cope—most agents but not, we may suppose, our robot—there are going to be variations in the impact of the data in any situation and so in the degree of confidence with which the agent holds this or that belief. We shall set aside this complication, however, noting only that it is obviously of great importance. What an agent does is bound to depend, not just on what they believe or indeed desire in an on–off sense, but also on how strongly they believe or desire it. In the final section of this chapter, although by way of an interlude in the overall presentation of the genealogy, we will discuss the relationship between on–off attitudes and attitudes that come in such degrees of confidence or intensity.

---

[6] If the desire is a final desire to X—if it broadly conforms to the idea of an intention, then the reference to 'other desires' will not strictly be necessary.

[7] Numbers can be used to track various quantities insofar as those quantities relate in a numerically describable way, with each being numerically related to others: this, in the way a magnitude or force may be twice or ten times that of another. And in the same way propositions can be used to track various attitudes, as we characterize a belief by a proposition it takes to be true or a desire by a proposition it seeks to make true. But this does not mean that the attitudes involve relations that require agents to be aware of the propositions used to track them. We will return to this issue in the next chapter.

Finally, our account of the functionalist model is over-simplified in implying, to focus again on belief, that every agent will believe every necessary truth: no one can act as if it were not the case that 2+3=5. If the model is to extend to such cases, there must be a range of action available to the agent such that within that range—and, no doubt, only within that range—they may or may not be disposed to act as if a necessary truth were false. By a standard account, that range of behavior will require language, as when someone makes linguistic moves in an argument that fail to respect necessary truths or the entailments of existing beliefs (Stalnaker 1984). This is an example of how the capacity to speak can affect mental performance and bears on the capacity for reasoning discussed in the next chapter.

2.1.3 Two forums for intentional action

Drawing on our simple model of agency, we may say that even an agent like our robot brings about an event intentionally—in the strict sense of bringing it about deliberately—just in case it desires that that type of event should be realized, believes that the behavior it displays will serve its realization, and those attitudes generate the event robustly, not as a result of some contingency.[8] That they generate it robustly means that they do not give rise to the event by any sort of accident; they would still have generated it had circumstances varied in a range of contextually salient ways.[9] In this sense the robot will intentionally raise a glass into an upright position, when it operates in such a way that it would still have brought about that effect if the glass had been just a little bigger, or had a different shape, or been placed at a different point, and so on.

In this sense of intentional action, most things that agents do involve intentionally changing the external world around them in various ways. The robot intentionally puts the glasses and bottles that lie on their sides into an upright position. The dog intentionally runs to the end of the garden, recognizing that that is where the ball has gone. The bird gathers twigs intentionally, seeing them as a means of building its nest. And human beings act intentionally in repairing a bicycle, in getting an errand done, or in searching out food or company. In all such cases agents act to change the world around them, their position in relation to the world, or their access to the resources that the world offers. They act intentionally in the forum of external things.

---

[8] There is another, looser sense in which an agent may do something like X-ing intentionally. In this sense, it requires, not that the agent act with the intention to X as such, but only that the agent know that whatever the aspect under which it is explicitly intended, their action will constitute X-ing, where that knowledge does not make them reluctant to perform it: they do so willingly. More on such a weaker notion of intentional action, and on the idea of voluntariness or willingness, in Chapter 6.

[9] The robustness required is designed to help get around the problem of deviant causation, as it has been called. See (Davidson 1980).

The striking thing about the sphere in which agents operate is that it is usually restricted to that forum; it does not normally include the forum of their own attitudes. The dog that sniffs around among the trees and ground cover at the end of the garden may be said to want to know where the ball is. But if we are to be parsimonious in interpreting its behavior there and in other contexts, we should say that all it intentionally desires is to locate the ball, intentionally running around and intentionally sniffing with a view to attaining that end; it does not desire as such to enter a state of knowing the location of the ball or forming a reliable belief about where it is. True, if it succeeds in locating the ball, it will have come to know where it is or have a belief about what it is. But, plausibly, that psychological state will materialize only unintentionally as a means essential for it to locate the ball: it will materialize in the way my muscles flex without my intending that they do so when they provide me with the means of grasping a cup.

By contrast with the dog, and plausibly with other animals too, we human beings perform intentional actions that are designed to change things in the internal, attitudinal forum. We do this when we seek out relevant evidence on questions that concern us and see whether we are ready in view of that evidence to make a judgment and form a corresponding belief and indeed, if the belief is supportive, a corresponding desire. We act in such cases with a view to making up our own minds, not changing anything in the world around us. We seek out evidence and aspire to make relevant judgments when we try to remember what someone's name is, or try to imagine how differently a scene would look from another perspective, or try to drum up enthusiasm for a new colleague by focusing on their positive attributes, or look at the sun in the attempt to determine how late in the day it is.

In seeking evidence and deciding on whether to make a judgment one way or the other, we exert intentional control over the exercise: we act out of the desire to achieve a certain effect within our own minds. But it is important to notice that we may exercise a similar degree of control over whether and how we make up our minds, without taking active steps toward that end. This is because we often control for certain effects intentionally but do so in a standby or virtual manner, not an active one.

Do I intentionally take a certain route when I walk home from work, even though I act out of sheer habit, thinking about other things? Of course, I do. If habit fails me and I take a wrong turn, then a red flag will go up, prompting me to wonder where I am, and will lead me to reflect and put things right. That shows that even though I take my course home out of brute habit, and without a moment's thought, I remain in standby or virtual control. Habit may be the motor but I as an intentional agent occupy the driving seat, being poised to assume active control if habit fails and a red flag goes up. I outsource the production of the behavior but do not give up control.

As I retain standby, intentional control over an action like finding my way home, so I may retain intentional control over the search for evidence, over making evidentially based judgments and indirectly over forming the attitudes that go with those judgments. I may let the judgments and attitudes appear under the motor of habit but still remain on standby, ready to take active charge should anything go amiss. They will go amiss in that sense if the process leads to such an unlikely result, for example, or generates such disagreement with others, that a red flag prompts me to look or listen again and to see if I misread things the first time around.

This discussion has given us a good overall sense of agency, belief, and desire, and of the role of judgment in our performance as human beings. We now turn to the humanoids, looking to see how far the advent of language might push them from a stage at which they do not intentionally seek to make up their minds about what to believe or desire to a stage at which they do. If it turns out that the mastery of language would push them in this direction, then that should be of the greatest interest. The mastery of language by this account would extend the range of their intentional control, enabling them to take charge—at least in some measure—of the attitudes they form. It would enable them in that measure to make up their own mind about things, freeing them from total dependence on unregulated inputs from the world around them.

2.2 Signaling and asserting

2.2.1 Signaling and informing

We argued in the last chapter that, given the range of competence we assume in the humanoids, there is no inherent mystery about how they might access signs that carry information about the environment: this, in the way in which the natural warning calls of vervet monkeys carry such information; and, more importantly, there is no mystery about how, unlike the vervets, they might use those signs intentionally to convey that information—strictly, that would-be information—to others. The vervets use their calls to convey information in virtue of the brute fact that the calls elicit corresponding beliefs among their conspecifics: they dispose them to form evidence-sensitive dispositions to act as if things were as the calls indicate. The humanoids, by the story told, would use their signs out of a desire to elicit such dispositions or beliefs among their hearers; they would signal intentionally that things are thus and so.

Having sketched how the humanoids might intelligibly get to use signs intentionally—initially, signs that come as naturally to them as their calls come to the vervet monkeys—we maintained that it is equally intelligible why the humanoids would then take a further limited series of steps. They would introduce conventional as well as natural signs to serve their purposes in eliciting beliefs about the environment; they would also use those signs with a different force or significance, as in employing a water-sign—saying 'Water!'—to indicate that they are thirsty; and they would each come to recognize that they and others may use their signs deceitfully as well as honestly, seeking to mislead rather than inform an audience.

As we saw, the humanoids would also take two further steps but under limitations that will only be lifted when they learn to reason. The need to register disagreement would lead them to introduce a way of negating a sign, thereby constructing a sentence, and to combine their signs sententially in other, simple ways—in a conjunctive or disjunctive manner, for example—though hardly in the complex manner of a conditional sentence. Finally, the humanoids might well have access to indexical signs, letting context shape the content of what they signal in a word like 'I' or 'here' or 'now', but there is no reason to think that they could resort to more radical forms of contextual shaping, as exemplified in metaphor or irony.

We noted that as the humanoids come to use such signs—in effect, words and sentences—in an intentional manner, they will inevitably practice communication in the sense illustrated by chimpanzees in a situation of targeted help. In signaling that something is the case, they will each have a response-centered intention to elicit a certain effect—the formation of a belief that that is the case—in their hearers. And they will issue that signal with the recognition-centered intention of getting their hearers to recognize the response they are seeking and, things going well, to make that response as a result: to form the belief that things are as the sign indicates that they are.

In these two respects, the act of signaling among the humanoids will resemble the communicative act of a chimpanzee in the scenario of targeted help: the act that it performs when it reaches for a stick in order to get its partner to recognize what it wants and to respond by handing over the stick. But there is an important difference to mark. The humanoid speaker seeks to get their hearers to form a certain belief, so that they must have a concept of the evidence-sensitive disposition that constitutes belief. The chimpanzee may have to elicit a suitable belief in its partner if the partner is to act appropriately but it need not aim at eliciting the belief as such and need not have a concept of such a state; it may simply aim at getting the partner to act appropriately, relying on it to respond as desired. Where the humanoid seeks to convey information—and perhaps on that basis to elicit a certain action—the chimpanzee seeks to elicit the action alone.

While their signaling activity will require the humanoids to be able to conceptualize beliefs, however, they need not yet make a distinction between the state of believing something and its content—the state of affairs that it posits, the proposition it endorses—treating them as separate items. Or at least they need not do so in the sense in which that would enable them to conceptualize and form beliefs about such a state of affairs or proposition—say, that it is true, or that it entails a distinct state of affairs.

We argue in the next chapter that if they are to be able to reason, then the humanoids must have this capacity to form beliefs about states of affairs or propositions: they must be able to conceptualize them as entities to which they can ascribe properties. But, as noted earlier, the argument in this chapter does not yet presuppose a reasoning ability. For all that is required at this stage, the humanoids will only have a functional view of belief, not one that presents belief as a relationship between the subject and a distinct entity that they can contemplate, like a state of affairs or proposition.[10]

To anticipate the next chapter, this will change when the humanoids become equipped, not just to believe that p in the dispositional or functionalist sense, but to reason from the purported fact that p to other facts. At that point they can still be said in the functionalist sense explained to act robustly as if p. But something performatively equivalent will also hold of them: that is, that they robustly treat it as true that p. And as they may be said in belief to treat it as true that something is the case, so they may be said in desire to treat it as attractive that it should be the case. Neither claim can be made about the humanoids at the current stage, since their conceptualization of beliefs and desires as functional states does not mean that they will be able to conceptualize propositions: it does not mean that propositions are entities about which they can form beliefs, desires, or other attitudes.

2.2.2 Informational exchange

It will clearly be in the interest of humanoids, living in a world of moderate scarcity like ours, to have as much information as possible—to form as many reliable beliefs as possible—about their surrounds. And that means that it will be in their individual interest to be able to access the information available to others as well as the information available to themselves. If they live in the sort of environment where our forebears operated before the agricultural revolution, for example, then they will want to know, not just about the food and other resources that they can register for themselves, but also about the resources that are registered by others. They will want to learn about how things are according to one another's beliefs—presumptively, reliable beliefs—not just according to their own.

In view of the appeal of gaining information about their environment, the humanoids will welcome any reliable information that others can provide in their signaling activities. And of course they will learn also to seek information from others, posing questions to them. As using the sign for water may indicate the presence of water, or indicate against a certain background that they need water, so presumably it may be used to ask a question: to indicate that the speaker wants information about where water is to be found.

---

[10] The way the belief-state posits things to be—something, to anticipate, that will be salient in the corresponding judgment that p—may figure among humanoids in identifying how it disposes the agent to act. But it need only figure at this stage like an adverbial qualifier of the original belief, in the sense that for them believing that p may mean nothing more than believing, being disposed to act, in a that-p way: being disposed to act, in our shorthand, as if p.

These observations suggest that it will be in the interests of the humanoids as a whole to exchange information or least reliable information with one another, so that each is as well informed as others about the opportunities and resources available in their environment. But exchanging will have its problems. For, on the assumption of moderate scarcity in relation to their needs, or the needs of their family, it will often be in the self-interest of any individual humanoid to gain as much reliable information as possible and give away as little as possible. Each will be tempted to free ride: to let others provide information without providing information in return, whether on a given occasion or over a series of encounters.

2.2.3 The economy of esteem

Happily, the existence of free-riding temptations will not undermine the prospect of informational exchange among the humanoids. There are factors that we may expect to push them into being cooperative with one another that are familiar from human life. They are related to tit-for-tat strategies, as they are known and, more generally, to the economy of esteem.

Suppose that you and I are humanoids, that we relate roughly as equals, and that on some occasion you ask me for information, say on where the hunting or fishing is best, and I provide it. And now imagine that then or later I ask you whether the fruit trees on a nearby hill are ripening and that you refuse to provide that information, or mislead me, whether through deception or carelessness. How am I to respond to this failure of reciprocity? If you are someone I can shun without serious loss to my own interests, shunning will make perfect sense. Why should I bother maintaining an otherwise unnecessary relationship with another that puts me at risk of being denied information available to the other or being duped and misinformed by the other?

Since the humanoids live in community, however, they will want to maintain good relationships with at least most of those around them. So what can I do, if you are someone I cannot shun without a loss to my interests: someone with whom I would like to maintain a relationship?

The most salient response available to me will represent a version or cousin of the tit-for-tat strategy mentioned in the opening chapter. I can penalize you for your failure of reciprocity by refusing information the next time around, for example, making clear at the same time that I mean only to teach you a lesson, and that I will respond cooperatively if you are cooperative in our next encounter. This penalizing tactic ought to be successful, given that the humanoids are taken to be mutually reliant individuals living under conditions of relative equality.[11]

---

[11] Did they not live in relative equality, then the stronger might have no incentive to provide information or to tell the truth in such an exchange. And on matters of a more complex kind, the weaker

If something like this tit-for-tat routine gets established among the humanoids, then they will each have a strong prudential motive to communicate information to one another and to be careful and truthful about what they say: to be ready to impart information and to be reliable in the information imparted. If someone fails in either manner, they scarcely expect the other to prove ready and reliable in their informational response.

But the humanoids will not only have this tit-for-tat motive to provide information to others and to be careful and truthful about what they say, they will also be motivated by the fact that third parties may witness how they behaved. For such witnesses may well treat them in later interactions on the basis of how they acted in that original encounter. The witnesses are likely to treat them as uncooperative if they were not ready to provide information or provided unreliable information; they will treat them as cooperative if they proved to be cooperative on those two counts. This being so, the humanoids will become aware that the esteem in which they are held by others, and the manner in which they are therefore treated, will depend on their general performance, assuming it cannot easily be hidden. They will live within an economy of esteem where the incentives should push them into cooperating with others in general, sharing information in a careful and truthful manner.[12]

The economy of esteem is likely to reinforce the cooperative dispositions of the humanoids in virtue of an added effect that language itself will make possible. This is the effect of gossip in spreading the word about anyone who defects on another in exchange, whether through a refusal to share their beliefs or a lack of care or honesty in doing so. Let the word spread about any defection and the class of those who take an individual to have misled someone will become much wider than the group of those who directly witnessed the failure.

Gossip is likely to be a robust phenomenon among the humanoids, as it is among human beings, since each will have an esteem incentive to gossip to others about anyone's failure to cooperate. Such gossip will give evidence, however defeasible, of the speaker's own cooperative disposition, since pronouncing on the failures of others will expose them to a particularly harsh penalty—that accruing to the hypocrite—if they fail themselves. By speaking out about others, they will communicate an assurance that they themselves are reliably cooperative. Why would they risk gossip, exposing themselves to the hypocrite's penalty, if they were not quite sure of their own cooperative disposition?

---

might suffer the epistemic injustice of not having their testimony taken seriously by the stronger; see (Fricker 2007).

[12] There is a long and deep tradition of thinking that human beings live within such an economy of esteem. For an introduction to the traditional belief in the power of esteem, see (Lovejoy 1961), and for more recent treatments, see (Pettit 1990; Brennan and Pettit 2004; Appiah 2010; Liebert 2016; Origgi 2018).

These observations indicate that as the humanoids meet in random pairs, they will display a pattern of reliable informational exchange. They will each be ready to share information with the other but will be generally careful in checking any information sought and generally sincere or truthful in communicating it: they will be ready as well as reliable interlocutors.[13] To the extent that an individual humanoid operates in that manner, they will benefit from the cooperation of those with whom they regularly interact. And to the extent that that is true, their performance will attract the attention of others, so that those others will have little fear about interacting with that individual in future. Or at least they will have little fear, provided they prove cooperative themselves. For as they will have learned that the individual is generally cooperative, so presumably they will have learned that others, including that individual, will tend to shun or penalize anyone who lets them down.

2.2.4 The norm of information-sharing

Assume then that as a result of these pressures, the ready communication of reliable information comes to be routine in the humanoid community. It comes to be routine that the humanoids give one another information and that they are careful and truthful in conveying that information. They do not play safe by saying nothing, refusing to share their beliefs about the environment with others. But they are careful and truthful about the beliefs they do share: they are not reckless enough to say almost anything.

Once such a regularity is established, the members of the community are more or less bound to recognize that it obtains among them. The evidence of general conformity with the regularity will be there for all to register. Indeed it will not just be evident that individuals generally conform. Since the existence of the evidence for conformity will be salient to all, it will also be evidently evident that the regularity obtains. And for similar reasons, this will be evidently evidently evident, and so on, opening up a potentially infinite hierarchy.

As the hierarchy materializes, each will believe that conformity with the regularity is general; each will believe that each believes this; each will believe that each believes that each believes this; and so on. As the point is often put, it will be a matter of common belief, a matter manifest to all, that conformity is general (Lewis 1969).[14] The notion of common belief is a technical concept and we will invoke

---

[13] Care and sincerity—in his terms, accuracy and sincerity—are two aspects of what Bernard Williams (2002) describes as truthfulness. In this text truthfulness is usually equated with sincerity.

[14] Suppose a common belief that p requires, at any level, that an individual be disposed to act as if it were the case that everyone believed that everyone believed ... that p, where the dots reflect the iteration required at that level. Common belief would be implausible if the requirement is that the person should be currently disposed in that way: that they should be ready to be triggered to act appropriately

it in many contexts. It answers broadly to the common-sense idea of something being a matter of public record but, for our purposes, need not be taken to match it exactly.[15]

Let it be granted, then, that the general regularity of readily and reliably sharing information will be recognized as a matter of common awareness among the humanoids. Once that regularity is in place, the humanoids are robustly likely to take a further important step. They will tend to introduce their young to the regularity rather than letting them have to learn the reputational lesson on their own. Equally, they will be disposed to warn potential offenders of the penalties that an offence will attract or indeed to threaten such penalties themselves. And with someone who has offended they will likely seek to correct their behavior by pointing to the reputational, penalizing consequences of their offence.

At this point the regularity will assume the status, intuitively, of a beneficial social norm. It will be a collectively beneficial pattern of behavior with three defining characteristics: it is enforced case by case by an esteem-based, prudential sanction; it is registered across the society—the presumptively equal society—as a matter of common awareness; and it is invoked to a regulative purpose in instructing the young, or correcting offenders, about how things are done. We shall argue in Chapter 5 that there are richer constraints that collectively beneficial social norms are also likely to satisfy among both humans and humanoids, but these need not concern us for now.[16]

The norm of ready, reliable information-sharing will impose different demands across contexts where the stakes at issue for those who rely on the information vary significantly. Thus, the humanoids will be especially anxious to be careful and truthful about what they say in answering another's questions when the person is manifestly likely to suffer a serious cost if the answers given turn out to be false. While remaining ready to share information with others, they will weigh the concern for reliability more heavily in such cases: they will be more concerned with what is at stake for hearers and with the strength of the evidence available to them.[17] We will address the issue of stakes-sensitivity in the discussion of belief and credence in the final section and in the discussion of reasoning in the next chapter but otherwise keep it in the background.

---

at that level. But all that need be required is that they should be predisposed to become disposed to act appropriately at any level, should they consider and understand the question at that level.

[15] On this issue, see (Lederman 2018). However unfaithful to the common-sense notion, the idea of something's being a matter of common belief can still isolate a pattern that is of theoretical importance (Pettit 2020).

[16] For this approach to norms, see (Pettit 2019; 2023b, Ch. 1), and the earlier work on which it draws, especially (Brennan and Pettit 2004).

[17] Does the sensitivity of humanoids to whether the strength of the evidence require, contrary to our assumptions in this chapter, that they can form beliefs about the evidence to which they respond? No, it does not. The humanoids may be more or less strongly disposed to respond in judgment to certain evidence and may let the strength of this disposition resolve the issue.

2.2.5 Informational exchange and assertion

With the norm of truth telling in place, each of the humanoids is likely to recognize that others hold various expectations about how they will behave in informational exchange, recognize that others will be surprised by any breach of the expectations, and recognize that such a breach is liable to attract a sanction within the economy of esteem. In other words, each will recognize that others, as we say, will hold them to those expectations.

As the humanoids recognize—indeed recognize as a manifest fact, a matter of common belief—that they each have those expectations of others and are disposed to hold them to those expectations, informational exchange will assume the character of a practice with its own rights and rules. Their expectations of one another will identify what the practice of informational exchange requires and what it allows. And the way they hold one another to those expectations within the economy of esteem will ensure that it has the stability of a practice: it is an institutional feature of their social life.

The fact that informational exchange constitutes a practice of this kind, means that any informational offer must purport to satisfy the requirements of the practice. And if it fails to do so, then it will not count as an offer, or at least not a bona fide offer; like counterfeit money it will be lacking in the credentials it advertises. Humanoid speakers will operate under conversational maxims like those that Paul Grice (1975a) takes to be honored in cooperative exchanges where human beings purport to convey ready and reliable information to one another.[18]

That the humanoids converse within a practice, under expectations to which they hold one another, does not mean that they will never fail to be ready to convey available information or fail to be careful or truthful about the information they provide: fail to prove reliable. As with human beings, they will presumably be subject to occasional temptations to defect from the requirements of the practice. But the existence of sanctions for such failures ought to mean that they will remain exceptional.

The fact that the practice of informational exchange requires the humanoids to be ready and reliable informants, and that this is manifest among them—that it is a matter of common belief—has a number of implications. It means that the humanoids will purport as participants in that practice to communicate only that which they believe, not something they disbelieve or have no beliefs about, so that a communication that something is the case will claim to reveal the speaker's belief that it is so. But the humanoids will not just purport to reveal

---

[18] These maxims prescribe broadly that speakers should be taken to aim at speaking informatively, and at conveying information that is suited in range and relevance to the purposes of addressees. For an influential, critical elaboration of Grice's maxims, see (Sperber and Wilson 1986).

that belief as they might if they reported or confessed it—'I find that I believe that such and such'—as an autobiographical curiosity. They will present themselves as willing to have others rely on what they say—as, presumptively, they will rely on it themselves—insofar as they accept the prospect of sanction to which a failure will expose them, or at least expose them if they have no excuse: if they cannot explain it in a reputation-saving manner. In short, to introduce a term of art, they will ratify the belief they convey; they will present it as something by which they stand.

This ratifying aim justifies us in taking the signaling acts of humanoids about how things are to count in the standard sense as assertions that they are thus or so. Such signaling acts will display the features commonly associated, by a range of philosophical accounts (Goldberg 2015), with assertions. They will be 'constituted by rules' or norms, fitting with the claim that assertoric practice is 'like a game and unlike the act of jumping' (Williamson 1996, 489). They will present any fact communicated by a speaker under those rules as a fact that provides a safe guide to action: in that sense, as a fact that they know to be the case (Hyman 2006). And they will explain why many are attracted to the view that knowledge is the norm of assertion: that to assert something is to claim to know it (Williamson 2000).

But there is another feature associated with assertion that the humanoid acts of signaling will also display. Under the rules of the practice, the humanoids will present any claim they make as one that they manifestly expect others to accept. And if others do not demur—if they do not exercise the right to demur that they have under the practice—it will be manifest to all that they effectively join the speaker in backing what was said. It will be manifest that not having demurred at what was said, as they had a right to do, they may be taken to believe it.

If others do not demur in such a case, we may say that the speaker will have established what they communicated as a matter of common ground among the interlocutors. It will be manifest to each—a matter of common belief—that they share this information. Every new offer that is accepted, then, every communication that passes without objection or challenge, will add to that common ground between them. Thus, each must recognize that any such intervention is a proposal to extend that shared ground and that the failure of any interlocutor to recognize this will prompt incomprehension or expulsion (Stalnaker 1978; Lewis 1979b). We will return to this aspect of assertion when we discuss the nature of commitment in the fifth chapter.[19]

---

[19] Our account of assertion also suggests that it is mistaken to think that testimonial evidence depends for its persuasive power on an effect of the kind that regular non-testimonial evidence would also have. For the epistemological issues in this area, see (Leonard 2023).

2.2.6 Disagreement and reconciliation

Our assumption in this discussion of signaling and assertion is that the humanoids will each be able to grasp the class or kind or property associated with any predicate and that no matter who is the speaker, one and the same signal will predicate the same property and have the same meaning. That assumption is supported by the account of rule-following that we offered in the interlude section of the last chapter but we have taken it as granted within the main genealogy. It means that, unless they have strong reason to think that someone seriously misunderstands the relevant words, the humanoids will take seriously any divergence between them in signaling that this or that is the case. They will generally take it to reflect, not a difference in the meanings they give to their words and sentences—not a difference in their respective idiolects, as it were—but a disagreement about what is actually the case.

That the humanoids will treat assertoric differences in this manner is scarcely surprising, under our guiding assumptions about their character, and their relatively egalitarian circumstances. Prominent among these is the assumption that they are capable of joint action and in particular of the joint action implicit in their teaching and learning from one another, taking on the roles of master and apprentice in the education of their young and even in their relationships as adults. This assumption will make sense only if they each face the same world and each display a capacity to learn about that world. And that assumption of a common world and a common access to competence will not allow them, except perhaps occasionally, to dismiss signaling divergences as differences of meaning rather than differences about the matter at hand.

They may naturally assume that if a person is a neophyte in some area of discussion, their assertion may be the one to dismiss in the case of divergence from others. And if the person is on their own in what they say and many others differ from them, they may equally assume that that person is the one that gets things wrong. But even in those cases, and certainly in cases where there are just two interlocutors involved, or there are similar numbers on each side of the dispute, they will want to identify a factor that can be seen as the cause of the discrepancy: a factor that may lead the individuals affected not to register all the evidence that is available or not to register and process that evidence properly.

There will be no problem about their recognizing and tagging cause–effect relationships in general, since non-human animals and young children have the ability to do this (Sperber, Premack, and Premack 1996). And presumably they, like us, will be in a position to identify disrupting factors like inattention, distraction, or bad lighting as causes of not registering all the evidence, and factors like intoxication, obsession, or color blindness as causes of not registering or processing the available evidence properly. And that being so, they will be able to explain why even careful and truthful reporters may make false assertions, even if they cannot always agree on who is at fault in the case of a dispute between individuals.

That explanation may prompt them to try to determine who is adversely affected and triangulate on one another's efforts in search of a resolution. But the disputants may be unable to achieve such convergence in some cases. And in those cases, they may take any of a range of views. They may treat the issue as one that is irresoluble in principle, for example, putting it out of the debate; take it to be resoluble and assume that it is others and not they who are misled; or see the predicate involved as vague like 'bald', and trace the divergence to the borderline character of the case on hand.

We will return to the issue of disagreement and negotiation in the discussion of reasoning in the next chapter. Once the humanoids gain the capacity to reason, they will have richer resources for negotiating differences in assertion, being able to think as such about the evidence available to each and about how far it supports one or other of the conflicting claims.

2.3 Assertion and judgment

By the lesson of the last section, the relationship between a humanoid subject and the belief state reflected in their signaling that things are thus and so is not just one of revealing or expressing, manifesting, or displaying that belief, since the speaker does more than make their believing that p visible to others. They present it in ordinary interaction as a belief they take themselves to be compelled to hold by the evidence, and a belief therefore on which they invite others to rely. They ratify the belief, as we put it earlier, endorsing it as worthy of being adopted by them and their audience.

That they take themselves to be compelled by the evidence for such belief need not imply, any more than with our simple robot, that they have a concept of evidence as such or that that they can form beliefs about how far evidence, suitably conceptualized, supports a belief. It only implies they take the belief to be elicited within them, not in a random way, but on the basis of inputs they naturally find relevant. We shall complicate this picture in the next chapter, arguing that they will be able to conceptualize evidence in many cases as evidence—this is required for reasoning—and to form beliefs about the degree of support it provides for this or that judgment. We shall also have more to say about inviting the reliance of others, and creating common ground with them, when we discuss normativity in Chapter 5.

The ultimate aim in this section is to explain how the practice of assertion tracked so far in the genealogy will lead the humanoids into a practice of judgment in the sense we have targeted. But in order to introduce judgment we must first look at how belief relates to assertion and assertion to belief; the relationship between the two offers a model of the relationship between belief and judgment.

2.3.1 From belief to assertion

When someone in the humanoid community affirms or asserts that p in an informational exchange, the fact that they thereby ratify the belief does not entail that they had not held it prior to ratification. They may have affirmed that p and ratified the belief previously, of course, and make the current assertion on the basis of memory; we may put that simple case aside. But even if they had not affirmed it previously, they may still have held the belief in the sense of instantiating the corresponding functional state: in our shorthand, the disposition to act as if p. Insofar as assertion involves ratification, however, the prior existence of the belief will not sideline the need for the subject to attend to the evidence that p before making the assertion. The assertion that a humanoid speaker makes in the course of an informational exchange may reflect a novel state or a pre-existing state of belief, where the pre-existing state may not have been previously ratified.

Even in the case when one of the humanoids holds a purely functional belief that something is the case, however, the act of asserting that it is the case will change their relationship to the belief. It will articulate the belief, perhaps for the first time. And, more importantly, it will give the belief a ratified status, casting it as one by which they stand.

The connection between asserting that something is so in informational exchange and ratifying the belief may explain a fact about human beings that is frequently noted in the literature (Evans 1982; Byrne 2011). This is that people often answer a question as to whether or not they believe that p by considering, not whether they have that belief, but whether it is the case that p. This should not be taken as evidence that that is a way in which people seek to determine whether or not they actually believe that p but rather as evidence that they understand the question in a special manner. They take it as a question about whether or not they ratify the belief that p—whether they are prepared to stand by it—not as a question about what they happen to have believed up to that point. Put in other terms, they do not take the question as a biographical query about their state of mind but rather as a query about what belief they think is warranted.

2.3.2 From assertion to belief

This is to say that when someone holds a belief that p among our humanoids and asserts that p, then the belief has a special status. But it is not to say that whenever someone asserts in honesty that this or that is the case, they must therefore have a belief to the effect that it is the case. It is not to say that a sincere assertion inevitably ensures the presence of a corresponding belief: that it presupposes an existing belief or is linked with the formation of a new belief. An assertion that fails to be careful or truthful may certainly materialize without a corresponding belief, of course. But it turns out that even a careful and truthful assertion may occur without being attended by a belief.

The assertion that p is a speech act but the belief that p, in broadly a functionalist sense, is a state: a disposition to act as it would be rational to act, given their desires and other beliefs, if it were the case that p. Thus, there is surely a possibility that someone might assert something carefully and truthfully yet fail to have a belief corresponding to the proposition affirmed. Nothing in logic would preclude the possibility of such a disconnection. And some examples of the disconnection in ordinary life testify to its occasional realization; we may assume that corresponding examples will arise among the humanoids as well.

Consider the case where you explain the gambler's fallacy to me (McGeer and Pettit 2002). You point out that each spin of the roulette wheel is independent of others so that if there is a run of blacks, for example, that does not mean the chance of a red on the next turn is higher than it would otherwise have been. And suppose that I am totally persuaded, asserting that the gambler's fallacy is indeed a fallacy. Isn't it possible that the affirmation I make does not elicit the belief proper: the evidence-sensitive disposition to act as if the fallacy were a fallacy? Suppose that when I go to the casino that evening I act as if it were not a fallacy, staking everything on a red after a run of blacks. Isn't it likely that that sort of behavior testifies precisely to the possibility envisaged: a failure of the daytime affirmation to resonate in my evening performance, a failure of the words I endorse to have an echo in my heart? I may have ratified the belief in subscribing to your argument, putting it forward as something by which I am ready to stand, but I will have failed to form the belief ratified.[20]

This example shows that assertion, even when it is careful and truthful, does not strictly ensure the presence of the corresponding belief. But cases like this, plausibly, must represent exceptions among our humanoid counterparts, as they do among our own species. In order to assert that something is the case, and to do so carefully and truthfully, a humanoid subject will have to pay attention to the relevant evidence—without necessarily being able to think of it as evidence—if they are to satisfy the requirements of informational exchange. But if the belief that that is the case consists in an evidence-responsive disposition to act as if it were the

---

[20] If this happens just once, a rival explanation of the failure would be that I did form the belief but that the unusual circumstances of the casino induced a temporary failure of performance: a bout of cognitive akrasia. But it is enough for our purposes here to register the real-world likelihood of the disconnect between careful and truthful assertion on the one side, and belief on the other. And in any case, the rival explanation will become less and less plausible if I continue to agree about the fallacy but repeatedly fail at the casino to display the belief that it is a fallacy.

case, then that consideration of evidence will be likely to elicit a belief as well as an assertion.

Suppose the humanoids search for evidence, and scrutinize what they find, trying to decide on how to answer the question of whether or not it is the case that p. If the evidence is up to the mark, their efforts will have two effects. It will lead them, first, to make a careful, truthful assertion, say that p; and second, to form the corresponding belief that p. The belief will be formed for the first time in the case where it did not already exist, it will be articulated and confirmed in the case where it did not. Hence we should expect the humanoids to be able to achieve a high degree of congruence between what they honestly say and what they actually believe.

If careful, truthful affirmations did not more or less ensure the presence of the corresponding beliefs, of course, then chaos would reign. Each individual would present to others in two profiles, one constituted by their actions, the other by their words. If the words were not a reliable guide to their actions—this, because of not being a guide to their beliefs—the words would be counter-productive at worst, unproductive at best. They would disrupt any coordination among humanoids by providing cues that misled agents about the likely actions of others. Or they would be irrelevant to coordination, constituting random, background noise.

In view of the fact that the humanoids will ground any careful truthful assertions in the same considerations that would support corresponding beliefs, we may expect that there will be a reliable, if not exceptionless connection between such assertions and the beliefs that they hold. Indeed, since that connection will itself be evident to the humanoids, indeed evidently evident and so on, we may expect that it will be registered among them as something manifest to all: that it will become a matter of common awareness in the community that someone who carefully and truthfully asserts that p will generally believe that p.

This argument raises a question as to the exact nature of the relationship between the exposure to evidence, the assertion on the basis of that evidence that something is the case, and the associated belief that it is the case. It may be that while the consideration of evidence is a common cause of the belief and the assertion, it does not lead by the same direct route to each. It may be, to take a plausible possibility, that it first leads to the belief and via the belief to the assertion. We return to an issue that this observation raises in the next section when we explore the relationship between judgment and belief rather than assertion and belief.

2.3.3 From assertion to judgment

With the notion of assertion in place, and its relationship to belief, we can finally introduce the idea of judgment. Suppose that one of our subjects makes a careful, truthful assertion that something is the case. That assertion will take the form of a public utterance, assuming that it is part of an informational exchange with another. But it is quite conceivable with any humanoid, as it is conceivable with any human being, that the subject, having exercised due care and formed the intention to utter the required words, has second thoughts and does not actually say anything or, worse, indulges a desire to deceive and asserts the negation of the sentence.

Whatever the reason for their silence or duplicity, we assume that in such a case the humanoid subject will still have done something in the internal forum: that they will have performed some mental act, albeit an act without its normal external counterpart. That act will have consisted in intentionally taking account of the data at hand, identifying approximately the words in which to assert in response to those data that this or that is the case, and ratifying the corresponding belief without using those words to voice it.

We may plausibly cast this mental act as a judgment that the subject makes, despite not voicing it in an assertion. Like an assertion, it will be subject to the agent's intentional control insofar as they can decide whether or not to look for the evidence that might elicit it and, if the evidence is available, whether or not to let it elicit the judgment. And like an assertion that something is the case, a judgment that it is the case will generally match up with the belief that it is the case. How could it be otherwise, given that both judgment and belief will be grounded in exposure to the same evidential factors?

But matching up generally does not mean matching up in every case. As careful and truthful assertion may ratify a belief without that belief actually materializing in the subject—this, as in the gambler's fallacy example—so the same will be true of judgment. It will amount to an exercise in which the agent ratifies the belief that corresponds to their judgment but unbeknownst to that subject, the belief ratified may not form within them.

How to think of the relationship between a humanoid's judgment that p and their careful and truthful assertion that p? If they are simultaneous, the natural line will be to take them as two aspects of the one act: assertion will be the act in an external form, judgment the act in an internal. If there is a brief temporal lag, however, the natural line will be that the assertion expresses the judgment already made; in this case, there will be two acts, not one act with two aspects. From our perspective it does not matter which picture applies.

As with assertion, of course, even the most carefully made judgment may turn out to be false. And as with assertion, the best response to that possibility, in the absence of resources for reasoning, may be to check on how far the judgment converges with the assertions and judgments of others or at least to check on whether it may be influenced by the sorts of disruptive factors that are liable to undermine convergence with others. This is because the judgments of humanoids will be subject to more or less the same norms as those that govern their assertions, at least when they are designed for interpersonal purposes; we look in the next section at the effect when they are recruited to intrapersonal purposes alone. Every humanoid will be ready to make judgments when they are ready to make assertions. And while the judgments they make are bound to be truthful, unlike assertions, they will call in the same way for care. The reliable assertion has to be careful and truthful, the reliable judgment has just to be careful; its truthfulness will come for free.

2.4 Judging and thinking

In learning to make careful and truthful assertions in response to one another's questions—in learning how to respond to evidence out of a wish to answer such questions—the humanoids, as we saw, will give rise to a social assertoric practice. But they will learn at the same time, as we have just seen, how to make judgments, where judging may constitute a social-cum-mental or a purely mental exercise. And as they learn that when they make careful and truthful assertions, they will generally hold the beliefs ratified, so they will learn that in making corresponding judgments, even making them within their own minds alone, they will generally hold the beliefs that they ratify in that way.

But with these elements in place, we can now begin to push a little further, revealing the full dimensions of the change that induction in informational exchange will realize for the humanoids. The change will materialize insofar as the humanoids are positioned to recognize three distinct but related facts about their situation. It will lead them to interiorize assertoric practice in a mental exercise that corresponds closely to what in ordinary language we would describe as thinking.

2.4.1 Extending the genealogy: three steps

The first of the insights available to the humanoids is that they can benefit, not only from gaining the information provided by others, but also by seeking to provide the information that others seek. Suppose that one of them is at a vantage point where they can see a range of features in the natural environment: the mountains rising in the distance, the plain in a haze below, the river meandering across the plain and some animals drinking from its waters. And now imagine that they are asked by someone on a lower level about the animals; that they are led thereby to focus on the animals for the first time; and that this focus allows them to see, as they report, that the animals are antelopes, or that they are lions.

The person asking the question will gain beneficial information as a result of this report. But the individual answering the question is also likely to benefit in the course of the exchange. Where they may not have been aware of the identity of the animals beforehand, although they were positioned to find out, they will gain that information by the very act of seeking to give it. Like the person to whom they made the report, then, they will become aware for perhaps the first time that the animals are antelopes they might hunt or lions they should avoid.

The lesson of this first observation is that for the humanoids exchanging information is not just a win–win game in the sense that each will gain information on some novel matters, even if they have to yield information on others. It will also be a win–win game in the special sense that participants will stand to benefit in seeking to give information to others as well as in gaining information from them.

The humanoids will naturally make a second observation in the wake of the first, or perhaps at the same time. They will recognize that the questions posed by others play a distinctive role in leading them toward the benefit they can gain in seeking answers. The questions lead them toward that reward by prompting them to adopt certain intentional activities that are designed to provide others—and this, as it may be, by providing themselves in the first place—with information: that is, reliable, ratified beliefs about their shared environment. The questions will do this in leading them to seek out and scrutinize what we naturally cast as evidence, although they will not see it under that aspect.

Like any animals, the humanoids will be disposed even before language to shift attention more or less automatically in the cause of maintaining a good sense of what is happening in their environment: literally and metaphorically, to keep their eyes open. Equally, they will tend to respond in automatic shifts of attention to indications that something is happening at this or that location, as when they are aroused by lights or noises or smells. And of course, they will be disposed in the course of seeking to track prey or evade a predator to adopt information-gathering tactics—say, staying still or listening keenly—that serve them in achieving their goal.

But while those tactics will be intentional attempts to track the prey or evade a predator, they will not constitute an intentional effort to form reliable beliefs—they will not be adopted with the aim of forming such beliefs—about the whereabouts of the animals targeted; in the absence of language the humanoids will not have the concept of belief that such efforts would require. All of that will change, however, once language is in place and the humanoids come to act intentionally with a view to answering the questions of others. In learning to make the intentional efforts required to answer such questions, they will learn how to gain the information that the answers require: how to form ratifiable beliefs on those issues.

And now to the third insight that the humanoids are bound to have. Assume that they will be aware of how the questions posed by others can prompt them toward intentional activities like seeking and scrutinizing evidence and can lead them thereby to gain the very information they provide for others in answering those questions. That will surely lead them to see that as others prompt them to achieve that informational goal when they pose questions to them, so they can prompt themselves to achieve such a goal by posing questions to themselves. They will realize that they may play interlocutor with themselves, raise questions on issues where they do not already have ratified beliefs, and prompt themselves to make the intentional efforts to generate answers when they take the evidence to permit this: that is, given they have no concept of evidence, when they find themselves strongly enough disposed in the wake of their efforts to be willing to ratify an answer.

The humanoids will have a ready means of intentionally exploring this possibility, making such self-benefiting judgements, and ratifying corresponding beliefs. Being able to ask questions of others, they will be able to ask questions of themselves. And being able to answer the questions of others, evidence presumptively permitting, they will be able on the same basis to answer questions they raise for themselves. Indeed they will be able to conduct this ask-and-answer exercise as the need or the wish strikes them; they will not depend on being pushed into doing so by the queries of others.

But not only will the humanoids have a means of exploring this possibility, making judgments, and ratifying beliefs, for themselves. They will also have a motive for doing so. Like the social practice of information sharing that it interiorizes, the mental exercise will naturally require them to be ready to seek information for themselves, and to provide only reliable information. And insofar as it has this character, the mental exercise is going to be enormously appealing for the humanoids. It will enable any one of them to extend the range of their ratified beliefs and to identify novel ways in which they may be able to advance their goals. Thus, their induction in the social practice of informational exchange will be robustly likely to lead them to interiorize it in the private exercise of raising and answering questions for themselves.

These final steps in our genealogy of judgment take the humanoids to a point where we can cast them as thinking subjects, for the mental ask-and-answer practice counts intuitively as an exercise of thought. If they constitute a nomadic community, it will enable them individually to think about when the trees in a given area are likely to fruit, or about whether the animals they are hunting are more likely to be in the hills than on the plains. And if they have developed agriculture, it will enable them to think about when it is best to let their domestic animals mate, when they should plant and when they should reap, and when the rains are likely to come this year. In the end, indeed, it may even enable to think about questions in the higher reaches of mathematics and science.

2.4.2 An aside: judging as a means to believing

Before looking further at the implications of this capacity to think for the humanoids, it will be useful to consider a question about the relationship between judgment and belief. Is it really reasonable, as this account of thinking suggests, to hold that the humanoids can intentionally control for the ratification and formation of certain beliefs in the presence of suitable evidence, by trying to make the corresponding judgments in light of that evidence? Is it plausible to think that the intentional practice of making judgments will constitute an instrumental means whereby they may hope to form ratified beliefs?

Suppose, to return to a possibility raised in the discussion of assertion, that paying attention to evidence in seeking to make a judgment leads first to the belief that p and only via that belief to the judgment that p. Suppose that the causal sequence runs from evidence to belief and then from belief to judgment. Would it still make sense, if that were the case, to say that the humanoids can control for the beliefs they ratify by relying, as a means to that end, on making the judgments that the evidence supports?

Yes, it would. The existence of an instrumental relationship between making a judgment that p—deciding in light of the evidence to judge that p—and forming a belief that p is consistent with the causal relationship running in the other direction, from the belief that p to the judgment that p. While this may sound bizarre, a simple example shows that it is not.

Suppose I am asked by a neurosurgeon who is scanning my brain to activate my motor cortex. How am I to do that, I ask. The surgeon says: just raise your arm. If I comply then I will use the action of raising my arm to activate my cortex, although the cause of my arm moving will be that very activation. I will move my hand out of a desire to ensure the activation in my brain, despite the fact that the causal relationship runs in the opposite direction. In the same way, our humanoids may make a judgment on a certain issue by attending to relevant evidence out of a desire to hold a ratified belief, even if attending to the evidence will lead them directly to form or confirm the belief and only via that belief to the judgment made.

The humanoids, by this account, will look at the evidence on various issues and make judgments on that basis, expecting thereby to form reliable beliefs on those questions. And they will rationally pursue this course of action, hoping to provide themselves with reliable beliefs about their environment, even if the judgments they endorse with a view to forming reliable beliefs materialize only in the causal wake of those beliefs. The judgments they make may be effects of the beliefs they form, yet seeking to make the judgments may count as a good means to adopt for the purpose of forming such beliefs.

This observation turns on the fact that the by-relationship of means to end, or action to consequence, is not necessarily causal (Goldman 1970; Pettit 2018d). By raising my hand I may wave to a friend, by returning a loan I may keep a promise, although in each case the antecedent action does not causally bring about the consequence; raising my hand constitutes waving, returning the loan constitutes keeping the promise. The neuroscientist example shows that things can go even further, when the action taken as means—moving a hand—will serve in that role only if it is a causal effect of the result sought as an end: the activation of the motor cortex. Things also go further in the possibility envisaged here. In that possibility, the subject tries to make an evidentially supported judgment as a means of forming an evidentially supported belief, despite the fact that if they do make such a judgment it may materialize as the causal effect of forming the corresponding belief.

2.4.3 Thinking and curiosity

There is a sort of curiosity, as Hobbes (1994b, 3.6) remarks, that is 'common to man and beast'—and we may, suppose, to our humanoids. This consists in a disposition to seek the immediate cause of a disturbing or surprising event—a noise, a flash, a smell, for example—or an available means of satisfying a desire or appetite. But Hobbes distinguishes this from 'the discourse of the mind, when it is governed by design'—that is, intentionally conducted in the manner envisaged here—describing this as 'a curiosity hardly incident to the nature of any living creature' other than human beings.

This, he says, is a 'a lust of the mind, that by a perseverance of delight in the continual and indefatigable generation of knowledge, exceedeth the short vehemence of any carnal pleasure' (Hobbes 1994b, 6.35). And, as we might expect, he associates this desire for knowledge—this desire to form beliefs fit to stand by—with language. 'As in the discerning faculties, man leaveth all community with beasts at the faculty of imposing names; so also doth he surmount their nature at this passion of curiosity' (Hobbes 1994a, 9.18).

Our observations on the power of thought that the practice of informational exchange will give to the humanoids argue that as Hobbes says it is with human beings, so it will be with the protagonists in our thought experiment. The humanoids will have a motive to want to learn about how things are in a range of domains that engage their interests. And equipped with language they will be able to go about acting on that motive, displaying the sort of curiosity described by Hobbes.

Equipped with language, they will ask one another questions and pose questions for themselves. And equipped with language they will also be able to answer those questions, whether together or on their own, if there is evidence enough at their disposal. They will be able to go out in search of more and more information about the world they inhabit and about the obstacles and opportunities it may represent for them.

2.4.4 Thinking and autonomy

Not only will the power of thought give our humanoids this desire for information and this capacity to satisfy their curiosity, learning about their world. It will also give them a distinctive form of autonomy: an ability to govern their own minds.

We saw in discussing agency that while all agents must be able to act intentionally within the external forum, satisfying their desires to achieve this or that result, there is little evidence that any beings other than humans can act intentionally to achieve a certain result within the internal forum: that is, in the realm of the mind. We can now see that the humanoids will gain this capacity with the exercise of judgment that language makes possible.

Like us, the humanoids will presumably have their minds made up for them passively on various issues—have their beliefs formed about those issues—on a more or less automatic basis, in response, for example, to the deliverances of memory or perception. Thus, they will not have to reflect on the darkness of the clouds, as we would not have to reflect on this, in order to hold that it will likely rain: that judgment and belief will come spontaneously to them under the stimulus of evidence. But on other matters where they pose questions for one another or for themselves, they will be able to take active steps to make up their own minds. They will operate like governors of their mental life, assuming a degree of active control over what to think about this or that issue; in relevant areas, they will achieve a sort of cognitive autonomy.

It would be a mistake, however, to hold that the two processes distinguished, one passive, the other active, will operate independently of one another. With their ability to make active judgment in the background, the humanoids can let many of their judgments and beliefs form in a passive manner, and still retain a virtual or standby form of intentional control. For example, they will be able to retain intentional control over the spontaneously formed judgment and belief that it will probably rain to the extent that two conditions are fulfilled. First, a red flag is likely to go up if the judgment is questionable: say, if the high altitude of the swallows indicates fine weather or another person challenges their expectation of rain. And second, they are poised to think actively about the issue if such a red flag is raised and to decide about what to judge and believe.

These observations show that the humanoids will exercise a degree of active or virtual control over their mental lives across a broad range of cases. But the control or autonomy they achieve, of course, will be limited in depth. The reason is that in making judgments they must depend on abilities that they do not themselves control, in particular the ability to register and respond appropriately to data or evidence. Being beyond the realm of their intentional control, such abilities will be sub-intentional or sub-personal: a gift of a nature that the humanoids, like us, will inherit from their genes.

Thus, the humanoids will remain in the debt of brute nature for the proper operation of those abilities and for the infrastructure it provides for judgment. They may intentionally seek to expand the realm of their understanding and knowledge, asserting a relative degree of autonomy, but they will depend on the proper functioning of their inherited, humanoid constitution for being able to do this. We return to the issue in the next chapter, where we will see that the humanoids may expand their control and autonomy even further—though still within a certain limit—by resort to the activity of reasoning.[21]

Notwithstanding this limitation, however, the humanoids will still stand in stark contrast, as human beings stand in stark contrast, to other animals. They will be within reach of the mental activity we ascribe to the figure in Rodin's famous sculpture, *Le Penseur*. We can well imagine any humanoid assuming the thinker's posture, with head on hands and eyes focused on an unseen question. We can hardly imagine any non-human animal assuming that posture or giving evidence of conducting such an activity. Not at least outside the Gary Larson cartoons in which dogs are taken to ponder things.

For all their capacity and charm, dogs do not ponder things. The dog that hears a noise may be automatically prompted to perk up its ears or quiver its nose, forming in consequence a belief on whether it is dinner time, or whether the family are home. But no dog raises questions for itself, so far as we can see, and no dog tries to prompt itself to make up its mind on such issues. Where the humanoids, like human beings, will be able to operate as thinkers, pondering this or that issue, there is little or no evidence of a similar skill among other species.

2.4.5 Thinking about what to desire

We have been discussing judgment and thought insofar as they bear on matters of fact that the humanoids will register in belief. But there are other matters of fact such that registering them in belief will be inherently relevant to the formation of desire, whether in the form of preference or intention. If the humanoids are truly counterparts of ours, they will be able to seek evidence in this area too and if it is available, to form suitable judgments: practical judgments, as we naturally call them, rather than theoretical judgments. Practical judgments may be expected to lead them, as they lead us, not just to the formation of belief, but also to the formation of desire.

The features or properties that are inherently relevant to the formation of desire are naturally described as desiderata. These will be taken on more or less all sides, or at least all sides within any single culture, to play a role in generating desire: say, to anticipate, in generating preferences over various alternatives, or even an intention in favor of one of the alternatives that figure as the options in a choice.[22] But while they individually tend to elicit desire, they may weigh differently in the degree to which they have that tendency relative to one another; some

---

[21] For an extended, insightful set of reflections on the way in which intentional control is always conditional on the operation of a non-intentional psychology, see (Ricoeur 1966).

[22] It may even be that they are features that would be shapeless, or at least not salient and prominent, for creatures who lacked the corresponding desires. For a thought along these lines, see (McDowell 1979). It fits with our discussion of properties in the sub-section interlude within the first chapter.

may be weighted more heavily, others less heavily, on the scale of an agent's concerns. Moreover, the way in which one agent weights desiderata may differ in some measure from how another does so and may even differ across times or contexts within a given agent.

This view of the role of desiderata is grounded in the fact that objects of desire do not attract us, and will presumably not attract the humanoids, in their particularity; they will attract agents under desiderative aspects, as we may call them, and may repel them under aversive. Focusing on attraction rather than aversion, desiderata are the features in virtue of which various possibilities prove appealing for an agent, eliciting desire in a functional sense of the term. This view is not uncontroversial, but we shall take it for granted here as a view that applies to humans and so also to humanoids.[23]

A core idea in the view is that there is no intelligible desire—no desire that humans or humanoids can intelligibly ascribe to others or even to themselves—unless there is an intelligibly desiderative feature to be discerned in the object of the desire, however differently that feature may be weighted by different agents. Examples of the desiderata that will make desire intelligible among the humanoids, as they make desire intelligible among us, come in many forms. They may include the feature of relieving the agent's current hunger or thirst, being a lot of fun, being exciting, or promising a pleasurable reward. But they may also include non-hedonic features that bear on the agent or those close to the agent: that something would ensure long-term health or would guard against poverty in old age, that it would help out the agent's family, or serve their country. And, still building on the similarity between humanoids and humans, desiderata may even include relatively neutral features: say, that an action will help to advance knowledge, relieve worldwide poverty or contribute to overall peace or prosperity.

The assumption that desiderata play an essential role in generating desire shows up among us human beings in the fact that we expect anyone who claims to want something to be able to explain why they want it by reference to a desideratum it displays. Thus, to take an example from Elizabeth Anscombe (1957), we would balk at someone who claimed to want to have a saucer of mud but could say nothing whatsoever about the aspect under which this appealed to them, reporting only that they wanted it in its particularity or for no general reason. Or to take an example from Warren Quinn (1993), we would be utterly perplexed by someone who just wanted to turn on every radio they came across and could say nothing at all about the aspect under which turning on radios attracted them.

---

[23] For accounts that support something close, see (Pettit and Smith 1990), (Pettit 2006), and (Dietrich and List 2013). That we adopt this view here need not mean that the enterprise in the book stands or falls with it, for alternative views are likely to preserve at least many aspects of the position defended.

These examples suggest that, on our ordinary way of thinking about human beings—and by analogy, about humanoids—the connection between forming a desire in favor of some state of affairs and seeing it under a recognizable, desiderative aspect is not merely inductive. Our conception of human and humanoid agency dictates that if someone is taken to desire a certain course of action, that must be in virtue of some intelligibly attractive feature that they see in it. The feature that makes one agent's desire intelligible to another, however, need not be one that also appeals to that other. The only requirement is that they can understand how, perhaps with different beliefs, the feature might move them, with whatever weight, in the same direction; they must be able imaginatively to take the perspective of such an individual. Thus, among humans, those of a secular mentality will surely find it intelligible that a religiously minded individual might seek a saucer of mud as a salutary reminder of their mortality.

Desire in the broad, action-relevant sense invoked appears in two distinctive forms. First, it may take the form of a preference ranking of possible alternatives. Or second, the form of an intention to take one option within a set of alternatives that constitutes a choice.

To form an intention or policy is to form an unqualified desire for one alternative over others in a current or foreseen choice or type of choice. Such alternatives must be taken to be mutually exclusive and jointly exhaustive options, such that the agent can presumptively realize any one of them and only one of them. With intentions and policies, as we use the terms here, the desire for a particular alternative, although prompted by the relevant desiderata, will be unqualified insofar as it is not subject to second thoughts. While it may later change, it does not operate under a proviso that other desiderata do not surface and give the agent pause (Bratman 1987; Holton 2009).

To form a preference, by contrast, is to form a qualified desire for one sort of alternative over others and for the desideratum or set of desiderata characterizing that alternative: say, a preference for working only in daylight hours, for speaking well rather than badly about colleagues, or for abstract over representational art. The desire for that alternative and that desideratum will be qualified to the extent that it operates within the agent under a proviso that other things are equal. Such a preference will give rise to an intention directed at one among a suitable set of action alternatives only when the agent lifts that proviso, focuses on the desiderata attaching to that alternative, and neglects or suspends the effect that rival desiderata might have had. To form an intention to take that option will be to desire it, not just under one or another desiderative aspect—not just, *pro tanto*—but to desire it, period: to desire it *pro toto* (Broome 2013).[24]

---

[24] This is a notion of a preference that makes it into something like a plan about how to choose in counterfactual circumstances, under the proviso mentioned; the proviso apart, it is akin in that respect to the notion of a super-plan in Allan Gibbard's (2003) sense.

Given our picture of the role of desiderata in the formation of preference and intention, we ought to expect the humanoids, not just to think about purely factual questions, but to think also about questions bearing on desiderative properties and to form practical judgments in response. And we ought to expect that making such practical judgments in response to suitable evidence—say, evidence of the presence and relative weight of certain desiderata—will offer a means whereby they can exercise some control over their preferences and intentions, as theoretical judgments will enable them to exercise a similar variety of control over the beliefs they form.

But in the case of intentions or policies, practical judgments may play a role that has no exact counterpart among theoretical judgments. They may enable the humanoids, not just to form an intention or policy bearing on options that lie to hand, but also to form plans of that kind for a time or times that they foresee in the future. In the role of such plans, as Michael Bratman (1987; 1999) has emphasized, those attitudes will put fixtures in place that determine in advance what else the agent may contemplate doing.

For reasons of simplicity we shall continue to focus in our genealogy on theoretical judgments and beliefs. But on the model sketched in the foregoing comments, the lessons we draw ought to carry over to practical judgments and desiderative beliefs and to the preferences, intentions, and policies that they support. We will return to a fuller consideration of such desires when we consider normativity and value in Chapter 5.

2.5 Interlude: degrees of belief

By the account developed so far, it is a great achievement on the part of our humanoid subjects that as a result of coming to language, they learn the practice of assertion, develop the associated habit of judgment and become, in some measure, the masters of their own cognitive lives. But the judgments that they make, evidence presumptively permitting, are associated with beliefs in a yes-or-no sense and this raises an issue as to how those states connect with beliefs in the sense targeted in ordinary talk of degrees of confidence and formalized in decision theory as *credences* or *subjective probabilities*. We address that issue in this final section, which counts as an interlude in the overall genealogy since it may be skipped without a serious loss in following that narrative.[25]

---

[25] There is now an enormous literature, some of it quite technical, on the relationship between on-off belief and degrees of confidence: that is, credences. My excuse for largely ignoring it here is not just that space forbids but that in any case the framework employed here, which introduces judgment as well as belief and credence, makes it difficult to compare the picture with those defended by others. I have benefited greatly in thinking about the issues by conversations with Alan Hajek.

2.5.1 Belief and credence: introducing the issue

The judgment as to whether something is or is not so is binary in character; either the judgment is made or not made: there is no spectrum between those extremes. The binary aspect of judgments is carried over to the beliefs they ratify, indicating that the subject stands by them. As humanoid or indeed human judge that p or that not p, period, so in tandem they will generally believe that p or not p, period.

The binary character of judgmental belief is more or less inescapable among the humanoids, since their judgments, like their assertions, have a binary nature. The only way in which one of their judgments might reflect the degree of the speaker's confidence is by making the content probabilistic, as in the judgment that it is more likely than not that p, for example, that it is likely to the point of certainty that p, or that the probability that p lies in a certain range. But the judgment upheld in such a declaration will still fail to register the strength with which it is maintained and will introduce an on–off belief, albeit a belief to the effect that probably p rather than not p, period.

It is conceivable even at this stage in our genealogy that, as a result of being aware of their disposition to respond to evidence, and specifically of how strongly the evidence elicits that response, the humanoids may introduce probabilistic markers of this kind. If their disposition is strong but not compelling, for example, it may lead them to judge that that it is more probable than not that p, or that it is very likely that p, or whatever.[26] For reasons of simplicity, however, we shall set aside judgments and beliefs with probabilistic contents. The claims we go on to defend can be adjusted to make room for such probabilistic judgments and beliefs but it is easier to uphold the claims with a focus just on probabilistically unqualified counterparts.

The binary character of judgmental belief means that it cannot properly or fully do a job for which belief in the functionalist sense introduced earlier is designed. That job is to make sense, in combination with their other beliefs, of what agents do in pursuing the satisfaction of their desires. What an agent does, however, is not just a function of the things they believe, period, but of the degrees of confidence with which they believe them; and not just a function of what they prefer but of the degrees of intensity with which they prefer them. When an agent is said to judge that p and to ratify an on–off belief that p—we may assume that the ratification is successful, so that the belief actually materializes—that tells us nothing about how confident they are and leaves us without important information. We noted this deficiency earlier, in discussing ways in which our account of agency—and the place it makes for beliefs and desires in the functional sense—is over-simplified.

---

[26] This account of how humanoids might come to form probabilistic judgments would explain why, as in the human case, they can only be expected to make quite coarse assessments of probability. Not having access in any detail to the strength of their credences, they could not be led by an awareness of that strength to assign fine degrees of probability to different scenarios.

Decision theory lifts this simplification in arguing, under any of a number of formulations, that in deciding what to pick among the options in a given choice, a well-functioning agent will choose that option—or one of that set of options—with the highest expected utility, as it is called. Setting aside the difference between approaches of an evidentialist and causal kind, as it is put, as well as the many other differences that appear among decision theories (Buchak 2015), the idea of expected utility is readily explained.

Each of the mutually exclusive options in a choice will be associated, typically, with more than one possible outcome. And the expected utility of any option for a given agent will be a function of the figures that give us the utilities that its possible outcomes promise to deliver. How to compute that function and determine the expected utility of an option? The standard decision theory approach, which comes in a number of variants, is to take the utility of the outcome, suitably quantified—the degree to which the agent prefers it—and to weight or multiply it by the probability—that is, the agent's degree of belief—that the relevant option, should it be chosen, would lead to that outcome. The expected utility of an option will be the sum of the figures generated by this procedure for its different possible outcomes. And an agent will maximize expected utility insofar as they choose that option in any decision—or one of that set of options—that has the highest expected utility; intuitively they choose the option that counts as the best gamble, given their degrees of belief and desire.

Our main focus is on belief and the question for us is how belief in the on-off or binary sense associated with judgment relates to belief in the scalar sense of a degree of confidence. Let us continue to use the word 'belief' for the binary state associated with judgment, and 'credence' for the scalar state recognized in common sense and formalized in decision theory. The issue before us, then, is how belief connects with credence.

We shall assume that there really are credences—that they are not illusory—and that they play a role in the generation of action, as decision theory assumes. This assumption is borne out by our everyday talk of degrees of confidence, as well as by a series of relatively formal results (Eriksson and Hajek 2007; Hajek 2008). How can this assumption be squared, then, with what we have been arguing up to now: that beliefs in the binary sense—beliefs that are successfully ratified in judgment—also play a role in the generation of behavior? How can the actions of humanoid or human agents be the product of credences, on the one side, and beliefs, on the other?

2.5.2 The stakes-sensitivity of assertion and judgment

In order to address this question, we must return to an observation introduced earlier in this chapter. This is that assertions among the humanoids, as among us human beings, are bound to have a stakes-sensitive character.

The practice under which humanoid subjects operate in making assertions, as noticed earlier, presupposes that they will want to establish a reputation for being willing to give information to others and information of a reliable kind. It is only if they themselves prove to be ready and reliable informants, as we argued, that they can expect to be able to rely on others or, when necessary, to get others to rely on them. But the desire to establish a reputation for being ready and reliable informants is bound to create a problem for the humanoids, given that they are confined to making on–off assertions in conveying how they take things to be.

The problem is that the concern for being a ready informant and the concern for being a reliable informant will often pull in different directions, given that the humanoids can share information only in a binary fashion. Yet readiness and reliability will each have a distinctive appeal for the humanoids. Speakers must be ready enough in making assertions to be worth engaging, but they must be reliable enough in the assertions they make to be worth heeding. If they are reliable enough to be worth heeding, however, they may not be ready enough to be worth engaging; and if they are ready enough to be worth engaging, they may not be reliable enough to be worth heeding.

Recognizing this problem, the humanoids must be ready to make assertions that something is so, even when the evidence fails to be compelling and may lead them to prove unreliable. But they must also be poised to inhibit that disposition when the danger of misinforming their audience weighs too heavily with them: when the evidence is not intuitively strong enough to warrant their taking the risk of misleading that audience. This suggests that the humanoids may find a way around the problem by judging on a case-by-case basis about where the balance lies.

Take the case where someone has a strong but not conclusive sense that the apple trees they saw yesterday on a nearby mountain were in fruit. What should they say, then, if others ask them whether the trees are in fruit, clearly intending to act on the reply? The case-by-case approach would require them to work out the chance that they make a correct judgment about the apples; the benefit to their interrogators of learning about the apples if indeed they are ripe; and the cost to them—say, the cost of time wasted in climbing the mountain—if they are not. And then they would have to do a cost–benefit analysis, making their decision on that basis.

Such a case-based approach to their problem would be close to infeasible for the humanoids, as it would be for us. The chance of error, and the degrees of potential benefits and costs involved, will generally be indeterminate, and even if they are not, working them out would require intuitively too much time or too much effort. Thus, we may expect the humanoids to evolve a more general, manageable strategy for handling the problem.

The salient strategy for the humanoids will be one that we human beings seem to follow ourselves. It involves two elements. First, a general readiness to make assertions, no matter what the subject matter, provided that there is a reasonably high chance that they are true. And second, an unwillingness to make an assertion where it is obvious that the costs of misinforming the audience would be unusually high; or at least an unwillingness to do this unless the evidence for the assertion is unusually strong and the chance of its being true unusually high.[27]

This two-step strategy will make great sense. It would guard humanoid speakers against the danger of being taken to be unreliable, by setting a relatively high constraint of reliability on all assertions. Still, it would ready them to make a wide range of assertions by not setting that constraint too high. And yet it would guard them against seeming reckless—perhaps the greatest danger of all—since it would raise the constraint to a higher level in any case where the foreseeable costs of misinforming an audience looked particularly serious.

The strategy may prompt the humanoids to offer their views readily in gossiping about newcomers to the group, in opining about the better of two foraging strategies, or in pronouncing on how the weather will be in the week ahead. But it will lead them to hold back on issues, even perhaps issues about which they are fairly confident, where their audience is deeply invested; or at least it may lead them there to make only probabilistically qualified claims. Thus, if one asks another whether an unfamiliar plant is poisonous, or whether someone they are getting married to is already attached to another, they may well play safe in such a manner. They may declare that they don't know or may offer a relatively uninformative probabilistic response.

So much for the two-step strategy that the humanoids are likely to follow in making assertions. What now of judgments, in particular judgments that they make for their own benefit only, not as preliminaries to assertion? As we noted in the last section, the humanoids will want to ratify a range of beliefs sufficient to guide them in pursuit of their various goals. But at the same time they will shrink from ratifying unreliable beliefs, particularly in cases where the potential costs of getting things wrong are high. Thus, as in the case of assertion, it will make good sense for them to embrace the two-step strategy described.

In the case of judgment, however, that strategy may lead them in a different direction from how it leads them in the case of assertion. It may allow agents to judge for themselves that something is the case—and so act generally as if it were the case—without necessarily being prepared to assert that that is so for an audience. They may be prepared in other ways to act as if p—that is, to act as it would be rational for them to act, given their other attitudes, were it the case that p—but not be prepared to take the action of asserting that p to a particular audience; such an assertion might impose too great a cost on that audience, did it turn out to be false. Thus, an individual may take care not to assure someone that a person they are

---

[27] Analogues of this strategy have been much discussed in relation to knowledge (Stanley 2005), with different positions on the question emerging in the epistemological literature. For an overview, see (Rysiew 2016).

marrying is unattached to another even while they judge without hesitation that the person is indeed unattached.[28]

2.5.3 Back to the issue

The stakes-sensitivity of judgment and assertion gives us a picture under which it is possible to situate both beliefs and credences at the origin of action.[29] The relationship between belief and credence will assume one form in contexts where the cost of error would be particularly high and another in more standard contexts where the cost of error is not high and indeed where the cost of silence—that is, of not making a judgment or assertion—might even be higher.

In a context where the risk of error is very high, a humanoid individual will be ready to judge and believe that p—we may focus for simplicity on judgment, whether it be public or private—only if they have a very high level of credence: say, a credence of 95 percent or even higher. In such a context the individual will judge that p only when the evidence to which they are exposed—the data they are naturally disposed to attend to in forming their beliefs—prompts them relatively strongly to make that judgment. In that context the evidence, considered as an abstract state of affairs, will provide a high degree of support, although the humanoids will not yet be able to think about it in that way; doing so, as we shall see in the next chapter, presupposes the ability to reason.

In standard contexts, however, where the risk of error is not particularly high—and where the risk of silence may be—the picture will be very different. If an individual is prepared to judge that p in such a context, ratifying an on–off belief that p, then that requires only that they have a credence above a moderately high level of support—say, 85 percent—but not necessarily a credence that is very high. They will be prepared to make the judgment that p and ratify the belief that p, because it will be rational for them, given their other beliefs and desires, to act in the manner associated with such a belief: that is, to act as if it were the case that p. In making that judgment and forming that belief, they will take a risk, for it may turn out to be the case that not p. But the risk involved is one they will be ready to live with, given that they have an interest in forming and ratifying a relatively rich range of beliefs, and that silence itself may be risky.

---

[28] Taking up the converse question, could someone assert without deception that something is the case when they do not judge it to be so? Perhaps, if the issue—say, whether p or not p—involves a high risk in their own life, a low risk in the lives of their audience. In that case, they might assert that p without judging that p: they might assert it insincerely but still benevolently and, to that extent, non-deceptively.

[29] The picture that follows is consistent with the constraints that Dietrich and List (2018) impose on the relationship between credences and beliefs. For an elaborate theory of the relationship that also meets those constraints, see (Leitgeb 2015; 2017).

For any on–off belief that an individual humanoid forms, according to this picture, they will have a degree of credence within a corresponding range. For high-stakes contexts, the belief that p will be paired with one or another credence in a very high, narrow range; for standard contexts, the belief will be paired with a credence in a wider range of only moderately high credences. For each case, then, there will be a corresponding class of credences that the agent may hold; these will be functionally equivalent insofar as they each prompt the agent to act as if p, displaying the same binary belief. Which of those credences will the agent actually hold? That may be hard to determine, for the way that the agent acts is unlikely to reveal which precise credence they have in the equivalence range.

This picture may seem to raise a problem for reasoning, to anticipate the topic of the next chapter. Within the framework of credences, it makes perfect sense that though the fact that p and the fact that q entail the fact that p-and-q, the credence someone gives to the conjunction will be lower than their credences in the conjuncts; where the conjuncts are independent, the probability of the conjunction will be the product of the other probabilities and, assuming these are less than 1, that will have to be less than either.[30] By parallel reasoning the individual who judges that p and that q, given suitably strong evidence and suitably low stakes, may not be able to judge that p-and-q, as the evidence for that conjunction, unlike the evidence for each of the conjuncts, may not be sufficiently strong.

This need not be a problem. That there is a logical relationship of entailment between two propositions is relevant to, but does not conclusively determine, whether someone will be rational to move from an on–off belief in the first to an on–off belief in the second. Also important in that determination is the strength of the evidence that evokes the belief in the first and, in the case envisaged here, that is going to be too low to sustain a judgment that p-and-q. This issue will come up again in the next chapter.[31]

One final, somewhat complex observation about our picture. The relativity to context postulated does not mean that judging-that-p-in-a-moderate-stakes-context is a different sort of act from judging-that-p-in-a-high-stakes-context; it does not mean that it is different in the way that accepting that something is the case for-practical-purposes is different from accepting that it is the case for-all-purposes (Stalnaker 1978). Thus, suppose someone later sees that the stakes are so high that they ought not to have judged that p as they did earlier when they took the stakes to be moderate. They will be required in that case to retract the earlier judgment. They will see that what was assertible earlier is not actually assertible: it is not assertible in light of the information available to them at the time of the later assessment.[32]

---

[30] A broadly similar lesson will hold if the conjuncts are not independent.
[31] For background on issues related to how reasoning relates to logic, see (Harman 1986).
[32] This view of the relativity of what is creditable/assertible parallels John MacFarlane's (2014) views on the relativity of truth.

2.5.4 The importance of both belief and credence

On this representation of things, credences combine with utilities to play a more basic role in generating action than that which on–off beliefs play. Whatever action an on–off belief is invoked to help explain in the presence of certain stakes, there will be a credence that underpins the explanation: the belief would not lead anywhere without the presence of that credence, or a relevantly equivalent credence. Given a suitable context, it follows that the presence of the belief, and ultimately the making of the judgment that successfully ratifies it, presupposes the presence of a credence that lies within the relevant equivalence class. It is the credence rather than the belief that does the heavy lifting.

One way of bringing this out is to notice that, on our picture, whether an individual decides to judge that p rather than not judging it to be so—to ratify the belief that p—will depend on whether doing so is rational in light of their credences and utilities: whether, in the standard formula, it maximizes their expected utility. Their making that judgment will maximize expected utility in standard cases to the extent that they put a sufficiently high utility on proving to be ready as well as reliable informants, whether in relation to others or to themselves. It will fail to maximize expected utility, however, in the high-stakes cases where misleading others or themselves has a disutility sufficient to offset the utility of promising to provide information readily.

But if credences do the heavy lifting on this picture, judgments and the beliefs that correspond to judgments are more significant in other respects. Judgments and the beliefs that generally go with judgments program for the actions that credences generate more directly. And that gives them an advantage that shows up on two fronts: *ex post* in supporting a useful explanatory perspective, and *ex ante* in facilitating the agent's intentional control over their actions.

The notion of programming is relatively straightforward.[33] A factor at a higher level in the organization of things—call it, H—programs for an effect, e, that is occasioned in a more basic way by a distinct lower-level factor L, when three conditions are fulfilled. One, H has to be realized, maybe in one way, maybe in another, at the lower level. Two, L, its actual realizer at the lower level, occasions the effect, e, in intuitively a more direct way. And three, if H had been realized at the lower level by something other than L, then the chances are that that realizer too would have occasioned e. When these conditions are fulfilled, then both H and L are causally relevant in the explanation of e. H is relevant insofar as it ensures that, no matter how it is realized, its realizer is likely to occasion e. But L—or LR, or some still more basic realizer of L—may be relevant in producing e in a manner that depends on no lower level.

---

[33] On this notion of programming, see (Jackson and Pettit 1990) as well as (Jackson, Pettit, and Smith 2004, Pt. I) and (Pettit 2017).

Judgmental, binary beliefs program in this way for the actions that credences occasion. In a suitable stake-setting context, such a belief will ensure that the agent has a corresponding credence: that is, a credence within the relevant equivalence class. And, more specifically, the belief will ensure that the credence present is fit—in combination with relevant utilities—to occasion any actions that it, qua belief, disposes the agent to take. The belief will be realized as a credence in the appropriate equivalence class, and no matter what the realizer—no matter what the degree of credence present—it will generally suffice to occasion the required action.

In virtue of playing such a programming role, an agent's judgments and beliefs serve a useful *ex post* role, providing a highly general explanation of why an agent acts in a certain manner. They identify an antecedent condition that serves to make that response intelligible, despite the fact that it may be realized in any of a variety of ways at the level of credences and utilities. Of course, it might be of some interest to recognize—if, unusually, that information were accessible—that an individual takes a certain line because of this or that precise credence. But it is likely to be of much more interest to know that they take that line because they hold by such and such a judgment and belief, regardless of how that psychological profile is realized at the level of credence (Jackson and Pettit 1992).

Suppose, for example, that a humanoid or human agent climbs a hill to pick some fruit. Others might naturally explain that behavior by saying that the agent judged and believed that the fruit was ripe, the assumption being that they wanted the fruit. Those others could assign that judgment and belief while recognizing that the agent may not have been fully confident about the fruit; they would be happy to do this, provided that the cost to the agent of being wrong—the time and effort wasted in climbing the hill—seemed to be relatively low. This explanation would serve those others well, remaining appropriate over possible variations in the agent's degree of confidence that the fruit was ripe: in other words, not requiring information about their exact credence on that question.

Compare by contrast the explanation that the agent had such a degree of confidence in the fruit's being ripe, and assigned such utility to getting the fruit and such disutility to climbing the hill, that the option at issue maximized their expected utility. This might provide more precise information about the agent's make-up at the time of action. But it would be informationally very costly and it is not clear how useful the extra information encoded in the explanation would be.

But judgments and beliefs will also serve agents better than credences in enabling them *ex ante* to exercise intentional control—active or virtual control—over how they respond to evidence. As we know, the humanoids will be able to intentionally make judgments and form beliefs in careful response to evidence, where the care they take is proportional to what is at stake in the context. But they cannot control in the same direct way for the credences that materialize within them. They can only control their credences indirectly by controlling for the judgments they make, and the binary beliefs they ratify, in response to evidence. And indeed they can only exercise that control over credences at a coarse level, determining that in a given context the credence they form will fall within such and such an equivalence class.

We saw earlier that even if trying to form a judgment leads first to the formation of a belief and only thereby to the formation of a judgment, it can still make good sense for a subject to try to form a belief—a ratified, binary belief—by trying to form a judgment. The means–end direction can reverse the direction of causation, as in the case where I move my arm, under a doctor's instruction, in order to activate my motor cortex. A similar point applies with judgment and belief on the one side, and credence on the other. It can make perfect sense for a humanoid agent to try to form a judgment on some issue with a view to ratifying an on–off belief, and thereby forming a credence, wittingly or unwittingly, in the relevant equivalence class. And they can do this, even if trying to form the judgment first leads to the formation of that credence and only as a result to the formation of the on–off belief and judgment.

That judgments and beliefs program for action, despite doing so only for relevant contexts, means that they can support the humanoids better than credences in seeking to exercise intentional control, not just over theoretical decisions, but also over practical. Humanoid agents will be able to judge intentionally that one of the options in a choice scores best in desiderata—in effect, they can intentionally decide on that option—without knowing the degrees of credence, or indeed the degrees of utility, that operate within them.[34] And that is just as well, since those states will normally be inaccessible. Thus, it is only via their judgments and beliefs that agents can actively make up their minds about what to do as well as what to think.[35]

2.5.5 A final observation

But apart from the utility of judgments and beliefs in explaining an agent's responses, and in supporting the agent's control over those responses, they will also play a role that often goes unnoticed, in supporting the evaluation of what an agent does for whether it is decision-theoretically rational. As we have seen, an agent will be rational in this sense when they choose an option, among the alternatives

---

[34] I am assuming that the members of the equivalence class related to a desiderative judgment by any agent will be credences in the presence of the desiderative property. Given the role assigned to such judgments in leading to preferences or intentions, the corresponding credences in desiderative properties will presumably be associated with suitable degrees of utility. Might the effect of these credences run counter to the effect of utilities, leading to the triviality result identified in (Lewis 1988)? Not on the picture we are relying on here, for how an agent weights desiderata at any time may reflect their corresponding degrees of utility.

[35] This explains why advising someone to maximize their expected utility may be as useless as advising them to buy low and sell high on the stock market. See (Pettit 1991).

available, that maximizes expected utility. But evaluating an agent for such rationality presupposes an account of what their options or alternatives are: specifically, what they are in the agent's own view. And it turns out that this will normally have to depend on what the agent is taken to judge and believe their options to be.

It might be thought that the agent's credences can play the role of determining that the options in a choice are X or Y: say, sending a message by email or by regular post. But those credences will typically be less than 1, since it may not be certain that the email server is operational or that the postal service is not on strike. Thus, despite being designed to allow for the uncertainties that the agent faces—their degrees of confidence or credence—the decision-theoretic evaluation of such a decision will have to ignore the uncertainty of realization attached to the options: it will have to take it to be certain that the agent can realize either X or Y.

A standard line in response to this observation is to assume that the evaluation of the decision can start from options like emailing a message or posting a letter when, by contextual criteria, the agent can reasonably *take* them to be the alternatives on offer. As I interpret this line, however, that is simply to assume that the agent makes a judgment and forms a belief—a stakes-sensitive judgment and belief—about the alternatives at their disposal. And that is just to assume, in a nice irony, that the very use of decision theory in judging on the rationality of such a choice—the appeal to the agent's credences and utilities in determining whether their choice of option maximizes expected utility—presupposes appeal to the very judgments and on–off beliefs that decision theory may have seemed to demote and dismiss.[36]

Can decision theory avoid this issue by reducing the options in any choice evaluated to attempts to do things like emailing a message or sending it by post? In that sense attempting or trying to do something X, when X is hostage to external contingency—say, that the internet is down or the postal system out of action—will not itself be subject to such a contingency. It will amount to a mind-restricted action that is so independent of environmental breakdown, even a breakdown in the agent's own body, that the agent cannot fail to pull it off.

One difficulty that such a proposal faces is that nothing would then be available to restrict the options in any choice in the way that the environment and body of the agent restrict available options to alternatives like emailing or posting a message. But this is not the place to evaluate the resort to attempts or tryings as the

---

[36] As decision theorists identify rational choice by determining whether the option chosen maximizes expected utility, so they usually identify rational updating by whether in response to the evidence that p, for example, they assign to any other proposition—say, 'q'—what had been the conditional probability that q-given-p. But this move presupposes that the agent can settle on what the evidence is, as the theory of rational choice presupposes that they can settle on what the options are. And for similar reasons, it suggests that the agent will take as evidence what they judge and believe in a stakes-sensitive way to be the evidence. The point is relevant to the topic of the next chapter, though we shall not be commenting further on it. For a complication about updating that is ignored in this footnote, see (Jeffrey 1983).

relevant options in a choice. Suffice it to observe that most of the choices to which decision theory is taken to be relevant do not involve such stripped-down options, so that we have to invoke judgment and binary belief to determine what the alternatives are.[37]

These observations should be enough to make sense of how the decision-theoretic picture can apply to the humanoids, consistently with their making judgments and forming beliefs on the lines tracked in the earlier sections of this chapter. We need not worry on decision-theoretic grounds about the picture of their psychology that emerges from the narrative developed here, as we need not worry about the counterpart picture of our own psychology.[38]

---

[37] There is a large literature on the trying-based approach. For a recent sympathetic account of the approach, which explores a rich range of related issues, see (Holguín and Lederman 2024).

[38] The position sketched here on the relationship between belief and credence can likely be mapped within the possibilities formally and fully characterized by Hannes Leitgeb (2015; 2017). On his theory, the belief that p corresponds to a suitably stable credence, or degree of confidence, in 'p'. It corresponds, specifically, to a credence that is stable in the sense that the agent's credence in 'p' conditionally on any in a range of selected propositions—the selection is context-sensitive—is greater than a half by a margin that is also selected by context. This approach, like that at which I gesture here, comes, as Leitgeb (2015, 176) says, at the price of 'a strong context-sensitivity of rational belief': 'what one believes rationally codepends on the context . . . of reasoning of the rational agent who has the beliefs'. I am grateful to Mario Günther for helping me to see this connection.

3
Rationality with reasoning

On the account sketched in the last chapter, those with access to language, in particular the humanoid subjects of our thought experiment, can take intentional steps, for example in researching evidence, to form a judgment on whether p or not p. And evidence presumptively permitting, they can intentionally judge that p (or not p); they will choose in that case between responding judgmentally to the evidence or withholding judgment. This, as we have seen, will give the humanoids a degree of intentional control over what beliefs they ratify, whether in forming them for the first time or raising them to ratified status. The humanoids can exercise control over the beliefs they form in one or another domain under the prompt of questions posed by others or under the prompt of questions they ask themselves. We may set aside for now the possibility, illustrated by the gambler's fallacy example, that ratification will not be successful in generating a belief. And, once again, we may set aside desires, both in the form of preferences and intentions.

In giving this account of judgment, we assumed that what our humanoids expose themselves intentionally to is the evidence or data they gather, whether gathering it from memory or perception or whatever. But we assumed that while they intentionally let themselves register and respond to that evidence, they do not have a concept of evidence as such; they are naturally disposed to attend to evidential inputs but not because of recognizing them as evidential. And in a similar fashion we assumed that while the humanoids may be more or less strongly inclined by the evidence before them to make a certain judgment—and may even register this in probabilistic judgments—they will not have the ability to assess the evidence as such for how far it supports the judgment.

In this chapter, we argue that the capacity to communicate with language will also give the humanoids an ability to monitor and manage their responsiveness to evidence. They can act intentionally, not just to make judgments on issues where the evidence presumptively permits—where they are strongly enough disposed to support a judgment—but to make judgments on those issues in light of judgments about how far the evidence is adequate. We will not say much on the varieties of evidence the humanoids can consider—we postpone until the next chapter, for example, the extent to which perception can be recruited to provide evidence—but we shall see that they will be positioned to conceive of whatever evidence is available as evidence, and to rate it for how far it supports this or that judgment.

The ability to make judgments out of a recognition that the relevant evidence is adequate amounts to the ability to make reasoned judgments: the ability to reason to the judgments made in virtue of recognizing that they are supported by what is seen as data or evidence. The ability to make reasoned judgments is one that the humanoids will certainly want to exercise for, as we shall see, it gives them a way of showing others that their assertions are credible, a means of checking on whether their own spontaneous, judgmental responses are reliable, and indeed a way of extending the range of their judgments and beliefs.

While we present reasoning as a later development than the appearance of the capacity to make judgments, that presentation is consistent, as we noted in the Introduction, with holding that the humanoids would be unlikely to develop the ability to make judgments without the ability to make reasoned judgments at more or less the same time; the two developments might co-evolve in mutual support. As we noted in the Introduction, the temporal order of the genealogy reflects the abstract possibility that judgment might appear without reasoning, but not vice versa, rather than the likelihood that judgment and reasoning will be temporally separated.

The chapter is in five sections. In the first, we look at rationality, both in the unreasoned form in which it is realized in simple agents and in the reasoned form that it assumes in us human beings. In the second, we show that the humanoids will be motivated to explain and reinforce their judgments to one another and, by courtesy of language, will have the means required for doing so. In the third, we explain how this will give rise to a social, interpersonal form of reasoning and by interiorization to a mental, intrapersonal counterpart. We look at the varieties that such reasoning may assume in the fourth section and we conclude with a fifth section on the connection between reasoning and following rules: this is an interlude in the genealogy and connects with the final section of Chapter 1, on the problem of basic rule-following.[1]

3.1 Rationality and reasoning

3.1.1 Agency and rationality

We introduced the idea of rationality in the discussion of agency early in the last chapter. In order to count as any sort of agent, a system has to pursue one or

---

[1] The argument in the chapter fits nicely in its general thrust with the elegant theory of the origin of reasoning in human beings developed by Hugo Mercier and Dan Sperber (2011; 2017). By their account the first function of reasoning among human beings is to 'indicate what motivates and, in their eyes, justifies their ideas and their actions', and the second 'to make communication effective even when the communicators lack sufficient credibility in the eyes of their audience to be believed on trust' (Mercier and Sperber 2017, 8–9). One point worth noticing is that they also use their theory to explain the pathologies as well as the powers of reasoning; their account connects with the Hobbesian claim, mentioned in the Introduction, that language may increase people's power but it does not necessarily improve their performance.

more purposes reliably according to the representations it reliably forms or maintains: this, at any rate, when the system counts on independent grounds as functioning normally. The two sorts of reliability involved constitute two aspects of rationality, as we saw: cognitive rationality in the formation of belief, executive rationality in the selection of the action to take.

Cognitive rationality argues that an agent should meet an evidence-to-belief condition and a belief-to-belief condition, as well as analogous conditions on related attitudes like desire. The evidence-to-belief condition requires that the agent's representations should be evidentially responsive to the data accessed by the agent, and the belief-to-belief condition that the representations of the agent should not be inconsistent with one another: if they were inconsistent, they would not depict any possible world and could not reflect all genuine data on the actual world. Executive rationality supports a third, belief-to-action condition, requiring that the agent's representations must shape their actions so as to produce suitable, purpose-promoting behavior.

If beliefs did not satisfy these conditions, at least up to some reasonable limit, it is not clear that they would fill the role that makes it right to treat them as the agent's representations. The evidence-to-belief and belief-to-belief conditions require belief to play a suitable role in responding to inputs and the belief-to-action condition requires it to play a suitable role in generating outputs.

The consistency required under the belief-to-belief condition is often associated with a desideratum of closure. Suppose that it cannot be the case that p without its also being the case that q; in other words, that p entails that q. Consistency will be breached when an agent holds the belief that p and the belief that not-q; closure when they hold the belief that p but fail to hold the belief that q: their beliefs will not be closed, as it is said, under entailment. Closure may be a desideratum of cognitive rationality—it would equip agents, after all, with rich, potentially useful beliefs—but it cannot be a general requirement. For while consistency is hard to achieve in certain cases and can be required only up to some intuitively reasonable limit, closure will often be downright impossible. If closure were required for rationality, then the fully rational agent could not believe a set of mathematical axioms, for example, without believing all the theorems they support.[2] Closure can be a requirement only in cases where we would expect any functional agent to register and respond to a relevant entailment.

---

[2] Another reason why it cannot be a general requirement, to recall a point from the last section of Chapter 2, is this: someone who judges that p and that q when their evidence is sufficiently strong may not be willing to judge that p and q, since the evidence for it will be weaker and may not be sufficient to support a judgment. In this particular case, their judgments—and the corresponding on–off beliefs—will not be closed under entailment. This comes up again later in the chapter. In considering this and related issues I was enormously helped by advice from Christopher Bottomley.

3.1.2 Blind rationality

Agents may be rational in the required way in virtue of how they are organized. They may display rationality without having to do anything, and without being able to do anything, to ensure or promote their own rationality; it may come to them spontaneously as a byproduct of their nature. Consider our simple robot again. Its organization, over which it has no control, will more or less ensure that as it perceives things to be—as its perceptual inputs indicate that they are—so it will believe them to be; that as it believes them to be, so will it act; and that the beliefs it forms at any moment will not be inconsistent in an action-related way: it will not believe both that a glass is on its side, for example, and that it is upright.

The robot will operate within a domain where it enjoys a certain control: an environment in which it can intervene or not intervene, depending on whether its purpose requires intervention. But that domain will not extend to include the robot's own rational processing: this will evolve on the basis of the organization introduced by the designers. The robot can act intentionally to affect things in the external forum, but not in the internal: not within its own make-up or mind.

Insofar as this is true, the robot may be said to be blindly rational, not rational in virtue of acting out of a desire to be rational and a belief that by taking one or another step it can promote the satisfaction of that desire. And as it is with the robot, so plausibly it is with non-human animals. There is no ground for ascribing to them a desire to be rational or a belief about the means of achieving rationality: they won't have the representational abilities—in effect, the concepts—needed to form such beliefs. Insofar as their rationality is beyond intentional control it may be said to be sub-intentional or sub-personal.

It is not surprising that a significant level of rationality should be sub-personally ensured in any agent. After all, there would be no prospect of a system attaining the status of an agent unless it had a minimum of rational organization. To the extent that such inbuilt rationality is a presupposition of agency, the rationality of an agent cannot be solely the product of their own agency; the inbuilt rationality that is guaranteed by their designed or evolved organization must come to them by nature and cannot depend on their own intentional efforts. But the fact that this is so does not rule out the possibility—illustrated, as we shall see, in the case of humans—that an agent should be able to act intentionally with a view to facilitating or enhancing their rationality: that they should be able to exercise a certain control over how far they display rationality.

3.1.3 Back to the humanoids

Are our humanoids going to be just blindly rational? For all we have said so far, they may be. We argued that as they will have the capacity to ask and address questions intentionally in interaction with others, so they will be able to ask themselves questions and, if they find the evidence sufficient, answer them as well. And we saw that insofar as they intentionally make judgments on the issues raised, they will generally have corresponding on–off or binary beliefs—beliefs that something is the case or is not the case—and the degrees of confidence, the scalar credences, that those beliefs presuppose. Will such judgmental control of whether they have beliefs on certain issues imply that they have a degree of control over their rational organization? No, it will not, at least not in the sense intended here.

Judgmental control, as we have characterized it so far, involves being able to act intentionally with a view to ratifying binary beliefs across a range of issues. That intentional action may involve seeking out the evidence available: say by looking around carefully; reflecting on the data collected; and, if the evidence is suitably strong, letting it elicit a judgment or not letting it do so: withholding judgment instead.

An agent may enjoy judgmental control over their judgments on certain issues without enjoying any degree of control over the rationality of those judgments. The point is nicely illustrated by certain *savants* (Battistutti 2021). On the issues where *savants* display their exceptional capacities, they can try intentionally to form true judgments—they do so with a remarkable degree of success—yet form those judgments more or less blindly. Consider, for example, the *savant* who can link a day of the week with any date they are asked to consider. Asked about the day on which a particular date fell in the past, they take a moment to reflect and then, without knowing how, come up with the right answer. Such a *savant* will act intentionally in considering the question asked and, while it is not clear how this happens—not clear, for example, that introspective evidence plays any role—they respond on a purely sub-personal, unconscious basis.

Our humanoids will be prompted by questions that others raise, or that they raise themselves, to pay attention to what we would consider relevant evidence: say, evidence in memory about whether the fruit trees they saw in the morning were ripe, or the evidence of their eyes as to the character of some animals in the distance. And faced with that evidence, they may make a judgment and ratify an appropriate belief. But for all that we have assumed so far, they may be prompted by those questions to seek out and respond to relevant evidence, yet be unable to make judgments about the grounds for the answer they give to a question, lacking both the concept of evidence and the concept of relevance. At no point, according to our story up to now, will they consider the evidence as such or ask how far it supports the judgment; they will resemble *savants*—albeit *savants* without special gifts—in the way they operate.

3.1.4 Reasoned rationality

Before looking at how humanoids might be expected to go beyond judgmental control and achieve a degree of control over their rational processing, it may be useful to look in the abstract at what such control involves among us human beings. In doing this, we may focus on the exercise of such control in its mental rather than social form and in an example where it is designed to secure an intuitively compelling form of closure. In that example, the adjustment involves moving from the belief that p and q to the belief that q. This adjustment illustrates such a simple and salient transition that we might expect any rational agent to be disposed—in most cases, just blindly disposed—to make it. The transition from a belief in such a conjunction to a belief in one of the conjuncts might be of interest if the conjunctive state of affairs, but not perhaps its conjunctive character, was salient and only one of the conjuncts—in this illustration, q—was contextually relevant and significant; the fact that p, by contrast, might amount to distracting clutter that an agent would do well to avoid (Harman 1986).

If you, a presumptively regular agent, exemplify this transition blindly, then what happens within you might be characterized as follows, in the language of binary beliefs. You have a standing belief that p and q, and this belief state leads you subpersonally to form that belief that q. At the personal level, to anticipate a theme from the next chapter, you may be conscious of now believing that q. But that belief will appear as if from nowhere; it may just seem obvious to you—you know not why—that q.

What would be involved, by contrast, in your transitioning to the belief that q in a personal manner that displayed a degree of control on your part? It would involve more than coming to believe that p and q and then coming to believe that q. It would also require you to believe of the first state of affairs, 'p and q', that it entails or in some way supports the state of affairs, 'q'. And it would require you to give that metapropositional belief—that belief about the relationship between the p-and-q proposition and the q proposition—a role in checking on whether to judge and believe that q. Or at least it would require this in the case of an actively controlled process; as we shall see, the process may also materialize under a virtual or standby form of control.[3]

Another way to put this is to say that in the process described, you will take the premised state of affairs to support the state of affairs posited in the conclusion, and be moved as a result—or at least partly as a result—to endorse the conclusion. Paul Boghossian (2012b, 5) describes the requirement as a taking condition on reasoning or, in his terminology, inference. 'Inferring necessarily involves the thinker taking his premises to support his conclusion and drawing his conclusion because of that fact'.

Following John Broome (2013), we might say that the main element required in agents who meet the taking condition is a linking belief that posits a relationship between the premise, p and q, and the conclusion, q. That linking belief will not generally be articulated in judgment: it may consist in just a functional belief that

---

[3] Is this too intellectualist a picture of reasoning? For considerations that suggest it is not, see the end of section 3.3.

disposes you to treat the presumptive fact that p and q as a reason to believe that q. The role of that belief in linking the premise judgment to the conclusion judgment will typically show up in your phrasing the conclusion in words like 'so, q' or 'therefore, q' or 'it follows that q' (Pettit 2007b, 500; 2016). Transitioning to the belief that q in such a manner amounts, in a more or less standard use of the word, to reasoning actively to the conclusion that q—concluding that q—from the fact, as you assume it to be, that p and q.

By this characterization of reasoning it is crucial that you form a belief in the relationship of support—in this case, entailment—between the premise proposition and the conclusion proposition, displaying a degree of logical or related competence in recognizing that relationship. But, of course, the exercise of such competence is not sufficient on its own for reasoning about the actual world. You might display it in just exploring such relationships between propositions—say, in logic or mathematics—without any interest in whether or not they are true. Or you might display it, more generally, in suppositional rather than actual-world reasoning: that is, in reasoning about whether a certain proposition would follow on the supposition, perhaps assumed to be false, that other propositions held.[4]

In reasoning about the actual world, you must draw a conclusion about what is actually the case, given that you take certain premises to hold. And in deciding about whether to draw the conclusion or not, you must take account, not just of the relationship between the propositions, but also of whether, in the context of whatever is at stake, you have sufficiently strong evidence for the premises to warrant using them as evidence to support the conclusion. Thus, as we saw in the final interlude section of the last chapter, you may have sufficient evidence to assert that p and to assert that q without having sufficient evidence to assert that p and q; it is always going to be more likely, after all, that either of two conjuncts holds than that both hold at once.

While we shall mostly focus on actual-world reasoning, this will give us the resources to make sense of suppositional reasoning as well. In actual-world reasoning you take account of the relationship of support, in our case the entailment, between the premises and the conclusion. And in addition you take account of the strength of your evidence for the premises and whether it allows you to assert the conclusion. In suppositional reasoning, you simply suppose that the premises are true and so have to take account only of the entailment. The example we have been working with, which involves reasoning from the judgment that p and q to the judgment that q, does not allow actual-world reasoning to come apart in this way from suppositional; if you have sufficient evidence to judge that p and q, you will

---

[4] It may be that some will use the term 'reasoning' of the computational exercise that is common to all forms of reasoning rather than focusing mainly on actual-world reasoning. That usage might require us to restate some of the claims made in this chapter and later in the book, but it would not enforce any substantive change of view.

have sufficient evidence to judge that q. That indeed is the reason for relying on this particularly simple and artificial example in our discussion.

By the emerging account, actively reasoning about the actual world makes three demands. First, that you believe the premise, on the one side, and believe or come to believe the conclusion, on the other. Second, that you have a meta-propositional belief *about* the different states of affairs in which you thereby believe—namely, that they are related suitably—giving expression to that belief in the so-character of the concluding judgment. And third, that the meta-propositional belief plays some part in eliciting or at least reinforcing the belief in the conclusion. You believe that the first state of affairs, now treated as itself a subject of predication—an object of thought—has a certain evidential relationship to the second state of affairs, also treated as a subject of predication; and that belief helps to generate or secure the belief in the conclusion, directing you to a reason, as we say, why the conclusion holds.[5]

Reasoning or drawing conclusions in the sense described presupposes access to a normative notion: the meta-propositional belief deployed holds that the premise entails or supports the conclusion, that it provides evidence for the conclusion, that it explains why you ought to endorse the conclusion, where those are all prescriptive ideas. In exploring how the humanoids might come to reason, then, our narrative must explain not just how they can form meta-propositional beliefs but beliefs of a prescriptive or normative character. The normativity involved, as we shall see, is not as rich as that which we address in Chapter 5, but it still calls for explanation.

3.1.5 The utility of reasoning

It is important to see that reasoning gives us human beings a benefit, not just socially in enabling us to explain and justify ourselves to one another, and to persuade others of our views, but even in the form it assumes within the privacy of the mind. Such mental reasoning provides us with a distinctive sort of intentional check and control over our attitudes. Thus, assuming that you are spontaneously disposed to believe something as a result of believing something else—as a result of the evidence provided for you by that prior state of affairs—you may conduct reasoning intentionally out of a desire to check on whether you should stand by

---

[5] In the example of reasoning provided, you might go one step further by articulating this linking belief in a judgment and letting it figure as an extra premise: namely, the fact that p and q entails the fact that q. But if you do that, and reason on the basis of the expanded premises to the conclusion that q, you will presumably have to rely on a meta-propositional, functional belief to the effect that the enhanced state of affairs that is now premised provides evidence that q. And so on, if you take yet further steps, so that a regress looms. The lesson, underlined by Lewis Carroll (1895), is that in order to avoid that regress, you will have to rely at some point on a purely functional, linking belief that does not figure as a premise.

the belief to which you are disposed. Suppose you are spontaneously disposed to believe that q as a result of believing that p and q, as in our example. You can intentionally try to check on that transition by taking steps to make a judgment and form a belief on whether there is a suitable relationship between the premised and the concluded state of affairs.

But you may conduct reasoning out of a desire, not just to check on whether a spontaneous transition in belief passes muster, but in order to determine what, if anything, follows from a given set of propositions; and this, indeed, whether you take those propositions as matters of actual judgment or just supposition. This will involve contemplating the premised state of affairs, perhaps analyzing its different aspects, and trying thereby to make a judgment on whether it links appropriately with one or another conclusion: whether it provides evidence that, or a reason why, something else holds.

Think about what is involved in resolving a puzzle. To take a parlor-riddle as an example, think about what you would do in seeking to resolve this riddle: 'Brothers and sisters I have none but that man's father is my father's son. Who is that man?' The answer as to the man's identity is unlikely to come to you spontaneously, as if generated sub-personally: not at least, if you are only talented in the typical way, and not a *savant*. But you can take certain intentional steps—you can reflect on the premised situation, for example, and break it down into its various components—in the attempt to form a judgment on what follows, ensuring the appearance of a corresponding linking belief.

One way in which the reflection could go, and could resolve the puzzle, is as follows. You start from the position of the speaker and notice that having no brothers and sisters, they are a lone child. And now you ask about who the son of the speaker's father is: in the words of the puzzle, who is *my father's son*. The answer, of course, is, the speaker. And who, to go to the core issue, is the speaker directing attention to: who is *that man*? Well, the answer to the earlier question makes it clear that *that man's father* is the speaker. And so, the conclusion leaps out: *that man* is the speaker's son: *my son*, as he might have said.

Like any human being, and like any humanoid subject, you will be able intentionally to make a judgment on certain issues where evidence is available: this, insofar as you may make or withhold the judgment, even when there is evidence to support it. But if you are a reasoning subject, then on at least some of those issues you will be able intentionally to make a judgment-in-view-of-the-evidence; you will be able to make a reasoned judgment in light of a linking belief. This linking belief will identify the state of affairs that constitutes the evidence as also being evidence enough for the conclusion, a reason why the conclusion holds.

These observations show that the ability to reason and make reasoned judgments increases your intentional control beyond the control grounded in the ability, evidence presumptively permitting, to make judgments, period. But you will not always exercise this ability, of course, in forming beliefs rationally. In many cases you are likely to update many of your beliefs in light of new evidence or data without any active reasoning whatsoever: you will update them more or less blindly. Even in those cases, however, you may retain intentional control of a virtual or standby sort: if a red flag goes up, as in your reaching an unexpected or a controversial conclusion, that may prompt you to reason actively about the transition.[6]

The ability to make reasoned judgments, like the ability to make judgments, period, rests on an infrastructure of sub-personal competence and gives only a limited degree of intentional control to an individual. While you may be able to exercise intentional control over whether to form a reasoned judgment on an issue—say, over how, assuming the data are sufficient, to resolve the parlor riddle—you will only enjoy that control insofar as you can rely on your sub-personal processing to operate properly: say, to make it obvious to you, at the appropriate point, that the man referred to in the riddle must be the son of the speaker.

The fact that we human beings rely on sub-personal processing in this way might seem to support a waiting-theory of reasoning, as we might call it.[7] This would equate reasoning with paying attention to the data on hand, letting beliefs form in response and then waiting to see what beliefs materialize as conclusions under their influence. But this neglects the social role of reasoning between people, since reasoning with one another or reasoning as a group can hardly consist in waiting together. And, even more important, it ignores the need for any reasoner to form a meta-propositional belief in the linkage of premises to conclusion: the belief that triggers a 'so' or a 'therefore'. Those who reason about anything, whether socially or mentally, do have to rely on their sub-personal processing. But they do not rely passively: they conduct intentional actions in seeking and attending to evidence—and in casting it in this or that way, as in the parlor game puzzle—with a view to catalyzing their sub-personal processing.[8]

We have been looking at examples of deductive reasoning where the premises actually entail the conclusion. But reasoning to beliefs—theoretical reasoning, for short—may be inductive or abductive as well as deductive: it may involve probabilistic reasoning to a generalization of certain presumptive facts or to the best explanation of those facts. And it may be practical as well as theoretical, taking

---

[6] This possibility argues for complicating somewhat the distinction made by Daniel Kahneman (2011) between system-1 and system-2 thinking, at least if that is equated with the distinction between sub-personal transitioning and reasoning.

[7] I use that name because of a challenge that David Lewis once made at a conference where Michael Smith and I had presented a paper on deliberation. The challenge consisted in the account he gave of his own processing. 'When I deliberate', he said, 'I let belief form about the options before me, about their likely consequences, and so on. And then I wait.'

[8] I borrow the usage of 'catalyze' here from Galen Strawson (2003). He recognizes the role of 'preparatory, ground-setting, tuning, retuning, shepherding, active moves or intentional initiations' in reasoning, while emphasizing—not uncongenially—that the 'rest is waiting, seeing if anything happens' (237). In fairness to David Lewis, he may only have envisaged this role for waiting.

desiderative judgments as input and yielding a practical judgment—in the most practical case an intention and action—as output. For the sake of simplicity, however, we shall concentrate initially on theoretical, deductive reasoning and look at other varieties only later, in the fourth section.

3.1.6 The challenge for the genealogy

The most striking requirements of reasoned rationality over blind rationality, on the account just presented are: first, that in reasoning an agent has to be able to form beliefs about contents or propositions or states of affairs, not just beliefs in them; and second, that the beliefs they form have to predicate a prescriptive relationship of entailment or support or the like. To believe that p, we may say, is to have a belief in the p-possibility: to be disposed, in our shorthand, to act as if it were the case that p. To have a belief about that proposition is to believe that it, cast now as the subject of predication, has one or another property or relationship. And in the case of reasoning, to revert to our example, it will be to have a belief about the proposition to the effect that it is connected prescriptively to another: that it is supported as a conclusion by the other or that it provides support as a premise for the other.

Can the humanoids come to form such beliefs and act on them in reasoning? Most regular beliefs, with a subject–predicate structure, target the subjects of those beliefs in the way that our simple robot's beliefs target things like glasses and bottles, assigning to them features linked with their orientation, direction, and distance. In order to reason theoretically to a conclusion—say to the judgment that q—the humanoids will have to be able to take the premised proposition—say, that p and q—and the conclusion-proposition, q, as subjects of predication, and will have to be able to form a belief about the relationship between them that is expressed in words like 'so, q', 'it follows that q', or 'therefore q'. The propositions or states of affairs involved will have to become objects of thought, as the glasses and bottles are objects of perception for the robot, and the humanoids will have to have beliefs about those propositions—in reasoning, prescriptive beliefs—as the robot forms beliefs about the objects on the table.

In virtue of being able to represent such states of affairs, the humanoids can be said to form concepts of them. Concepts are representational abilities, by the account offered in the last chapter, and the concept of an abstract item like a property may vary in sophistication—it may be stimulus-independent rather than dependent—insofar as it supports richer abilities. It may enable the subject merely to form beliefs about currently perceived scenarios—the object is a glass—in which the property figures in predicate position and the concept counts as stimulus-dependent. Or it may also enable the subject to form beliefs about unperceived scenarios—that object was a glass—in which it figures in predicate position, counting to that extent as a weakly stimulus-independent concept. Or it may enable the subject to form beliefs about scenarios—presumably unperceived scenarios—in which it figures as the subject of predication: being a glass correlates with being fragile; in this case it counts as a strongly stimulus-independent concept. In order to reason, the humanoids will have to be able to form strongly stimulus-independent concepts, holding beliefs about the abstract entities constituted by propositions.[9]

The same picture holds with practical as distinct from theoretical reasoning. In order to reason practically, say to the action of X-ing, a humanoid agent will have to target a premised proposition like 'X-ing would be fun' and be led thereby, say in the case of intention, to form a practical judgment that might be expressed in the words 'so, I shall X'. That the intention has been reached by such reasoning will appear in the fact that the agent can back it up in the practical judgment that, promising to be fun, X-ing has the most attraction or appeal.

The question before us now is whether our humanoids will not just be able to make up their minds in judgment but also to form linking judgments and beliefs and to reason their way to judgments. Will they be able to act intentionally, not just in making judgments on certain issues where the evidence presumptively permits, but in making those judgments-in-view-of-that-evidence: in short, in making reasoned judgments?

We shall deal with this question over the following three sections. In the next section we look at why the humanoids will want to explain and reinforce their assertions in many cases and, more importantly, how they will manage to do this. We shall see in the third section that this will lead them to reason socially or interpersonally and, by interiorization, mentally or intrapersonally. And in the fourth section we shall look at other varieties of reasoning that the humanoids will also come to practice. The fifth section, which has the character of an interlude to the genealogy, explores how far reasoning involves a variety of rule-following akin to that which we discussed in the last, interlude section of Chapter 1.

3.2 Reinforcing judgments

3.2.1 The motive for reinforcing assertions and judgments

We have seen that the humanoids will routinely make assertions for one another's benefit, often presumably in response to one another's questions, and that they will

---

[9] The proposition 'p' will figure predicatively within the property characterizing various beliefs—the that-p beliefs—and will figure as the subject of predication when the agent is able to believe that the proposition itself has properties that may be predicated of it: that it entails or is entailed by something else, that it is true or false, and so on.

generally do so, on pain of reputational damage, carefully and truthfully. This will certainly put pressure on them to give adequate, accurate reports on how things are for audiences that may not be independently aware of how they stand. But sometimes those reports may fail to convince the audience. The speaker may have proved careless or insincere in the past, so that their credentials are suspect. Or the report they give may clash with the independent presumptions of the audience. Or someone else may have given a conflicting report.

This means that in such cases the humanoids will often have a motive for seeking to reinforce the reports they give to others. To reinforce assertion, in the sense assumed here, will be to explain why they made it, thereby prompting others to accept it as well. And in view of the salient possibility that others may suspect their credentials, or find their report dubious, or receive contrary indications, this motive is likely to have a stable place in their make-up and performance.

3.2.2 The challenge of finding a means

How might the humanoids find a means of acting on that motive, providing reinforcement for their claims? The salient way for a speaker to achieve the effect would be by making the audience aware of the evidence—the presumptively persuasive evidence—that caused them to report as they did. But will the humanoids be able to provide such an explanation of their claims? We may presume, as noted in the last chapter, that they will be able to make assertions about causal connections, since these are salient even for non-human animals and young children (Sperber, Premack, and Premack 1996). But will they be able to identify the evidence at the causal source of a claim, and will they be able to invest it with the capacity to win over their hearers?

Suppose that the original claim the speaker made was that q. And suppose that the evidence that prompted them to make that claim is the apparent fact that p and q. Suppose, in other words, that the speaker judged that q, because p and q; they judged that q because of registering in perception or memory the fact that p and q. How might a humanoid in such a case come to be able to identify that evidence as a cause of their judgment? And how might they invest it with persuasive force? We tackle these questions in turn, describing them, respectively, as problems of identification and investment.

3.2.3 The identification problem

There is a problem about how the humanoids might be able to identify the evidence at the causal source of their judgment because the evidence that plays this role will always be a would-be state of affairs. This will consist in a certain property being realized in a certain object, or in a certain relationship obtaining between certain objects, or in certain properties or relationships being co-realized together, or in something of the kind. In other words, it will constitute an abstract entity that contrasts with the concrete objects that will populate the environment of the humanoids. There is no problem about how the humanoids will form beliefs about *concreta*—even the simple robot of our example forms beliefs about glasses and bottles—but there is a problem about how they will be able to form beliefs about *abstracta*: a problem, equivalently, about how they can conceptualize them as the subjects of certain predications. How on earth will the humanoids be able to take a would-be state of affairs as an object of attention and predicate a causal relationship of it: cite it as the cause of their judging that something is the case?

The answer to the problem, as we shall now see, is that their access to language will not only enable the humanoids to make assertions and judgments about concrete objects, it will also provide them with new *abstracta* about which to make judgments and form beliefs: new items to conceptualize in a strongly stimulus-independent way (Pettit 1993, Ch. 2). And, as we shall see, such items may include pieces or bodies of evidence.

The reason why language will be helpful in this regard is that it will enable the humanoids, as it enables us, to put sentences to a double use. They will not only be able to use a sentence, to assert that something is the case. They will also be able to use it, with the help of explicit or implied quotations marks, to refer like a name to what it can be used to assert.[10]

Consider the way we do this in our own language. When we can use a sentence to assert something, say that Sydney is north east of Canberra, we can put it in quotation marks—'Sydney is north east of Canberra'—and use it as a name for its assertoric content. We do this implicitly when, for example, someone asks what another said and we report: Sydney is north east of Canberra. That we use the sentence just as a name for the assertoric content of what the person said shows up in the fact that we may not endorse or believe what they said. In a case like this we make the content of the assertion available as an object of reference, conceptualizing it as the proposition expressed in those words or the state of affairs postulated by them. And with that object picked out in this mode—with that object being conceptualized by us—we can predicate various properties besides the property of being what someone said. Thus, given a familiar disquotational principle—'p' is true if and only if p—we can say that that proposition is true or, equivalently, that that state of affairs obtains (Davidson 1984).

Being in quotation marks, the sentence is not used in these cases to make an assertion itself but is employed off-line and recruited to serve in a different,

---

[10] This capacity parallels the capacity to refer to classes or kinds or properties that we took simple signs to support in the case of basic rule-following in the last section of Chapter 1.

referential role. But there is one important qualification. We may use the sentence offline in this non-assertoric way but indicate at the same time that the content picked out is true. We would do this, for example, if we said that someone knows that Sydney is northeast of Canberra. What they know is a state of affairs, which the sentence in quotation marks picks out, but the knowledge relation requires that it be a state of affairs that obtains: that it constitute a fact.

As we human beings have the capacity to do this sort of thing, so too will the humanoids have it. They will be able to use a sentence to serve as a name to identify the proposition that in online, assertoric usage it would serve to assert: the presumptive state of affairs it would record. And using sentences in that way they can put themselves in a position to treat the states of affairs or propositions identified as conceptualized objects of thought: items about which they can form predicative beliefs.[11]

The simplest case in which the humanoids are likely to use sentences in this offline manner is in answering a third person's question about what a speaker said. Suppose the speaker had said that the apples on a certain tree are ripe. The individual who is asked what they said may not believe that the apples are ripe and may not be willing to assert that they are. But they would certainly be able and willing to use the sentence to provide the third person with the content of what the speaker said, as in responding to the query with the words, quotation marks understood: the apples on that tree are ripe. Indeed, that will be an appropriate sentence to use even if those were not quite the words of the speaker, provided that it refers in that usage to what the speaker intuitively asserted.

As the humanoids will be able to use sentences offline to refer to what someone says, they will also be able to use them to target states of affairs or propositions as the subjects of predications or as the terms of a predicated relationship; they will be able to conceptualize them in a strongly independent manner. Thus, like us, they will be able in principle to introduce a predicate such as 'true'. If they are disposed to judge that p, for example, then their ability to target and conceptualize the p-proposition will enable them to judge that p is true: this, insofar as 'p' is true if and only if p. At that point, believing that p can assume the form of treating it as true that p. And as this is true of belief, something similar can hold of desire: desiring that q can assume the form of treating it as attractive that it should be the case that q. In other words, to return to an issue raised in the last chapter, their functionalist beliefs and desires can assume a relational character: they can become states in which the humanoids take themselves to be related to propositions or states of affairs.

---

[11] A sentence in quotation marks is taken here to refer to the proposition asserted, which is plausible, but in certain contexts it may be taken, more specifically, to refer to what that particular sentential expression asserts, not for example to the proposition that might equally well have been asserted by an equivalent sentence or by a translation of the sentence in another language.

This humanoid capacity to conceptualize propositions, forming beliefs about them, will bring with it a capacity to conceptualize the elements of propositions in a similar, strongly stimulus-independent way: for example, the class or kind to which something is assigned within a proposition, the property that is predicated of it. As a sentence in quotation marks may refer to the proposition, for example in reporting what someone said in talking about an object, so the predicative part of the sentence may be used to refer to what they said about that object: it is red, it is bulky, it is a stick, or whatever. Thus, they will be able to form beliefs about a property to the effect, for example, that it is instantiated here or there, or that it is always co-instantiated with some other property.[12]

Back now to our explanatory question. How can the humanoids invoke a state of affairs that caused them to assert that something is the case in explanation of that judgment? In our simple example, how can they identify the state of affairs that prompted them to assert that q?

We know from the observations just made that they may simply reply: p and q. In that reply, as it is understood here, the sentence is used offline, with quotation marks understood, to cite the relevant state of affairs rather than to assert it. But because the state of affairs is cited as a prompt or trigger or cause of the assertion it explains, the presupposition is that it actually obtains. As the knowledge relationship presupposes that any known state of affairs obtains, so the explanatory relationship presupposes that the same holds of any state of affairs that does explanatory work. A state of affairs cannot be known unless it constitutes a fact, and equally it cannot be invoked to explain something unless it has such a factual status.

This makes sense of how the humanoids might get over our first problem, enabling them to identify the relevant evidence as the explanation of why they asserted that something is the case. As creatures able to make judgments intentionally, they will be in the habit of relying on this or that cue—an evidential cue, as we will think of it—to prompt the answer to one or another question raised by others or by themselves. And so, if they are prompted to explain the answer they gave, whether at another's request or because of a felt need of their own, they can pay attention to what did the prompting and, assuming that they have access to a corresponding sentence, can use that sentence off-line to identify that state of affairs as the explanation. They will be able to say that they were led to assert that q by the fact, as they will see it, that p and q.

---

[12] We argued independently that given the ability to tag things for the properties they display, the humanoids will have this ability as a requirement of rule-following in the final, interlude section of the first chapter; see too the final section of this chapter. We will return to this ability in the next chapter when we consider the effect of language on the humanoid perception of certain properties.

3.2.4 The investment problem

But we are not yet out of the woods. For why might a humanoid speaker expect a causal explanation of their assertion in a given case—their assertion, as they can now see it, that a certain state of affairs obtains—to lead an audience to accept that state of affairs and give credit to what they said? Why might they think that the audience will be moved by that explanation to silence doubts raised by the speaker's history, the implausibility of the assertion, or the counterclaims of another?

There are many possible causal explanations of an assertion that an individual might offer—say, by reference to a gut feeling or to a dream the previous night—that they could not expect to move their audience. So, what is it about the sort of explanation postulated here—the appeal to a distinct, presumptively actual state of affairs—that would lead them to invest it with a reinforcing power?

There are two assumptions humanoid speakers will have to make if they are to invest their explanation of an assertion with that potential. First, they must assume that the fact that they explicitly invoke—say, that p and q—is one that their audience believes as well, or at least will believe as a result of their invoking it and, strictly speaking, that the same is true of any implicitly assumed facts that they may or may not articulate. And second, the humanoid speakers must assume that as the actual state of affairs—that p and q—causes them to believe that q, so it will cause their audience to believe it too.

If the humanoid speakers have grounds for holding by both the first, factual assumption and the second, causal assumption, they may and must expect that their explanation will serve to reinforce their original assertion that q, helping to win around their hearers. At least that is the case in contexts where the speaker and hearer have a shared sense of what is at stake for each of them; in this discussion, we shall take only such contexts into account. So, the question is whether the humanoids will be entitled to make the two assumptions.

Consider the factual assumption first. If others have a reason to doubt a given assertion, prompting the speaker to try to reinforce it, aren't they equally likely to doubt any assertion the speaker makes about the state of affairs cited in defense of the original claim. So, what will entitle the speaker to think that their hearers will accept whatever fact they cite in explanation of their original assertion?

On the specifications of the humanoids from which we began the genealogy, they are capable, not just of ascribing agency to one another, but of acting for shared goals, including the goal linked to teaching and learning. If the humanoids are to live up to those assumptions then, like us, they must be able in general to tell what others in any group are likely to assert and believe: what states of affairs they will probably take to be actual. It will have to be a matter of shared assumption, indeed, that members all hold in common by a certain range of beliefs. Otherwise, they could hardly make sense of one another as agents, let alone share with some others in the pursuit of common goals.

That means that whenever a speaker seeks to explain an assertion they made by citing an alleged fact at its origin—this, as in explaining why they said that q by citing the fact that p and q—they may reasonably expect to be able to identify states of affairs that they and their audience accept in common. And, of course, they will be careful to draw only on a state of affairs that they have reason to think their audience does actually accept. Thus, they will have no general problem about endorsing the factual assumption.

There may be occasions, of course, where the audience turns out not to believe in the alleged fact that the speaker invokes in explanation of an assertion. In such a case, assuming that they take the audience to satisfy our specifications, the speaker may go back a step and try to explain their belief in the rejected evidence—in our example, that p and q—by reference to further evidence that the audience does accept or believe: say, that r. Presumably, they will find common ground at that level or at some deeper level; if they diverged at every level, then they would not satisfy the specifications introduced in the first chapter and sharing information with one another would be an impossible enterprise.

But will the humanoids be entitled to make the causal assumption as well as the factual assumption, as they must do if they are to be able to invest their citation of evidence with a reinforcing capacity? Will they be entitled to assume that as they were caused by the evidence that p and q to judge and assert that q, so their audience will experience the same effect? What if the audience is not prompted as they are by that evidence? What if they agree that p and q but display no disposition to come as a result to the judgment and belief that q?

This possibility is also ruled out by our specifications on humanoid capacities. If the humanoids did not share a disposition to move from believing that p and q to believing that q—if they did not share dispositions of that general kind—they could not effectively learn from experience. And, as a consequence, they could not hope to exchange information with one another, act as the members of a joint enterprise, or serve one another as teachers and learners. That they are all disposed to make that sort of move will have to be a matter of common assumption, indeed, if they are to presume that the messages they communicate have the same significance for all; that a report on the presence of predators, for example, will cause everyone to recognize the danger and flee for their lives.

This suggests that as the humanoids will cite in explanation of an assertion only states of affairs they expect their audience to believe, so they will cite only states of affairs that they expect their audience to be moved by. And it suggests that those expectations will often be quite plausible. The background, shared assumption is that they are close to one another on both fronts. They are close enough to warrant the belief, indeed the common belief, that they will respond to a shared world by generally forming the same beliefs. And they are close enough to warrant the belief, and again the common belief, that they will display similar dispositions in how they respond to believing one state of affairs by forming a belief in another.

All of this suggests that in many cases the humanoids may expect to be able to reinforce certain assertions by successfully explaining the assertions on the lines explored. They will achieve success in such a case when the state of affairs that causally prompted them to make the assertion is one that their audience also believes, and when it moves the audience, as it moved them, to accept the assertion, believing in the state of affairs it affirms.

3.2.5 Negotiating divergence

Insofar as they are like us, the humanoids will often find that they do not share a premise-belief required to explain an assertion or do not share the disposition on accepting that premise to hold a relevant conclusion-belief. What are they likely to think in such a case? And how are they likely to respond to such divergence?

Our specifications on the capacities of the humanoids require us to say that when there is divergence on any such issue, the humanoids are bound to balk. According to those specifications, it will be a matter of common assumption among them that they each confront a common world and that they are each relatively competent or rational in forming beliefs about that world. Given that shared assumption, they must respond, and expect one another to respond, by believing that there is something amiss on one or another side when they diverge. This will most obviously be so, if the divergence is on a more or less straightforward issue and involves one judging that something is the case, and another judging that it is not: this, rather than withholding judgment. How could equally competent agents respond so differently about such an issue in an equally accessible world, and this, indeed, within a relatively equal society?[13]

But while divergence is bound to lead humanoid interlocutors to balk in this way, it is equally likely that they will develop a sense of how to explain differences, consistently with the assumption that they face a common world and that, in general, they are each competent in making their judgments. Although they are otherwise competent in making judgments and forming beliefs, the humanoid interlocutors will naturally explain a particular divergence among them by one of two sorts of failure, as we already noted in the last chapter. One, a failure of the evidence to show up clearly on one or another side and so a failure of those on that side to register all the relevant evidence. Or two, a failure of one or another party

---

[13] In our story, the humanoids are focused on judgments and beliefs that turn on how things are in a world salient to all and that are important insofar as they are urgently needed to guide action. Thus, we may assume that the burdens of judgment that John Rawls (1993, 55–56) invokes to explain differences on more complex issues are not generally going to be relevant here.

to respond to that evidence reliably: a failure in other words to register and process the evidence properly; for simplicity of presentation, we may ignore the possibility that such failures occur on all sides.

It is only an explanation of this kind that can save the assumptions of a common world and of a common evidential competence in plumbing that world. Those assumptions, embedded in the very nature of the humanoids, as they are embedded in ours, will make it natural for them to try to triangulate with others in determining what's what, and only this sort of explanation will enable them to persevere in that project of triangulation. Thus, any breakdown between them is likely to prompt a search for the explaining factor that can make sense of their failure to reach a common mind. They will want to achieve convergence with one another as a test—based on triangulation with others—of what is likely to be true.

It is not hard to see how the humanoids might develop a sense of the disrupters that are likely to get in the way of one or another party to an exchange. If those on one side were obstructed from seeing all the evidence available to those on the other, that will suggest that they were disrupted by lack of access to all relevant evidence; this may be because the light was poor, for example, an echo was distracting, or there was something in the way. Or if it turns out that those on one side were subject to a processing difficulty in making their judgment, then that will stand out as the likely explanation; this may consist in the fact that the party or parties on that side were intoxicated, for example, or subject to duress, or affected by a condition like color blindness. The humanoids may even learn in time that there are other, less prominent factors, such as confirmation bias, that may affect their judgment, as they often affect ours (Kahneman, Slovic, and Tversky 1982; Gilovich, Griffin, and Kahneman 2002).

If the humanoids come to be familiar with the idea of evidential disruption of broadly these kinds, then while they will continue to balk at any divergence between them on some issue, they need not be dismayed by it. For they will be in a position to negotiate about it, so to speak, seeking together to identify a disrupter that may account for their divergence from one another and may lead those affected to change their minds and agree with those not affected. Negotiation of this kind may reveal that one or another party to the dispute neglected some facts—some potential premises—relevant to the conclusion drawn. It may reveal that they were careless about what they took the premises registered to support, perhaps because of time pressure or distraction or the like. Or it may even reveal that due to a deeper form of carelessness they were operating with an invalid pattern of reasoning, as in treating the fact that 'p' entails 'q', and that q, as providing a reason to conclude that p.

The humanoids in any exchange may fail to find a plausible explanation for their difference, of course. But in that case, as we noted before, they may seek to suspend judgment on the dividing issue, pending further inquiry. Or, sticking with their own judgment, they may judge that those on the other side are affected by some distorting, if unidentified factor. Or they may decide that the predicate involved is vague and undefined for the borderline case on hand.

3.2.6 From explanation to justification

Once it is clear among the humanoids that disruption of this kind is possible, then that will have an enormous impact on anyone who seeks to reinforce an assertion by citing an alleged fact in explanation of why they made that assertion. Someone who seeks to reinforce an assertion in that fashion will realize that the explanation they offer will not carry weight with any audience if they or that audience are subject to some evidentially disrupting effect. And that is bound to make a difference to how they cast the reinforcing explanation they offer: this, at any rate, if they are not being devious or deceptive.

They will have to advertise their explanation of the assertion as one that is not distorted on their side by any disrupting effect; they will cite the piece or body of evidence that moves them as evidence that has that effect in the absence of any disrupter. It is only if they present themselves as registering or responding to the evidence in a disrupter-free way, that they can expect an audience to be moved in a similar, judgmental direction to theirs.

But equally, there will be no reinforcing point in explaining an assertion to others, if they believe that those others are subject to disruption by one or another distorting factor. That means that they will have to offer the explanation as likely to be successful only if those they address are not affected in such a manner. The message they convey to the audience will be: this will lead you to accept my earlier assertion provided you have avoided or suspended disrupting influences.

At this point, it should be clear that what we characterized earlier as a causal explanation of why the speaker made an assertion will amount to a prescriptive or normative justification of that assertion in functional terms. The explanation will no longer aspire to account merely for why, as it happens, the speaker made the earlier assertion. It will aspire to explain why they made the assertion and to induce the audience to accept that assertion, on the assumption that they and their audience are operating in a functional manner: specifically, on the assumption that they are all able to register and respond to evidence in the absence of disrupters.

The move made by the humanoids from explaining and reinforcing their assertions to justifying them comes out nicely in the distinct success conditions associated with those activities. A speaker will successfully explain an assertion insofar as they identify a body of alleged evidence that is at its causal origin. They will reinforce the assertion insofar as they identify a body of evidence that moves their audience as it moves them. And they will justify the assertion insofar as they identify a body of evidence that would move any normally functioning, disrupter-free individuals.

In seeking to reinforce an assertion, on the assumption that they and their audience are normally functioning, the humanoids will be seeking in effect to justify it. For if a belief is one that any normally functioning, disrupter-free humanoid would endorse or ratify, it is a belief that all of them ought in a familiar sense to satisfy. It will be in their nature as agents with manifestly common access to a manifestly common world to cherish normal functioning. And insofar as they are creatures of that type, they will be required to endorse or ratify any belief that a normally functioning agent would endorse. That will be an epistemic imperative that binds each of them.

At this point in the genealogy, we can reasonably expect the humanoids to introduce a normative word to answer to our use here of 'ought'. And with that concept and its cognates within reach, they will be able to single out the responses to this or that alleged state of affairs that, on their view, they or others ought to make, or should make, or have good reason to make in light of relevant functional standards. This functional or rational normativity, as we might describe it, is intuitively weaker than the sort of injunctive normativity we characterize later in Chapter 5. But it marks a crucial step in the development among humanoids that our genealogy seeks to track.

3.3 Reasoning, social and mental

3.3.1 Reasoning socially

We may conclude from the previous observations that the humanoids will be robustly likely, on suitable occasions, to offer justificatory explanations of the assertions they make. They will have a motive to provide such justifications, particularly when the audience has any doubts about the claim. And they will also have a means of acting on that motive, for they will be able to get over both the problem of how to identify the evidence at the origin of their assertions and the problem of finding a basis on which to invest their explanatory appeal to that evidence with a reinforcing effect.

When the humanoids engage in such justificatory explanations of their claims, they come close to reasoning with one another in support of those claims, on the model of reasoning introduced in the first section. We make the point in this discussion, with a focus on straightforward theoretical reasoning rather than theoretical reasoning involving probabilities, for example, or practical reasoning about what to do; we look briefly at other varieties of reasoning in the next section.

For any assertion that q, in our formulaic example, the humanoids will be able to cite the fact that p and q as sufficient to explain the assertion, provided disrupters are absent; they will cite it as justifying the assertion that q to other humanoids. This is not quite an instance of reasoning, in which we might expect them to relate the fact that p and q to the fact that q, not to its being explicable and justified for them to assert that q. But there is a reason why that difference will soon disappear.

It will be manifest among the humanoids that when a speaker seeks to reinforce any assertion, like the claim that q, they will assume the absence of disrupting factors in their audience and will assume that that audience will accept that q. And that means that they need not present their case as: p and q, so everyone ought to believe that q. They can say, more simply: p and q, therefore q. Or, given their ability to conceptualize and refer to the states of affairs involved—this, by the argument in the last section—they can say: 'p and q' entails 'q', or the fact that p and q entails the fact that q. When the humanoids make this move, they take up the project of reasoning proper, making connections between different alleged facts, not just between an alleged fact on the one hand and what people ought to assert or judge on the other.

We said earlier that, like assertion, judgment will be intentional among the humanoids insofar as it is intentional on their part, first, that they search for evidence in judging on whether or not something is the case and, second, that they choose to make a judgment rather than not when the evidence is in. Something similar will be true of their reasoning or, if you like, their making reasoned judgments. They will exercise choice in looking for the propositional linkages that might license reasoning and in drawing or refraining from drawing the supported conclusion.

It may even be that with these developments, the humanoids will be enabled and motivated to introduce the broad range of conditionals into their language. Spelling out why they connect the fact that p and q to the fact that q, a natural development will be for them to begin to say things like: if p and q, then q. Such a development would enable them to give concise expression to the linkages recognized. And it would enable them to offer fuller statements of the connections they see, as in: if p and q, then q; p and q, therefore q. These developments would enable them to introduce a conditional connective into their language, filling a gap we left open in our account in the first chapter of the language from which they begin.

As the humanoids will be able to register the implications of a presumptive fact in a conditional—broadly, an indicative conditional, so called—so they will be able to trace the implications of a merely supposed fact, even one admitted as false, in a subjunctive conditional. This is because the entailment relationship holds between states of affairs, independently of whether the entailing and entailed states of affairs obtain. As the actual fact that p and q entails the fact that q, so the supposed fact that p and q, did it obtain, would entail the q state of affairs. There will be a motive for such suppositional as distinct from factual reasoning insofar as the humanoids will often have an interest in knowing what would follow from it being the case that such and such, even when they do not know that it is the case; it will be in their interest as agents, for example, to know what would follow if they were to take an action X and what would follow if instead they were to take the alternative, Y (Vetter 2022).

While the humanoids will have a motive to reason that derives from their interest in explaining and reinforcing their assertions to others, they will also have other motives for engaging in the practice once it has emerged among them. They will not only be able to justify to others the assertions they are evidentially prompted to make. They will also be able to explore how far things currently supported by evidence, states of affairs they take to obtain, support further states of affairs. And they will be able to explore how far states of affairs they are unsure about may be supported by states of affairs they take to obtain: in other words, how far currently open questions can be resolved by currently acknowledged facts. On these two fronts, they will be able to pursue closure in their belief system. And in the same way, they will be able to check on how far their beliefs are inconsistent with one another; two states of affairs will be inconsistent, after all, when one entails that the other does not obtain.

3.3.2 Reasoning mentally

In line with the general thrust of our genealogy, we have been offering a narrative according to which the social practice of reasoning would be robustly likely to emerge among the humanoids. As in the case of assertion, language will provide the means of social reasoning, and the humanoids will have incentives to explore the possibility as it becomes accessible. But the humanoids will not only have an opportunity and incentive to reason with one another. They will also have a means and a motive for interiorizing that social practice, and reasoning with themselves. And in doing this, they will develop a capacity that would make Rodin's *Le Penseur* an even more fitting image than the capacity for judgment alone.

As a truthful or sincere assertion will reflect or constitute a personal judgment among the humanoids, so a sincere train of social reasoning is bound to reflect or constitute a mental counterpart: a personal endorsement of the argument presented. As judgment may occur in the absence of assertion, so the personal endorsement of an argument—the personal ratiocinative process—may occur in the absence of reasoning with others. And, to turn to a third parallel, as humanoids will be able to raise questions for themselves and, evidence presumptively permitting, make judgments in response, so they will be able to reason with themselves about issues that they raise for themselves as well as issues presented by others.

Thus, the humanoids will be able to reason with themselves about whether they have evidence that supports a certain judgment. They will be able to reason about whether various facts they endorse provide evidence for further facts that they ought to accept as presumptively functional agents. And they will be able to reason about whether any currently open questions can be resolved by currently recognized facts: about whether any states of affairs they are unsure about are supported by things they believe already. In short, they will be able to reason mentally about any issues that might arise in reasoning with others.

This suggests that social reasoning can be readily interiorized among our humanoids, as they learn how to relate to themselves, as a distinct individual might relate to them, debating with that figure—with themselves—about what to believe or desire or do. Mental reasoning will be a form of inner speech: a form of conversation and debate within the inner forum. But assuming that the humanoids will have a means of reasoning mentally, will they also have a motive to do so?

Yes, of course, they will. By reasoning with themselves, the humanoids will be able to achieve many of the appealing goals that reasoning with others would deliver. They will be able to check the judgments they form on the basis of this or that evidence, asking about whether that evidence really supports the judgment; they will be able to explore how far the various judgments that they currently make provide evidence for further judgments; and they will be able to look at how far open questions can be resolved by the judgments they currently endorse. They will have all the resources required to solve intellectual problems and puzzles.

The appeal of such mental reasoning, like the appeal of social, is that it will enable the humanoids to achieve a degree of intentional control over what they believe and desire that exceeds the degree made possible by judgment alone. Their cognitive autonomy, as we called it earlier, will be enhanced in a further dimension. The point is nicely illustrated by the contrast between what they will be able to do and what *savants* do in considering questions within the range of their special competence.

When *savants* intentionally consider such a question and provide an answer they do so relatively blindly: they wait passively for the answer to bubble up within them rather than making an intentional effort to help the processing along. The humanoids may not be able to answer the esoteric questions within the *savant* domain. But in considering questions within their own area of competence, they can actively explore a range of connections likely to be relevant to the resolution and when an answer comes to mind, they will be able to explain why indeed it is the answer: they will be able identify the evidence that supports it.

We must enter a cautionary note at this point, however, as we did in discussing the autonomy achieved in judgment. The autonomy that reasoning may enable the humanoids to achieve will always be relative or partial in character. In order to make judgments on any issue, the humanoids will have to rely on having dispositions that are reliably triggered by evidential cues, where it is ultimately their inherited nature that ensures the presence of such dispositions. And in order to reason mentally, or indeed socially, about any question, they will have to rely on having dispositions, inherited on the same genetic basis, that make them sensitive to the evidential connections between states of affairs and to the responses those connections trigger. They will have intentional control over whether to seek out the propositional linkages that license reasoning and over whether or not to draw any conclusions supported.

But they will not have any intentional control over whether or how far they have the sub-personal dispositions on which any such reasoning depends.

3.3.3 Reasoning without effort

While the humanoids must be expected to resort to mental reasoning as we do, however, their reasoning should not be taken—as our human reasoning should not be taken—to demand a sustained effort on their part. We may presume that, like us, the humanoids will not have the energy to devote themselves very often to racking their brains over the various issues they may face.

That mental reasoning may play a major role in humanoid life without requiring sustained effort appears in the fact, to reintroduce a familiar distinction, that it may impose control in a virtual, not an active manner. We saw in the last chapter that even without intentionally forming a judgment, a subject may control in a virtual or standby manner for the formation of a judgment and belief in response to evidence. And, as that is possible with unreasoned control of judgment, so it is also possible with control of a reasoned kind.

When the cowboy in the classic Western movie rides herd on his cattle, he lets them follow their head so long as they are on the right track, and intervenes only if one of the cattle wanders off track, raising a red flag. In the same way, the humanoids may ride herd on how they transition between judgments, as they may ride herd on judgments they independently form. They may let those transitions materialize on a spontaneous basis, confident that if they go awry that will raise a red flag, and prompt them to check the connection in active reasoning.

The fact that reasoning may assume a virtual as well as an active form means that it can shape the minds of humanoid agents on a very wide front. Reasoning can govern the humanoid updating of their beliefs and desires, not just when it is actively present, but also when it is virtually present—that is, on standby—ready to be activated by a red flag: say, by the flag raised when the agent draws an implausible conclusion, draws a conclusion under feelings of duress, or draws a conclusion that others challenge. However rare it is for the humanoids to reason actively, the capacity for reasoning and the sensitivity to such red flags will massively transform their mental and indeed social lives. Reasoning will be pervasively present as a means whereby the humanoids can control their mental lives, even if it is often present only in an unreflective, standby way.

3.3.4 Reasoning without sophistication

Even on this picture, however, active control remains important and, for all we have seen, it apparently requires an unlikely level of sophistication among humanoids.

In particular, it may be thought to require that they be able to articulate principles of the kind that are often spelled out in logic. An example might be the *modus ponens* principle that the truth of a conditional and its antecedent—the truth of the propositions that if p, q and that p—ensures the truth of the consequent: the proposition that q. It turns out, however, that even active reasoning does not require this.

We saw that when a subject reasons from a premised to a concluded state of affairs, they must be acting on a meta-propositional, linking belief—ultimately, a purely functional belief—that posits a suitable relationship between the two: the sort of relationship that makes it appropriate for a conclusion to be formulated in a so-form or a therefore-form. But it is now worth noticing that among the humanoids, as among our own kind, that belief may govern reasoning in a case-by-case rather than a once-for-all-cases manner. It may operate without requiring the subject to be able to articulate and assent to a principle that spells out the general form of relationship that the belief postulates between the premise and the conclusion.

The meta-propositional belief involved in reasoning posits a universally reliable relationship between the type of premise involved and the corresponding type of conclusion. But it is possible to believe a universal proposition like 'all Fs are G' either in a once-for-all or a case-by-case way or indeed in both modes at once. To believe the proposition in the first manner is to be disposed to assent to the universal formula, 'all Fs are G'; to believe it in the second is to be universally disposed with anything recognized as an F to treat it consequently as a G also.[14]

It may be a requirement on the humanoids that in order to conduct appropriate reasoning they must believe in the general sort of relationship that the *modus ponens* principle articulates. But they may believe it only in a case-by-case way. They may be disposed on recognizing the truth of a conditional and of its antecedent, to ratify a belief in its consequent in the 'so' or 'therefore' manner. And they may have this universal disposition without recognizing or even understanding the *modus ponens* formula. Suppose that they reason, for example, from the assumption that if the streets are wet this morning it rained last night, and the observation that the streets are wet, to the conclusion that it rained. And suppose moreover that they reason on that same pattern in example after example. They will certainly conduct *modus ponens* reasoning in that event, but they may do so without being able to understand or subscribe to the relevant formula.[15]

---

[14] Jonathan Bennett (1976), and in a different context David Lewis (1969), both make use of this distinction, relating it to the medieval distinction between someone's holding a universal belief *in sensu composito*—that is, in the once-for-all-cases way that requires endorsing a universal formula—and holding it *in sensu diviso*: that is, in the case-by-case manner that merely requires the believer to be universally disposed to endorse each instance.

[15] This observation may help to make the picture adopted here more acceptable to those who have argued in response to earlier versions of the picture (Pettit 1993; 2007b), that it is over-intellectualized (Boghossian 2012b; Broome 2013); see too (Pettit 2016).

3.4 Varieties of reasoning

We concentrated in the last section on how the humanoids would come to practice theoretical reasoning rather than practical reasoning, and theoretical reasoning that is not probabilistic in any sense. We look in this section at other varieties of reasoning, arguing that the humanoids would be robustly likely to develop these as well. In exploring these varieties, we need not distinguish much between social and mental forms of reasoning, as the answers sketched will generally be relevant to both.

We look first at probabilistic reasoning, then at practical reasoning and finally at a sort of theoretical reasoning that promises to be of particular importance for the humanoids, as it is for us. This is the interpretive reasoning that allows speakers to break away from purely conventional signs, relying on the reasoning capacity of hearers to discern messages they want to convey that require departures from the literal meaning of their words and sentences.

3.4.1 Probabilistic reasoning

One variety of theoretical reasoning, as already mentioned, involves inductive reasoning to a generalization of presumptive facts, another abductive reasoning to an explanation of such facts. These forms of reasoning are associated with one another to the extent that they are both probabilistic in character. Such a style of reasoning does not conclusively support a conclusion in the manner envisaged so far. It may be said to give support to a conclusion that probably something is the case or to give probabilistic support to the conclusion that it is the case.

The humanoids, as we noted briefly in the last chapter, will be able to make a claim that something is probable insofar as they can let the probabilistic qualifier reflect a strong but not irresistible disposition to judge that it is so. And that ability will be even more saliently accessible once they have the concepts that would allow them to predicate probability of a state of affairs. As they will be positioned to say that a state of affairs obtains, a proposition is true, when they actually judge and believe that that is the case, so they will be positioned to say that the state of affairs probably obtains, the proposition is probably true, to the extent that they are more or less strongly inclined to judge and believe that it is so.

If they can formulate a proposition in that probabilistic manner, they will be able to argue from a premised state of affairs, say that probably p and q, to a state of affairs that is probabilistic in character: say, to the conclusion that probably q. And equally they will be able to recognize that the support provided by a non-probabilistic premise for a certain conclusion may not be conclusive in the manner of an entailment but rather probabilistic: it may justify only a probabilistically qualified conclusion.

This is to say that the humanoids will have access to a means of reasoning probabilistically in an inductive or abductive fashion. Would they also have the motive to do so? Yes, because the motives that make conclusive reasoning attractive for them will do the same for probabilistic. Such reasoning will enable them to vindicate certain assertions to others, partially if not completely. And it will enable them, albeit in a tentative manner, to pursue closure in expanding the range of their beliefs, as well as checking their beliefs for consistency.

But probabilistic reasoning about the actual world may be taken to include something other than induction or abduction, on the view of judgments adopted, according to our genealogy, among the humanoids.

Suppose there is a deductive linkage between certain propositions, with some figuring as premises, another as a conclusion. And suppose that someone is willing to assent to the premises, judging that they actually hold. Will that individual be led to assent therefore to the conclusion about the actual world? Not necessarily, in view of the stakes-sensitivity of judgment. For the strength of evidence that suffices in the context of relevant stakes to support their judgment in favor of the premises may not be preserved under entailment. The evidence for the entailed conclusion may turn out to be weaker than the evidence for the premises, and to be so weak that the individual is not willing to judge in favor of the conclusion.

This problem does not arise in the simple example on which we have been relying, where the subject reasons from the presumed fact that p and q to the conclusion that q. The evidence for the entailed conclusion cannot be weaker in such a case than the evidence for the premise. And so, assuming that the stakes are the same in each case, the fact that the subject finds the evidence sufficiently strong to make a judgment that p and q means that they will also find the evidence sufficiently strong to draw the conclusion that q.

But this is not always the case with deductive reasoning, as we already noted. Suppose that someone judges that p and that q, where they hold the linking belief that those conjuncts entail the conjunction, p and q. And now imagine that the individual judges that p and that q because the evidence that the world offers for each, while it is not overwhelming, is sufficiently strong in the context of relevant stakes to support each judgment. Will their linking belief lead them, assuming the stakes remain constant, and no extra evidence appears, to judge that as it is actually the case that p and that q, so it is actually the case that p and q? Not necessarily, for the evidence that a conjunction holds—the evidence that both conjuncts hold—is not going to be as strong as the evidence that either conjunct holds. But if the evidence for the conjunction is not going to be as strong as the evidence supporting the conjuncts, it may well be that it is not strong enough to support a judgment in favor of the conclusion.

What may we expect the humanoids to do in reasoning from conjuncts like p and q to the conjunction in a case like this? They will find themselves disposed, if they are clear about the situation, to judge that p and that q but not, despite the entailment, to judge that p and q. Since the reasoning bears on the actual world—it is not just suppositional in character—they will be responsive, not only to the entailment registered in their belief linking premises to conclusion, but also to the fact that their judgments in favor of the premises are made on the basis of less than overwhelming evidence.

Will the humanoids just fail to draw any conclusion in such a case? Hardly. With the concept of probability available, they will be able to do more than just fail to conclude that p and q on the basis of their judgments that p and that q. They can be more positive and conclude that probably p and q, giving a probabilistic cast to their reasoning. By doing so in a case like this they will register, however indeterminately, that the evidence that p and q is relatively strong, albeit not strong enough to elicit an unqualified judgment. And since taking that line would be more informative for any audience, or indeed for themselves, they will presumably be led to adopt it.

3.4.2 Practical reasoning

On the account that we sketched in the last chapter, practical judgment will involve the agent's ascribing a desiderative property to an object—say, a prospect, an option, or whatever—where this judgment tends to elicit a desire for that object: a desire for it under that desiderative aspect. The desire formed may be qualified in the manner of a preference for a certain sort of alternative, or unqualified in the manner of an intention or policy to take one of a set of options in a certain choice or type of choice. We assumed that while humans may weight such desiderata differently—or even vary over time in their individual weightings—they will scarcely find an agent intelligible unless they can see desiderata at the source of their choices. They may be unmoved themselves by those desiderata, but they must at least understand how the agent could be moved by them, say as a result of having different beliefs; they must be able to take the perspective of such an agent.

On this model of practical judgment, it is clear that as the humanoids will learn to reason theoretically in matters remote from desire and action, so they will learn to reason practically. They will make a judgment on the balance of desiderata across relevant alternatives and, reasoning from that judgment as from a premise, they will judge that one alternative or subset of alternatives scores over others. Insofar as it follows this pattern, practical reasoning will resemble theoretical. What makes it practical is the fact that the conclusion drawn will typically trigger or, as we may prefer to think, constitute the formation of a desire, whether that be a general preference or a specific intention or policy.

Different individuals may reason to different conclusions and desires, of course, as a result of weighting desiderata differently; they may reason from their own perspective, as we say, or perhaps from the perspective of a group with which they identify. But while that makes for a deep difference from theoretical reasoning, it also leaves many similarities in place.

These remarks suggest that the humanoids will have the means of reasoning practically as well as theoretically. But will they have the same motives to do so? They will not need to reinforce their practical judgments and desires as they might wish to reinforce other assertions and judgments, except in the case of acting jointly with others: more on this in Chapter 5. But, on our assumptions, they will want to make their practical judgments and desires intelligible to others, if only in the manner of the ascetic who claims to want a saucer of mud as a reminder of their mortality.

Moreover, as theoretical reasoning will enable the humanoids to extend their intentional control over the judgments and assertions they make, looking at what follows from what, so practical reasoning will enable them to extend their intentional control over their practical judgments. They will be able to look at what desiderative judgments follow from ones they already hold and at what to desire as well-functioning agents in view of their judgments on desiderata. Where data are going to be firm enough for the humanoids to be able to agree generally on their significance, however—evidence for one subject will tend to be evidence for all— the same need not be true of desiderata. The humanoids may agree on the presence of certain desiderata but differ on the weight they assign to them and on their practical significance. Still, it will be true in this case, as in the other, that the greater intentional control it provides will naturally make it appealing for humanoids.

3.4.3 Interpretive reasoning

There is a specific form of reasoning, albeit broadly theoretical in character, that is worth discussing in its own right, particularly since it will likely play a major part in the trajectory of humanoid development. This is the sort of interpretive reasoning required to recognize, for example, that the assertion that no man is an island does not express a banal truth; that to say that a horse is tall is not to compare it with skyscrapers; or, in an example from earlier, that Marc Antony means to pillory Brutus and his fellow conspirators, when he casts them as honorable men.

Why does the recognition that an assertion carries this sort of non-literal message require reasoning? Plausibly, because the fact that that is the message derives from contextual assumptions that are likely to be manifest among speakers. In the examples given, the relevant assumptions are that a speaker is unlikely to want to communicate something as banal as that no man is an island, unlikely to be interested in placing a horse among any entities whatsoever in speaking of its height, or in Marc Antony's case, unlikely to want to praise Caesar's assassins. Presumably hearers will only be able to pick up those messages—at least in their first exposure—by making a series of adjustments: taking the assertions at the face value established by convention; seeing that in the context of the exchange—and as a matter of common belief—the speaker cannot wish to communicate that face-value message; concluding that the speaker must therefore have wished to convey something different; and then arguing, inevitably in a probabilistic fashion, that they likely intended such and such an alternative.

We argued earlier that the humanoids, on their first introduction to conventional, intentional signaling, would be restricted in their mutual understanding to taking signs or sentences as their conventions established that they should be taken. That reading of their capacity fitted with our stipulations about their nature and no richer construal was plausible.

Once reasoning is in place among the humanoids, however, their mutual understanding will cease to be restricted. Sharing beliefs about one another's likely intentions and about the literal message a speaker's words would convey in a given exchange, they will be able to conclude that the speaker is not using those words conventionally or with their conventional intent. And of course, they will thereby sponsor a search for what the speaker must have meant, re-using their shared beliefs to work out what that can be. It will be manifest to all that this is the case and so each will be licensed, whether as a speaker or hearer, to exploit the new resources of communication that are thereby made available (Sperber and Wilson 1986).

The humanoids will not merely be licensed to put the new resources to work. They will be motivated to avail themselves of those resources in expanding the range of messages they can convey and in conveying them to a finer, more nuanced effect. It will enable them to enrich and embellish their reports on how things are, for example, and to provide accounts of things that can clearly not be intended as reports and get to be taken as stories: say, tales designed merely to entertain. And at the limit, it will enable them to explore poetry, reflecting on their situation with the help of figurative devices—even varieties of ambiguity (Empson 1949)—that the austere discipline of conventional meaning would not have allowed.

With these developments, communication among the humanoids will continue to depend on the conventions that have emerged between them, including conventions governing presumptions about what they are doing in certain speech acts—say, communicating or seeking information—as well as conventions determining the meanings of their words. But henceforth those conventions will provide a framework that they may put in the service of different purposes. Most of the time they will speak to conventionally recognized purposes, in conventionally familiar ways. But they will be enabled, as occasion demands, to exploit shared assumptions in speaking to a novel purpose say, in spinning a tale or speaking ironically, or in resorting to metaphor to express what they have in mind.

It may seem that this sort of innovation in signaling will make linguistic communication exceedingly challenging and hazardous. But as conventions emerge to standardize the literal meanings of words, so they are likely to emerge at a further level, causing metaphors to die, for example, and ironical modes of speech to be recognized by emphasis or intonation (Lakoff and Johnston 2003). And even where the speech is quite innovative, interpreters need have little difficulty in understanding it. They will begin with the presumption that the speaker intends to use their words in a standard, conventional way but be ready to lift that presumption as this turns out to be the best way of making sense of their speech. Interpretation will have the character of an art rather than a science, under this account of what it involves, but it will be an art that we may expect the humanoids to master naturally in the course of managing their lives together.

3.5 Interlude: the role of rules

3.5.1 Following rules in reasoning

It is common to associate reasoning with rules and there is good reason to do so (Broome 2013). In every instance of reasoning, the subject relies on a linking belief in a systematic connection between the premises and the conclusion that is meant to hold over variations in the precise ways in which those propositions are or might be made true. This will be a probabilistic relationship in the case of inductive and abductive reasoning, a relationship of entailment in the case of deductive, including the deductive form of reasoning where, as we have seen, the subject's evidence may be strong enough to support assent to the premises but not, except in a probabilistic variation, to the conclusion.

The subject may not be able to formulate the systematic pattern to which they are faithful in reasoning. They may believe it only in a case-by-case way, as we saw, not being able to articulate it in a universal formula to which they can assent. But they will reliably and intentionally conform, instance by instance, to what the pattern requires of them, as they endorse a conclusion in recognition of the support provided by the premises. Thus, they will count as following it—following the rule involved—as they reason, under intentional control, in a reliable fashion.

The rules of reasoning that the humanoids follow will normally be valid rules, by the tests of logic or methodology, since the humanoids will be positioned, like us, to learn over time that other rules can lead them to false beliefs and unsuccessful actions. But in a given case the rule that an individual follows in reasoning may be invalid; it may be like the rule of affirming the consequent, as in reasoning from the facts that if p, q, and that q, to the conclusion that p (Broome 2013).

How does the rule-following in this case compare with the rule-following involved in the use of signs in assertion and judgment? We discussed this in the final section of the first chapter, which was also an interlude in the genealogy. And how far does rule-following in this case raise a similar problem?

The two forms of rule-following are distinct in the following respect. When someone intentionally signals that something is the case—say, that an object is red or bulky—they must follow the rule of doing so only when an abstract entity, the relevant property, is concretely present; otherwise, they could not communicate anything by their use of that sign. When one of our humanoids follows a rule in reasoning, they will also have to register the presence of an abstract entity—a certain premise–conclusion relationship between propositions—now in this instance, now in that. But registering that entity will have an extra effect in reasoning that it need not have in simple signaling. It will not only prompt the subject to use a word like 'entails' or 'supports' or whatever in response, as in any case of signaling, it will also dispose them determinately or probabilistically to move, other things being equal, from endorsing the premise or premises to endorsing the conclusion.[16]

Expanding briefly on this feature: when a subject takes certain propositions as premises and another as conclusion, that will go hand in hand with their becoming disposed, at least in general, to draw the conclusion. The relationship will be presented to them as an affordance, to use a term introduced by the psychologist J. J. Gibson (1979). It will serve as a stimulus that simultaneously primes them to register that something is so—the relationship is present in this instance—and to respond as its being so prompts them to respond: to become strongly or weakly disposed to move from endorsing the premises to endorsing the conclusion.

So much for how rule-following in reasoning compares with the rule-following required by any intentional signaling. How far does the problem of basic rule-following arise in this case, as we saw that it arises in the other?

The problem arises in the signaling case, because the rules governing when and when not a subject is to use certain signs cannot all have a definitional status. Some must be basic in the sense that the individual grasps them directly, identifying and intentionally tracking the relevant classes, kinds, and properties. The problem is to explain how it can be possible for any subject to target something abstract that has an indefinite range of instances and let it determine what to signal or not to signal in a given instance.

A similar problem is going to arise in the case of reasoning. There may be some patterns or rules of reasoning that are defined for an individual in terms of other rules: the definition would explain how to follow the defined rule in terms of steps that required following the other rules. But for any subject there must be some basic rules of reasoning that cannot be defined in that way, as there must be some basic rules of signaling that cannot be defined in terms of other rules. And there is going to be an issue here, as in the other case, about how the humanoids can get to follow such basic rules.

---

[16] When they have independently mastered the art of reasoning, the humanoids may learn under pressure to explain or justify an assertion or judgment that something is red by reference to the fact that it looked red. But that will not be required as a prerequisite of their ability to signal that something is red. All they need to register in order to make the assertion or judgment is just the presence of that property in that instance.

If the problem has the same character in the two cases, the solution that we found in the earlier case should work here as well. In this section we try to explore the form that the solution will take. We first look at an applicational theory of reasoning and show that it raises even more problems than its counterpart in the signaling case. And then we explain how the materials provided in this chapter are enough to support an implementation model of reasoning that nicely parallels the implementation story about the rule-following involved in signaling. Unlike the signaling case, the model here constitutes a how-probably explanation of the emergence of rule-following in the reasoning of the humanoids, not just a how-possibly account; this, as we shall see, is because it is implicit in the how-probably account of reasoning itself.

3.5.2 The applicational model

Socrates asked Euthyphro whether the gods love the holy because it is holy or whether it is holy because the gods love it. Echoing a similar theme in our discussion of signaling, we may ask whether reasoners reason because of following suitable rules or whether they follow such rules because of reasoning. The question is whether rule-following is present as a means of reasoning or whether it arises on some other basis as a byproduct of reasoning. The applicational model of reasoning holds that rule-following is a means of reasoning, the implementational that it is a byproduct.

On the applicational model, following a rule requires accessing something akin to a formula that summarizes the rule; relying on that formula to indicate, perhaps fallibly, the requirement of the rule in any particular case; and then acting according to that indication in intentionally, if fallibly, seeking to meet the requirement. The model is applicational insofar as it takes the reasoner to have a grasp of a rule, and to seek to apply that rule, now in one situation, now in another.

This model is faulty on a number of counts. A first obvious problem is that it leaves in place the same problem that arises with the basic rule-following involved in signaling. A second problem, equally obvious, is that it rules out antecedently the sort of case-by-case reasoning that we mentioned in the third section. And a third, as others have recently argued, is that it raises a serious regress problem (Boghossian 2012a; b; Wright 2012).

Suppose, to take up this third problem, that someone aims to reason by following a rule of the form: if in circumstances C, make response R. How might a reasoner follow such a C-R rule? Presumably by recognizing situations that instantiate the antecedent feature, C, and by reasoning in those situations to the R-response. But this requires the subject who applies that rule in reasoning, to do so by virtue of reasoning: that is, by reasoning from the C-feature of a situation to the R-response it requires. The model opens up a regress, with an initial exercise of reasoning depending on rule-following, that exercise of rule-following depending itself on an exercise of reasoning, that later exercise of reasoning depending in turn on rule-following, and so on *ad infinitum*.

3.5.3 The implementational model of reasoning

On the alternative, implementational approach, the humanoids will not follow rules as a means of reasoning but rather as a result of reasoning; they will not apply but rather implement rules in the course of reasoning. Such a model is supported by the picture of humanoid reasoning that we sketched in previous sections. We can make the point with reference to the example of deductive reasoning that we have been using—from the premise that p and q to the conclusion that q—where, as we know, there is no problem raised by the fact that the evidence supporting a conclusion may be weaker than the evidence supporting the premises from which the conclusion is deduced.

On the view of reasoning developed in the chapter, the humanoids will get to reason, whether socially or just mentally, in virtue of six dispositions, where the first is widely shared among agents of any kind and the other five will have evolved, according to our genealogy, in the wake of language. These factors enable and dispose them, respectively:

1. to be led from believing that p and q to believing that q;
2. to believe that the propositions are linked: in effect, that 'p and q' entails 'q';
3. to conclude in view of 2 that q—'so, q'—reinforcing the belief in 1;
4. to correct that step, if it is undermined in negotiating divergences with others;
5. if no correction is needed, to accept that q, as in step 3 above;
6. otherwise, to rerun the earlier steps in light of the correction.

The first element is a disposition to believe a proposition whose truth is rationally supported by the presumptive truth of propositions already believed, if only in the manner of a blindly rational agent. The second presupposes a conceptual capacity to hold beliefs about abstract entities like states of affairs and posits a disposition to display this capacity in forming a belief in the reinforcing linkage—the relationship of entailment—between the first two propositions and the third. And the third element is a disposition to assert and believe the third proposition in a manner that casts it as a conclusion from the supporting propositions.

The fourth and later elements in our list introduce a moderating disposition to balk at divergence with others, and to search for a resolution by identifying possible disrupters: factors that would explain the divergence consistently with the assumption of a common world, a generally shared competence on the part of all and a wish to triangulate with others in determining what's what. And finally, if the correction envisaged in the fifth and sixth stages is achieved, the humanoids will come to think that when they transition from acceptance of the one state of affairs to the acceptance of the other, they move in a justified way: in the way that properly functioning humanoids—humanoids unaffected by disrupters—would move.

On this account of reasoning the core elements that make it possible are two inclinations. One, supported by stages 1, 2, and 3, is a transitional inclination to reinforce the conclusion-belief on the basis of a premise-belief. The other, introduced in stages 4, 5, and 6, is an interrogative inclination to question the transitional inclination if there is a divergence from others that constitutes potential evidence of disruption. These inclinations are the counterparts in this story of the extrapolative and balking inclinations in the story about intentional signaling.

The extrapolative and balking inclinations in our resolution of the intentional-signaling problem enable the humanoids to be able to track the abstract class or kind or property associated with any simple sign. The extrapolative disposition will help them to home in on that entity, letting instances of the sign exemplify for subjects the class to which they are disposed to extrapolate. And then the balking disposition ensures that they will take divergence between them seriously, as a result of operating with an assumption that any class to be tracked is the same for all, and that they will come to treat their extrapolations as fallible indicators of its presence that may be discounted in the course of triangulating with others.

The transitional and interrogative inclinations play a very similar role in our account of reasoning in this chapter. The transitional inclination, like the extrapolative inclination in the other case, will provide the humanoids with a first take on the patterns to be followed in reasoning. The interrogative inclination will give them pause in the case of divergence from others, leading them to look for disrupters on one or another side, to triangulate with others and, if that proves possible, to validate one particular transition and invalidate others.

We can see from the parallel between basic rule-following in signaling and basic rule-following in reasoning that as our story in the first chapter can make sense of its possibility in the signaling case, so our story in this chapter can make sense of its possibility in the case of reasoning. In each enterprise, the humanoids have to idehtify an abstract entity that can be realized in a potential infinity of cases and let it guide them reliably but fallibly. If the guidance is successful, that targeted entity will lead them to signal intentionally only when that entity is instantiated in the world before them, and to reason from some propositions to another only when it is instantiated in the relationship of those propositions to that other.

On this model of rule-following, the humanoids will not follow independently identified rules as a means of conducting the relevant exercise: signaling or reasoning; they will not apply rules in the manner envisaged within the applicational model. On the account given in each case, what they do will be to implement rule-following in their practice. They will seek to track their target on the assumption, encoded in how they see the world and one another, that they may miss or mistake it in a given case. And they will count thereby as seeking to follow the corresponding rule: it will be manifest to all that remaining faithful to the signaling or reasoning practice that emerges between them constitutes following such a rule.

In concluding this discussion, however, we should stress that basic rule-following, taken as a general topic, naturally encompasses following basic rules in both signaling and reasoning. We have stressed at a number of points that the capacity to reason cannot emerge prior to judgment but that for all we need assume they may co-evolve, emerging in tandem among the humanoids. This holds too of the basic rule-following presupposed to judgment and reasoning.

It makes good sense to think that the capacity to follow basic rules in judgment will be closely followed by the emergence of a capacity to follow such rules in reasoning. And it is worth noting that the rule-following in signaling that we characterized in the first chapter will be much more plausible once it is accompanied with rule-following in reasoning. This is because the negotiation of divergence between individuals or groups can be much more explicitly and effectively conducted, once those parties are capable, not just of explaining a divergence in their judgments, but of explaining why one side in a dispute is justified, the other not, and why those who are not, ought to alter their view. Basic rule-following will be able to come into its own, so to speak, only when the humanoids gain access to the resources associated with being able to reason.

4
Perception with percipience

We saw in Chapter 2 that, equipped with the use of language for exchanging information, our humanoids will be able to make judgments on a range of issues. They will be able to answer one another's questions by looking at relevant data, thereby forming or confirming their beliefs, and they will be able to ask themselves questions and, on the same basis, answer those questions for themselves. This will constitute an ability to make up their own minds intentionally on issues where the data—and, in the case of practical judgment, the desiderata—are appropriately rich. The humanoids will be able to form judgments in response to those data and desiderata, ensuring that they have theoretical and practical beliefs, indeed ratified beliefs, on issues of concern to them.

For all we said in the first chapter, however, the humanoids' capacity for judgment might be as unreasoned on the routine issues addressed as the judgments of *savants* on the esoteric questions they master. But, as we saw in the last chapter, the humanoids will have a capacity to register the linkage that enables certain data to support their judgments and beliefs and to conclude on this or that evidential basis that *therefore* things are thus and so. This ability to form reasoned judgments on various issues will serve them well. It will enable them to explain and justify their judgments to others and to themselves, and it will enable them to recognize that reasoning from those judgments may enable them to draw conclusions that might not otherwise have been accessible. Moreover, it will enable them to reason in this fashion across a range of areas, including reasoning in a practical mode from desiderata to action, and thereby forming preferences and intentions that the desiderata support.

In our presentation of their capacity for judgment and reasoning, we emphasized that the humanoids will enjoy intentional control over the exercise of those capacities. They will not be able intentionally to judge or reason as they wish, since the functionally appropriate belief to hold, theoretical or practical, will depend on the data or desiderata available. But they will be able to seek out relevant data or desiderata to support judgments on whether this or that is so and, even when adequate support is available, they will be able to decide to go ahead or not to go ahead in making a judgment.

We turn now to the effect that the presence and the exercise of the capacities for judgment and reasoning will have on the perception of the world that the humanoids, like human beings and other animals, will certainly enjoy. We argue that the effect will be transformative, enabling the humanoids to perceive a new range of properties in a new way, to exercise intentional control over what they bring to attention within perception, and to question their perceptions for whether they reflect reality or constitute mere appearance. The enjoyment of this new ability is derivative from their enjoyment of the more basic capacities for judgment and reasoning but, as we shall see, it marks a development in the life of the humanoids that is worthy of attention in its own right. We draw on the term 'percipience' to register the new level of ability achieved, arguing that percipience enhances humanoid consciousness and gives them access to art and science.

The chapter is in three sections. In the first we offer a general picture of perception as it is common across a range of animals, humans and humanoids included. Then in the following section, we explore the three aspects under which perception will be transformed among the humanoids, as they are enabled to enrich judgmentally the range of properties presented, to regulate perceptual attention in the service of reasoning from those properties, and to authorize the dismissal of a perception as missing or misrepresenting things; these developments reflect salient aspects of human perception and exemplify the different dimensions of percipience, as that capacity is understood here. Finally, in the third section, we turn to the connection between percipience and consciousness, arguing that it will elicit a kind of perceptual consciousness in humanoids over and beyond that which is available to non-percipient animals.

The capacity for percipience will inevitably appear among the humanoids insofar as they bring the capacities for judgment and reasoning to bear on perception; indeed, it consists in the presence and exercise of those capacities in the perceptual area. The social provenance of the capacities means that percipience is sourced ultimately in the interaction of humanoids with one another, including their interaction in checking with one another on whether they have perceived properties correctly, on what attentional moves are needed to identify the answer to certain questions, and on how far they are mistaking appearance for reality. But perception is a mental rather than a social reality, and while percipience gives perception a new quality, it is not something distinct from it in the way judgment is distinct from belief and reasoning from rationality. Thus, the chapter will not start, as the others do, with the emergence of an interpersonal practice and then look at its intrapersonal counterpart. It will focus on perception in its essentially intrapersonal character and show how it is bound to be transformed by the socially sourced presence of judgment and reasoning.

As we argued in the discussion of demystification in Chapter 1, the genealogy should help to counter the non-naturalistic view that there is more to the six capacities than natural science is equipped to explain. But, as we registered earlier, it will not do anything to make naturalistic sense of the perception that percipience presupposes and, in this area, it will leave open the debate between naturalism and non-naturalism. For all that the genealogy demonstrates, there may be something in non-percipient perception—and in the consciousness, as we shall see, that it can involve—that lies beyond naturalistic explanation. And, of course, there may be something of that irreducible kind to other non-perceptual states such as sensations and moods and the like that generally count as conscious; we say nothing here about such states.[1]

4.1 Perception in general

4.1.1 Perception is presentational, attentional, and dismissible

Perceptual activity supplies subjects with information about their environment in the sense that its character is generally indicative of how things are. It involves a range of sensory channels which are coordinated so that the environment is accessible to the subject as a single perceptual field, with different aspects of that field corresponding to how it presents in different channels. Sometimes the activity may fail to be indicative of how things are, giving rise to a misperception that such and such, but we may still think of the activity involved as broadly perceptual in character. This is despite the fact that by ordinary criteria we cannot say in that case that the subject perceives that such and such.

Although it evolves continually over time, perceptual activity gives rise to episodic perceptions, or indeed misperceptions, at different times. These are distinctive in a number of ways (Dretske 2006). First, they are direct in the sense that they involve unmediated causal contact with the environment. Second, they provide information of a kind that can interact with the agent's desires in controlling behavior, whether by operating like beliefs or giving rise to beliefs: we leave open the question of which is the case. And third, they generate that information along recognizable sensory routes; while these include the five familiar senses in human beings, they may involve quite distinct channels in other species (Yong 2022).

In this section, we try to provide an account of perception as it may figure in a variety of animal species, not just in humans or humanoids. We assume that the humanoids will begin with perceptual abilities of a kind that are common to many animals, human beings included, and we shall argue in the next section that their capacity for judgment and reasoning in the perceptual area—their capacity for percipience—will transform those abilities to give them a distinctive quality.

In this first section, we sketch three claims about perception, arguing, in terms defined as we progress, that it is presentational, attentional, and dismissible. Some of the claims we sketch are controversial, and we outline them here without a

---

[1] My thanks to Daniel Stoljar for illuminating discussions of the material in this chapter, and for extremely helpful comments on an earlier draft.

proper defense.[2] Moreover, we sketch the claims at a level of abstraction that ignores detailed debates in philosophical and empirical psychology. These faults are inevitable, given the nature of our project. They may be unobjectionable insofar as the view we develop in the following sections is likely be defensible under different assumptions about perception, and on rival accounts of the details ignored in our sketch.

The account offered in this discussion is primarily built on a phenomenological appeal to our own perceptual experience and, by observationally based extension, to that of other animals.[3] What holds for us and for other animals will presumably hold for the humanoids as well, given the assumption that they share our pre-linguistic nature. But we will not focus on the humanoids as such in the current discussion. We shall need to do so only in the later sections when we investigate the difference that judgment and reasoning are robustly likely to induce in humanoid perceptions.

4.1.2 Perception is presentational

Perceptual activity is presentational in the first place to the extent that like many beliefs and judgments, the perceptions it generates routinely take the form of predicating properties of objects. They depict things as thus and so, homing in on one or more objects and predicating properties or relationships of them; these objects may be enduring substances, temporally located events, temporally extended processes, or whatever. It is common to distinguish between perceiving an object, of course, and perceiving things to be thus and so. But for our purposes here, we may assume that to perceive an object is always to perceive it as such and such, at least if the perception is commissioned in the manner of a belief to shape how the subject behaves. As the point is often put, to see is always to see-as: seeing an object means seeing it as something.

If this is right, then a perception will always have accuracy conditions, its role being to depict things as being thus and so. By our account in the second chapter, the belief that p has the role of disposing the believer on an evidence-responsive basis to act as if p: to act as it would be rational to do, given their other beliefs and desires, if it were the case that p. Subject to a qualification related to its dismissible character, the perception that things are thus and so will generally have the same

---

[2] There is no single overview of the enormous literature on the claims made. But for a collection of relevant contributions, see (Haddock and McPherson 2009), and for useful review papers, (Siegel 2016) and (Soteriou 2020).

[3] I lack the space and the expertise to offer a scientifically informed account of what sentience amounts to in different non-human species. For a wonderful, evolutionarily structured introduction to the area, see (Godfrey-Smith 2020). For an overview of recent developments in the cognitive study of animal consciousness, see (Birch, Schnell, and Clayton 2020). And for an overview of the varieties of perception across the animal world, see (Yong 2022).

role of disposing the subject, on the basis of responsiveness to perceptual inputs, to act as if things were thus and so. In doing this, the experience may have a role resembling that of belief or may elicit a corresponding belief in that role; as noted, we can set aside the issue as to which is the case.

But while a perception is predicative in the manner of a belief—and counts as presentational to that extent—it is presentational in a direct manner that makes for a contrast with belief. By the account to be assumed here, it is presentational, first, in relating subjects directly to the properties—including, the relationships—it predicates of objects and, second, in relating them directly to the objects of which it predicates those properties. We look first at how a perception directly presents properties, and then at how it directly presents objects.

4.1.3 Presenting properties directly

According to one possible view of perceptual processing, which might assume any of a variety of forms, what it delivers in predication of a property is something that can be understood and grasped by the subject only if they have a perceptually independent concept of that property. The perception involves passive submission to something given from without and it will assume the profile of predicating one or another property only insofar as it prompts the subject to form a belief in which that independently grasped property is predicated.

On this story, then, the subject must be possessed of a concept on a basis that is independent from its perceptions. It will be that concept that provides a grasp of the property predicated. The perception will not present the property to the subject in any literal sense, it will serve merely to nudge the subject into believing it is present.

According to the view that I shall adopt here, this is a misleading picture. We saw in an interlude on demystification and metaphysics in the first chapter that a property will be constituted by a set of patterned instances: a set that is patterned in the sense that other members can in principle be determined from a proper, finite subset. And we saw at the same time that even a simple animal can be sensitized to such a pattern, becoming disposed in the wake of exposure to some instances to be able to identify others in the set. That disposition may be grounded in nature, as when the set is a natural similarity class for the creature, or it may be grounded in a history of conditioning: say, that which occurs when a simple pigeon is conditioned to peck for food at little doors of a triangular shape.

Sensitization of this kind establishes that the set of items targeted constitutes a property; it shows that it is possible to determine other members of the set on the basis of exposure to a finite sample. But it also gives the sensitized creature a rudimentary grasp of a property, offering a model of how perception may present a suitable property directly. The animal's sensitization to a property consists in a disposition to extrapolate from some instances—the sample set that enables it to cotton on to the property—to others. But that disposition cannot itself be explained, without an explanatory circle, by its grasp of the property; it must be explained by an independent, neuropsychologically intelligible responsiveness to the triggering, sample instances. The animal will grasp the property in virtue of being disposed to extrapolate appropriately to instances; it will not be disposed to extrapolate in virtue of its grasp of the property.

Suppose a simple animal is sensitized in the manner envisaged to different perceived instances of this or that color or shape or sound, or indeed to perceived instances of conspecifics, predators or prey. Its sensitization in each case will give it an ability to identify the property instantiated, predicating it of one or another object in perception and belief. Thus, the subject will perceive that property in the inputs it processes, without having to bring an independently formed concept to bear on those data.

The simple animal's concept of the property will be stimulus-dependent if it can form only beliefs predicating the property, and only predicating it in the presence of perceived bearers. But even if it gives the creature a weakly stimulus-independent ability—even if it enables it, say as a predator, to have a concept of its prey that can apply in memory or anticipation—that concept is still likely to presuppose sensitization to the pattern and to be reactivated in every perception where it is relevant. The animal that forms a perceptual belief that predicates the property, now in this instance, now in that, may do so in virtue of seeing that pattern within its perception; it does not need to have access to an independently supported concept that it brings to that perception from outside.

How will it be, in phenomenological terms, for any animal, including a human or humanoid, to have a property directly presented in perception? Returning to the example of the pigeon, what it sees will be a particular triangular door, not the property of triangularity. But if that particular door is to make the property itself accessible—accessible as a predicable feature—then it must impact on the pigeon, not just as a particular instance of the class or property, but as an exemplar of what it involves. And presumably it can do this in virtue of a natural history of sensitization or a history of conditioning that elicits sensitization. That history will let each instance play the role of displaying or exemplifying the class or type to which it belongs: the class or type that corresponds with the sensitization (Goodman 1969).

On the account supported by these considerations, it appears that every perception of the kind envisaged must do two jobs at once. It must present a property to the subject and at the same time it must predicate the property presented of the object perceived. The instance of the property in the object that is perceptually registered will exemplify and thereby present the property to the suitably sensitized subject. And at the same time, it will confirm for the subject the instantiation of that property in the object perceived. In exemplifying the property, it will give the subject access to the truth-condition of the perceptual predication: the general condition such that its realization in any particular case will make the predication accurate. And in being taken as an instance of that property, it will enable the subject to register that the condition is actually realized.

Does the approach suggested make it impossible for a perception to mislead? Well, the fact that a particular identifies a certain property for a perceptual subject may seem to imply that it has to realize the property identified. But that need not be so. Suppose the pigeon is tricked by the light into taking a square door to be triangular and pecks at it. Plausibly, in that case, it makes a mistake about the shape of the door that is there. The simulacrum of a triangular door serves, as a regular instance would serve, to present the property of triangularity, but the reality of what is actually there fails to confirm the predication of that property.

4.1.4 Presenting objects directly

Perception presents objects directly insofar as it does not posit the existence of the object and then go on to predicate a property of that posited object. It does not break down, as many judgments and beliefs break down, into two distinct claims: first, a claim that there is an object there, at one or another locus in the subject's space; and second, a claim that that object is predicatively thus and so. Perception presents the object—whether a substance, event, or process—as something presupposed, whose existence is not in question, and then it makes a predication of that presumptive object. It is like demonstrative belief—but not belief more generally—insofar as it presupposes the existence of the very object it characterizes (Evans 1982). In the absence of that object, there would be no perception: the predication apparently involved would not predicate any property—it would not amount to a predication—since there would be nothing of which to predicate the property.[4]

We shall assume that perception is presentational of objects, not just in this presuppositional sense, but in the deeper sense that it relates the perceiver directly to the object presupposed. On this picture, the object I see as I reach for my coffee is the actual cup that is there, not the look of a cup, not the silhouette of a cup, not a sense-datum of a cup: not anything supposedly seen that might survive the absence of the cup itself. Equally what I hear is the music playing, not the sound that reaches my ears; what I smell is the soup, not the smell of the soup; what I taste is the wine, not the taste of the wine; and what I feel is the dog's fur, not the feel of the fur. What is presented to me in each case is the worldly object itself, not any sort

---

[4] The picture of perceptual experience as representational of objects in the two-claims sense seems to be implied in Fred Dretske's (2003, 74) remark: 'a visual representation can represent a pink rat in the corner without there being anything—certainly nothing pink and rat-shaped—it represents to be that way'. The picture may appeal insofar as it enables him to make sense of hallucination as a perception that goes wrong in the first claim, and of illusion as a perception that goes wrong in the second.

of go-between. We shall see later that percipience will enable humans and humanoids to identify and enjoy appearances as such—to savor the effects that perceived objects may have on them—but that is not to say that it is the appearances that they directly perceive rather than the objects themselves.

Of course, there is a sense in which people may be said to see looks, hear sounds, smell smells, taste tastes, and feel feels, as they may be said to jump jumps as well as jumping hurdles (Ryle 1949). But that is irrelevant to the central claim, which is that the perceptual relation subjects have to an object perceived is just as basic as the relation they might be thought to have to such appearances. It is not the case that the subject's experience reveals the appearance directly and that a subject can be said to experience the object only in a derived sense.

Why embrace this presentational view? Well, first, it fits with the phenomenology of perception, as registered in a long tradition (Merleau-Ponty 1965). I do not see or otherwise perceive objects as a result of having an independent experience of appearances they generate. Rather, I see the objects simultaneously with registering the appearances, not as a result of having a prior experience of those appearances: I see the object in the appearances, as it is often put. These observations are consistent, of course, with acknowledging that I will perceive objects in virtue of effects they generate within my brain, since such effects are not likely to register with me.

Phenomenology apart, there is a problem facing other views of perception that the presentational view nicely avoids. If the look I see or the sound I hear is the direct object of perception, is there some way it in turn has to look or sound? If there is no special way it has to present, what makes it so different from that of which it is the look or the sound or whatever: what makes it intrinsically perceptible, so to speak? And if there is a way it has to look or sound in order to be perceived, why doesn't a similar problem arise at the next stage, thereby opening up a regress? The presentational view that it is the objects of perception that directly look or sound or appear avoids such issues, for it does not imply that there is any way that looks have to look, sounds have to sound, or appearances have to appear.

A more general consideration also supports the presentational view of perceptual experience. Perception often involves a number of sensory modalities and that which is commonly perceived across such modalities will have to be something that exists for the subject in all of those different ways. But only the perceived object itself—the thing or event or process identified—can serve in that unifying role, at least at the level where I register things, not at the level of sub-personal, unregistered processing within the brain. Thus, if I hear a trumpet around the corner, what I hear is the same object that I see when I reach the corner. If I feel the dog on the bed, it is the same animal I see when I turn on the light.

Does the view entail that there can be no hallucinatory experiences, as in Macbeth's experience as of a dagger before him? No, it does not. There surely are hallucinatory experiences that are indiscernible for those undergoing them, at least at the moment of experience, from the perceptual experience of an actual object. But whatever accounts for these, and whatever they have in common with counterpart perceptual experiences—at the least, they must have much in common at the neural and computational level—they need not tell us much about what happens in the veridical, perceptual case. They certainly do not show that in each case the same appearance is perceived and that it conforms to a reality in the veridical case but not in the hallucinatory.[5]

4.1.5 The attentional character of perception

This discussion of how perceptions directly present objects and properties to a perceiver might suggest that perception consists in a series of temporally discrete events, involving the perceptual ascription of particular properties to individual objects. But this would obviously fail to register the continuity of the perceptual activity within and across sensory modalities, and the extent to which that activity projects a single, more or less enduring perceptual field. Once this is put into the picture, the perceptual predications of the subject present as episodes in which certain objects in that background field, and certain properties of those elements, are brought into the foreground and given prominence as matters that the subject registers.

On this picture of perception, the subject's activity makes a range of objects and properties continuously accessible for perceptual predication, but even when the subject predicates this or that property of this or that object, the other objects and properties remain within reach of perception. The perceiving subject retains a general sense of the perceptual field, so to speak, but attends now to this part of the field, and now to that other part, as it forms distinct perceptual predications. That the perceiver attends to one or another part of the field just means that it forms a belief about what is the case there, putting itself in a position to act on the basis of that belief. According to this conception, as one author puts it, if a subject selects a feature of the perceived world to guide how it behaves, then the subject attends to that feature (Wu 2023).[6]

---

[5] Michael Martin (2006) argues that in recognizing that a hallucination is phenomenologically indiscriminable from its veridical counterpart, we need not be able to recognize a feature—presumably, a phenomenologically accessible feature—that is common to the two. It is worth noting, however, that the line taken here on how properties are directly engaged in perception might be taken to support the view that hallucination and veridical perception each engage the same complex of properties. For something close to such a view, see Mark Johnston (2004).

[6] As in other matters covered here, we abstract from many differences between competing psychological and philosophical theories of attention. For a useful overview, see (Mole, Smithies, and Wu 2011). For a recent, congenial account of attention and its relationship to consciousness, see (Watzl 2017).

The attentional nature of perception is readily illustrated. The cat that hunts mice in the long grass will rely on the flow of its experience across visual, auditory, and olfactory channels; it will vary its position in order to get a better take on its would-be, often moving prey; and it will seek out its quarry as a predator, not in the spirit of a playful kitten. And as it adjusts in these ways, different aspects of the situation will come to its attention, and prime it for action, if an occasion for action materializes. What is true of the cat in this simple illustration, of course, is also going to be true, with some differences of detail, of other animals, human beings and humanoids included. Their perceptual activity will also project a more or less enduring perceptual field but allow them to make a predication of one or another element in the field, where such a predication will serve like a belief to ready them potentially for action.

We have seen that perception contrasts with judgment and belief in its presentational engagement with the properties it predicates and, demonstrative beliefs apart, with the objects it tracks. But the attentional aspect of perception marks a starker contrast again, at least with on–off beliefs associated with judgment. Such beliefs typically evolve in stops and starts as new evidence appears, novel insights materialize, or the subject undergoes some transformative shocks. Perceptual predications evolve on the basis of a continuing flow of processing with each predication condensing out of that flow, as the subject resolves attentional focus now at this point, now at that.

In view of its attentional structure, the information that perceptual processing offers the subject can be cast as analog or rich in character, while the finer information distilled in this or that predication, and suited for the guidance of action, can be seen as relatively digital or austere. An analog watch, a picture, or a map will enable a user to extract relatively finer, digital detail, expressed in a judgment about just how many minutes remain before noon, about the precise color of the sky in the picture, or about whether a point, A, in the map is nearer to B than to C. Similarly, the sensory processing of a perceptual field may be taken to enable the subject to explore relatively finer aspects of that field, attending to this or that object or feature or relationship and making an appropriate perceptual predication.[7]

4.1.6 The dismissible character of perception

The presentational and attentional aspects of perception mark important points of contrast between perception on the one hand and judgment and belief, on the

---

[7] The analog idea derives from (Dretske 1999) but is variously analyzed in the literature; for an overview of different approaches, see (Beck 2019). For general background, see (Braddon-Mitchell and Jackson 1996).

other. But there is also a third difference between how those different states are likely to figure in the psychology of an agent.

Suppose that an agent who previously held the belief that p ceases to be disposed to act as if it were the case that p: they cease to act as it would be rational to act, given their desires and other beliefs, if it were the case that p. By the functional account of on–off belief presented in Chapter 2—perhaps by any plausible account—the belief will cease at that point to be present in the agent. That it ceases to play the role associated with belief—the role by which belief is defined, on the functionalist story—means by almost all accounts that it will not survive the loss of that role. The belief may remain and occasionally fail to exercise its role—this by a sort of cognitive failure or akrasia—but there is no ground for holding that it remains in place without playing that role at all.[8]

Perception is very different insofar as it can apparently retain a place in a subject's psychology while failing to play its response-shaping role. This will manifestly occur when an experience is cognitively impenetrable, as Jerry Fodor (1983) puts it. A perception as of something being the case may remain obstinately present despite the fact that the agent does not believe that it is the case, or believes that it is not the case, and denies the perception a response-shaping function. Thus, in a familiar example, the stick in water will continue to look bent even after I learn that it is not bent. And the sun will continue to look like it is crossing the sky even after I learn that it is the earth that is rotating, not the sun moving.

Do non-human animals undergo perceptual experiences that they dismiss in the way in which you or I might dismiss the bent look of the stick or the apparent movement of the sun? It seems, just on the basis of everyday experience, that they do. Consider the young puppy that barks at its reflection in the mirror and then pays it a lot of attention, licking and sniffing at the mirror and trying to look behind it. But the puppy will not take long to learn, as it matures, to dismiss that perceptual appearance. The failure of the experience to deliver the goods—to give it a satisfying, response-shaping take on the world—will lead the dog to ignore the reflection altogether.

It may be in such a case that the mirror continues to impact perceptually on the dog—this, as the stick in water impacts perceptually on us—so that while in some sense it has an experience as of a dog when it looks in the mirror, it loses interest in that experience. Or it may be that it simply ceases to have an experience as of a dog: this, in the way we cease to see our train as moving backwards when we realize, as in a familiar mistake, that it is the neighboring train that is moving forwards. Whatever happens, the perception ceases to play a role in guiding the dog's

---

[8] This comment bears on belief, strictly understood, and not on judgment. Someone may continue to say or even think that they hold by a judgment, even after it has ceased to sustain a corresponding belief. Think of the case we discussed in Chapter 2: the gambler who continues to commit the gambler's fallacy, despite judging and continuing to judge that it is a fallacy.

action, although in some sense the perception—certainly the neural interaction involved—remains in place. Like our experience of the stick in water, or our experience of the train moving, it is deprived of a role in guiding action: it is decommissioned or dismissed.

The dismissible feature of perception may be manifested among perceptual subjects in either of two responses. One will require the subject not to believe that the stick in the water is bent or that the train is moving. The other will require them, more specifically, to believe that the stick in the water is not bent or the train is not moving. Making the first response, the subject will not believe the apparent content of the perception; making the second, they will believe the negation of that content.

Which response does the dog take when it stops barking at the mirror? If we are to be guided by parsimony, then we will naturally take it to respond in the first way, not the second. This explanation does not require us to ascribe a mastery of the negation concept or a sense of what an apparent content would be, and yet it is adequate to explain the dog's subsequent behavior. It may be that the dog registers things in the same way before and after its change of belief, as in the case of the stick in water; or it may be that the perception itself shifts when its belief changes, as in the case of the apparently moving train. Under either scenario the dog may dismiss its perceptual experience, and yet not form a belief with a negative content.

We return to this point in the next section, arguing that the humanoids will be equipped to make the second response in such a case: to come to believe that things are not as they appear to be. It turns out that this capacity is of great significance and marks a salient divide between the restricted capacities of non-human animals, on the one side, and the capacities of humans and humanoids, on the other.

4.2 The advent of percipience

4.2.1 Recruiting perception

We assume that like many other animals, including human beings, the humanoids will enjoy and display the perceptual abilities sketched in the previous section. They will engage in the causally supported, sensory process of gathering information about their surrounds, ascribing immediately presented properties to immediately presented objects. They will make those predications on the basis of exercises in which they shift attention across the properties and objects in their perceptual field. And they will routinely dismiss predications that prove unreliable as guides to action, denying them any role in determining how to satisfy their desires and achieve their goals.

We turn now to the issue of what difference the capacity for judgment and reasoning will induce—strictly, is robustly likely to induce—in the perceptual processing and predication of humanoids: in its percipient exercise. We shall look in turn at the differences it will bring about for them in perceptual presentation, attention, and dismissal, arguing, in a sense to be explained, that it will lead them to enrich presentation, to regulate attention, and to authorize dismissal. Those differences correspond to distinctive aspects of perception among humans, and we may take them together to constitute the distinctive effects of percipience.

Percipience will make its appearance, so the argument goes, insofar as the humanoids recruit perception in the service of judging and reasoning about things. We have already assumed that in making judgments the humanoids will rely on having access to what proves effective for them as evidence, in community with one another, and that in reasoning they will rely on being able to consider how far such evidence is present or persuasive for them across that community. The evidence relevant in many cases will involve perception and perceptual recall, so that perception will inevitably be recruited in the service of such judgment and reasoning. What we explore in this section is the likely effect that its recruitment to that purpose among the humanoids will have on the quality of their perception.

4.2.2 Enriching presentation

We saw that the subjects of perceptual experience are not just going to see things but see them as such and such, not just going to hear things but hear them as such and such, and so on. Explicitly or implicitly, they are going to predicate properties of those objects—those substances, events, processes, or whatever—that they register.

The explanation of how perceptual subjects understand the properties that they predicate in experience, so we argued, is that when the instance of a property justifies the perceptual ascription of that property to the instantiating object, the instance does double duty. Assuming it is indeed instantiated, the instance not only makes the perceptual ascription of the property correct, it also enables the subject to grasp that property and understand the truth-condition or content of the ascription.

This story makes sense of how perceiving subjects, even simple animals, can be attuned to natural similarity classes, perhaps innately, perhaps in the course of maturation. But it also makes sense of how they may be trained to be responsive to other similarity classes, on the basis of habituation or training. In illustrating this idea, we suggested that insofar as a pigeon is conditioned to peck among various doors at those with a triangular shape, the property of triangularity can be exemplified for it by this or that example. By virtue of being sensitized to that pattern robustly over variations in the color or size or form of the triangle—by virtue of being trained up to extrapolate appropriately from suitable examples—the pattern is there for it as a property to recognize and predicate in its perceptions. The extrapolation does not require a prior conception of the pattern, which would make the explanation circular, but evolves on an independent basis; this basis, presumably, is provided by the pigeon's neuropsychological profile: an inherited profile in the case of a natural similarity class, an induced profile in the case of conditioning.[9]

The first effect of induction in language and reasoned judgment on the perception of humanoids is likely to be that it will train them up in sensitivity to a very rich array of properties, enabling them to grasp and ascribe those properties perceptually, as the pigeon grasps and ascribes the property of being triangular. When humanoids acquire the use of a word in response to perceptual inputs, then like humans, they will be sensitized to the class of items to which it applies and be positioned to grasp or understand the property involved. Such word-based sensitization will put more and more properties within range of the perceptual understanding of the humanoids and make them available for perceptual predication. And, of course, it will reinforce the perceptual sensitivity of humanoids to any properties associated with previously established similarity classes.

It is important that on this account, the means whereby the humanoids will gain perceptual access to the patterns to which their words cue them is at base the same means whereby any property is perceptually presented. That means will be the sort of sensitization whereby the distinct particular items to which the word attaches assume a commonality: they each get to be seen as an example of the property that is accessible, instance by instance, to a suitably sensitive subject.

Thus, let the humanoids be trained up in the use of sortal words like 'chair' or 'house', or 'square' or 'triangular', and they will quickly cotton on, becoming disposed to apply or withhold the word in an open range of instances. Whatever the perceptual inputs that prompt them in its use, now on this occasion, now on that, those inputs will become unified for them—unified perceptually—around the corresponding pattern and property. The inputs to which they are sensitized will assume a commonality for each insofar as they prompt the same response, disposing the individual to extrapolate from examples to other instances and to use the same word of those instances.

If this line of argument is correct, then the appearance of language and of the cascade of perceptually cued words to which it gives rise is bound to expand the range of properties that the humanoids will be able to identify in perception and predicate of this or that object perceived. The pigeon may depend on being conditioned by a food reward in order to be able to grasp and ascribe the property of being triangular. But the humanoids will be able to grasp and ascribe that property perceptually just on the basis of being trained up in the use of the word 'triangle'. And of course, their training will not restrict them to doors, as the pigeon's

---

[9] For an account of how things might look to be of the same color in virtue of such an independently sourced tracking disposition, see (Pettit 2003).

conditioning may restrict it. With a word for the property in hand, they will be able to see triangular shapes in any of a range of objects: in cut-out pieces of wood, in the waves created by a boat, and in drawings and diagrams.

The range of perceptually cued words that humanoids will be able to access is presumably as open-ended as the range of such words that we human beings learn to master in perception. Like us human beings, they may not have the same range of sensory sensitivities as other animals, not having the olfactory capacities of the dog or the visual capacities of the eagle. But they will be able to expand their perceptual skills or capacities well beyond the range that nature makes available.

They will be able, not only to see triangles, but also to detect ellipses and trapezoids and, if they are suitably trained, the shape of a piece of art deco sculpture or the sign of a fracture in an X-ray display. They will be able, not only to hear the calls of prey or predator, but also to recognize the resolution in a melody, the syncopation in a rhythm or, if they are suitably trained, a morse code signature, or a word pronounced in different accents. And they will not only be able to taste sour and sweet, salty and bitter, they will also be able, with habituation, to taste the distinctive flavor of a chardonnay or a pale ale, a fresh oyster or a lemon meringue. Even the range of what they can smell or feel will expand with increased skill in the use of a perceptually cued vocabulary. It can expand to enable them to recognize the many scents distinguished by the trained parfumier or the feel of things that is salient to someone who can read braille.

On the story told of how the perceptual competence of the humanoids will be expanded under the influence of newly learned words, it is important that the properties perceived for the first time will be perceived on the basis of the same sensitization to instances that operates in other cases. True, some of the properties perceived under the impact of linguistic tuning will be grounded—and this, perhaps, as a matter of definition—in the presence of more basic, perceptible properties: this, in the way the presence of a triangle is grounded in the presence of a closed figure of three straight sides. But, on the account sketched, there is no reason to think that the humanoids will perceive the grounding properties in a phenomenologically distinct sense from that in which they perceive the grounded. High-level and low-level perception, as they are sometimes called, are going to be on a par in that respect. It may well be, of course, that there is a sub-personal difference in the neural and computational processing of high-level as distinct from low-level perception: that is certainly very likely. But by our account there is going to be no difference that registers in how the humanoids perceive the two sorts of properties; there will be no difference in the way the perceptual contents present.[10]

---

[10] For a useful introduction to this issue in psychology, see (Rogers 2017). For a philosophical discussion, which offers a full defense of a view akin to that taken here—she describes it as the rich-content view of perception—see (Siegel 2016). And for a grasp of the case for and against that position, see the debate in (Siegel and Byrne 2016).

We have been looking at how the properties perceived by the humanoids will expand under the influence of linguistic tuning. But the availability of perceptually cued words will not only impact on the number of properties that perception can present for subjects, it will also affect the mode in which the properties are perceived, whether they be properties already perceptible or properties made accessible by words. It will enrich perceptual presentation in a qualitative as well as a quantitative manner.

Perceptual presentation, in and of itself, confers only quite limited abilities on perceivers. It will enable the perceiver to form beliefs about instances, as the pigeon's ability enables it to form beliefs that this or that perceived door has the triangular shape it tracks in its pecking disposition. But it will not enable the subject to form beliefs about the property itself, for example, giving them a strongly stimulus-independent concept that identifies it as such. Thus, while the pigeon's concept of the property will serve it in forming beliefs about this or that door, it will not enable it to form such stimulus-independent beliefs: say, that it is a property that is normally co-instantiated with the property of being made of wood or metal or whatever.

We saw in the last chapter that as whole sentences can be used in quotation marks to refer to propositions, making them available as objects of attention, so the words that figure in sentences can be used to refer to the properties predicated in the propositions, making such properties available in the same way; the point was more fully elaborated in the interlude discussion of rule-following in the first chapter. Thus, humanoid perceivers will be enabled by access to language to make perceived properties available as objects of attention and to form beliefs about them of a kind unavailable to the pigeon. They will be able to conceptualize the properties in a strongly stimulus-independent way and to form beliefs about where they are instantiated, for example, about their relationships with other properties, or about their distinctive features.

Thus, when the humanoids perceptually predicate a property that is made accessible by the use of a suitable word—or indeed a property whose perception is reinforced by the use of a suitable word—they will not be subject to the limitations of a word-less perceiver. Able to identify a perceived property answering to the word—and able to have a stimulus-independent concept of the property as such—they will also be able to make reasoned judgments about the property itself: say, judgments to the effect that it is realized in different sizes or colors, that it is often co-instantiated with certain other properties, and even that its presence ensures the presence of some such properties. And in virtue of being able to make such judgments, the humanoids will enjoy an enhancement of their perceptual abilities.

They will presumably be able to take a particular color or shade of color, for example, as a perceptually salient referent and compare it with a color or shade present elsewhere or just remembered from past experience. They are going to have the capacity to let their perception focus, not on the objects of which it normally predicates certain properties, but on those properties themselves.

Again, their capacity for reasoned judgment, will enable the humanoids, if they wish, to imagine the different ways and places in which certain perceived properties might be realized together or apart, by sensorily simulating the realization of the possibilities: say, to give precedence again to the eye, by visualizing them. While the range of possibilities will be fixed by consistency with reasoned judgments about the properties, the humanoids will be able to intentionally control the imaginative rehearsal and exploration of such perceptual possibilities.

Their capacity for reasoned judgments about perceptual properties will also have an effect on how much information their perceptions give them. It is very likely that the perceptions of many creatures are going to be affected by their sense of what is or is not a live possibility in any perceived scenario; many animals show evidence of surprise in looking-time experiments where such expectations about what can and cannot happen are apparently breached (Winters, Dubuc, and Higham 2015). This background sense of live possibilities presumably enhances the perceptual take-away: the perception that something is an F will be informatively richer to the extent that the subject has a sense of what being F rules in and rules out. And that being so, we may expect the perception of humanoids to be especially enriched by the backgrounding that they can bring to bear on perception in virtue of their capacity for reasoned judgment.

Returning to the case of the triangle, the humanoids will be able to perceive any given triangle against a background of possibilities that will be as rich as their reasoned judgments allow. If they are relatively well informed, for example, the triangle may present as equilateral, isosceles, or scalene, right-angled, acute-angled, or oblique-angled; whichever form it assumes, that form will stand out against a background sense of the forms it might have assumed.

These observations support the view that the introduction of language, and of the capacity for judgment and reasoning that it brings in its train, will not only have an impact on the range of properties the humanoids can learn to perceive. It will also transform the mode in which those properties get to be perceived, making it possible for the humanoids to treat the properties normally predicated in perception as items of perception themselves, to explore in intentional imagination the ways in which they can or cannot be combined, and to enrich their perceptions informatively by situating them within an expanded range of the possibilities they rule in and rule out.

4.2.3 Regulating attention

By the account so far, then, the advent of language among the humanoids will make an expanded range of properties available to the humanoids and available in a relatively sophisticated mode of perception. But the humanoids will also be able to use the words at their disposal to raise perceptual questions for one another and, with interiorization, for themselves: that is, questions that they will expect to be able to resolve by appeal to perception. They will be able to interrogate their perception and, as we shall now see, to regulate the exercise of perceptual attention with a view to finding perceptual answers to the questions raised.

In order to explore the possibility of regulated attention, we need to look briefly at a prior issue. How exactly should we expect perception to connect with judgment and, via judgment, with belief? On the approach taken here, the relation between a perception and a corresponding judgment and belief consists in a match between their contents; the relation is propositional in character, as Susanna Siegel (2016) puts it, when she defends just that sort of model.

On the propositional model, predicating a property of an object in perception is an exercise that parallels the corresponding judgment, with the object and property being conceptualized by virtue of their linguistic markers in a way that makes them available for judgment and reasoning. Thus, the perceptual ascription of the property to the object can elicit its judgmental ascription directly, providing the subject in such a case with a perceptual counterpart to the judgment that the object has that property. The perception will make it evident that things are as that judgment presents them as being. It will invoke the perceived state of affairs in justificatory explanation, to return to that idea, of the subject's belief in that state of affairs.

On the presentational view of perception that we sketched in the last section, we will naturally expect the humanoids to form judgments in response to their perceptions on the lines of this propositional model. The linguistically tuned and regulated perceptions of judging and reasoning subjects like the humanoids will predicate of perceived objects the very properties ascribed to those objects in their corresponding judgments. Perceptual experience will play a causal role, of course, in giving rise to those judgments and beliefs. But it will do so, specifically, by presenting in perception the very states of affairs that are ratified in judgment. It will enable the humanoids, as reasoning subjects, to treat how they perceive things to be as a justifying explanation of why they judge and believe them to be that way.

According to Wilfred Sellars (1997), it is a common mistake—the myth of the given, he calls it—to think that perception only enables the perceiver to register a brute datum: something that can play a causal, prompting role, but nothing like a justificatory role, in relation to judgment. Our genealogy suggests that as a story about the humanoids, this story certainly is a myth. The matters given in the linguistically tuned perception of the humanoids will already be conceptualized and available for confirmation at the level of judgment. In moving from perception to judgment, the humanoids will not have to cross a gulf between the pre-conceptual and the conceptual: their perceptual experience of the world will already have been seeded with the resources of judgment and reasoning.

But this does not mean that the humanoids will be restricted to perceiving only properties named in their language. Once they are primed by the words at their disposal to gain perceptual access to certain properties, they will also be able to introduce new expressions and concepts to use for related, unnamed properties. Thus, given the perceptual salience of a particular shade of red—say, that which corresponds to the word 'scarlet'—they will be able to conceptualize and identify the property that consists in being of a marginally brighter hue. And having a sample available of the brighter color, they will be able to conceptualize the property—and do so for others as well as themselves—that consists in being of the same color as that sample (McDowell 1996).

These comments indicate how the exercise of attention in perception, and the perceptual predication that attention supports, can serve the purposes of the humanoids in judging and reasoning about related matters. But for all we have said, the exercise of attention need not be intentional in character; it may not be an activity that they can regulate. They may pay attention to this or that part of their perceptual field in the course of intentionally pursuing other ends, but it need not be an activity that they can aim at conducting or controlling under its attentional aspect.

The cat that smells a mouse will shift its attention to different points in its perceptual field as it looks in different corners of the room and listens carefully for the noises a mouse is likely to make. In intentionally pursuing the goal of finding the mouse, it will vary its attention in these visual and auditory modalities as a means to that end. But it need not intentionally vary its attention under that very description: it may not aim at varying its attention as such, and may not see that what it does in tracking the mouse involves that activity. A more parsimonious account of what the cat does would hold that it shifts attention in the automatic way in which I adjust my muscles—I know not how—when I reach out to take a sip from my coffee mug. It shifts attention under the indirect, unwilled control of what it intentionally does.

Will the humanoids be restricted in this way, having only intentional control of this indirect kind over where and how they pay perceptual attention? No, they will not. Pursuing a practical goal, as in the cat's search for the mouse, they may adjust their efforts as this requires, with shifts of attention coming about automatically as its efforts require. But when they consider a question about whether something is so, they will naturally resort to the intentional direction of their attentional efforts, at least when perception promises to hold the answer. They may do this together or on their own but even when they act on their own, they will depend for identifying the best attentional move to make on how far it enables convergence with others; we documented this sort of dependence and triangulation in the last chapter.

Thus, when they consider whether the animals approaching in the distance are wolves or pigs, predators or prey, they will intentionally scan those in front, look for individuals that stand out from the pack, scan those individuals for the telltale signs of their species and, if possible, compare their judgments in an attempt at mutual checking. They will take charge of the exercise we describe as paying attention, making it into something that they can intentionally do under that very description. They may do this without doing anything else intentionally as a means—they may do so by way of a basic action (Hornsby 1980)—or they may do it in a normal means–end fashion: say, by moving to a vantage point that gives them a better view.

As the humanoids will be able to regulate their visual attention in this way, so they will be able to do it in other modalities too, controlling what they attend to in what they hear or touch, taste or smell. To take familiar human examples, they will be able to listen for the transitions that mark a Mozart concerto, feel the linen to tell if it is mixed with polyester, savor the cheese to determine if it is ripe, or sniff the milk to learn whether it has gone off. They will remain dependent like other animals on what their perceptual senses tell them about the world. But they will be able to call up the voice of those senses and compel it to speak on matters where they have questions to resolve.

We mentioned in the discussion of judgment and reasoning that these activities will enable the humanoids to gain a certain degree of control over the beliefs they form and the transitions they make between those beliefs. Rather than letting the world make up their minds for them—willy nilly, so to speak—they will be able to choose between seeking out evidence or not on certain issues and, with sufficient evidence available, between ignoring that evidence or letting it prompt them to make a judgment. What we have been documenting is the form that such intentional control will take in the perceptual realm, as it leads the humanoids to negotiate with one another in interrogating what they perceive, regulating their attention, and letting perception serve up answers on the issues that concern them.

As the language that makes judgment and reasoning possible is bound to enrich the range of properties presented in perception, and to transform the mode of the presentation, so we see now that it will also enable the humanoids to take ownership of the attention in which perceptual processing issues predications, regulating it for their own distinctive purposes. Freud once said that the goal of therapy is to suspend the impersonal 'it' that normally guides us from below, giving authority instead to the personal 'I': *Wo Es war, soll Ich werden*; where It was, there shall be I. The slogan may be adapted to describe what language and converse enables the humanoids to achieve when it gives them the capacity to make judgments intentionally, to reason intentionally about their judgments, and to interrogate their perceptions in intentionally co-opting attention.

4.2.4 Authorizing dismissal

We have been documenting how their access to language and judgment will transform the perceptual experience of the humanoids in two distinct ways. First, it will enable them, by reliance on the mastery of perceptually cued words, to identify ever more numerous properties, and to represent them in a conceptually sophisticated mode. And second, it will enable them to rely on its attentional structure to recruit perception to the resolution of relevant issues, searching intentionally for whether various judgments pair with perceptual predications or follow from them.

A further distinctive feature of perception, apart from its presentational and attentional quality, is its liability to be dismissed by the subject. We illustrated this with the puppy that learns to disregard its reflection in a mirror: to cease, after various unsuccessful searches, to let the reflection occasion the belief that there is a dog to be found there. As access to language and judgments makes a great difference to the presentational and attentional aspects of humanoid perception, so too it will induce a big change to its aspect as a fallible and dismissible depiction of how things are.

We noted in the case of the maturing puppy that, while it certainly ceases to register the dog in the mirror, depriving the perceptual input of a belief-forming role, the most plausible explanation is that it ceases to believe that there is a dog in the mirror: it simply neglects the deliverance of its eyes on that issue. This is more parsimonious than the salient alternative: namely, that it comes to believe that that reflection in the mirror—or in demonstrative mode, comes to believe that *that*—is not a dog. Any account in which the dog does not-believe that something is the case will be more parsimonious than one in which it believes-not that it is the case; not-believing, unlike believing-not, does not require the dog to have a word or concept for negation.

Another way of making the parsimony point is that in order to not-judge or not-believe that something is the case, a subject will not have to do anything in particular: the judgment and belief may just not materialize. But in order for them to judge-not or believe-not that something is the case, the subject will presumably have to find evidence that it is not the case, perhaps negotiating any initial differences with others. And that means that when they dismiss a perception that something is the case, they will have to own or authorize the dismissal.

The parsimony consideration shows that simple animals like dogs can hardly be expected to respond to failures in their perceptions by coming to believe that things are not as they perceptually appear to be. But things will be very different with our humanoids, for they will be in the habit of making judgments that something is not the case, as they negotiate divergence with one another and recognize that anyone, themselves included, may be misled by the evidence on which they rely in judging that it is the case.

Many of those conflicting judgments will be perceptually based and, given our account of how perception relates to judgment, that means that any individual is liable in negotiating differences with others to conclude that it is they who are mistaken. If they do draw that conclusion, of course, then they must come to think that whereas they registered a certain state of affairs in perception, having a presentation as of things being thus and so, actually things are not as they seemed to be. The perceptual appearance did not correspond to what they later recognized as reality.

This may happen in the sort of situation illustrated by the stick that seemed bent in water, where the presentation continues to survive the revised, opposing judgment. Or it may occur in the situation exemplified by the train that seemed to be moving, where the presentation fades with ratification of the revised judgment. Regardless of which of these scenarios obtains, the humanoids will clearly learn that how things appear to be in perceptual presentation is not always how they are in fact, and indeed that how they are in fact is not always how they are perceived to be. It will be manifest that their perceptions may mistake some features of reality and may miss or overlook others.

With this possibility established among the humanoids they will be in a very different position from that of animals that are unable, as we took the dog to be unable, to question their perceptions in this way. Simple animals will use their perceptions to help them navigate their way around the world and, while they will neglect or dismiss perceptions that do not serve any purposes for them, that dismissal will materialize non-intentionally and doubtless, unconsciously. Thus, by this parsimonious story, they will not make a distinction between how the world is presented in perception—that is, in undismissed perception—and how it is in fact, let alone recognize the possibility of divergence between the two. Berkeley's famous dictum will hold of them in quite a radical sense: in their perspective, it really will be the case that *esse est percipi*—that to be is to be perceived and to be perceived is to be.

Things will be very different in the perspective of the humanoids, alive as any mutually correcting subjects must be to the possibility of mistaking or missing things in perception. This possibility will reveal to them that there is indeed a distinction between how things are perceived and how they actually are, and that how things are perceived and how they actually are may often diverge. They will be forced to recognize the conceptual distinction between *esse* and *percipi* and to acknowledge their actual divergence in various cases.

The acknowledgement will appear at its sharpest in the explanations that those who agree that they misperceived things are likely to offer for their mistakes. Like us, they will have to appeal to how things looked or sounded or felt, how they smelled or tasted, while agreeing that those appearances were misleading. Thus, they will naturally introduce words and concepts that can refer to the appearances in abstraction from whether they revealed corresponding realities.

This development is essentially cognitive in character, deriving from the humanoid exercise of judgment and reasoning. But it will generate a rich range of effects in their general psychology, impacting on how they construe various sensory inputs and let them resonate in their affections. Recognizing the difference between appearance and reality will put them in a position to attend to appearance independently of reality, savoring the way things present regardless of whether that is the way they are. And equally it will enable them to ask about reality independently of appearance: to wonder about whether the appearances are misleading in certain cases and about the reality that underlies them.

4.2.5 Percipience, speculation, and aesthetics

In making these possibilities accessible, the percipience of the humanoids, and in particular their capacity to distinguish appearance from reality, will open up a range of opportunities for further pursuit. These will not connect with their deepest individual or social needs but may still prove appealing, at least if their environment and society gives them a degree of leisure. There are two sorts of pursuit that they will be able in principle to explore, whether or not they do so in practice. One is of an aesthetic character, the other of a speculative.

Take the speculative possibility first. Once appearances are held up for question, then speculating about how far they may deceive will begin to make sense. And once that makes sense, it will be possible to look beyond appearances—or at least first appearances—in an attempt to explain the puzzling, or to accommodate the unsettling.

The humanoids may exploit this opportunity to best effect in the sort of science that human beings have developed over the past few hundred years. Does the sun move across the sky in the course of the day, as it surely seems to do, making it plausible that the earth is at the center of at least our local area of space? Or, as Copernicus speculated, does the earth rotate in the course of each day, making it look to those on its surface that the sun moves? The humanoids will not necessarily raise that question, of course, let alone adopt the Copernican response—think how long it took for human beings to do so—but the recognition of the reality-appearance gap will at least make it possible for them to do this. And it will make other scientific developments accessible also, as in theorizing about hidden forces like gravity and electromagnetism, or the atomic structure of matter, or the cellular organization of living organisms.

However unlikely it is that the humanoids will develop such scientific theories, the recognition of the appearance–reality divide will at least make it possible. But as it will make scientific theory possible among the humanoids, so it will enable a style of conjecture designed, not to resolve puzzles, but to reconcile them to unsettling aspects of life. Thus, the humanoids will be able to ruminate to a religious purpose, looking for a ground on which to make sense of their nature and destiny, and to identify ideals to guide them in life. They will be able to generate myths to explain their particular traditions, to celebrate their way of life, and to mark their place on earth. And, to move to less salutary possibilities, they will be able to speculate in the wayward fashion of the alchemist, the astrologist or the fortune-teller, or in the scapegoating manner of those who invoke sorcery or witchcraft to explain their misfortunes.

But their percipience will open up aesthetic opportunities for the humanoids as well as enabling them to speculate in such ways. Distinguishing appearance from reality, the humanoids will be able to savor appearance in its own right as well as speculating about the nature of reality. The look of the stars will now be conceptually distinct from the stars in themselves. The sound of the waves will be something that might break apart from the sea. The smell of the flowers will be separable from the plants, the taste of the wine from the drink, the feel of the fur from the animal that bears it.

There may be little for a community to learn from looking up at the stars, by contrast with what they will learn from looking out for predator or prey. But there will now be a look to the stars that can be dwelt upon and enjoyed, attracting predicates in description of them as bright or winking or warm, and even eliciting elaborate comparisons: say, with the look of a forest canopy as the sun shines through its chinks. Similarly, the sound of the waves will no longer be tied to the sea it lets them hear. It will be identified with the sound that a shell mimics when held to the ear; it will be remembered, perhaps with longing, if humanoid folk move into the hills.

As it is with sight and hearing, so it can be with all the other senses. In each modality, the humanoids will now be able to recognize the appeal of the sensory presentation, assuming that it has an appeal for them, independently of whether it is serving its practical purpose. If they are like us, they will be able to smell the roses and cherish them just for what they present to the nose. They will savor the taste of wine, regardless of whether it conveys the liquid that sates their thirst. They will be able to relish the feel of the wind in their faces, even as they wish they were out of the cold.

With this development, art and craft may come into their own, giving humanoid culture a texture to go with the myth or religion or science that it may also support. Not only will they be able to enjoy the look of the stars or the sound of the sea; they will also be able to recreate looks in paint, for example, and to recreate sounds in music. Indeed, they will even be able to create looks and sounds that break away from any realities they are likely to confront, exploring ways to outdo nature rather than just reproduce it. And of course they may do that, not only for the sake of a felt appreciation of sensory form, but also for the sake of challenging standard modes of thought and evoking novel modes of perception.[11]

---

[11] It is often remarked that the affect that human beings enjoy in response to how they find the world depends on how the world appears, not on how it is: this explains why we may feel real joy or sadness in the fate of a purely fictional character. The appeal of the art envisaged here may spring from the way it engages such real affective responses, not just the simulacra of those responses.

As art will become accessible to the humanoids, so too will craft: for example, the craft involved in preparing food, making clothes, or constructing buildings. For it will become possible and appealing for the humanoids to meet the basic needs served by food or clothing or shelter in ways that generate appearances to savor. The food that pleases the palate, the clothing that catches the eye, the shelter that provides an elegant space will likely prove preferable to alternatives that merely serve the function of relieving hunger, keeping the body warm, or guarding against the elements.

We saw in the last chapter that the humanoid capacity to reason will enable them to explore the novelties of story-telling or even poetry, coming culturally into line with familiar human practices. We see now that their percipience in perception will also allow them to approximate human culture in the realms of religion, mythology, and science, as well as in those of art and craft. If the genealogy we have followed is sound, language may be the secret that allows such developments to unfold.

4.3 Percipient consciousness

4.3.1 Two sorts of consciousness

While the focus in preceding chapters has been on the way the humanoids will gain a degree of intentional control over how they judge and reason, the considerations rehearsed also support some conclusions about consciousness. The issue of consciousness arises with many different states, some content-bearing, some not. On the assumptions with which we have been working, perception is similar to belief and judgment insofar as it has a content: in a particular case, for example, the predicative content that something is F. Thus, we focus here on consciousness insofar as it may be present in such a content-bearing state, ignoring the sort of consciousness associated with states like bodily sensations or emotional moods that do not apparently have a content. There may be cases of unconscious perception, as when we recognize only later that we had previously registered perceptually that something was the case, but we shall focus here on cases where we are positioned at the time of the perception to register what we perceive.

The basic notion of a conscious state is that of a state with which a distinctive sort of awareness or knowledge is linked. The linkage is registered in the Latin 'con', 'with', and 'scio', 'I know', from which the word 'conscious' is derived. But there are two ways in which awareness may be linked with any content-bearing state in a sense that would legitimate the ordinary use of the word.

The state may be said to be conscious insofar as the subject not only instantiates the state but is also aware of instantiating it. Such a subject will enjoy consciousness of the state: consciousness of believing or judging or perceiving, for example, that such and such. But a content-bearing state may also be cast as conscious insofar as the subject is aware of the content of the state in a distinctive manner: they know what it is that they believe or judge or perceive. Such a subject will enjoy consciousness in the state: consciousness in believing or judging or perceiving that something is the case. We cast the first sort of consciousness in any content-bearing state, S, as consciousness-of-S, the second as consciousness-in-S.[12]

4.3.2 Consciousness, with and without feel

The points we have made about how the humanoids ratify their theoretical and practical beliefs in reasoned assertion or judgment are enough to show that with such states they will be able to enjoy both consciousness-in-belief and consciousness-of-belief. Take the latter first. There is no reason to think that ordinary animals must be conscious of having the functional beliefs that show up in how they act, since it is possible to be disposed to act as if p, for example, without being aware of the disposition. But just in virtue of making judgments, taking judgments to ratify belief-dispositions, and recognizing that they may differ from others in those respects, the humanoids will each be aware of the evidence-sensitive dispositions within themselves—their beliefs in the functionalist sense— that may mark them off from one another. They will have consciousness-of-belief.

This consciousness among humanoids of holding beliefs will be enhanced as they learn, not just to make judgments, but also to reason about the judgments they make. They will then become capable of recognizing their beliefs as relating them to propositions at the same time that they dispose them to action. But with the development of reasoning, and the ability to conceptualize belief-contents as propositions, the humanoids will also achieve consciousness-in-belief: they will be able to invoke such propositions to identify what it is that they believe.

When they enjoy such consciousness-in-belief, the humanoids will be able to identify the content of that belief: the *representatum* it endorses. The content will become accessible in this way to the humanoids, as we saw, only with the advent of reasoning and the development of strongly stimulus-independent concepts of propositions. We shall see later that there is a special pre-conceptual way in which the humanoids, and indeed other animals, may be able to know what they perceptually believe to be the case, but we can put that aside for now.

When they enjoy the consciousness-in-belief that reasoning makes possible, the humanoids will also enjoy an enhanced form of consciousness-of-belief. Being able to identify the content of a belief, they will also be able to identify the subjective state within themselves as representational, not just dispositional, in character: it

---

[12] This line on two senses of conscious states, in particular perceptual states, reflects Daniel Stoljar's (forthcoming) arguments on a range of related topics, although he himself does not explicitly make the distinction.

will appear as the *representans* in which the *representatum* is registered. They will be aware of it as the state within themselves in virtue of which things seem to be thus and so: the state that marks them off from those with whom they disagree on whatever question is at issue.

Consciousness transforms the character of beliefs and related attitudes. If we think of the most basic form of on-off belief in functional terms—if we think, roughly, that to believe that p is to be disposed in an evidence-sensitive way to act as if p—then it is clear that an agent like an ordinary animal may instantiate a belief without awareness that they do so. And equally such a simple agent may not be aware in a conceptualizing way of the content believed. Ignoring for the moment the exception promised in the perceptual case, they will be unable to enjoy either sort of consciousness.[13]

But while consciousness is a significant feature in belief, it has a purely cognitive character, like belief itself, and may fall short of the expectations raised by the word. This is because there is a usage of the term, given philosophical currency by Thomas Nagel (1979, 166), in which a creature will have conscious states just insofar as 'there is something it is like to be that organism—something it is like for that organism'. On the best interpretation of what this means, the state will be conscious when there is something it feels like to the subject to instantiate that state (Stoljar 2016). Consciousness in that sense is often described as phenomenal consciousness.

There need be nothing it is like in this sense to hold a belief or any such purely cognitive state, however conscious in either sense it is. Consciousness of or in belief does not have anything like the feel associated in this usage with consciousness; it does not give a belief a phenomenal character. But perhaps things are different in the case of perception, especially percipient perception, given that it operates in sensory channels. Perhaps consciousness in perception, or consciousness of perception, does have a phenomenal character.

We now explore that possibility. We argue that consciousness-in-perception is going to be phenomenal, whether the subject is percipient or not, but that percipience will enhance such consciousness. And we argue that consciousness-of-perception requires the subject to be percipient and is also going to be phenomenal in character, though phenomenal only perhaps by somewhat relaxed criteria.[14]

---

[13] The line taken in connecting conscious belief with reasoned judgment belongs with the set of approaches in which a person's knowledge of the attitudes they hold is said to depend on their ability to make up their mind about what to believe rather than on a special epistemic access to their own attitudes. See for example (McGeer 1996; 2008); (Moran 1997); and (Boyle 2009). There is more material relevant to this issue in the discussion of avowal in the next chapter.

[14] By many accounts, consciousness-of-perception will not be an instance of phenomenal consciousness and will not raise the same difficulties for physical reducibility (Block 2002). We differ in taking a broader view of phenomenal consciousness but also in ignoring the issue of whether it is reducible in physical terms. For a nice introduction to different ways of conceptualizing consciousness—though not quite the same as ours—and to different views on the reducibility issue, see (Kind and Stoljar 2023).

4.3.3 Blind-sensed subjects

Before we come to those arguments, however, it will be useful first to follow the lead of Ned Block (1997), and begin by contrasting perception as it occurs in percipient or non-percipient animals with an imagined sort of perception—perhaps better cast as quasi-perception—that we might describe as blind sensing. This is a form of perception or quasi-perception—a mode of causal, information-yielding interaction with the environment—that is not displayed by any known creature. It is a philosophical construct, built on the model of blindsight among humans, a clinical condition recognized only in relatively recent times (Weiskrantz 1986).[15]

A patient who suffers blindsight, typically in one half of their visual field, will report that they cannot see anything in that area: that they are quite blind there. But they often form beliefs on the basis of their blind perceptions—and to that extent their perceptions serve a standard response-shaping role—despite the blindness they report. Registering that there is a table in front of them, for example, they may step around it if they want to move forward. Moreover, if they are asked to guess at what is present in their immediate environment the blind-sighted patient will be able to guess at what is there with a relatively high success rate.

Imagine now a subject who is wholly blind-sighted but, having the capacity to make reasoned judgments, learns that they respond reliably when asked to guess about what they see. In particular, imagine someone who is super blind-sighted in the sense of becoming adept in asking themselves questions about what they see, and forming relatively reliable answers, they know not how, in response to those self-initiated prompts. Pushing things even further, indeed, imagine that they suffer a parallel to blind-sight in other sensory channels and that they also develop a self-prompting capacity there: they are blind-sensed, indeed super blind-sensed.

Why introduce these imaginary subjects into the discussion? They count as perceivers or quasi-perceivers who may enjoy consciousness-in-perception and consciousness-of-perception. Yet, however conscious they may be of or in their perceptions, they are not phenomenally conscious by any half-plausible criteria. How, then, do they differ in performance or functioning from regular conscious perceivers? How in particular do they differ from percipient subjects like our humanoids that are capable of perceptual judgment and reasoning; we may ignore what a capacity for judgment only would ensure? If the differences point to features that are intuitively relevant to whether consciousness is phenomenal or not, they may give us a reason for thinking that conscious perception in regular subjects, or at least regular, percipient subjects, is associated with such differences.

---

[15] There is an empirical issue about whether blind-sight is an intuitively unconscious form of visual processing or whether it is a degraded form of conscious vision, as suggested for example by (Phillips 2016; 2021); for a reply, see (Michel and Lau 2021). While I write here of subjects who answer better to the first theory, the choice does not require a commitment on that issue.

4.3.4 Consciousness-in-perception

Blind-sensors will be able to enjoy consciousness in their form of perception insofar as they can judge and reason—and can therefore exercise an analogue of percipience—as we have been assuming they can. Thus, the blind-sensor who learns that their guesswork is generally reliable and is prompted to say that there is a door in front of them may be aware of what they are registering perceptually. Yet intuitively this consciousness-in-perception is not phenomenal. How then does it differ from the consciousness-in-perception that more regular perceivers display? And might the factors that make for a difference in performance mark the divide between non-phenomenal and phenomenal forms of such perceptual consciousness? We shall explore those questions, first with percipient subjects like our humanoids, and then with their non-percipient counterparts.

4.3.5 Consciousness-in-perception: the percipient case

There are two striking, and related, ways in which blind-sensors will differ in matters broadly of functioning or performance from regular percipient perceivers. The first is attentional in character, the second explanatory, and both are intuitively relevant to whether or not the form of consciousness-in-perception they enjoy is phenomenal in character.

The first, attentional limitation is the more salient. By the account given earlier in the chapter, percipient, humanoid subjects will be able to direct another's attention to this or that aspect of the perceptual field, as indeed they may direct their own, when trying to prod them into registering some perceptually accessible feature. Trying to alert another to a particular constellation in the night sky, for example, they can tell them to look just above that tree before them and then slightly to the right. It is impossible to imagine being able to do any such thing with the blind-sensed subjects of our imagination. While they may be able to guess at the presence of this or that familiar sort of object in their surroundings, there will be no point in anyone's instructing them, or in their instructing themselves, to direct their attention to this or that part of their perceptual field; it is not even clear that the notion of a perceptual field will apply in their case.

This limitation in the attentional instruction someone might give to blind-sensors is closely connected with the second, explanatory limitation. How percipient, humanoid subjects perceive things to be, by the account we sketched earlier, will provide them in the normal case with a reason for judging and believing them to be that way. Fred Dretske (2006) highlights this feature of ordinary perception when he distinguishes between, on the one side, the way in which perception can provide a reason-for-someone to believe that things are such and such and, on the other, the way in which a prior event, perhaps unnoticed by them, may be a reason-why they form that belief. Clearly, the blind-sensors will be causally prompted to form various beliefs—say, that this is a table in front of them—with the processing behind that effect being hidden in the sub-personal operation of their minds. In that sense it will be the case, with any belief they form, that there is a reason-why they came to form it. But, by contrast with percipient perceivers, there will not be a reason for the blind-sensors to form the belief: there will not be a perceived way things are that is a reason-for-them to believe that they are that way.[16]

Neither of these limitations shows up in the performance of percipient perceivers like our humanoids. Being like us, they will be ready for attentional direction, whether issued by others or by themselves. And their mode of perceiving the world will offer a reason-for-them to form a certain belief—a reason that grounds the belief, so to speak—not just a reason-why they form it?

The source of these abilities is that unlike the blind-sensors, the humanoids will take the world to be a certain way, not just when they make judgments or form beliefs about it, but also when they rely on the materials delivered in their sensory channels to identify objects in their perceptual field and predicate properties of those objects. Their perceptual activity will be attention-ready insofar as it will be possible for them, whether prompted by themselves or others, to move attention across that sensory field and form predications at the points where they stop. And it can ground the beliefs that it supports by providing perceptual, sensory predications that correspond directly with beliefs; it can provide a *presentatum* that matches the *representatum* of the belief, referring to identifiably the same object or objects and predicating identifiably the same property or properties.

By this account, the consciousness-in-perception available to percipient perceivers will be strikingly different from that which would be available to blind-sensors. It will have an attention-ready character insofar as the sensory presentation of things in perception will be available as a field across which the subject can have their attention directed. And it will have a belief-grounding aspect insofar as that presentation will provide a ground for supporting a corresponding belief: it will be a presentation in sensory materials of the way the subject takes the world to be when they let perception guide their beliefs.

There will be nothing it is like for a subject to have a blind-sensed perception: nothing that might allow them to pay attention to this or that aspect of the presentation, nothing that might be taken as a way they ought to believe things to be. But there will be something available to fit the something-it-is-like bill if there is a sensory presentation involved in the perception that can play the attention-attracting, belief-grounding role. What, then, will such a perception be like for the subject? The materials for the answer will be provided by the look or the sound, the texture, the taste or the smell—for short, the feel—of the sensorily registered

---

[16] Dretske (2006) himself takes the condition to be a test of whether or not perception involves consciousness.

world. Like us, the humanoids will know exactly what to think, if they are asked whether there is anything it is like to perceive the world to be thus and so. There may be nothing it is like to register or perceive unconsciously that something is the case, but there will certainly be something it is like in the regular sort of perception envisaged here.

4.3.6 Consciousness-in-perception: the non-percipient case

This line of thought suggests that percipience is sufficient for consciousness-in-perception. But is it also necessary? The evidence is that no, it is not necessary, for a little reflection argues that even non-percipient animals can conduct perceptual monitoring in the attention-ready, belief-grounding manner, inevitably sensory in character, that is required for consciousness-in-perception.

The perceptual activity of a dog will be attention-ready insofar as we can get it to see where the ball has gone by pointing beneath the chair and instructing it to fetch, and the perceptual activity of animals in general will be attention-ready insofar as we can get them to notice things in this or that part of their perceptual field by directing a light, making a noise, or whatever. And how we take such an animal to perceive things to be when it exercises attention is how we will naturally take it to believe that things are; the perception will ground the belief, perhaps even ground it to the extent of playing the belief role itself. Thus, how we take a dog to perceive another dog—whether it sees the other as friendly or unfriendly, for example—is how we will take it to believe that things are, expecting it to behave as if things were that way, perhaps by assuming a friendly or unfriendly posture in response.

On this picture, other animals resemble humanoids and humans, and differ from blind-sensors, insofar as they can perceive things in the attention-ready, belief-grounding manner that involves sensory presentation. They may not be able to intentionally direct their own attention or intentionally seek to ground their beliefs. But there will be a way the world can present to them, as it presents to humans and humanoids, whether in the familiar, sensory array of color and sound, smell and taste and texture, or in alien sensory modes that it is hard for us to simulate or imagine. In virtue of how that surrounding world—that *Umwelt* (Yong 2022)—presents, it will guide non-human animals when they pursue their prey, search for shelter, seek willing mates, or look after their offspring; it will ground the beliefs on the basis of which they pursue those goals. Indeed, how that *Umwelt* presents may also elicit pleasure, as when adult animals relax in the sun or splash about in the water, or their young cavil or play with one another and irritate the grown-up group.

If this line of thought is sound, then we may conclude that many animals, and not just percipient subjects, can enjoy consciousness-in-perception. Of course, they will not always perceive things with the attention and the grounding linkage with belief that ensures consciousness. But unconscious perception is also likely among us human beings, as we noted, and will be equally common among our humanoid counterparts. The important point is that this need not always be the case and that perceptual consciousness in the relevant sense will be entirely within the reach of non-percipient animals.

We mentioned in the case of belief and related attitudes, that the humanoids will be able to identify the content of a belief—and enjoy consciousness-in-belief—by virtue of their capacity to conceptualize propositions and to be able to cite a proposition as the item to which the belief relates as content. We can now see that there is also another, pre-conceptual way in which an agent, even an agent of a non-percipient kind, may be able to identify the content of a perceptual belief. As they can be aware of the content of a perception by virtue of being able to attend to it, so they can be aware in a corresponding sense of the content of a belief that the perception grounds. This mode of consciousness-in-belief is going to be available to any subject that enjoys the corresponding mode of consciousness-in-perception.

These observations argue that percipience is not needed for consciousness-in-perception, since non-percipient animals can display the attention-ready, belief-grounding capacities that make perception conscious in the relevant sense. But that conclusion is quite consistent, of course, with holding that percipience has a significant enhancing effect on such consciousness. And, as we saw in the second section, there is every reason to hold that it will have such an impact.

Their percipience will enable the humanoids to perceive—and as we can now see, consciously perceive—a much larger range of properties than those that will be accessible to the simple animal. It will enable them to conceptualize the properties perceived in a strongly stimulus-independent way, viewing them as items about which to raise and answer a range of questions. And it will enable them to regulate their attention with a view to answering perceptual questions about those properties and their instantiations. It will transform what and how they perceive in attention-ready, belief-grounding perception: what and how the world consciously presents to them.

4.3.7 Consciousness-of-perception

As we saw, blind-sensors will be able to enjoy consciousness in their form of perception insofar as they can judge and reason. They will be able to recognize that something they register before them, however sub-personally, is a door or a table or a tree. Because they can judge and reason, blind sensors will also be able to enjoy consciousness of their registering or perceiving things in that way. They must recognize that sometimes they differ from others in what they register and that sometimes they are wrong: what they take to be a door is actually a window. And that being so, they must recognize that how the world presents to them may not be how it is, and that it must be in virtue of a subjective state within themselves—a perception or quasi-perception—that it presents in that way.

But this consciousness-of-perception clearly fails to have a phenomenal character. And so we return to questions parallel to those asked in the other case. What is the difference between the blind-sensed enjoyment of such consciousness and its enjoyment in regular perceivers? And might the factor that makes for a difference mark the divide between phenomenal and non-phenomenal forms of consciousness-of-perception? Again, we explore those questions, first with percipient subjects like our humanoids, and then with their non-percipient counterparts.

4.3.8 Consciousness-of-perception: the percipient case

Percipience is certainly sufficient to enable the humanoids to enjoy consciousness-of-perception. As we saw, it will enable them to recognize that how they judge and believe things to be is often grounded in how things perceptually present; that how they judge and believe things to be can be mistaken, as highlighted in disagreements with others or indeed with themselves over time; that how things present perceptually can therefore be mistaken; and this being so, that when the world presents in one or another sensory fashion, it must do so in virtue of subjective states of their own: specifically, states of perception. Thus, their percipience will ensure that not only can the humanoids identify the *presentatum* in any attentive perception, they can also register the *presentans*: the presenting state that perception requires.

But the humanoids can achieve this form of consciousness-of-perception on broadly the same basis as the blind-sensors. And doesn't that mean that the consciousness-of-perception they achieve amounts to nothing more than what blind-sensors can achieve: namely, a non-phenomenal form of awareness? No, it does not.

The blind-sensor's recognition of the role of their quasi-perceptual states will be wholly cognitive, resembling the consciousness-of-belief that any percipient subject can display. But the consciousness-of-perception available to the humanoids will not have the same purely cognitive character. And it may well count as a form of phenomenal consciousness.

In percipient perceivers, the *presentatum* of a conscious perception will have a sensory profile, being constituted out of colors and sounds, textures, tastes and smells, and coming to awareness in sensory sensitivity to those features. The consciousness-of-perception available to those perceivers would not be phenomenal if it merely consisted in a belief that they are undergoing otherwise featureless states that dispose them to act in this or that manner; it would resemble the consciousness-of-perception available to blind-sensors. But the consciousness-of-perception available to them is going to be much richer than that.

Aware of having perceptual states in which things present under sensorily constituted properties, percipient perceivers will be able to identify and enjoy an awareness of those states by rehearsing or simulating within themselves how those states present the world. Such a perceptual simulation occurs in remembering how things presented in perception or imagining how they might present: remembering how it was to perceive some mountains in the distance, for example, or imagining how they might look from the perspective of a soaring eagle. As humanoid perceivers will presumably be able to rehearse perceptual states in those extended ways, they will be able to rehearse them in the course of perceptual activity itself. They will be able to let perceptual activity unfold, enjoying an awareness of the way in which the relevant sensory properties assemble and shift and assume one or another form. They will be able to let the *presentans* come to awareness—to savor it, we might say—as a form of exposure to the *presentatum*.

Achieving awareness of a perceptual state in such a rehearsing or simulative mode need not be unusual. The sensory properties registered when the subject is conscious-in-perception will naturally double as the properties by which the percipient subject will individuate their perceptual states. If the object seen is red, seeing it will have a red look; if the sound heard is sweet, hearing it will be sweet as well; if the fruit tasted is bitter, tasting it will be bitter too; and so on. Although the redness, the sweetness, and the bitterness are properties of the objects perceived, they will also provide the salient means of characterizing their perceptual states for the perceivers themselves (Harman 1990; Dretske 2003).

This observation suggests that whereas the consciousness-of-perception that is available to blind-sensors is wholly cognitive in nature, that which the humanoids enjoy with perceptions that are already conscious in that other sense will have a rich sensory character akin to that of consciousness-in-perception. The humanoids will identify such perceptual states by their sensory, content-dependent properties, making their consciousness-of-perception in those cases into something that will count, if only by somewhat relaxed criteria of plausibility, as a phenomenal experience.[17]

4.3.9 Consciousness-of-perception: the non-percipient case

So much for the claim that their percipience will suffice to give the humanoids consciousness-of-perception, and specifically consciousness of broadly a phenomenal kind. But is percipience necessary for consciousness-of-perception? Is there

---

[17] A perception may have some content-independent properties that are sensory too, as when the brightness of an object seen dazzles the eyes, or the volume of a sound hurts the ears. But insofar as the states are characterized in this way for perceivers, they will count as sensations that, by many accounts, are not content-bearing; unlike the content-dependent properties mentioned in the text, they will not mark out the perceptions as perceptions.

any variety of such consciousness that non-percipient animals might be able to enjoy? The answer suggested by the considerations of this chapter is that there is not, and that percipience is necessary for consciousness-of-perception, if not for consciousness-in-perception.

Non-percipient animals will enjoy consciousness-in-perception insofar as their perceptions engage the sensory world accessed by humans and humanoids. The world presented to them will be articulated in simpler similarity classes, to be sure, not in the rich categories accessible to humanoids. And it will be presented to them as a passive source of information by which to navigate, not as one they can intentionally probe, determining how and where they give their attention. But the question is whether or not such animals will recognize the role of their perceptual states in determining the character of that *Umwelt*.

We argued in the last section that while non-percipient animals will be prompted to dismiss certain perceptions, they will do so by ceasing to form or act on the perceptions dismissed, not by recognizing that how things are perceived to be may not be how they are. This means that those animals will not be positioned to enjoy consciousness-of-perception. They will be lost in the world revealed in their senses, unable to recognize that perceptual appearance may deceive, and unable indeed to have even a conception of how things might appear to be thus and so without actually being that way. Their *Umwelt* will be an immersive world that locks them within its walls, denying them the capacity to stand back and recognize that how it presents is a function of their own potentially misleading perceptual states.

Things will display for such animals the colors and sounds and other sensory qualities to which humans and humanoids are responsive. But they will display those properties through a perceptual medium that is as transparent and invisible to the animals as clear glass. Where the possibility of perceptual error will make that medium detectable to the humanoids, overcoming the transparency that might have kept it out of view, there will be nothing to serve that purpose in the case of these animals. Their perceptual world will be sensorily engrossing by contrast with the world of the blind-sensors, having a phenomenal feel that gives them consciousness-in-perception. But they will be lost in that world, captive to how it reveals itself to their senses; they will have no inkling that it presents as it does in virtue of states, in particular potentially misleading states, within themselves.

4.3.10 Conclusion

The argument in this third section of the chapter emphasizes the important impact of percipience on the perceptions of the humanoids, and its role in relation to their consciousness-in-perception and their consciousness-of-perception. It will enhance the first, marking a contrast with non-percipient animals, and it will enable the second, marking a gulf between percipient and non-percipient perceivers. The consciousness it enhances in the first case will certainly be phenomenal in character, meeting Nagel's test that there must be something it is like to be the subject of such a conscious state. And the consciousness it enables in the second will count as phenomenal also, if only by somewhat more relaxed criteria.

One of the most controversial issues in contemporary discussions of consciousness bears on whether its existence is explicable on the basis of the sorts of entities and regularities envisaged in natural science: whether in broadly that sense it is naturalistically reducible. The humanoid capacities for judgment and reasoning are naturalistically explicable on the account offered by the genealogy, as argued in the discussion of demystification in the first chapter. And, as we have seen, those capacities can certainly explain much about the perceptual consciousness enjoyed by the humanoids, and presumably by human beings, when they are exercised in percipience. But the fact that that is so does not support a wholesale naturalism about perception and perceptual consciousness. Percipience presupposes perception and indeed the consciousness-in-perception that is available to animals that lack percipience. Thus, our account of its impact, however naturalistically explicable that impact is, leaves open the question as to whether perception itself, and the pre-percipient consciousness it allows, lends itself to naturalistic reduction.[18]

---

[18] For the record, I do not find non-naturalism on these issues persuasive. I am loathe to treat consciousness as in no need of naturalistic explanation (pace Strawson 2024). And I find that the standard arguments against naturalism about consciousness (see Chalmers 1996), are hostage to future developments in scientific knowledge (Stoljar 2006), fall short of being compelling (Pettit 2003; 2004a), and are often in tension with one another (McGeer 2003).

5
Normativity and value

We have been looking at the effects that the appearance of language is robustly likely to have on the psychology of the humanoid protagonists in our genealogy. We saw in the second chapter that it will be likely to elicit the capacity to make judgments on matters of fact and to enable the humanoids, assuming the availability of adequate data or desiderata, to make up their own minds intentionally on whether this or that is the case, or whether this or that is to be done: in effect, to ratify a belief or desire on that matter. We then went on to argue in the second chapter that equally language will be robustly likely to elicit the capacity to reason from judgments made or supposed to other judgments and beliefs or, where the premised judgments involve desiderata, to preferences or intentions.

Finally, in the previous chapter, we argued that in supporting reasoned judgments, language will elicit percipience in humanoids and with it a distinctive form of consciousness. This development means that the humanoids will be able to enrich the range of properties presented in perception; to control where and how they pay attention to the presentation, making suitable perceptual predications; and to determine on their own authority—perhaps as a result of negotiating with others—that some presentations are to be dismissed, others embraced. This will give the humanoids a sense of the difference between appearance and reality and enable them to enhance and extend the consciousness that is available to non-percipient animals.

These likely effects on the psychology of our counterfactual humanoids—and perhaps the corresponding effects on our human forbears—all involve capacities in broadly cognitive processing. In the final three chapters we will be looking at capacities of a different character. The practice emerging in each case is an explicitly relational or interactive practice but, as we shall see, it allows of being interiorized in a familiar, psychological fashion. Thus, the discussions will continue to emphasize the main motif of our genealogy: that the distinctive way of thinking that the humanoids develop in face of the opportunities presented will appear first in a social or interpersonal guise and only second, in a psychological or intrapersonal role.[1]

---

[1] This and the next chapter draw on themes from (Pettit 2018a), while always recasting them and often revising them. I was greatly helped in rethinking those themes by the discussions in a symposium on that book, edited by Tristram McPherson and David Plunkett in *Inquiry*, Vol. 67, 2024.

In this chapter, we look at the appearance of a sense of injunctive normativity and value as distinct from the prudential, reputational normativity assumed in the economy of esteem, or the functional, epistemic normativity associated with reasoning and, more basically, with any form of ratified assertion or judgment. In the next chapter, we explore the way in which this will lead them to hold others and themselves responsible for their actions, introducing a notion of free will in the course of doing so. And in the seventh and final chapter, we argue that as a result of those developments the humanoids will have a capacity to relate and conceive of themselves as persons, each with a characteristic self; as percipience is enabled by the capacities for judgment and reasoning, so the capacity associated with personhood is enabled by the capacities associated with normativity and responsibility.

This chapter is in three sections. In the first section, we argue that the humanoids will be robustly likely to develop a sense of the injunctively normative in the course of evolving social norms, applying it to others in the first place, themselves in the second. In the third section, to jump forward, we explain why they will naturally explicate this injunctive normativity, and some related variants, in value terms, where valuing is distinct from desiring. And in the second, middle section we build the bridge between those two discussions, explaining why the humanoids will make commitments to others and to themselves, and invoking commitments to create a link between normativity and value. The chapter is complex insofar as it introduces three distinct practices and concepts that may be expected to appear among the humanoids, but the complexity is unavoidable since, as we shall see, normativity, commitment, and valuing are deeply interconnected.

In this chapter and in the two that follow, we will be relying saliently on an assumption introduced in the first chapter and engaged indirectly in the genealogy of processing capacities. This is the assumption that the humanoids in our genealogy enjoy a relative degree of equality among themselves. We relied on the assumption when we took it for granted that the humanoids will evolve tit-for-tat reciprocity across their membership, that they will care about the esteem of others generally, and that consequently they will make assertions and judgments, and practice reasoning, under the constraint of one another's expectations. This assumption takes on a higher degree of salience as we look in this chapter at how the humanoids are likely to generate common norms, a pattern of mutual commitment, and a shared practice of valuation, and as we build on that claim in the following chapters, exploring their practices in relation to responsibility and personhood.

We shall proceed, as we have done up to now, on the assumption that the humanoids enjoy relative equality in power across their whole society and that the society exists in isolation or at any rate is not subject to other societies. That assumption does not apply in our own world, since human societies have been long marked—at least since the agricultural revolution—by inequalities of power. And that raises an obvious question. Does the assumption of a wholesale, if relative equality of power among the humanoids entail that the counterfactual story can have little or nothing to tell us about our world? Happily, as we indicated in the first chapter, it does not.

It is quite likely in human history that even in hierarchically organized societies, there were always subgroups among whose members a degree of equality prevailed. And that would be enough to let the counterfactual story carry lessons for the actual world. It can still carry significant implications for how we should think of human capacities for judgment, reasoning, and percipience. And it can still teach us lessons about the relational capacities explored in this and later chapters. Thus, to focus on this chapter, the sorts of norms, commitments, and values that figure in the story may have counterparts in the norms, commitments, and valuations made by humans within one or another subgroup. And, looking ahead, the same holds for the practices associated with responsibility and personhood.

5.1 Injunctive social norms

5.1.1 Ideas of the normative

We introduced a notion of prudential normativity in recognizing that things will be appealing or attractive for the humanoids insofar as they answer to their self-regarding desires. Thus, we assumed that they will each have a desire to be held in reputational esteem rather than disesteem among their fellows; and that this goal will make it practically rational for them to treat one another well, as in reporting on things carefully and truthfully. We may say of them in this sense that they ought to treat others well, where that statement is an implied, prudential conditional: they ought to treat others well, if they are to win the social acceptance they want. And we may imagine that they will readily learn to use a similar idiom in speaking among themselves: say, in giving advice to another, as in the advice of a parent to a child, about how they ought to behave.

We operated with a different idea of normativity when we addressed the demands of rationality at the basic level of judgment and assertion as well as the demands, at the more sophisticated level, of reasoning from certain asserted or supposed premises to conclusions they entail or otherwise support. In these cases, we spoke of the way the humanoids will take themselves to be required, assuming they care about functioning normally, to make a certain judgment or to draw a certain conclusion, on the basis of where triangulation with others leads them. And as we spoke in this idiom, so we may imagine that the humanoids will also speak, representing such a mode of judgment or reasoning as one they ought normatively to display.

Both prudential and functional normativity are recognized among human beings, so that these earlier discussions directed us to ways in which the humanoids will be led, ultimately by grace to language, to develop important aspects of familiar human practices. But the story so far has left the humanoids without anything corresponding to normativity of a distinct kind that is routinely recognized among human beings. This is the injunctive normativity implied when humans register that something is obligatory: that they must do it, as a matter of normative rather than physical or psychological or situational necessity. It is the normativity allegedly registered by Luther in the refusal, as he saw it, to go against his conscience: *Hier stehe Ich, Ich kann nicht anders*; here I stand, I can do no other.

There is a long tradition among human beings of recognizing some requirements as injunctive in this sense. They are requirements of the kind associated with orders or commands. For to tell someone that they must do something is another way of ordering them to do it, or of registering that an appropriate authority orders them to do it. Unsurprisingly, this injunctive notion of normativity is often associated with the appeal to a god as the authority that dictates their duties or obligations—commandments, as they are aptly named—to human beings. There has long been a well-established tradition, of course, of questioning the reality of such obligations, often linked with a denial that there is a god. But with some exceptions—Nietzsche (1997) comes immediately to mind—the notion of obligation has generally survived such skepticism. This being so, it is significant that at least a relative of injunctive normativity will be robustly likely to appear, as we shall see, among our humanoid subjects.

How best to relate injunctive normativity to the prudential and functional forms of normativity discussed earlier? Prudential normativity imposes requirements that are conditional on the subject's having a certain purpose: you ought to do this or that, if you wish to promote your personal welfare, or perhaps the welfare of those who are near and dear. Such requirements may be cast as conditional or hypothetical. Functional normativity also imposes requirements that can be expressed in a conditional form: you ought to make this judgment or draw that conclusion if you are to operate functionally or rationally. But those requirements are best cast as categorical or non-conditional—you ought to make this judgment, period; you ought to draw that conclusion, period—since they do not apply conditionally on the purposes of an agent but in virtue of the agent's functional nature.

Unlike its prudential counterpart, then, injunctive normativity is not conditional on the purposes of the agent to whom it applies. And unlike the functional normativity, it does not apply to someone in virtue of their functional nature, or not in virtue of that nature alone. Its demands are categorical, like functional demands, but they apply to an agent as demands made by a certain external authority. This may be the authority of a particular agent or agency, or the authority of something like a regime of positive law or, if there is one, a natural analogue of law.

The paradigm of such a categorical, authoritative demand—such an injunctive demand, as we may cast it—is the command or injunction issued by an individual with authority over the agent addressed. This might be the command that a divine creator is taken to issue to human beings under their aspect as creatures. Or it might be the command that an authorized ruler issues to subjects under their aspect as members of the society. Unlike prudential requirements, both sorts of demands are categorical insofar as they are not conditional on the purposes of those to whom they apply. And unlike functional requirements, they are authoritative insofar as they apply in virtue of the status of the individual or body at their source.

While injunctive demands are categorical and authoritative in these respects, however, that does not imply that they bind individuals in an absolute manner. Qua categorical, such a demand will not apply conditionally on an agent having a certain prudential purpose or indeed a purpose of any kind, even a goal of universal benevolence. But it need not bind the agent regardless of the circumstances under which they have to act. Even if the agent is able to comply with a given demand, for example, they will hardly be bound to satisfy the demand when, as a red flag may indicate, doing so would mean breaching a presumptively weightier requirement.[2]

When we make demands of an injunctively normative kind, we usually support them by an appeal to the values that might make the obligatory option worthy of being chosen. Indeed, many take the notion of the injunctively obligatory to be just the same as the notion of that which is most choice-worthy: that which is best supported by values or reasons in general or in the moral domain. We shall see in the third section that the humanoids will certainly have access to the notion of value—this, by virtue of the commitments explored in the second—and that they will naturally recognize a linkage between the injunctively obligatory and the evaluatively choice-worthy. But it is important, as our discussion will suggest, that the obligatory and the choice-worthy are distinct categories.[3]

5.1.2 Conventions, norms, laws

The notion of normativity to be addressed here will first gain a hold among the humanoids, so we argue, as a result of the practices associated with social norms. As we conceptualize them, social norms contrast on the one side with conventions and on the other with laws. All three consist in regularities with which most people in a community comply, where compliance is supported in part by considerations of self-interest. But they differ in the way in which they engage the parties involved.

Conventions, as we noted in Chapter 1, consist in regularities that enable people to solve coordination predicaments. In such a predicament each has an interest in acting on the same pattern as others, regardless of which pattern that is. Thus, they will have such an interest in traveling on the left or on the right side of the road, or

---

[2] I thank Garett Cullity and Nic Southwood for helpful conversations on these issues.
[3] This distinction is overlooked, or at best backgrounded, in (Pettit 2018a).

in greeting one another by the same form of physical contact: say, a handshake, a hug, or a kiss. If a convention is to arise among people, then they must solve the epistemic problem of identifying a common pattern of response on which they can all converge. Once that emerges as a matter of common recognition in the community, however, they will each naturally have a self-interested motive for conforming; they may conform out of brute habit, but that motive will always be there to serve as a backup.

Social norms, as we shall understand the term, differ from mere conventions in this regard. Even if they are collectively beneficial in the sense that each will do better in the presence of conformity by others than in its absence, still they are likely to be individually burdensome. Any individual is liable to be tempted to free ride: that is, to try to benefit from the conformity of others without themselves paying the cost of conformity. Thus, to take some obvious examples, each may do better under a pattern of non-deception, non-coercion, and non-violence by all than in the absence of such a pattern; yet even if the pattern is established, each may be occasionally tempted, when it gives them some advantage, to be deceptive, coercive, or violent.

Social norms of a collectively beneficial kind are likely to be articulated and sometimes expanded or altered in formally enacted laws (Hart 2012; Pettit 2023b). Paradigmatic laws are backed up by the threat of a material penalty, where this is defined on a central, organized basis, and imposed under centrally dictated procedures. Social norms will often double as formal laws, and laws may often introduce regularities that have the same collective appeal as familiar norms. But nonetheless they are distinct categories, and our focus here will be on social norms alone.[4]

More specifically still, the focus will be on norms that have a reasonable claim to being collectively beneficial for the sort of humanoid community that we are imagining. There are malign norms that are also likely to appear among the humanoids, as they appear among humans. For example, norms of honesty among crooks or cronies that benefit a section of the relevant community only; norms of revenge that benefit few if any, and then only in the short term; norms of pluralistic ignorance—we illustrate these later—that are sustained on the basis of a mistake that each makes about what others expect; and, if we lift our regular assumption and allow the humanoid society to be hierarchical, norms governing how those in dominated groups should relate to their dominators.

In what follows, we stick with our genealogical project, explaining how collectively beneficial norms would be robustly likely to emerge in humanoid society. We do this in two stages, first explaining why in prudence the humanoids would be likely to conform to beneficial norms, and then explaining why those prudentially

---

[4] For a genealogy of law and of the state needed to establish and enforce law, see (Pettit 2023b, Ch. 1).

supported norms would be likely to gain a categorical and authoritative status, giving rise to an injunctive sense of normativity.[5]

5.1.3 The emergence of social norms: first stage

We already sketched a story in Chapter 2 about how one particular social norm—that which requires ready and reliable information-sharing—would be likely to emerge, under the pressure of prudence. Sticking with that example here, we first give a little more structure to that story, and then go on to show that it will apply in a range of other cases too, explaining the emergence of norms against violence, coercion, and fraudulence, for example, and against breaking promises or stealing the property of others.

The first stage in our genealogy of beneficial norms begins with the observation that the humanoids will often relate to one another in pairs, and that in such interactions, something like a tit-for-tat pattern will hold (Axelrod 1984; Nowak 2006). Under such a pattern each will respond to the indifference or malevolence of another by treating them harshly in future interactions, returning to a cooperative stance only when the other proves willing to be cooperative. As we saw in the case of information-sharing, each will have a motive to shun any other who refuses to give some information, or deliberately misinforms them, if shunning is a realistic possibility. And if it is not possible to shun such an offender, on the grounds that there are bound to be further interactions between the parties, then each will have a motive to teach them a lesson, as the human idiom has it: to impose some sort of penalty on the other—if only a refusal to provide some information they request—on the assumption that the other can recognize that that treatment is meant as a lesson and that future cooperation will be reciprocated.

This tit-for-tat motive for behaving beneficially toward others is going to be reinforced among the humanoids in a special manner. Each will recognize that they must treat any interactant well, not just because of a concern for their reputation with that individual—this is the core element in tit-for-tat—but also because of a concern for their reputation with others in general. This is because there will often be others who witness an offence against that individual, are loath to expose themselves to the risk of being treated in the same way, and are likely to spread the word about the offender's behavior.

---

[5] For an earlier version of the conception of norms developed here, especially in stage 1, see (Pettit 1990; 2008b) and (Brennan and Pettit 2004); for a version that distinguishes the two stages, see (Pettit 2023b, Ch. 1). The stage 1 notion picks up points made in a variety of approaches. See for example (Hart 1961; Winch 1963; Coleman 1990; Sober and Wilson 1998; Elster 1999; Bicchieri 2006; Shapiro 2011; Bicchieri 2017). For an approach that takes the notion of the normative to pre-exist norms, see (Brennan, Eriksson, Goodin, and Southwood 2013); the stage 2 version of norms presented here is designed to explain the normative aspect rather than taking it to be independently sourced.

Why will witnesses be likely to spread the word in this way? Because doing so will promote their own reputational standing. By reporting on how the individual behaved, and particularly by reporting that they were uncooperative, a witness to the behavior may hope to communicate the message that they themselves are a cooperative type: they will signal their own virtue. And the same will be true of anyone who passes on that message in an expanding circle of gossip. By praising cooperation or denouncing an offence, the witnessing or gossiping party will manifestly expose themselves to the extra sanction of being denounced as a hypocrite should they themselves behave malevolently. And in exposing themselves to the risk of such a special sanction, they will advertise their own disposition to be cooperative.

These considerations argue, as we saw in the information-gathering case, that in every interaction where they might hurt another, the humanoids will each be motivated by a concern for their general reputation with others. Let others come to think badly of them as a result of word spreading about how they treated one or another individual, then they will suffer serious consequences: they will be unable to rely on others taking them to be reliable partners in cooperation. Let others come to think well of them, however—if only for lack of any word in discredit—and their opportunities for cooperative relationships will expand. As they will want to avoid being held in disesteem by others, so they will want to stand as high as possible in their positive esteem. They will prefer to be esteemed and will have a policy or intention of doing nothing to jeopardize their standing with others.[6]

This argues that in any domains where it is important to score well in the economy of esteem, the humanoids will individually adjust their responses to ensure such a score. The lesson we drew about reliable information-sharing in Chapter 2 applies across a much larger range, offering reason to think that the humanoids will be reliably averse to violence, coercion, fraudulence, and the like, as well as being reliably averse to under-informing or misinforming others.[7]

One observation in passing. While we shall concentrate on the ways in which the humanoids will be averse to these malevolent forms of behavior—and later concentrate on norms that rule against them—the economy of esteem is also likely to motivate an aversion to forms of behavior that are collectively damaging but, unlike the cases envisaged, not particularly harmful to any single victim. Thus, it can explain an aversion to forms of free riding that harm others generally in a marginal

---

[6] For an introduction to the traditional belief in the power of esteem, see (Lovejoy 1961), and for more recent treatments, see (Brennan and Pettit 2004; Appiah 2010; Liebert 2016; Origgi 2018).

[7] They may have to learn the lesson about the importance of esteem in the manner depicted here. Or the lesson may also come to them by nature, under our assumption that they are like human beings. For it may be that humans are disposed to care about esteem by their very nature—ultimately, perhaps, on the basis of genetic assimilation prior to the appearance of language—and not just by noticing and alerting their young to its importance.

measure but no one to a serious degree (Pettit 1986). And it can explain an aversion to free riding on the collective efforts of others to deal with a communal crisis like that of flood or fire. Anyone who free rides in these sorts of situation is likely to attract the notice of others, to become a fair target for complaint and gossip, and to find themselves moved by the desire for esteem, or the aversion to disesteem, to maintain a cooperative stance.

What we have seen so far is that the humanoids will adjust to one another on a pattern that secures cooperative behavior in situations where free riding might otherwise be attractive. They will respond to instances of malevolence in a way that threatens the reputational status of offenders and makes it rational for agents in general to behave in a cooperative fashion. It will lead them to be cooperative in giving information, in avoiding coercion and violence and fraudulence and—a type of case we shall generally set aside—in playing a collectively cooperative part within the community as a whole.

If the humanoids adjust to one another in this fashion, however, they will be very likely, as we saw in the information-sharing case, to give rise to what intuitively count as social norms.

The first point to note in charting this development is that the adjustments the humanoids make in giving information readily and reliably, or in avoiding violence or fraudulence, will aggregate across the society to generate a social regularity: a pattern with which each will generally conform. It will be a fact about the society that as a rule the members are cooperative in the relevant domains.

But when a social regularity emerges from the adjustments made by different parties, to introduce a second point, the regularity will come to be recognized as a matter of common awareness across the society. Assuming that the humanoids are as perceptive as human beings, it will be evident to each that members are generally cooperative in that domain; it will be evidently evident to each that that is the case; indeed, it will be evidently evidently evident that that it is the case; and so on in the familiar hierarchy of common awareness.

This takes us to the denouement. Once the regularity obtains, and is registered in common awareness, it will offer a device of regulation in the relevant domain. Parents will be aware that their offspring will suffer reputational damage if they do not conform to that regularity and will naturally hold out the regularity as a rule or guideline for the children to follow; they will prefer that the children be taught the lesson in advance than that they should have to learn it for themselves. Humanoids will also be motivated to do the same with any newcomers to the society who might not be aware of the rule; in doing this, they will protect themselves, win the approval of others for teaching a welcome lesson, and signal their own virtue. And for similar reasons they will each be disposed, first, to make the lesson clear to would-be offenders, whether in giving a warning or making a threat of dire reputational consequences; and second, to make it clear to actual offenders by triggering such consequences.

As we suggested in the discussion of information-gathering, a recognized social regularity that is invoked to a regulative purpose in instruction of this kind, or in the associated form of correction, will count intuitively as a social norm. It will do so, as we may note for mnemonic purposes, in an A-triple-R pattern. Beginning from the *adjustment* that leads to cooperative behavior—this is represented in the A—it shows that that adjustment will lead to three further developments, each marked by an R: the appearance of a *regularity*, that attracts *recognition* as a matter of common awareness, and that comes thereby to serve in *regulation*.

But now we need to notice that A-triple-R norms of the kind envisaged so far are limited in a salient respect. They can be presented in instructive or corrective regulation only as maxims of prudence. For all that is presupposed in the account given, the only ground on which one individual can seek to elicit the conformity of another is that otherwise the other will be in reputational trouble, losing the capacity to rely on others or to get others, when they wish, to rely on them. This will be true of the humanoids in instructing children or outsiders, in instructing would-be offenders, or indeed in correcting those who have already offended.

The mode of regulation involved here is described by Thomas Hobbes (1994b, 25.3) as counsel or advice. He is worth quoting fully on the topic: 'COUNSEL is where a man saith *do*, or *do not this*, and deduceth his reasons from the benefit that arriveth by it to him to whom he saith it. And from this it is evident that he that giveth counsel pretendeth only (whatsoever he intendeth) the good of him to whom he giveth it.' Thus, as Hobbes goes on to say, an individual 'cannot be obliged to do as he is counselled, because the hurt of not following it is his own'. In other words, the individual can be required to act as they are advised to act only in the prudential sense that that is in their interest.

The fact that A-triple-R norms can only be presented in regulation as maxims of prudence—recommendations made in the addressee's own interests—means that they do not introduce any normativity among the humanoids other than the prudential kind with which, as we saw, they will be familiar already. That ceases to be so, however, as these norms begin to assume a novel status, which we explore in the second stage of our genealogy of norms.

5.1.4 The emergence of social norms: second stage

The first stage of our genealogy of social norms begins with the sorts of adjustment that the humanoids will be naturally led to make in light of the economy of esteem under which, like human beings, they will inevitably live. The second stage builds on the A-triple-R norms that have already emerged, as we may assume, starting from an attitude to those prudential norms that each is likely to display. This response consists in the internalization of those existing norms and triggers a series of further developments; these appear in an I-triple-R pattern, as we shall see, where the 'I' stands for internalization.

The humanoids will internalize a prudential norm, in the intended sense of the term, insofar as they each come, not just to have an intention or policy of conforming themselves, but also to prefer that others should conform as well.[8] When a norm is collectively beneficial, as in the case of our targeted examples, it is unsurprising that they should internalize it. For in that case there are three benefits that general conformity will provide for each.

First, everyone will do better insofar as it is the case that in each encounter they will enjoy the other's information-sharing or non-violence or non-fraudulence. Second, everyone will do better in virtue of enjoying that treatment robustly, as the norm requires, not just contingently on the other feeling benevolent or indulgent; they can rely on being treated in that welcome manner, robustly over certain variations in the independent inclinations of the other (Pettit 2015). And third, everyone will do better insofar as they will enjoy the status, as a matter of common awareness, of manifestly attracting such robust treatment by others in general.

Given the prospect of benefitting from the compliance of others, everyone is likely to prefer that others in general should conform. In that sense they are likely to internalize each of the norms we have been discussing.

The same will not be true, however, of norms that are not collectively beneficial. Thus, it is hardly likely that every humanoid will want crooks or cronies, if there be such a minority, to be honest with one another; they may much prefer such a subgroup to be riven by mutual deception. And equally it is hardly likely that every humanoid will want everyone in general to abide by a norm of revenge, should such a norm emerge among them. While an aggrieved party may passionately desire the satisfaction of exacting revenge against an offender, the humanoids in general will presumably recoil from the cycle of harm it threatens and the danger such a cycle may constitute for them individually.

Perhaps the clearest case where internalization is going to fail involves pluralistic ignorance, as it is often called. A norm will obtain as a result of such ignorance under two conditions: first, everyone conforms to it, despite a degree of reluctance, because of expecting that otherwise they will suffer the disesteem of others; but second, that expectation is mistaken: as a matter of fact, few or none have the attitudes of esteem and disesteem that are ascribed to them. Under those conditions, it will not be the case that everyone prefers that others should generally conform; given their reluctance to conform themselves, a general failure of conformity would release them from the reputational pressure they currently experience.

---

[8] To internalize a norm, on another use of the term, is not just to conform to it, but also to approve of conformity (Cooter 1996). I avoid the language of approval since the availability of evaluative language is only explained in the third section of this chapter. But my non-evaluative account of internalization clearly connects with this alternative characterization.

Thus, to draw on a psychological study of the phenomenon (Miller and Prentice 1994; 1996), a group of students who regularly go drinking together may each drink more than they wish, because of the mistaken belief that otherwise their fellows will hold them in disesteem. In that sort of scenario, there is a salient and feasible alternative to the norm in question, such as drinking according to personal preference or drinking up to a lower limit. And it turns out that many or all the relevant individuals would prefer this to be the general pattern. Thus, while the students abide by the norm—and while it becomes a norm on the A-triple-R pattern—they do not internalize it in our sense: they do not prefer that others in general should conform.

Clearly, the sorts of collectively beneficial norms on which we are focused here are going to be internalized among the humanoids, unlike the sorts of norms just illustrated. But once we grant that internalization is in place, we can see further developments that are robustly likely to materialize. They will do so in an I-triple-R pattern that parallels the foregoing A-triple-R pattern.

Let internalization materialize as a regularity among the humanoids on the grounds that the social norms at issue are collectively beneficial; let them each come to want others to conform in view of the benefit that such conformity will promise in their own case. In that event, it will be evident to the humanoids themselves, not just to us as outside theorists, that this is so: that there are grounds for each to internalize the norms; to think otherwise would be to deem them inexplicably unperceptive. But not only will it be evident to the humanoids that they each have grounds for internalizing the norms. It will be evident, assuming that they are perceptive, that this is evident to each of them; indeed, it will be evidently evident that that is the case, and so on. By our account, then, it will be recognized as a matter of common awareness that the internalization is universal.

But such *recognition* is only the first of three likely developments to follow on internalization, each marked by an R. To advertise the further developments before charting them fully, recognition of the internalization will generate the opportunity for an appealing form of *regulation* in the name of the society as a whole. And then, with the prospect of such regulation being itself *recognized* as a matter of common awareness, the norms will gain a novel social status. They will no longer serve only to support prudential maxims for the guidance of self-interested individuals: they will represent injunctive demands or obligations that society lays upon all its members. We look now at these further developments.

With manifestly internalized norms, to take the regulation development first, there will be clear motives for anyone to invoke them in instructing or correcting others, even others in whom they do not have the interest of a parent or a friend. By doing so, they will protect themselves, perform the welcome service of protecting others as well, and advertise their own disposition to conform. But despite the continued relevance of these motives, the regulation possible and appealing in this case will assume quite a different character from that which applies with an A-triple-R norm.

In order to see why it will be different, we need to recall an observation in Chapter 2 about the common ground that is going to be established among interlocutors in the course of any successful informational exchange. We noted that when anyone conveys information—strictly, alleged information—to others, and none of their interlocutors questions it, all of them will share that information, and share it as a matter of common belief: it will be manifestly common ground between them. This being so, every new offer that is accepted in the course of informational exchange, every assertion that passes without challenge, will add to that common ground between the interlocutors. And so each will be able to recognize that any assertoric intervention they or others make is a proposal to extend that shared ground—a proposal to speak for all—and that they will be expected to recognize that that is the case (Stalnaker 1978; Lewis 1979b).

This observation means that in contributing to the conversation, each party will aspire to speak for all. If they expect to win the acceptance of others, they will presume on the authorization of others to purport to speak for all. And if they actually win that acceptance—if no one objects to what they say or to their presumption in saying it—they will have succeeded in speaking for all. The others will be recruited as virtual or standby supporters to the extent that they could and would have demurred had the assertion raised a red flag—had it appeared in any way dubious—and chose not to do so.

Thus, any contributor to a conversive exchange can purport to speak for all—for example, in saying that p—under circumstances where they can plausibly assume that others will agree that p. In the same way, any individual who issues an instruction to another—say, to do X—can purport to speak for all in giving that directive, if they can plausibly assume that others will support it. And as any contributor to a conversation whose intervention is not challenged by others can claim to have spoken for all, so any instructor whose directive is not queried by others can claim to have given that directive in the name of all; others would have demurred if the instruction had raised a red flag, so it is assumed, and they chose not to do so.

With these points in the background, we may return to the sort of regulation that will materialize with norms that are manifestly internalized on all sides, with each manifestly preferring that everyone conform. By the observations made, anyone who seeks to instruct another on the demands of such a norm will be enabled to do so in the name of all. And importantly they will also have a motive to present the instruction as one with that sort of communal status. By giving it that status, after all, they may hope to make a novel and deep impression on the youth or newcomer, the would-be or actual offender, whom they wish to inform or reform.[9]

---

[9] In any case, they will be presumed under the maxims of conversation discussed in Chapter 1 to aim at conveying reliable and useful information, and not to indicate the depth of social support for their instructive or corrective intervention would represent a failure to provide relevant and useful information. It would breach Paul Grice's (1975a) maxim of quantity, which requires that the cooperative

The lesson for that advisee will be that regardless of whether they are independently motivated to conform, the community requires them, as it requires everyone, to do so.[10]

Under A-triple-R norms, as we noted, the instruction or correction that any humanoid issues will have the character of counsel, in a term borrowed from Hobbes. As those norms begin to assume an A-triple-R profile, they will display the instructive character of commands rather than the advisory character of recommendations. 'COMMAND', as Hobbes (1994b, 25.2) puts it, 'is where a man saith *do this*, or *do not this*, without expecting other reason than the will of him that says it': that is, without offering the addressee any reason to obey other than that that is the will of the speaker.

Hobbes's characterization assumes that the person giving the command is doing so in their own name. But it can be extended to apply to the case envisaged here where the person who instructs or corrects another speaks in the name of all and conveys the will of all. In this case, they will speak in the name of all, giving a command or issuing an injunction that is presumptively backed by all. Thus, the message conveyed to the addressee of a regulative speech act will be: we the community order or command you to conform; this is a requirement on you as someone subject to the authority of the society.

At this point, it is clear that the regulative intervention of someone in instructing a child or newcome or would-be offender, and in correcting an actual offender, will have the status of an injunctive demand. It will impose a categorical requirement that is not conditional on the purposes that the agent may have. And it will impose a requirement in the name of an authority, casting the person as subject to that authority: namely, the society as a whole.[11]

The regulation development we have been discussing provides the second R in our promised account of I-triple-R norms; it follows the I of the initial internalization and the first R associated with the common recognition of that internalization. The third R in our account involves a further level of recognition: the common recognition of the regulation development and the depiction of the norm as having a special authorization across the community in whose name the instructor claims to speak.

---

speaker should not give less or more information than that which would serve the presumptive purposes of the conversation.

[10] This observation explains why the prudential counsellor is not taken, in our genealogy of stage 1 norms, to speak for all in advising someone that they will suffer reputationally in the event of breaching a norm. They could do this, but it would not serve any point. The counsel is designed to motivate an agent by drawing attention to what the agent's own interests demand and it need make no difference that it is offered by one or many. But the requirement or command imposed in this case will be more effective for being backed by the community rather than just a single individual.

[11] This line of argument may suggest an account of what David Enoch (2014) describes as robust reason-giving, a genus of which he takes authority to be a species.

Let it be granted in view of the regulation development that just about anyone may enjoin conformity with a suitable norm, not just in their own name, but in the name of the community. Under our assumptions about humanoid perceptiveness, the fact that this is so will be evident to all, evidently evident to all and so on in the usual hierarchy. In other words, it will be a matter of common belief among members of the community that other things being equal no one, themselves included, will object to an individual's issuing such an injunction in the name of all; everyone, themselves included, will stand behind that injunction. This means that each will acquiesce in being cast, not just as a subject of the norm enjoined, but also as a co-sponsor: as someone ready to uphold the norm.

This final development implies that the norms that are available for injunctive regulation by anyone in this or that case will now be recognized across the community as regularities that the members of the society manifestly stand by, seeing them as a source of injunctive demands on everyone. Not only will they each internalize the norms, seeing universal compliance with the norm as personally and collectively beneficial. As a matter of common awareness, they will also see universal compliance as something that they join with others in universally demanding.

The injunctive practice that these developments support is interpersonal in character, but it is ready for interiorization in the intrapersonal demands that an individual humanoid can make upon themselves. Being a sponsor of a relevant norm in tandem with others, and being subject like others to that norm, each will be positioned to speak for all in enjoining themselves, as they may enjoin any other, to conform with the norm.

Will they have any motive, however, to interiorize the practice? As a private individual they will certainly have a prudential motive to self-enjoin conformity: let them not do this, and that may lead them to defect and risk the penalty of disesteem.[12] But in co-sponsoring the norm with others, recognizing it as the demand of a societal authority with which they identify, they will also have a motive in that public identity to enjoin conformity for themselves. They would have to be of a schizoid mentality to be able to look askance at the defection of others while remaining complacent about their own.

At this point we can see that as norms in their first guise will emerge among humanoids on an A-triple-R pattern, so norms in their second will emerge on an I-triple-R pattern. The norms will assume their new injunctive status in virtue of first, the *internalization* of the norms across the community; second, the *recognition* as a matter of common awareness that the norms are widely internalized; third, the consequent availability of a form of *regulation* in which anyone can

---

[12] With the development of injunctive norms, detected offenders can expect to go down in the opinion of others in two ways. In their role as potential partners others will cast them as imprudent and unreliable. And in their role as co-sponsors of an injunctive norm that they broke, others will condemn them for their offense.

issue a command or injunction in the name of all; and fourth, the *recognition* of this availability as a manifest fact, which forces each to register that together with others in their society, they sponsor obligations to which each is subject.

The fact that A-triple-R social norms invite injunction in the command mode means that they are both categorical and authoritative: they require a person to do something, period, not just to do it if they wish to pursue this or that goal, whether of prudence, benevolence, or anything else. And they impose that requirement in the name of an authority: the community as a whole. But that does not mean, of course, that the demands they support are absolute or exceptionless. Consistently with being categorical and authoritative, as we noted, they may be outweighed in certain circumstances, as when complying with a norm requires breaching a norm of intuitively greater importance.

The fact that a norm has exceptions, however, need not mean that the humanoids will need to add those exceptions to the different norms, as in assigning exact weights for example to each. It will be enough to have the norms in existence, and their demands recognized, provided that individuals are alert to red flags indicating that there is a problem, as in the case of conflicting norms, and can achieve a degree of convergence on how the problem should be resolved. Thus, the humanoids might agree with Kant in ruling that the injunction to tell the truth is categorical and authoritative in form, yet disagree with him in holding that the information-sharing obligation may be suspended if someone asks about the whereabouts of a person they clearly intend to kill.

5.1.5 Back to the normative

With this final development in our genealogy of social norms, we are returned to the idea of the normatively obligatory discussed at the beginning of this section. Those who believe in a supreme law-giving god will take themselves and others—if there are any non-believers in the world—to be subject to injunctive obligations that correspond to the imperatives or commandments that their god is taken to impose. Similarly, as we can now see, those humanoids who belong to a relatively equal society or community in which certain social norms are manifestly internalized and invoked in regulation will take themselves and others—if again there are any outsiders within their group—to be subject to obligations that their society imposes via its norms: norms, as it happens, that they stand by with others.

In this picture of how injunctive normativity gains hold in the psychology of humanoids, it is striking that the interpersonal comes first, the intrapersonal second, reflecting the general thrust of the genealogy. This aspect of the picture comes out nicely in contrast with Kant's famous image of how human beings are engaged by the morally normative.

Kant (1998) insists that the moral laws to which people are subject are necessarily laws that they each legislate for themselves. Focusing on ideal laws that unlike social norms may fail to elicit universal compliance—we ourselves consider such requirements in the third section—Kant argues that while each person lays them down as laws for themselves, they must lay them down at the same time as laws for everyone else. Focusing on laws that already exist as social norms, the claim here is that each backs them as laws or norms, not individually but jointly with others, and that as they back them as laws for all, so they back them as laws to which they also are subject. Where Kant takes the lone individual to be the first sponsor and the first subject of each moral law, this approach takes individuals in community to be the first sponsors—this, at any rate, with socially established laws—and individuals across the community to be the first subjects.

Our story about how norms and normative demands will come to be recognize does not ascribe to humanoids a capacity to form value judgments about compliance with those norms. But this shortfall can be rectified. As we shall see in the next section, the humanoids will be disposed to commit themselves on various fronts, and in particular to commit themselves to abiding by their social norms. And being committed in such ways, as we shall see in the final section, they will be able to develop evaluative concepts for the assessment of one another's behavior—or indeed their own—in complying with such norms or indeed with other sorts of commitment.

The evaluative concepts they develop may also serve them well if we lift our standard assumptions and allow that there may be inequalities among the subgroups of humanoid society or that there may be different, relatively unequal societies. As we shall see, they can provide the humanoids with the resources for assessing different sets of social norms against one another and even with the resources for advocating the adoption of novel principles—morally ideal principles as they may be cast—in the role of social norms.

5.2 Norms and commitments

5.2.1 Avowing and reporting attitudes

We saw in Chapter 2 that it will be manifest to humanoids—a matter of common assumption—that judgment generally ensures the presence of a corresponding belief, whether a pre-existing belief that it confirms or a novel belief that it generates. The only exception is the sort of case we illustrated with the casino example where someone who judges firmly that the gambler's fallacy is a fallacy does not display in action a belief that that is so. The fact that the judgment–belief connection is generally present and manifest means, as we mentioned, that the humanoids will not just communicate that such and such when they judge and assert that that is so: they will also communicate that they believe that such and such, ratifying that belief in the process.

Drawing on regular idioms, we will say in such a case that the speaker reports the alleged fact that such and such and expresses their belief in that fact. Assuming that the speaker expresses the belief knowingly and willingly, we can describe it as an instance of avowing the belief. Where an agent may reveal or express an attitude without realizing that they are doing so, or without being happy or willing to reveal it, we may take the notion of avowing an attitude to require that it be both witting and willing.

This observation means that the humanoids will have two distinct ways in which to convey the information that they are in a certain belief state. They may avow the belief by reporting the correlated fact, say that p, or they may report their believing that p as a fact about themselves in the way that they might report any fact about the world. It turns out, however, that when evidence for the correlated fact is sufficient the more appealing way for them to communicate a belief state will be by avowing it. And, as we shall see later, the two modes of communication involving report or avowal will also be available with certain desires states, whether of preference or intention, and that in those cases too avowal will often be more appealing.

5.2.2 The appeal of avowal: a lesson

There are three reasons why the humanoids will want to avow rather than report their belief states. First, the avowal of the belief in such a case will come as easily to them as the judgment about the correlated fact; it won't require them, as a self-report might do, to search around introspectively or otherwise for independent evidence that the belief state is present within them. Second, as noted already, the avowal of the belief will convey the belief as a state that they ratify in affirming the correlated fact; they will not convey it, as a self-report might do, in the spirit of a biographical observation that would say nothing on the status, ratified or otherwise, of the belief state reported. Third, and most significantly, the avowal of the belief will be a more costly and therefore credible way of communicating the presence of the belief state than a self-report. This last consideration requires some background and elaboration.

As we know, a humanoid speaker will put their reputation on the line whenever they make an assertion, reporting a would-be fact, and so the economy of esteem will provide them with a motive for being careful and truthful in making their reports. That will be true of attitudinal self-reports as well as reports about their environment. Such a self-report might take the form, 'I think I hold that belief', or 'It seems that, yes, I do hold that belief'. But there is an important observation to add at this point that was not relevant earlier.

The observation is that insofar as they are like human beings, the humanoids will be able to salvage their reputations even when it turns out that things are not as they reported them to be. There are two salient, reputation-salvaging explanations—if you like, excuses—that a speaker can offer in the wake of being proved to have made a misreport. One is the misleading-evidence excuse that the evidence did seem to support their report at the time they made it: 'there really did seem to be fruit on the trees at twilight'. And the other is the changed-fact excuse: 'someone must have picked the fruit since I observed it'.[13]

Such reporter excuses will need to be backed up if they are to enable those who make false assertions to salvage their reputations as generally reliable reporters. Insofar as they are hard to back up, they won't offer an easy exit and will ensure the continued effectiveness of the economy of esteem in motivating speakers to be careful and truthful. But the reporter's excuses will be very readily available to explain false self-reports: these will be false insofar as the agent does not act as if they had the belief they report. In any such case the speaker can claim that the evidence about their own mind misled them or that they changed their mind since making the self-report. And it will often be hard for others to reject such a claim, bearing as it does on a realm to which the speaker will generally have readier access.

This being so, those humanoids who wish to communicate their states of belief to others can hardly hope to be taken seriously if they merely offer self-reports on those attitudes. For such reports will be too cheap to be convincing. The speaker will always be able to get off the reputational hook in a case where they do not go on to act appropriately; they will be able to cite a self-reporter excuse, invoking a misleading-mind or a changed-mind to explain the divergence between their words and their actions. How can the humanoids counter this problem, as they must do if they are to establish relationships of mutual reliance with others? Easily, as it turns out. They can resort to avowing rather than reporting their beliefs.

When a speaker avows the belief that p—that is, their being in the state of believing that p—they will do so by asserting, presumably with care and sincerity, that p. But that means, as a matter manifest to all, that they will not rely on evidence of an introspective or related kind about their own minds in making the avowal; they will rely on the worldly evidence that p, not on psychological or behavioral evidence that they hold the belief that p. Thus, by avowing the belief, they will foreclose the possibility of later explaining a failure to live up to it by holding that the evidence about their own mind misled them; it couldn't have done so, given that they didn't consult such evidence in the first place.

For these reasons, a speaker's avowal of the belief that such and such will be more costly and credible than an introspective report that they hold that belief. It will be manifest to all that by choosing to avow the belief rather than just report it, the speaker forecloses the misleading-mind excuse for any failure to act on the

---

[13] For convenience, I ignore here a third sort of excuse that someone might offer for having said something or indeed for having failed to say something: that they mistakenly took the stakes to have supported their assertion or their silence.

belief. And by denying themselves access to that excuse, they will raise the cost of communicating the belief in a corresponding measure, and can expect thereby to improve the prospect of winning the credence and confidence of others.

In avowal, as this makes clear, speakers will bet on themselves to be true to their words, where the stake in the bet is the reputation they show themselves willing to put at risk by foreclosing the misleading-mind excuse. In a game theory sense of the term, they do not just communicate their belief-state: they commit to it by showing themselves willing to pay a certain cost, should they not display that belief in action. In speaking of commitment in relation to avowal, and later in relation to pledging, we shall use the term only in this austere sense, which figures across a range of social and evolutionary theories.[14]

The commitment involved in avowing a belief will bind the agent more closely than a report and will communicate the belief much more credibly. But, of course, it will bind the agent only to a limited extent. The agent may be able to explain not acting on the belief avowed by invoking the other self-reporter excuse—that they changed their mind since making the avowal—or by invoking a distinct obstacle as an excuse: say, that they were blocked from acting as it required or that they were deceived about its relevance.

So much for the appeal that the avowal of belief will have for the humanoids. But it turns out that insofar as avowal is appealing for them, so will three further initiatives be appealing too, and we need now to look at these. As the humanoids will see the appeal of avowing their beliefs, so they are bound to see the appeal of seeking when feasible: first, to avow their personal desire states as well as their states of belief; second, to avow beliefs and desires in a virtual or standby manner rather than in an active mode; and third, to go beyond avowing certain attitudes to pledging them also: to committing to the attitudes in a way that forecloses the changed-mind as well as the misleading-mind excuse. These developments are going to be so attractive for the humanoids, and so accessible, that it is hard to see how they could fail to materialize.

5.2.3 Extending the lesson, 1: avowing desire

The reason why humanoids will choose to avow and commit to their belief-states, when evidence for the correlated facts is appropriate, will also motivate them to

---

[14] For an overview of the literature on commitment in social science, see (Nesse 2001). There is a large literature in evolutionary theory on the linkage between expense and honesty in animal signaling, which is a continuing subject of debate. This is often expressed in the handicap principle (Zahavi and Zahavi 1999). According to this principle, roughly, the relative expense of a wasteful or handicapping signal—say, the peacock's tail, the exaggerated jump of the gazelle—conveys the wealth of resources at the animal's disposal and its significance for the presumptive recipient: for the peahen in the first example, for the predator lion in the second. See (Maynard Smith and Harper 2004). In such cases the the expense is undertaken non-intentionally by nature, of course, where in the case of concern to us it is undertaken intentionally by the relevant individual.

avow and commit to desire-states, when supportive desiderata are in evidence. By registering publicly the desiderata that support a general mode of action in comparison with alternatives, they will commit to a preference for that activity; and by registering publicly the desiderata that support one option in a certain choice or type of choice by comparison with the other options, they will commit to an intention or policy to take that option. Or at least that will be the case in the absence of contextual indicators that they are merely ruminating on those possibilities, not looking at them with a view to supporting or making a choice.

The assertions of the humanoids in such a case may leave a good deal to be understood from context. For example, in the case of a preference they may merely assert that, yes, teaching would be a fulfilling vocation; in the case of an intention, that yes, helping out this person now would be the kind thing to do. In either case, they may be presumed to judge that the desideratum they cite silences other considerations that might argue against the favored possibility, or to judge that that desideratum makes the crucial difference in weighing up the competing considerations that favor the different alternatives.

While avowal will always be costlier and more credible than a self-report, the avowal of the preference is going to be cheaper than that of the intention, since its presence or absence will not show up so sharply in how the speaker behaves. By their nature, as noted earlier, preferences have looser behavioral implications than intentions, so that it may be unclear whether an agent fails to enact a preference they had communicated: they may always invoke the presence of countervailing desiderata present in the context of action that were not there in the context of avowal. The humanoids may remedy this, however, by taking any preference that an agent avows—and so any preference that they themselves avow—to be a reliable preference or, to reuse a now familiar word, a robust preference: that is, a preference that may be expected to remain effective across a range of contextually salient variations on the context of avowal. This will help to raise the cost of avowing a preference and to make it more credible.[15]

One final observation on the avowal of beliefs and desires. Given the manifest appeal of avowal in each case, it may be expected that the humanoids will often treat utterances that look syntactically like self-reports as avowals. Asked about whether p, or even about whether they believe that p, some may respond with the words: 'I believe that p'. And in many circumstances that will be taken to avow the attitude that 'I believe that p' strictly reports. The same will hold plausibly of many utterances that look syntactically like reports of the person's preference or

---

[15] This difference in the utility of avowal with desire-states has a parallel in the case of beliefs. If a humanoid avows a belief that it is likely that p, that will be less costly and credible than the avowal of a belief that p, period, since the presence or absence of the probabilistic belief will not show so clearly in the actions of that speaker. In such a case, the motive to avow the belief rather than just report it will have a radically diminished force. This consideration may complement the case, outlined in the last section of Chapter 2, for risking reliability in choosing to be a ready interlocutor: it will argue for resisting the temptation to resort frequently to probabilistic assertions.

intention. This is another example of how we can expect reasoned interpretation to build on context as well as convention in enabling the humanoids to make sense of one another's utterances.

5.2.4 Extending the lesson, 2: avowal, virtual as well as active

The second way in which the lesson about how avowal extends takes us back again to some observations we made in discussing the idea of common ground. Suppose that some humanoids are engaged in an exchange of information, debating about how things stand, perhaps out of a wish to know more about imminent opportunities or dangers, perhaps just for the sake of building up a sense of the world in this or that dimension. As each purports to give further information in an ongoing exchange, their assertion may be questioned by others and, whether questioned or not, may or may not be rejected. But, as we saw, it will be a matter of common assumption that if no one rejects such a proposal about how things stand, then everyone holds the belief involved (Stalnaker 1978; Lewis 1979b).

This observation about assertion, such as the assertion that p, teaches a lesson about avowal as well: specifically, about the avowal of the belief that p that such an assertion would constitute. It means that when any participant makes an assertion and avows a belief in its content, they will purport, not just to say something that they expect others to accept, but to avow a belief that they expect others to stand by. They will purport not just to speak for themselves, as we put it earlier—not just to avow a belief that they individually hold—but to speak for others too: that is, to avow a belief as one that they each already hold or will be stimulated to hold by the speaker's testimony. The individual will presume to avow the belief in the name of the group, as we might put it; and, if no one objects, what they say will go down among all the parties as something they each manifestly avow: something to which they are each committed.

This means that when anyone takes the risk of purporting to avow a belief in the name of all, and no one else demurs, then by dint of not demurring, those others will be as committed to the belief as an active, individual avowal would have committed them. If they could have indicated that they did not go along with what the speaker said, or with how the speaker presumed to speak for all—we say more on the could-have condition later—then their failure to do so in the context of the exchange will portray them as parties committed equally with the speaker to the belief expressed.

In such a case, then, the control of other interlocutors over the commitment made in their name by the speaker will be of a standby or virtual character. It will materialize by virtue of their not demurring at what the presumptive speaker says, or to the belief to which the speaker thereby made a commitment, given that they would presumably have demurred if they had seen any indication—any red flag indicating—that the assertion or avowal was questionable.

In this sort of standby case, the others will go along with the speaker's avowal of belief on the grounds, presumptively, that the evidence for the fact correlated with the belief was sufficient to support it, at least given the relevant stakes; this may or may not be due, in whole or in part, to their taking the speaker to be reliable. And so, it will be evident to all, evidently evident to all, and so on, that none of them will be able to invoke the misleading-mind excuse for failing to act later as that belief would require. Not having consulted the evidence of their own mind in going along with the speaker, they will not be able to claim that that evidence misled them.

As the member of a group may speak for others when avowing beliefs, so they may also do that when avowing desires, at least under suitable conditions. To gesture at those conditions, they will do this with desires only when there is a high degree of convergence among group members about both the presence and the weight of relevant desiderata and only when there is sufficient coordination between them for it to make sense for all of them to be disposed to act—whether individually, jointly, or within an organized group—as those desiderata would make it rational to act.[16] When someone presumes in this way to speak for all, each will be implicated in the commitment insofar as it is the case that had they found the commitment unappealing—had it raised a red flag for them—then they would demurred.

One final observation. The reason why an individual will be implicated by what someone says in their name, whether by way of avowing a belief or a desire, is that the speaker will manifestly elicit in others the expectation that unless that individual gives a contrary indication—unless they demur—they must go along with that commitment. But it may be a matter of manifest expectation among others that an individual will be happy with such an assignment of attitude, even when no one has elicited that expectation by speaking in the individual's name. This may be the case, for example, when the evidence for a particular belief is manifest to all or when the desiderative stimulus for holding by a certain desire—say, the evidence that a third person is in dire need—is a matter of common awareness.

In such a situation the individual will also commit in a virtual or standby way to the attitude manifestly expected unless they take active steps to indicate that they do not actually hold it. Thus, virtual commitment may materialize either on the basis of what a would-be spokesperson says about the individual or on the basis of what manifestly goes without saying. It may materialize by dint of another's active initiative or as a result of what passively emerges as a matter of common assumption.

---

[16] For more on these conditions, see (Pettit 2018a), and for background, see (List and Pettit 2011).

5.2.5 Extending the lesson, 3: pledging, active and virtual

But not only will the lesson about the avowal of beliefs lead the humanoids to avow desires as well, and to avow both sorts of attitudes in a virtual as well as an active fashion. Turning to a third way in which the lesson extends, it will also lead the humanoids to resort as appropriate to a second form of commitment: the pledging as distinct from the avowing of an attitude. Someone will pledge an attitude, as we understand the idea here, by committing to it in a stronger way than mere avowal would involve, specifically, by foreclosing access, not just to a misleading-mind excuse for failing to display the attitude in action, but also to a changed-mind excuse for such a failure.

Pledging will not make sense with beliefs, since belief is evidence-sensitive, and no one can be sure in advance of all relevant data that later evidence will not lead them to change their minds.[17] Pledging will make sense with preferences to the extent that someone can pledge to give a certain weight to alternatives that display some desiderata. But it is unlikely to have a point, as we saw in the case of avowal, unless it takes the form of pledging to give a really significant weight to such desiderata. In other words, it must involve pledging, not just to preferring in the current context that those desiderata carry the day, but to preferring that they do so robustly across a variety of situations where there are contextually salient competitors.[18]

By contrast with these cases, pledging will make straightforward sense, and have an obvious point, with intentions and policies. Acting on an intention or policy pledged will make sense for an agent whenever they are likely to remain responsive over the relevant period to an enduring consideration that will support action: the consideration is not subject, as we might say, to a sunset clause. In most cases, at least the following consideration is likely to enjoy such a continuing presence: the fact that by acting in the specific way indicated, the individual will establish a reputation for reliability. In appropriate circumstances that agent, and those to whom the agent makes the pledge, can be assured that that individual will not change their mind to the extent that they are assured of the lasting importance to them of the desideratum of proving true to their word.

The humanoids will have a powerful motive in many contexts to pledge their intentions and policies and indeed, in the sense explained, their robust preferences.

---

[17] The humanoids, by this observation, will be unable to commit to believing even logical, apparently definitional propositions insofar as the weight of evidence across the whole web of their beliefs may argue for altering the way of thinking those propositions embed. But while they may be unable to commit to beliefs of this kind, they will be able to commit to a policy of interpreting new discoveries in light of one or another framework of logical assumptions, as they may commit to making judgments in light of available data. On these matters, see (Quine 1970; Quine and Ullian 1978; Priest 2008).

[18] The discussion of pledging in the case of beliefs, preferences, and intentions breaks from that defended by (Pettit 2018a) in a number of ways; it does so most significantly, in allowing for the pledging of suitably robust preferences, a feature that will be relevant in the next chapter. The impact of the change on the overall view defended, however, is not particularly deep.

Such a pledge will be more costly and so more credible than a corresponding avowal. It will foreclose the changed-mind as well as the misleading-mind excuse and it ought thereby to increase the assurance of those to whom the pledge is made that the agent will live up to their word.

But not only will it be appealing for the humanoids to pledge such attitudes: it will also be relatively easy. The humanoids will have ready access to a means of indicating that they are not just avowing but pledging the attitude. Suppose someone avows an intention to go to a party, saying, 'That party should be fun', or 'I'll be there'. If another is unhappy that the avowal leaves open the possibility that the person will change their mind, the speaker can strengthen the avowal by adding, 'You can depend on it, I'll be there.' That would clearly constitute a pledge and, if pledging becomes common, we may expect the humanoids to mark it in a specific word or phrase, corresponding to our word 'pledge' or 'promise'.

While avowing an attitude forecloses appeal to a misleading-mind excuse for not displaying the attitude in action, it does not foreclose appeal to the changed-mind excuse or to an excusing obstacle for any failure. Pledging an attitude will foreclose both forms of self-reporter excuse—the changed-mind as well as the misleading-mind excuse—but it will resemble the avowal of any attitude, of course, in not foreclosing excusing obstacles that lie beyond agential control. The individual who pledges to be at a party, as in the example just used, will be able to excuse their failure to attend if they can explain, for example, that they were obstructed in some way: they broke a leg, they misunderstand the date of the party, a family member fell ill, or whatever.

As avowal can assume a virtual as well as an active mode, so the same is true of pledging. With a suitably coordinated group, we may expect someone to be able to make a pledge, not just in their own name, but also in the name of others. Presuming to speak for others—with success manifestly depending on the absence of a demurral—they may say, 'That party will be fun', or, 'Depend on it: we'll be at the party', and make what counts in the context as a pledge. The context may be one where someone within or outside the group wants to know what everybody is going to do, for example, not just what the speaker means to do.

As in the case of avowal, others in any collectivity will be committed in a standby manner by their failure to balk or demur—we assume for the moment that demurral is an available option—when someone presumes to make a pledge in the name of each. It will be manifest to all that the failure of others to demur at the time of the pledge was based on their sharing in the considerations moving the speaker, and in their taking those considerations to support a pledge on their part. They will not be able to cite the missing-leading mind excuse for a failure to act appropriately later, since they will not have gone along with the speaker because of the evidence about their own attitudes or minds. And they will not be able to cite the changed-mind excuse for such a failure either, since the salient desideratum that made the pledge attractive—presumably, a consideration without a sunset clause—will remain in place come the time for action: for example, the desideratum of proving true to the robust preference, or the intention or policy, advertised.

But not only may someone find themselves pledged to a robust preference, or to an intention or policy, by not demurring at what another says in their name: that is, by acquiescing in the manifest expectation, elicited by the spokesperson, that the individual spoken for will not excuse any failure by appeal to a self-reporter excuse. They may also be pledged by acquiescing in such a manifest expectation, even when the expectation is not elicited by a would-be spokesperson but appears on a passive basis: it just happens to be a matter of common belief that the person is expected to act in a certain way and not to appeal to a self-reporter excuse for failing to do so.

It may be a matter of common assumption in a situation of communal danger, for example—say, the danger of a flood—that each will play a part in helping out: they will not free ride on the efforts of others. Under that assumption, no one who fails to demur in such a situation—more later on the possibility of demurring—will be plausibly able to excuse a failure to provide any help by appealing to a misleading-mind or changed-mind excuse. If they say nothing to demur at the assumption, then they will be taken on a standby basis to be pledged to play their part.

5.2.6 The case of norms

We may assume on these grounds that the humanoids will evolve a practice and a concept of commitment in our sense of that term. They will consciously avow beliefs and other attitudes and consciously pledge attitudes like their robust preferences, their intentions, and their policies. They may do so in the active sense in which they speak for themselves individually or indeed for others as well. And they will certainly do so in the virtual sense in which they do not demur at the manifest expectation of others that they will display the commitment, whether that expectation materializes spontaneously or is elicited by a would-be spokesperson.

Their access to the practice and concept of commitment will enable the humanoids to think in a novel way about the collectively beneficial norms that evolve among them, by our argument of the last section. The existence of such a norm will make it unsurprising that any individual humanoid will intend to comply with it themselves; will have a robust preference for universal compliance; and will embrace a policy of upholding it in the sense of being ready to stand by suitable norm-related instructions or corrections that anyone might issue in the name of all. That was the lesson of the first section. But we can now see reason why they will not just be moved by such desires but be pledged to them as well: be pledged, in effect, to acting on them.

To be pledged to an intention to personally comply with a norm, to a robust preference for universal compliance or to a policy of upholding the norm in tandem with others is to foreclose an appeal to either a misleading-mind or a changed-mind excuse for failing to display that desire in action. To be virtually pledged to the desire will consist in the agent's being pledged on the basis of having failed to demur—more on this condition in a moment—at the manifest expectation on the part of others that they will act on that desire, and not appeal to a misleading- or changed-mind excuse for any failure.

Assuming that a certain collectively beneficial norm, say of information-sharing, has emerged among the humanoids, others are bound to assume that each individual will have the intention of conforming to it themselves, if only for reputational reasons; that they will robustly prefer that others conform to it, because of the benefits for each of universal conformity; and that they will have a policy of standing by the norm—upholding it—because of those same benefits. At least that will be so, in general; there may always be exceptional cases where the individual's self-interest, for example, may get in the way.

When the individual acquiesces in such a manifest ascription of desires, they will effectively pledge themselves to those attitudes. First, others will ascribe that desire to them—and they will acquiesce in that ascription—on grounds of their manifest exposure to the relevant desiderata. And second, others will take the desire ascribed to have the character of a reliable intention or policy—and they will acquiesce in that ascription—on the grounds that the desiderata at work are manifestly enduring and lack a sunset clause. Appeal to a misleading-mind excuse will be ruled out on the first count, appeal to a changed-mind excuse will be ruled out on the second.

The observation extends beyond the norm of information-sharing, of course, so that the upshot is of general significance. Once collectively beneficial social norms get to be established in humanoid society—this, under the pressures charted in the first section—the humanoids will each be virtually pledged to an intention to conform to them, to a robust preference that others conform as well, and to a policy of upholding those norms, being ready to stand by anyone who issues norm-related instructions or corrections in the name of all.

5.2.7 The could-demur requirement

We have argued at various points in this chapter that someone can get to be assigned an attitude, even to support an avowal or pledge, by not demurring at what is manifestly expected of them, whether the manifest expectation is triggered by what someone says in their name, or is spontaneously generated. But on every occasion where we made that claim, we noted an accompanying assumption: that it is possible for the person to demur and that their not demurring—their acquiescence in the expectation held of them—represents a choice on their part; it is not forced upon them by any sort of natural necessity, for example, or social pressure.

The assumed requirement in each case is that the agent enjoys discretion over whether to acquiesce in the expectation or to demur. Thus, in taking someone to acquiesce in being construed as avowing or pledging an attitude on this or that matter, others must assume that the individual could have done something other than acquiesce: they could in some sense have demurred at the expectation. But is that assumption justified in the various cases relevant? That depends, as we shall now see, on what is taken to be necessary for someone to demur at a manifest expectation that another makes.

On a strong interpretation, demurring at an expectation will mean rejecting or resisting it, and there certainly are cases where people acquiesce in an expectation when they could just as easily have rejected it. This will presumably hold in the case of the open conversation where interlocutors seek to identify the common ground between them: to establish what they are each prepared to assert or accept, ratifying and avowing shared beliefs and, if relevant, shared preferences or intentions. It is in the nature of such an open enterprise that each is taken to have personal discretion over whether to agree or disagree with what another says: whether to acquiesce in their expectation of agreement or to reject it outright.

But there are other cases among those rehearsed, where that will not be so. Take the manifest expectation among humanoids that in the normal run of things each of them will comply with shared norms, robustly prefer that others comply with them too, and uphold those norms in the sense of being ready to stand by anyone who invokes a norm in the name of all. Or take the manifest, stronger expectation, that each of them will be pledged to suitable desires on those three fronts, having effectively set aside misleading-mind or changed-mind excuses for any failure to act on those attitudes. It may well be in a case like this that if the individual were to reject or resist that expectation, they would face the prospect of being shunned or ostracized, even perhaps derided. And it may be, therefore, that the option of rejecting the expectation would carry a cost sufficient to inhibit any presumptively ordinary agent: that, in that sense, it would be an unacceptable alternative (Olsaretti 2004).

This raises a problem, since it suggests that if the humanoids individually go along with established norms, meeting communal expectations, they may do so under the sort of social pressure that should inhibit others from taking them to be pledged to satisfy and uphold the norms. It suggests that their acquiescence to communal expectations will testify, not to a virtual commitment on their part, but to their fear of breaking ranks with others. Someone will count as committing to a certain line of action, by our account, only if they choose to commit themselves. And if they are to count as choosing to commit, then they must have been free to do something else instead: in this case, as it seems, to reject or resist the expectations that are held of them.[19]

---

[19] This sort of objection is raised by Rae Langton (2007) to a similar line that I had defended elsewhere; for an attempt to respond, see (Pettit 2007a).

The problem raised here is not as daunting as it may seem. Imagine that in the case of shared norms it will often be unacceptably costly for an individual to reject the manifest expectations of others, breaking ranks with them. Even in that case the individual may be able to demur at the expectations in a different, weaker mode, thereby meeting the could-demur requirement.

Suppose that in view of the sorts of desiderata listed earlier a particular individual acquiesces without complaint in the manifest expectation that they will comply with a norm, prefer that all comply in the same way, and uphold the norm in dealing with newcomers or offenders. Assume furthermore that they would face such an unacceptable cost if they rejected those expectations, adopting the role of a rebel or renegade, that rejection is not a viable option. They would still count as meeting the could-demur requirement if there were some alternative to acquiescing without complaint. And in most realistic scenarios, there is such an alternative: they can acquiesce under protest, displaying their reluctance in any of a range of ways, subtle or unsubtle, at least to their intimates and friends.

The could-demur requirement does not mean that the individual who goes along without complaint with the norm-related expectations of others must be capable of not going along with the norm if they are reasonably taken to endorse those expectations and to pledge a desire to meet them. It only means that there must be something other than going along without complaint that they are capable of doing. And obviously there is, since they may go along under a form of protest that they make clear to others.

Thus, assuming that the humanoids go happily along with the relevant expectations of others in view of the benefits associated with doing so—assuming they go along without complaint—they may be taken to sign up to the pledges that correspond to those expectations. They will count as being virtually pledged to the intention to comply with each norm, to the robust preference for universal compliance, and to the policy of upholding the norm appropriately. The could-demur requirement need not raise a problem for the general line we are taking in our genealogy of commitment.

5.2.8 Self-commitment

We have been looking in this section at how the humanoids will be able and willing to speak for themselves or even for a group of individuals, committing in avowals and pledges to the attitudes they communicate. That focus raises a question about commitments to the self that will become more prominent in the final chapter. Is there any sense in which the humanoids are likely to be able to make commitments, not to others, but to themselves? When they make sincere commitments to others, there is clearly a sense in which they commit to themselves to act as those commitments require; otherwise, the commitments would hardly count as sincere. But is there a sense in which they might make commitments to themselves alone?

They will certainly be able to make avowals to themselves, and will do so willy nilly. Someone will publicly avow a belief that p by asserting that p, as we have seen, and publicly avow a desire for X by asserting in a suitable context that X uniquely realizes some desideratum; in each case, a world-directed assertion will constitute a mind-revealing avowal. But the internal correlate of sincere assertion is judgment. And so, a person who makes a purely private judgment that p or that X is attractive in this or that respect will privately commit themselves to the corresponding belief or desire; they will avow the attitude for themselves alone.

Reporting that attitude to themselves—perhaps judging on an introspective basis that they hold it—will allow them to think with equanimity that a later failure to display the attitude shows that they got themselves wrong. But if they fail to act on the belief or desire when they had avowed it to themselves—when they had made up their minds that p, for example, or that X-ing is attractive—they cannot view the failure in such a relaxed manner: it was a failure, after all, to act as the world, in their earlier judgment, required them to act. They may think, of course, that they had gotten the world wrong and change their mind about whether p or about whether X is attractive. But that will be to invoke an explanation for the failure that an avowal does not rule out.

There is no problem, then, about how the humanoids might make avowals for themselves alone; this will happen by virtue of their making judgments for themselves alone. And as the humanoids will have a motive to make judgments for themselves, as we saw earlier, so they will have a motive to make corresponding avowals for themselves alone. But what now about pledges for themselves alone? Will they have a means and a motive for making such pledges too? Will they be able to privately self-commit in that stronger sense?

With pledging in mind, Thomas Hobbes (1994b, 26.6) argues famously that the idea of self-commitment in any literal sense of the term is incoherent: it is not 'possible for any person to be bound to himself, because he that can bind can release; and therefore he that is bound to himself only is not bound'. In a social pledge, so Hobbes suggests, an agent like one of our humanoids puts themselves under the power of the addressee, since that individual may register and advertise the agent's unreliability if the pledge is broken. In self-pledging, by contrast, the agent will not expose themselves to a similar sanction: they will be bound only to themselves and that, in Hobbes's view, will mean not being bound at all.

This is hardly a persuasive claim. If a humanoid makes a pledge to themselves to tell the truth, however inconvenient, or to remain faithful to a partner regardless of temptation, or just to stick with a difficult diet, then any failure to live up to that commitment will cause them to be disappointed in themselves: to berate themselves for failing in that way. They will be unable to cite a misleading-mind excuse in explaining the failure, as they might have done had they merely predicted that they would behave in the relevant manner. And they will be unable to cite a changed-mind excuse, had they merely formed an intention to act in that way. They will have formed a resolution in making such a self-commitment, not just formed an intention. And failing to act on a resolution carries its own intrapersonal sanction.

Self-pledging of the kind envisaged will clearly have an appeal for the humanoids. Making pledges for themselves alone will enable them to plan and control their own future dispositions to act. They will adopt an attitude in self-pledging such that they will be exposed to a distinctive sanction, should they not live up to the pledge: the sanction of being disappointed in themselves. By exposing themselves to that sanction, they will be able to give force and effect to the self-pledging or resolution, and provide themselves at any time with an ability to control for how they will perform in future. They will bind themselves at later times to their current self, although the bond will surely be less constraining than that engaged in social commitment.

While these observations give us a reason to reject or modify Hobbes's claim about the impossibility of committing to oneself, however, there is something in the neighborhood of his claim that is likely to be true of the humanoids in our genealogy and true, if the parallel holds, of human beings. This is that the practice of commitment, and the concept of commitment that will surely emerge in tandem among the humanoids, presupposes the social life that we have been charting. There is every reason to hold that in raising the cost and credibility of their communications with one another, as they have a motive and means to do, the humanoids will be able to conceive of commitment in a way that allows them to make sense of self-commitment. But there is little or no reason to think that they would develop this capacity or this concept in the absence of a social life.[20]

5.3 Commitment and value

We have seen that humanoids will be led as individuals, whether actively or in a virtual fashion, to avow certain beliefs, preferences, and intentions and to pledge robust preferences as well as intentions and policies. And we have seen that the regime of collectively beneficial norms that is likely to be established among humanoids will require them to make virtual pledges to comply with those norms themselves, to robustly prefer universal compliance, and to uphold the norms, demanding compliance from others.

---

[20] Social commitment may assume an active or a standby form. Is that also true of self-commitment? I set aside that question here, and in later discussion, because nothing much turns on it and the resolution is not obvious.

In this final section, we situate the practice and notion of valuing in relation to the norms and the commitments already in the picture. We show that the picture we have developed implies that the humanoids will value satisfying and upholding the norms to which they are committed, treating the desiderata that support the norms as values shared in their lives. But before we introduce shared values of that kind, we will look at valuing more generally, first as it appears among humans and then as it is likely to appear among our humanoid counterparts.[21]

5.3.1 Value in human life

The notion of valuing is closely connected in our own human usage with that of desiring. There are a range of similarities worth noting.

- As desiring connects with choice, so valuing does as well.
- As we can desire any of a variety of things, so equally we can value them.
- As we may desire things from an individual or group or other perspective, so we may value things from one or another standpoint.
- As desiring in our usage may assume the form of a preference, an intention or a policy, so valuing may vary in a similar way.
- As we desire things for the desiderata they promise to realize, so we value things for desiderata to which we give importance, casting them as values.
- As we give different weights to distinct desiderata and vary among ourselves in how we weight them, so we may do the same with values.
- And as any desiderata may conflict with one another within any agent, so too the agent's values may compete with one another in a similar fashion.

How then does desiring differ from valuing? Well, by all accounts what a human agent desires may or may not coincide with what they value: they may desire something and not value it, or value something and not desire it. And by all accounts this is not a competition that the agent should view with detachment, waiting to see which side wins out. It will count as a victory for them as an agent if what they value prevails, and a failure if what they desire is triumphant.

There are various accounts in the literature that seek to explain the role of valuing or some cognate in relation to desire. Although he does not use the terminology of value, Harry Frankfurt (1971) may be taken to argue, roughly, that to value something is to desire it and at the same time to desire to be moved by that desire (Watson 1975). Others, like Michael Bratman (2000), hold instead that to

---

[21] The discussion in this section draws heavily on the discussion in Chapter 5 of (Pettit 2018a), as other parts of the chapter draw on Chapter 4. As in other parts of this chapter, however, the discussion follows a similar line—one supporting the same general view—but not exactly the same line.

value something is to desire it from the perspective of a planning, self-governing agent, not just from a more temporally restricted viewpoint. Yet others, focusing in particular on moral valuation, hold like Michael Smith (1994), that to value something is to believe that your suitably idealized self, if not you as you actually are, would want you as you actually are to adopt it.[22]

All of these accounts seek in different ways to explain, on the one side, why valuing can lead to action in the manner of desire and, on the other, why it is going to count as a sort of victory for an agent to act on what they value rather than a conflicting desire. This will count as a victory on Frankfurt's account insofar as higher-order desires are supposed to reflect the identity of the agent better than lower-order, on Bratman's to the extent that an agent's long-term plans are given priority over passing desires, and on Smith's insofar as an agent may be expected, even as a matter of rationality, to give a special place to the desires for how they should act here and now that they would have, were they ideally rational and informed.

It is time to look now at how the humanoids might come to develop a practice of valuing, conceiving of it as something distinct in appropriate ways from desire, and at how they might develop a corresponding sense of the valuable—or equivalently, the desirable—as distinct from a sense of the merely attractive. It turns out that such a development is close to inevitable and that it offers a novel view of why an agent might want to prioritize what they value over what they desire.

5.3.2 From desiring to valuing

The key that gives valuing an entry into the lives of the humanoids is provided by the practice of commitment, specifically, that of pledging, and more specifically still, that of pledging to desire something. Suppose that an individual pledges, actively or virtually, to one among a number of courses or types of action they might take—pledges to a suitable intention or policy—whether in their individual identity or as the member of a group, and whether in committing to others or to themselves. In virtue of making that pledge they are likely to find, come the time for action, that the pledged desire, as we might describe it, is not a desire that they are spontaneously moved by at that moment. They may experience a desire at that time that conflicts with the desire—the intention or policy—to which they are committed.

The striking thing about the conflict they will face in such a case is that it bears a strong resemblance to what we would describe in our own experience as a conflict between what we value and what we desire. Suppose that a humanoid pledges to a certain dietary policy, whether in committing to a medical advisor,

---

[22] For a very helpful overview of the idea of valuing, see (Scheffler 2010, 15–40).

or self-committing in a private resolution. The committed policy or desire for the diet is very likely to conflict on many occasions with the experience of the desire that goes with feeling hungry or with having a yen for something sweet. And it will relate to the experienced desire in just the way that we take valuing to relate to desiring.

In particular, the committed desire will conflict with the experienced desire in such a way that acting on the first will represent a victory on the agent's part, acting on the second a failure. Acting on the committed desire will count as an achievement insofar as it shows that the agent lives up to their character as a commissive being. They stand with the enduring identity to which they aspire in making the commitment and resist an inclination that must count by contrast as a temptation: an inclination such that giving in to it would be a betrayal of the commitment.

In view of the role played by committed desires in relation to experienced desires, we may describe the humanoid individual in this case as valuing the diet while having a desire that would lead them to break it. They will count as valuing the diet regardless of what they do. But they may or may not live up to what they value in how they behave: they may resist the temptation or succumb to it.

In committing to a desire like this, the agent pledges to keep the diet or, as we also say, pledges an intention or policy to do so. That means, as we understand pledging, that if they fail to live up to valuing the diet, they will be unable to excuse a later failure, whether in relating to others or to themselves, by claiming that they were misled about their policy or that they had changed their mind since forming it. But it does not mean, of course, that they must stick to the diet, no matter what transpires. They may cease to value dieting, withdrawing the pledge implied. They may claim still to value the dietary plan when failing to keep it due to an excusing obstacle that the pledge did not foreclose: say, a temporary digestive condition that made it almost impossible to keep the pledge. And they may claim still to value it when failing to act because of a conflict with something they value even more: say, not disappointing a generous host.

5.3.3 From desiderata to values

When a humanoid agent commits in this sense to desiring a particular option or type of option—when they pledge an intention or policy—they will do so on the basis of the desiderata they see in that alternative. Those desiderata must weigh strongly in favor of the adopted alternative, if the agent is operating rationally, and they must be desiderata that the agent expects to retain that weight when it comes time to act on the intention or policy: as we put it earlier, they must not be subject to a sunset clause.

If desiderata are to serve in this demanding role then the individual must have a robust preference for realizing them: a robust preference for scenarios in which they are realized over scenarios where they are not. Consider again the case of the diet. If the commitment is rational, then there must be a desideratum such as losing weight or reducing cardiac stress that the agent robustly prefers to realize. That desideratum must present as a property that will retain its motivating power robustly over contextually salient situations where rival attractors pull in other directions.

If committing to an alternative in a choice or type of choice means valuing it, then it is natural to identify the robustly preferred desiderata that move agents to make such pledges as their values. Valuing an option or policy will amount in human terms to taking it as the right or appropriate option—the thing to do—by the agent's lights. The desiderata that robustly support the agent's valuing of the option—their pledge to realize it—will count in that case as the values that matter to the agent in that choice: the values that by the agent's own lights make the option the right one for them to choose.

The humanoids may find it intelligible that someone should act on certain values only if, as we noted in the case of any desiderata, they can imagine being personally moved by them. But consistently with that being the case, as we saw, they may differ from one another in many of the desiderata that robustly appeal to them and count as values; those factors may vary in the degree and robustness of their attraction for different parties. The humanoids will likely hold personal values that differ in that way, as we humans differ in the values associated with our hobbies and projects, and they will certainly hold values that differ insofar as they reflect their different family and other affiliations. As we shall see when we reintroduce social norms to the discussion, however, they are also likely to share some values, and indeed to do so as a matter of common awareness.

The values on which we have been focusing are the practical values that we may expect to shape how humanoids choose to conduct their lives. But the desiderata that robustly appeal to them will also include epistemic desiderata that bear on how to make their judgments, how to reason, and so on. They will presumably treat it as appropriate that they should check the judgments they tend to make by reference to the support—the stakes-sensitive support—provided by evidence, that they should seek to rectify any inconsistencies that they find in their beliefs, and that they should be open to identifying the implications of their judgments for questions that they currently take to be open. Their robust preference for realizing such properties will show up in the epistemic strategies to which they pledge themselves.

On this account, it is because of robustly supporting the agent's valuings—their pledged intentions or policies—that certain desiderata count as values; in relying on them in this way the agent displays a robust preference for realizing them. That means, of course, that individual humanoids, like human beings, may miss some of the values that actually move them or mistakenly believe that they are moved by other values that do not shape their behavior. They may fail to identify, or even misidentify, the desiderata that really matter to them: the desiderata that deserve to be counted as their values.

In the cases which we have been considering, a humanoid individual's values show up as the robustly supportive desiderata on which they actually rely in pledging to more specific intentions or policies. But an agent may also be proactive on this front. They may select certain desiderata and invest them with the status of values, pledging to robustly prefer them: that is, pledging to let them play a robust role in shaping the pledges they make at the level of intention or policy. An individual may assign great value to the welfare of their family, robustly preferring to help them, without ever having occasion to pledge a robust preference for that welfare. But they may have to rely on reflection and active pledging to invest a property like candor with colleagues with the status of a value in their lives. Speaking of someone's values in ordinary human usage—and, we may assume, in the usage that the humanoids are likely to develop—is ambiguous to the extent that it may refer to those properties that are robustly effective in the person's psychology or to those properties—likely, a set that overlaps massively with the first—that the person commits to robustly preferring.[23]

5.3.4 Values and social norms

As we have seen, individual humanoids may vary widely in the desiderata that they treat as values, differing in the perspectives within which those desiderata figure as values. But they are also likely to share certain values. And these will certainly include values that fit with their commitments, documented in the preceding sections, to satisfy and uphold established, collectively beneficial social norms.

As we saw in the first section, various social norms will appear initially as a result of the humanoids adjusting to one another out of a strategic concern for their own reputation, thereby generating regularities that are recognized across the society and invoked in prudential regulation. Consequently, it will have to be a robustly attractive desideratum for each—a prudential value—that they should enjoy a reputation fit to induce the reliance of others. But, as we also saw in the first section, their social norms will attain an injunctive status among the humanoids and this development will make room for collective as well as prudential values to assume a role in their psychology.

---

[23] That ambiguity is likely to generate the sort of puzzle raised by Mark Twain's story of Huck Finn's failure to betray his friend, Jim, a runaway slave. Huck fails to act on something to which he commits as an overriding value—the property of abiding by the law—acting instead on what really is a value in his make-up, albeit one that he does not recognize: keeping faith with his friend, Jim. By this account, his failure consists essentially in a failure to recognize that he values his friendship with Jim more than he values fidelity to the law (Arpaly 2015; Joshi 2017).

In virtue of this development, the humanoids will come to be pledged on a virtual or standby basis, not just to complying with such beneficial social norms, but also to preferring universal compliance, and to upholding or sponsoring the norms: this, by standing with anyone who enjoins them in the name of all. Qua sponsors of the norms, the humanoids will assume a standpoint from within which compliance, their own and that of others, will present as valuable as such, not just valuable conditionally on its serving their own prudential interests, though it will often serve those interests as well.

What robustly motivating desiderata—what collective values—will be relevant in supporting the humanoids in their pledge to a policy of upholding these norms? They will certainly include the robustly attractive benefits, recognized or unrecognized, that make the relevant norms collectively beneficial. As we saw earlier, the relevant values will include, first, the benefit for each of being treated benevolently or cooperatively in the different encounters governed by the norms; second, the benefit of their enjoying a robust form of such treatment on the part of any other; and third, the benefit of their enjoying the manifest status of being secured in that way by their society.

We noted in the first section that while the social norms that are given an injunctive status among the humanoids will be enjoined as authoritative, there are bound to be possible circumstances where a red flag would indicate that their demands have to be set aside. A similar point applies, of course, to the collective values that move the humanoids, as indeed it will apply to their prudential values as well. The desiderata involved may be appealing in themselves for anyone who sponsors the corresponding norms—as almost all will do—but there are likely to be conditions where that appeal fails to be conclusive, as when it is outweighed by the appeal of conflicting values.

5.3.5 Social and moral norms

In our common human usage, we distinguish the social demands that our collectively beneficial norms may make from what we identify as moral demands: the demands, as they are often put, that are made by moral as distinct from social norms. Moral norms are generally taken to be richer in content than the sorts of social norms we have been discussing. Moreover, they are taken to apply, not just to the members of this or that society, but to all human beings. And, since they need not be established or entrenched as social norms, it is generally acknowledged that they may represent idealized rather than actual realities: norms that people should ideally follow, whether or not they actually do so.

How likely are the humanoids of our genealogy to adopt the moral perspective that is characteristic of human beings? There are three observations worth making in response. The first is that the humanoids are certainly likely to enrich their collectively beneficial social norms beyond those on which we have focused, bringing them into line with standard moral norms. The second, however, is that they are unlikely, short of political developments uncharted here, to extend the social norms that evolve in their home community to relationships between humanoids generally; this assumes, exceptionally, that there are a number of humanoid societies. And the third is that they will have an opportunity for a form of moral advocacy—and a motive to practice it—that is common among human beings. We now look in turn at these three observations.

In illustrating collectively beneficial norms, we focused on norms against harmful forms, deception, violence, coercion and the like. But, as we noted, there is every reason why those norms should also require some forms of helpful behavior, such as participating in collectively important enterprises: say, in efforts to combat dangers to which a society is exposed. The economy of esteem will support conformity with such norms, so that the A-triple-R pattern will apply. And since those norms will be collectively beneficial, by assumption, that means that the I-triple-R pattern will apply as well. The humanoids may be expected to endorse fair-play norms, as they are often called, that bear on participation in socially important projects.

As the humanoid norms may be expected to expand on this front, so they will surely expand on other fronts as well. Once the practice of commitment is in place, for example, the humanoids are bound to evolve norms of fidelity that rule against the breach of commitments and require individuals to honor their avowals and pledges. Moreover, if some conventions emerge to establish titles to ownership, as may be essential for guarding against resource conflict, that should trigger the emergence of norms of respect for property; property conventions may be quite variable, of course, depending on how far they put resources under common ownership and how far they place them within private. And if conventions arise in any specific area, as in queuing or friendship, they should equally trigger the emergence of norms for respecting the rules of queuing or the expectations of friends.

If collectively beneficial social norms are enriched in these and perhaps other ways, they will begin to approximate the sorts of norms that are commonly conceptualized among human beings as morally demanding. But the most distinctive thing about moral norms, as conceived among human beings, is that they are taken to obligate everyone and to promise a benefit to all. A crucial question, then, is whether we might expect the humanoids to support norms that extend beyond the boundary of their home community and apply to relations between any individuals.

This takes us to a second observation. If the humanoids enjoy a relative degree of equality within any society, we may expect them to apply their norms to all relationships between members. But we cannot expect this if they live in different subgroups, distinct or overlapping, within a hierarchy of domination. And we cannot expect it if they live in a world of societies—even internally egalitarian societies—that relate to one another under a hierarchical order of domination or in mutual hostility.

We have been operating with an assumption that the humanoids live in an isolated society where relative equality prevails across all members, arguing that the genealogical lessons that apply in that idealized society may also hold of human beings, if only within subgroups of a hierarchical society. But if the humanoids did not live under society-wide, let alone world-wide, conditions of relative equality, there would be no guarantee that they would extend the collectively beneficial norms established within their home community—perhaps just the community of a subgroup—to relations between humanoids more generally. To the contrary, sadly, the nature they share with us would presumably give them the in-group partiality, and the out-group hostility, that make such relations difficult within our own kind. Looking at human history, we might speculate that only the advent of constitutionally, democratically, and justly ordered states, and the development of a suitably ordered world, could provide a ground for optimism on this front.

A third observation to make about the humanoids and morality is that they are going to be enabled to practice moral advocacy, as we might describe it, in the manner of human beings. On the story told, they will have access both to the idea of a socially mandatory requirement—a requirement that anyone can make in the name of others—and to the conceptual resources that might support such a requirement by reference to shared values. And as they may seek to value things from the shared perspective of their own community, so they will be able to think of valuing things from a perspective shared by all humanoids, no matter where they belong.

That will enable them to argue for the importance of certain desiderata for humanoid welfare in general—perhaps even for the welfare of other species—and to make a case for investing them with the status of common values. And it will enable them to draw on such values when arguing in favor of various standards that are currently not entrenched as social norms—they may even be violated by some malign norms—and to demand, as if in the name of all, that individuals should conform to such standards: to present conformity with the demand as an injunctive obligation. They may impose that demand on themselves in particular, arguing that they should seek to join with others in furthering an ideal like democracy that requires joint action and that they should individually act on an ideal like helping those in need, which applies no matter what others do.

The humanoids will not only have the means of practicing such moral advocacy with both others and themselves, they will also have a motive to do so. For if they have become committed beyond the reach of mere prudence to the collective benefits or values that support their shared social norms, those values may lead them to favor and support standards of behavior among humanoids that are not generally entrenched as social norms. Those or analogous values would lead them to support standards they expect to serve all humanoids well, or indeed standards they take to be conducive to the welfare of other species.

The moral advocacy that the humanoids, or at least some groups of humanoids, might be led to support on this basis resembles the sort of advocacy that we human beings often practice, as we argue from shared values—sometimes on different lines—to the case for one or another ideal. As values like those supporting collectively beneficial social norms will give the humanoids reason to abide by those norms, acknowledging the injunctive obligations the norms underwrite, so they would give them reason, at least in the view of advocates, for abiding by the moral norms advocated. If fully successful, moral advocacy of that kind would entrench the moral norms as social regularities that support injunctive obligations. It would generate what from the viewpoint of shared, impartial values would count as social progress.[24]

---

[24] The social progress envisaged here as a possibility for the humanoids would not have to flatten the cultural landscape, however, making different societies into replicas of one another. A common ideal of individual freedom may argue for specifying basic liberties differently in culturally different societies (Pettit 2014, 86–89). A common concern for reducing poverty may argue for different levels of provision in economically different contexts (Sen 1983; 1985; Nussbaum 2011).

6
Responsibility and free will

We have seen that the advent of communication in language will tend to elicit the basic processing capacities of judgment and reasoning and the derived capacity of percipience. But, as the previous chapter has begun to reveal, the advent of communication in language will also lead the humanoids to develop powers of a more relational kind.

We saw in that chapter that they will evolve collectively beneficial social norms that members see as enjoining requirements of conformity on all, including themselves; that they will commit themselves to various attitudes and actions and, in particular, pledge themselves to comply with, and uphold, those requirements; and that the practice of commitment will put them within reach of valuing things in the sense of pledging to desire them. The humanoid practice of valuing, and the associated concepts of value, will apply to the demands of their shared norms but can also be deployed in less comprehensive personal domains as well as in the aspirationally universal domain of morality.

We go on in this chapter to argue that humanoids will complement this battery of normative, valuational practices, and the associated concepts, with a practice of ascribing responsibility to one another, and even to themselves, for living up to the norms to which they commit and to the underlying values. And we show that as they come to hold themselves and one another to account in this way, they will naturally come to countenance a humanoid capacity that deserves to be described as free will, where the exercise of that capacity in doing something makes an agent fit to be held responsible for it.

The chapter is in three sections. In the first, we look at the received human notion of what it is to take another, or indeed oneself, to be responsible for doing something; this takes some time, as it is a much discussed, and contested, topic. In a second, long section, we argue that the humanoids will have the motives and the means needed to develop a practice that models this familiar mode of treatment and to access associated concepts like those of censure and commendation. And then we look in the third section at how their fitness to be held responsible means that the humanoids will enjoy free will in a perfectly intuitive sense of that term, and be disposed to ascribe it to all, including themselves.

6.1 The notion of holding responsible

6.1.1 Initial clarifications

In the relevant sense of holding someone responsible for an action, it amounts to much more than thinking or saying that they were at the causal origin of the event. In that purely causal sense, other animals and even inanimate objects can also be responsible for one or another result. Questions of responsibility in our sense arise only with human beings or human-like agents or indeed with the joint or corporate groups they form.

While only agents of this kind can count as responsible, however, they can count as responsible only for things they do. It may be reasonable to hold someone responsible, of course, not just for an action of X-ing, but also for a foreseen consequence of X-ing, C; but this is just to hold them responsible for the action, as we may also describe it, of bringing about C. And it may be reasonable to hold someone responsible, not for X-ing, but for failing to X; but this failure can itself constitute an action. Again, it may be reasonable to hold someone responsible for an attitude or condition—say, for believing something or for being awake or asleep—but this is to hold them responsible, so we shall assume, for acting in a way that produces that result or for failing to act in a way that would have prevented it.

There are two forms that holding responsible may take in familiar human practice, one negative, the other positive. To hold someone responsible in the negative form is to blame them, where blaming may refer to a mental act—the adoption of an attitude—or an overt action, such as a speech act, that is expressive of that attitude. And to hold someone responsible in the positive form is either to praise them, where this necessarily involves an overt act, or to adopt the attitude that praise would express.

For reasons of simplicity, we may concentrate on the negative form of holding responsible, as in blaming or censuring or condemning someone for an action or just remonstrating with them about what they did. There are some asymmetries between the negative and positive forms of the activity but it is much easier to focus on just one form, and the negative is the more salient of the two: people go in for censure, after all, far more often that they do for commendation. The lessons of our genealogy for blame, as we shall see, carry over naturally to praise as well. But it will be easier to concentrate for most of the chapter on blame alone.

While holding someone responsible always involves a mental or overt act, on the approach sketched, that act, whether negative or positive in form, is normally associated with a corresponding emotion (Strawson 1962; Wallace 1996). When you blame another, you will generally feel resentment if their action was personally unwelcome and indignation if it was unwelcome to another. When you praise someone, you will generally feel gratitude for an action that you yourself welcome and a more diffuse form of approval for an action that is primarily welcomed by another. Finally, when you blame yourself for an action you will routinely feel guilt or shame or remorse or something of the kind, and when you have the feeling that goes with praise for something you did, you will naturally feel a certain sort of pleasure or pride in the action.

But you may clearly feel a relevant emotion—say, resentment at how someone has treated you—without any corresponding mental or overt act. Are we to say that just feeling that emotion toward someone involves holding them responsible: that feeling resentment, for example, is already blaming them? No, we should not say this. After all, you may confess to feeling resentment at someone while admitting that you do not know why, and in that case you are surely not blaming them. The presence of an emotion like resentment will only signal blame in the presence of at least a mental act of acquiescence. You must adopt that emotion mentally: you must endorse it as a fitting reaction to what another has done. Or you must fail to dis-endorse it in a context where that is a consciously accessible option.

6.1.2 The elements of blameworthiness

There are three elements associated with believing that someone is responsible for a deed. In the negative form of believing that the agent is blameworthy for what they did, those elements are as follows; all have counterparts in the positive form too.

1. A belief that the person acted in an undesirable manner.
2. A belief that they acted in that way rationally, knowingly, and voluntarily.
3. A belief that they could have done otherwise.

When we hold these beliefs of someone, by the account to be defended here, we will believe that they are blameworthy. But by all accounts, to believe that someone is blameworthy will not yet amount to blaming them; to believe that someone is fit to be held responsible will not yet amount to holding them responsible.

All theories of responsibility offer an account of the beliefs involved in deeming someone to be blameworthy, treating them as conditions that are necessary but not sufficient if blaming is to materialize.[1] What more is required to blame someone as distinct from just believing that they are blameworthy? Different theories give

---

[1] There are a number of senses in which blameworthiness or fitness to be held responsible, is understood in the literature. In David Shoemaker's (2015) terms, and putting the distinctions roughly, someone may be deemed responsible for something when it is intuitively *attributable* to the person; or, more specifically, when they are *answerable* for justifying it; or, more specifically still, when they are *accountable* and exposed to sanction. As will become clear, we take responsibility broadly in the sense that equates it with accountability. For background to these distinctions, see (Watson 1996), (Scanlon 1998), and (Smith 2012). Among the kinds of blameworthiness distinguished in (Mason 2019) it is closest to her notion of ordinary blameworthiness.

different accounts of what is required, and we may put aside the issue for the moment. We shall return to it in the course of the genealogy that follows but we may concentrate at the beginning on just explaining how the humanoids would come to believe that someone is blameworthy.

Regardless of differences about what the act of blaming requires, existing theories agree about a range of cases where someone would lack the standing, as it is usually put, to blame an agent. We shall also return to this topic in the course of the genealogy. By all accounts, to illustrate the idea, no one ever lacks standing to blame themselves for having done something blameworthy. But by most accounts, someone will lack the standing to blame another for acting in a certain way if, for example, they are themselves guilty of doing the same sort of thing; if blaming them would be meddlesome, involving trespass on an intuitively private domain; or if blaming them would be inconsistent with a professional role, say that of a therapist exploring the motives that prompted the offence.

That our three numbered beliefs are elements in believing someone to be blameworthy—in ascribing responsibility—shows up in the fact that if any of them were missing, then we could not take the emotion associated with blame to be fit to be adopted. To endorse an emotion like resentment or indignation toward a given individual involves holding a belief about them that, in effect, posits or implies the realization of those three conditions (Rosen 2015). Thus, suppose we decided that actually they did not act in an undesirable way, or that they did not do so rationally or knowingly or willingly, or that for whatever reason they could not have done anything else: intuitively, they were not in control. Under any such supposition, it would be manifestly inappropriate to maintain any resentment or indignation we might have initially felt at how they behaved.

Suppose on the other side, however, that we believe that each of these conditions was satisfied. The person did behave in an undesirable manner, they acted in that way rationally, knowingly, and willingly, and in a relevant sense of the phrase—more on this later—they were in control and could have done otherwise. It would be entirely intelligible in that case that we should feel resentment or indignation at what they did, even if we did not endorse it in actually blaming them. The conditions are jointly sufficient as well as individually necessary for making that feeling a fitting one to have and for believing the person to be blameworthy.

The numbered claims presented have not passed without challenge and we should at least address a well-known objection, made in a classic paper by Harry Frankfurt (1969), to the third claim that to believe that someone is blameworthy for what they did implies believing that, in some sense, they could have done otherwise.[2]

---

[2] The Frankfurt line of argument has led John Fisher and Mark Ravizza (1991; 1998) to develop a distinctive view of what makes someone fit to be held responsible and gives them free will.

The challenge is illustrated by the following sort of case. Suppose that an agent faces a choice between doing X and doing Y, where X is manifestly undesirable but unbeknownst to the agent unavoidable: they will be stopped by an interferer from doing Y if they try to take that option. Suppose, however, that the agent does X. Surely we would blame them for taking that route, despite the fact that they could have done nothing but X. And doesn't that show that an agent can be blameworthy for having done something even when there was no alternative to their doing it?

No, it does not. The agent in the example had the alternative, not of Y-ing, but of trying to do Y: they would count as having tried to do Y, after all, if interference had been necessary to force them to take the X option instead. But as it happens, the agent did not try to do Y since interference was not needed to get them to do X. Thus, contrary to the suggestion, they faced two options in the choice—doing X or trying to do Y—and they can be blamed for taking the first rather than the second.

A response that is sometimes made to this argument is to change the imagined scenario and postulate that by grace of a neuroscientific device, the interferer will stop the agent from even trying to do Y, should interference be necessary. But that will not work either. The agent will be able to try to do Y if they believe that they can do Y, desire to do Y, and that intentional profile, by virtue of their nature, is fit to prime them to Y or to try to Y. But if the interferer blocks them from even trying to Y, then that interference must remove those intentional states or deprive the states of their functional role. In other words, the interferer must deny them rational agency and undermine our disposition to judge that they were blameworthy for choosing X rather than Y: on the picture assumed, making such a choice was no longer a possibility for them.

These initial remarks provide a broad justification for taking the belief that someone is blameworthy to involve the three elements listed: a belief that their action was undesirable, that the agent did it rationally, knowingly, and voluntarily, and that in a distinct sense they could have done otherwise. But we need to look in greater detail at what each element requires, if we are to have a good sense of what the genealogy must do to show that the humanoids would be robustly likely to adopt the practice of holding responsible.

6.1.3 First condition: an undesirable action

That an action is undesirable means that it flouts relevant values overall; we may take the notion of value to be available within our genealogy in light of the development charted in the last chapter. This element in the characterization of blame requires that the person who finds an action blameworthy must themselves think that it is undesirable; they would hardly blame someone for doing something that they did not take to be undesirable. But values, as we know, may be personal, group-specific, society-wide, or advocated as moral or universal standards, so that, depending on the standpoint adopted, people may differ in whether they take a given action to be undesirable, flouting relevant values.

Thus, the member of a business cartel or a criminal group may think that another member's failure to contribute to a joint enterprise is blameworthy, where members of the wider society would not agree. Again the citizen of a given society may hold that another's failure to play their allotted part, say in supporting a war, is blameworthy where outsiders would disagree. Those who advocate morally for different universal values may differ on whether or not an action is morally undesirable and blameworthy. And of course, someone may think that an action they took is undesirable and blameworthy, say because it breaches a personal project or a prudential value, where others might judge it differently.

These comments all bear on differences in the values of those who ascribe blameworthiness, since these will bear on how far they take the first condition on the ascription of responsibility to be satisfied. But what of the values of the person they judge to be blameworthy? Does that alleged offender also have to hold values on the basis of which their action counts as undesirable?

Assuming that the person ascribing responsibility is distinct from the alleged offender, the basic answer assumed here takes an either–or form. Either that would-be offender holds values in virtue of which their action counts as directly undesirable: they value honesty so that a lie by their lights will be directly undesirable. Or they hold more basic values in virtue of which their not holding such an action-relevant value counts itself as undesirable: they value mutual reliance between people so that it will be undesirable by their lights that they fail to value honesty; in this case the lie counts, by their lights, as indirectly undesirable. If neither of these things obtains, then treating their action as blameworthy is plausibly inappropriate.

In most cases of ascribing responsibility, the assumption is that the person is blameworthy because of offending against values to which they in some sense subscribe: the action is directly undesirable by their lights. But in other cases this will not be so, as for example in the case where we invoke anti-racist values to deem a racist's actions blameworthy. In such a case, presumably, we take the person to hold by more basic values that make their racist values inappropriate. Those more basic values might be the epistemic demands of evidential responsiveness or of treating like cases alike, or the practical demands of interpersonal respect, and the agent's endorsement of those values means that the racist action is indirectly undesirable even by the offender's own lights (Williams 1995, Ch. 3).[3]

---

[3] This would represent perhaps the harshest form of blame, since it excludes the blamed from the inner circles of the blamer's society: in effect, it excommunicates them from that community (Pettit 2018a).

If we did not share any values at any level with someone who does something that is undesirable by our lights—if we did not even share the sorts of basic values listed—then it is unclear that we could still blame them. We might deem them irrational, for example, or treat them as monsters of some kind, but we could hardly relate to them as other human beings whom we are entitled—entitled by the ground shared between us—to call to account.[4]

So much for the first condition that must be satisfied by another if we are to judge them blameworthy for what they did. The action must be undesirable by our own standards, of course. And it must be undesirable by standards that the other holds or that it would be desirable for the other to hold by independent standards that they hold. The action for which we hold that agent responsible must be directly or indirectly undesirable by their own lights.

6.1.4 Second condition: an action rationally, knowingly, and willingly taken

The second condition in our starting analysis of assigning responsibility is that whatever undesirable action the agent performed, they must have acted rationally, knowingly, and willingly in taking it. Each of these aspects of the condition—each of these features—needs further commentary.

First, rationality. You will do something X rationally, we may say, if you act successfully out of a desire or intention to do something that constitutes X-ing—say, Y-ing—and you do so on the basis of a belief that the behavior adopted will lead you to Y. There must be some description of the action, in other words, under which your desires and beliefs combine to lead you robustly towards realizing that description; we commented briefly on this in Chapter 2. You will do X rationally by this account, however, even if the description under which you take that action does not involve X—you may take it under the Y-description instead—and even if you do not see that by Y-ing you will X.

Notice that the issue of rationality arises in relation only to alternatives that you are presumed to have the capacity to realize. And so it will arise even if those alternatives are inappropriately restricted, by criteria most of us would endorse: say, restricted to the point where we think that you are deprived of political freedom. Assuming you have the required capacity in relation to the options defining the choice, however restricted they may, you will still meet the rationality assumption insofar as you act rationally on the basis of rationally sensitive beliefs and desires. You have a reason to choose as you do—say, that Y-ing appeals to you—and you act on that reason.

---

[4] Such a construal of an agent is implied in the view that Nazi concentration camp guards were monsters who failed in this way. See (Clendinnen 1999) for a critique of that approach to those guards.

You will fail the rationality assumption if you do not act on beliefs and desires at all: if those attitudes do not robustly generate the action, as we put it in Chapter 2. And you will fail the assumption if the desires on which you act are not responsive to recognizable desiderata or the beliefs are not responsive to suitable evidence; you do not hold those states in the manner of a properly functioning agent. The desires must not be the product of disturbing influences like compulsion, impulse, addiction or whatever. And the beliefs must not be the product of the disturbing effects of obsession, paranoia, *idées fixes*, and the like.

We turn now to the knowledge condition. While it may be rational for you to do something like X-ing without doing it knowingly—without recognizing that Y-ing in our example constitutes X-ing—we would scarcely blame you for X-ing in the absence of such knowledge. In order to do an action like X-ing knowingly, you must either desire and intend the action under that description—in this case, you will do it deliberately, as we may say—or you must foresee that if you realize the description under which you do desire and intend it, you will also realize the X-description. Thus, you may be blamed for bringing about a consequence knowingly, even if you did not desire or intend it as such. Suppose you deliberately go rock-climbing but, knowing that this will make your family anxious, you worry them by doing so. We may blame you for worrying them, even though you do not worry them deliberately.[5]

The third feature required under the second condition is that you must not only perform the blameworthy action rationally and knowingly, you must also bring it about voluntarily or willingly. Relying on an intuitive sense of the idea, this requires that you do not do that action, X, because it appears that every alternative to X-ing is unacceptable in comparison with X-ing. The apparent unacceptability of not X-ing by comparison with X-ing must not be an essential part of your reason for doing X. The idea is that if you choose the X-option because of the unacceptability of doing anything else—because hardly any agent could be expected to bear the cost associated with doing anything else—then you were not really in a position to choose whether to X or not: you had little or no choice, as we say, but to take that option.[6]

---

[5] Will you take the action intentionally in that case, even if you do not take it deliberately? Perhaps yes, on the loose sense of intentionality that we distinguished from acting deliberately in a footnote in Chapter 2. You will do something X intentionally in this sense if you do it knowingly and willingly—more on this, in a moment—even if the act you deliberately intend to perform is that of Y-ing. See (Scanlon 2008).

[6] This account of voluntariness builds on (Olsaretti 2004) but is meant to avoid some tricky issues. That there need only *appear* to be an acceptable option to make a choice voluntary means that you may choose one of two options willingly even when, unbeknownst to you, you would have been blocked from taking the other had you tried to do so (Frankfurt 1969). That the alternative need only be *comparatively* acceptable for a voluntary choice means that you may choose either of two equally repulsive options willingly on the grounds that neither is unacceptable in comparison with the other: this, as in Sophie's choice to give up one child rather than another to the Nazi guard. And that it is enough that you do not make your choice *because* of the apparent lack of a comparatively acceptable option means that you may make a voluntary choice, even when you believe (perhaps rightly) that there is no acceptable

Summing up the three requirements of the second condition, the blameworthy agent must have chosen to act as they did—must have taken the undesirable action involved—rationally, knowingly, and willingly. They must have performed the action deliberately under some description, as rationality requires. They must have been aware of the action under the description that casts it as undesirable, as the knowledge condition dictates. And, as voluntariness requires, their choice of that action must not have been motivated in any essential part by the fact that there appeared to be no comparatively acceptable alternative.

6.1.5 When the second condition fails: excuses

When rationality, knowledge, or willingness fails, the agent will no longer be blameworthy for performing an undesirable action. A lack on any of these fronts will constitute a blame-lifting explanation for why they took that action. It will figure in that sense as an excuse, but not one that can be foreclosed by the agent, by contrast with the self-reporter excuses considered in the last chapter. More strictly, it will excuse or exonerate the agent if the failure of rationality, knowledge, or willingness is sufficiently radical: if the excuse is full rather than partial, final rather than incomplete, and fitting rather than unfitting.

Full excuses remove the opportunity for blame altogether, partial excuses reduce the level of blame that is taken to be due: they may cite a factor that lowered but did not eliminate the agent's rational capacity, or their claim to a lack of knowledge, or the acceptability of the alternative. For simplicity, we may set aside the consideration of partial excuses, both here and later, in discussing the humanoids. The points to be made can be readily extended to the partial case.

But excuses may also be incomplete in the sense that while they strictly excuse an action taken in their presence, the agent is fit to be blamed for their presence. Thus, intoxication might make the behavior of an agent irrational, missing evidence might mean it was adopted in ignorance, and being blackmailed to act in that way might mean the behavior was involuntary. But the person may still be blamed for what they did insofar as they can reasonably be blamed, and perhaps blamed in full, for being intoxicated, for missing the evidence, or for exposing themselves to blackmail. As we set aside partial excuses, however, so we may set aside incomplete excuses of this kind; doing so will make for greater simplicity in the exposition, and the account given can be readily extended to such cases as well.

---

alternative; you may make it because of some appealing feature in the chosen alternative itself. My analysis of voluntariness or willingness here differs from that in (Pettit 2018a) on this last point. There I take the apparent absence of an acceptable alternative to be sufficient to make a choice involuntary; I do not require for involuntariness that you must also make the choice because of the apparent absence of an acceptable alternative.

But excuses may fail to be fitting, as they may fail in whether they are full or final. They will fail in this way to the extent that the comparative cost that allegedly forces the agent to reject an alternative and do something undesirable may not be intuitively great enough to make the alternative comparatively unacceptable. We might excuse someone for refusing to retrieve a child's toy from a river by the cost associated with getting their clothes wet. But we would hardly excuse them for refusing to rescue a drowning child from the river on the basis of that cost. As we set aside partial and incomplete excuses in our discussion, so for simplicity we shall set aside unfitting excuses too. If some cost introduces an unfitting excuse, of course, it will be a partial excuse at best. Thus, while it is worth mentioning unfitting excuses separately for the sake of clarity, they will be set aside in any case as excuses that are only partial in their effect.[7]

Assuming it is full, final, and fitting in these senses, an excuse may exonerate someone for having performed an undesirable action by showing that they were effectively obstructed from doing otherwise because of a factor compromising their rationality, their knowledge of what they did, or their willingness to do it.[8]

Thus, any factor that induced irrationality would mean that they could not have done otherwise. They could not have done otherwise if they had not acted rationally on the basis of their beliefs and desires, for example, or if those beliefs and desires were not rationally sensitive: if they were irrational counterparts of beliefs and desires proper. Any such factors would imply a rational incapacity on the part of the agent to have acted otherwise than they did.

Again, any factor that meant that the agent was ignorant of what they were doing would also mean that, given what they believed, and given their desires, they could not have done otherwise than they did. They might have been in ignorance of the undesirable character of what they did. Or they might not have recognized that the action they took was likely to have a consequence that would make it undesirable. Any ignorance of such a relevant fact will excuse the behavior taken, unless the agent happens to have foreclosed the excuse, as in avowing or pledging an attitude.

As the first two sets of excuses invoke irrationality or ignorance, the third invokes the comparatively unacceptable cost or expense to which the agent would have been exposed—or would apparently have been exposed—if they had done otherwise than they did: if they had told the truth, for example, rather than telling a lie. Thus, suppose they were coerced to lie under the apparent threat of losing their life, or by the apparent danger of losing a child or facing financial ruin. Under any such scenario, it is likely to be accepted that however undesirable the action,

---

[7] Non-radical excusing factors, qua non-radical, would be resistible in the same way as the disrupting influences that, by the third condition, a blameworthy agent has to be able to counter; but qua excuses, they would mitigate the blame accruing to the agent in a way that relates them to excuses that are full, final, and fitting.

[8] It may be useful in some contexts to cast factors that deprive an agent enduringly of their rationality as exemptions rather than excuses; see (Gardner 2007). For reasons of convenience, I set aside the distinction here.

they could not have been expected—no one in that situation could have been expected—to tell the truth: telling the truth was not a voluntarily accessible option.

With the notion of an injunctive demand in place, and the sort of value that would support it, we can see that there is also another form that this third sort of excuse may take. If someone would have had to breach a weightier obligation by telling the truth then they would be able to cite that as an unacceptable cost and as a factor that obstructed them from telling the truth and thereby provided them with an excuse. Telling the truth would not have been an option available on a voluntary basis.

While someone may not be blameworthy for lying when they did so for fear of the unacceptable costs of telling the truth, what will we say of the heroic person who insists, despite the costs, on telling the truth? Clearly, we will praise or commend them for their heroism, since there will be no reason to withhold that accolade: they will not have been forced by fear of those costs—to the contrary indeed—to speak truly: they will have done so voluntarily. The heroic person envisaged here stands in contrast to the regular sort of agent we invoked in defining an unacceptable cost as one that just about anyone might have been expected to recoil from.

6.1.6 Third condition: the agent could have done otherwise

Suppose now that the second condition for blameworthiness is satisfied in a given case, so that the agent does something undesirable rationally, knowingly, and willingly. That in itself means that the agent has no excuse for taking the undesirable action and that there is a sense in which they could have done otherwise. It was possible for the agent to have done otherwise—say, told the truth rather than telling a lie—in the sense that there were no recognized excusing factors that stood in their way. It was possible for them to have told the truth so far as such full, final, and fitting excuses are concerned: it was possible-relative-to-those-obstacles.[9]

When we take someone to be blameworthy for telling a lie, however, we also assume that it was possible for them in a more demanding sense to have told the truth. Assume plausibly that there is an open range of factors other than those that are recognized as excusing obstacles that may disrupt an agent's choice, leading them to go astray. If we are to deem someone blameworthy for making an undesirable choice, and if we think that in all likelihood they were affected by such a disrupter, then we must assume that they had the power to resist that influence; otherwise, we would take it as an excuse.

---

[9] This approach fits with a familiar style of semantics, according to which ascribing possibility to an event X amounts to saying that X was possible relative to the absence of certain obstacles or the presence of certain means (Kratzer 2012). For an overview of the treatment of abilities that situates that approach in relation to others, see (Maier 2022).

We acknowledge the presence of such a disrupter when we acknowledge that a person did something undesirable because of laziness or akrasia, for example, irresolution or caprice. But we do not treat those conditions as excusing and, other things being equal, will blame the person for what they did. Although we acknowledge that the disrupter associated with such a condition led the agent astray, we still think that they could have done otherwise. We take them to have had the capacity to neutralize or resist such a disrupter: to have had the ability to do otherwise in spite of its presence.

Making sense of this capacity while explaining why blame or censure is appropriate, constitutes what has been called the hard problem of responsibility (McGeer and Pettit 2015). The problem is hard because it is difficult to provide a naturalistic analysis of the capacity ascribed in taking someone to be blameworthy for lying that would explain why we blame them for not having exercised it and told the truth.

On perhaps the best standard analysis, that capacity is identified with a disposition on the offender's part to tell the truth in most circumstances that was unfortunately frustrated in the actual situation. Something like a glitch in their functioning or a mishap in their processing made them unusually vulnerable to temptation and disrupted their normal disposition. But why should we hold an agent blameworthy for lying just in virtue of their having had a general capacity to tell the truth that happened, unluckily, to be derailed? It would seem to be more plausible to offer them words of consolation rather than condemnation: to point out to them that while they did something undesirable, that was wholly out of character and does not reflect badly on who they are.[10]

One response to this problem has been to argue that the capacity of the blameworthy human agent to have done something desirable rather than undesirable is not naturalistically analyzable: it is constituted by a non-natural form of free will that puts them in principle beyond the reach of natural disruption. But for naturalists, of course, this will be a recourse of despair. We argue in the next section that humanoid fitness to be held responsible does not require non-naturalism and in the final section that the humanoids will be possessed of a significant but still naturalistic kind of free will.

6.2 Responsibility in the humanoids

So much for how we human beings think of responsibility and associated topics. We turn in this section to look at whether something resembling the practice of

---

[10] Michael Smith (2003) offers an illuminating account of the issues in the area, while defending that line on what makes it true that a blameworthy agent could have done otherwise. For a critique of his line, see (McGeer and Pettit 2015) and (Pettit 2018a, Ch 6).

holding someone responsible for an action is likely to emerge among the humanoids. Such a practice will emerge, so we argue, from the active and standby commitments they make to one another. This is true in particular of the commitments implied in their sharing collectively beneficial social norms and we shall concentrate for the most part on this case; later we will look at how far the lesson can hold with other forms of commitment as well.

We begin the discussion with observations on the discipline by others to which the commitment to norms will expose any humanoid; then move on to how others will have reason to give this discipline an active form in exhorting an individual to comply with the norms; and turn finally to an argument that holding an individual responsible for an offense is the ex post counterpart of such ex ante exhortation: it plays a similar role in crediting the agent with control over the choice for which they are held blameworthy. The discussion will enable us to make sense of why it is appropriate for humanoids to hold an agent blameworthy and of what blaming someone actually involves.

6.2.1 Commitment, control, and discipline

The humanoids must assume that they have a significant degree of control over how they perform in the domain of their active and standby commitments, especially their pledges; otherwise, they could hardly take the risk of foreclosing the misleading-mind and changed-mind excuses for failure. They will enjoy that control insofar as the desiderata they target are robustly motivating and promise to support them, more or less regardless of changes of circumstance, in the discharge of those commitments. A presumptive sensitivity to those considerations will ground their willingness to make the commitments, casting robust conformity as something fully and effectively within their reach.

What are the desiderata to which we may expect the humanoids to be sensitive, motivating them to live up to the collectively beneficial social norms to which they are committed? By our earlier account, the likely desiderata or values will include the prudential value of gaining a good reputation and earning the reliance of others; the value of proving themselves true to their commitment, which will have an impartial value for them as the co-sponsors of corresponding norms; and the value assigned to a range of collective benefits. These benefits, as we saw, will include the three sorts of benefits available to each humanoid under the envisaged regime of norms: being treated well by others, being treated well by them on a robust basis, and enjoying the status of being entitled to expect such treatment.

The humanoids will be ready to make commitments to one another insofar as they assume the capacity to control in choice for the expected satisfaction of such values, acting in any situation so as to enact the option that promises to do best overall by those standards. They will assume a form of valuational control, as we may say, and will vindicate the assumption insofar as they do actually live up to the commitments they make. This capacity for valuational control need not be absolutely surefire—they may always succumb to temptation or the like—but it must be fairly robust if they are to have the confidence to make associated commitments, betting on themselves to live up to their avowals and their pledges; it must be proof against disruption across a range of contextually salient scenarios that they take to be possible.

That the humanoids make commitments, and assume control in the domain of their commitments, means they will raise expectations in one another about how they are likely to perform. They will raise such expectations by the commitments they actively make but also, and even more pervasively, by acquiescing without resistance or reluctance in the manifest, independently generated expectations of others. The manifest presence of such expectations will mean that their control over how they perform will be reinforced by the discipline of having to live up to their commitments and values or suffer a reputational loss.

Given that the norms enforced under this expectational discipline are taken to be collectively beneficial for the community, the discipline will be benign in its effect. But there will have to be a relative degree of equality within that community, of course, for such norms to materialize among the members. We shall continue to assume that this equality prevails across a whole society, and is not compromised by subjection to other societies. But the lessons derived under that simplifying assumption may carry also, as we stressed, for a hierarchical society of humans, provided the members of each subgroup enjoy the required equality with one another and evolve norms within that group that are beneficial for all its members.[11]

The discipline to which the humanoids subject themselves in committing to shared norms means that each will be bespoken on numberless fronts and beholden to others for performing appropriately on those fronts. But this discipline has a compensating side. For while it subjects each to a discipline imposed by others, it will give each a disciplinary power in relation to their fellows. They will each have this power over others insofar as those others take them to observe and assess their performance, however unintentional the observation and assessment may be.

---

[11] In focusing on beneficial norms, we set aside the oppressive norms that might emerge across the subgroups in a hierarchical society or within a hierarchical world where internally egalitarian societies do not enjoy equality with one another. The members of a dominated subgroup will likely be subjected to oppressive norms—norms that favor others only—and be held by others to the expectation of conformity: say, the expectation that they should give way to various claims on the part of others against them. While we ignore such cases in our genealogy, it might be readily extended to explain how things could go awry in such a manner, directing us to parallels with how they often go awry among human beings.

6.2.2 Discipline goes active

This disciplinary power may materialize and have an impact in a purely passive manner, not requiring any effort on the part of those imposing the discipline. But it is always likely to assume an active form. Each of the humanoids will often have the motive, and will always have the means, to use their disciplinary power in an active attempt to exercise influence over another and shape their behavior.

The motive for actively using this disciplinary influence derives from the fact that while individuals may generally be expected to conform to shared, beneficial norms, successfully exercising their valuational control, still it is always possible that someone will succumb to the temptation to free ride on the conformity of others for the sake of a personal advantage; they will be susceptible to a variety of influences that may disrupt their performance. This fact provides an opportunity for any humanoids who are concerned about how someone may act, to reinforce that individual's commitment to conformity.

Why might other humanoids be concerned with the conformity of a particular individual or group of individuals to such norms? Any of a number of considerations is liable to support the concern. The other humanoids may be invested in the welfare of the individual, in the way parents are invested in their children, and might want for that special reason to direct them on the path of conformity. Or they or theirs may be exposed to harm in the event that the individual breaches the norm: in that sense they may be potential victims who naturally care about how the individual behaves. Or, more generally still, the high value they put on universal compliance—their commitment to robustly preferring such compliance—may give them a concern that any other agent, the addressee included, should abide by the norms.

What are the means whereby other humanoids might try to reinforce the commitment of a particular individual to conform to shared norms? The individual will have pledged to comply with such a norm, putting aside misleading-mind and changed-mind excuses, out of a concern for the rewards that commitment will secure. And so there is an obvious way in which other humanoids may hope to influence them and induce them to conform on this or that occasion. They can do so by reminding them of their commitment and reinforcing the sensitivity of the agent to the rewards that it promises: they can act so as to sensitize them further to those desiderata or values.

It may be that the individual is ignorant of the role of one of those goods or benefits in their life, as is possible under our account; it may be that the commitment is supported by the motivating role of such a personal or impartial value without their being aware of it. In that case other humanoids may be able to get the agent to act as the norm requires by making them conscious of the commitment they made and the unrecognized reward, collective or personal, that they would jeopardize by a failure of compliance.

But even when an agent is conscious of the appeal of a valued reward, they may overlook or neglect it in a given instance. Other humanoids will be able to guard an agent against such neglect as they can guard them against ignorance. They can do so in each case by pointing out the importance of the benefit involved, reminding them of what is at stake.

In these two cases, the humanoids will rely on an epistemic intervention, as we might call it, to sensitize the addressee to the values—values that the addressee already relies on—that support conformity. But there is also another dimension in which sensitization may prove an influential way of reinforcing the agent's own sensitivity to relevant values and their control over what they do. It may play an energizing, as distinct from an epistemic role, in getting the agent to respond to those values and conform to the norms they support. Others will be able to energize a humanoid agent by impressing on them the claims of the considerations at issue, eliciting a refreshed sensitivity to those concerns; they can make the considerations more imaginatively gripping and motivating.

The effect of the epistemic and energizing interventions that other humanoids adopt in this sort of exercise will be to prompt that agent to pay attention to the presumptive values by which they hold, thereby awakening or reawakening the appeal of complying with one or another shared norm. The interventions are not meant to elicit conformity, bypassing the agency of the individual addressed. On the contrary, they are designed to rouse the agent to the mental act of focusing on the relevant values, letting those desiderata renew the appeal of complying with the relevant norm.

6.2.3 Sensitization, scaffolding, and exhortation

What form of verbal address is likely to mediate the attempt by other humanoids to sensitize a given individual to comply with one or another norm? It will presumably consist in invoking relevant values and saying to that individual: you should or ought to recognize and respond to those values, conforming to the norm-based demand that they support; or, where those values are contextually salient, to say simply: you should or ought to conform to this or that norm, you should tell the truth or keep your word or avoid violence, or whatever.[12]

The notion of what someone should or ought to do may be understood in a purely evaluative or injunctive manner. In evaluative usage, telling someone that they ought to do something may not play a direct role in prescribing action, as in telling them that they ought to know how to repair a bicycle or ought to have

---

[12] Even if the other humanoids do not mention reputational considerations in seeking to elicit compliance, their intervention in mentioning impartial considerations like these will make it salient that the agent will suffer a reputational cost in relation to them, and in relation to those among whom they spread the word of their offense.

learned a certain language. In this usage, what makes the remark true is simply that things would be better in some way if the condition mentioned were realized: if the addressee knew how to repair a bicycle or had learned that language.

In the usage ascribed here to the humanoids, the message is not evaluative in this manner but injunctive. When the humanoids tell an individual that they ought to tell the truth or ought to refrain from coercing someone, they do not merely intend to say that it would be better if they did those things. Taking the agent to have the required capacity, they intend specifically to get the agent to exercise that capacity and act as they ought to act.

What other humanoids say to an agent in this sensitizing role may be cast in the following format: you should and can do X, where the supportive considerations for X-ing are contextually salient. You should and can tell the truth; you should and can keep your commitments; you should and can refrain from violence or coercion. Indeed the remark may plausibly take an even simpler form when it is assumed that certain contextually salient considerations support the requirement. It may then take the form: you can X, you can tell the truth, you can keep you word, or whatever.

As the 'ought' of sensitization is special, by our account, so is the 'can' that may be used to sensitize an agent to relevant values. To make the point vivid, we may take a particular example of sensitization as it might arise among humans or humanoids. Suppose that you are about to be interviewed by a committee of some kind—say, an investigation—and that it is important to me, for whatever reason, that you tell the truth about some embarrassing event. It may be important to me because telling the truth is a value we both recognize; or because you will protect me or others from some harm—say, an inquiry into our behavior—if you tell the truth; or because it is essential for you to tell the truth if you are to be sure of retaining your good name. In an example like this, whether among humans or humanoids, I am likely to say: you should and can tell the truth for such and such reasons; or, you should and can tell the truth; or even more simply, you can tell the truth.

The 'can' in any such remark is special because it is designed to serve a scaffolding role (McGeer 2018). By sensitizing you to relevant values, whether explicitly or by implication, I aim to scaffold your capacity to tell the truth, getting you to register those values mentally and to respond with an appropriate action. I do something that may be expected to make it more likely that you will exercise the capacity in these circumstances and to reinforce that capacity in the sense of making it more resistant to possible disturbances. I assume the role of a co-helper or influencer in prompting you to manifest the capacity and tell the truth.

On the face of it, 'You can tell the truth' is a purely descriptive report, on a par with, 'You are healthy', or 'You are tall', where the attribution of the property—in this case, the capacity to tell the truth—has no effect on whether the property ascribed really obtains. But, 'You can tell the truth', used among the humanoids in an attempt to sensitize and scaffold an individual appropriately—in a word, to exhort that individual to perform the action identified—is clearly not merely descriptive: it is designed to affect the very capacity ascribed, not just to record its presence. Is it like a performative attribution in that case: an attribution that ensures the presence of the property it ascribes, as in, 'I resign' or, 'You're fired'? No it is not, for while it is designed to increase the likelihood that the capacity ascribed is present, it is not guaranteed to make it present. Rather than being purely descriptive or purely performative in character, it falls somewhere in between. It has the character, as we might cast it, of an evocative attribution (McGeer and Pettit 2015).

An evocative or exhortatory attribution is made in the expectation that it will help to elicit the very property it ascribes: the capacity in this case to tell the truth. The descriptive attribution ascribes a property that obtains independently of its being ascribed or not, and the performative attribution ascribes a property that depends entirely for its obtaining on that ascription. The evocative attribution, falling in between those extremes, ascribes a property that becomes more likely to obtain in the presence of that ascription. Typically, then, an exhortation will be issued with a view to helping to ensure the realization of the property: the exhorter will play influencer to the agent in the exercise of the capacity.

Thus, suppose I seek to get another to tell the truth, saying that they should and can do so. The capacity I ascribe will presumably be present at a high level within such a humanoid agent—it will be reliably present and ready to be exercised—in view of their commitment to the norm of information-sharing and the expectational forcefield that reinforces that commitment. I can be fairly confident, then, that by reminding them that they should and can tell the truth, I can push them that further step and make it still more likely that they do tell the truth. Given that they are exhortable, as we might say, I will have reason to hope that by exhorting them I can get them to register and respond to the values in play and as a result to abide by the norm. I can increase their level of valuational control.

If the utterance is strictly needed to get the addressee to conform, it may elicit conformity by sensitizing and scaffolding them in the extra measure required: it may push them over the edge. And whether or not it is strictly necessary to elicit conformity, it should strengthen and reinforce the capacity; it should increase the probability of conformity and make the capacity less vulnerable to disruption. In either case, the utterance will constitute an effective act of exhortation.

6.2.4 Capacities and colors

Think now about how I, as a humanoid, must conceive of the capacity I ascribe to the agent when I exhort them in this way to tell the truth or abide by any shared norm. It is a capacity that I express in the words 'you can', but since those words are exhortative it cannot just be the capacity that a descriptive report, say from a third-person standpoint, would ascribe equally well. The best way to think about it is this. I presuppose and rely on my use of those words in an evocative way, rather than registering the evocative effect as such, and I see the capacity ascribed in light of that assumed evocative power. A third person might see that in the presence of my exhortation the agent's capacity has a certain increased strength: that it is more likely to be exercised, for example, or more resistant to disruption. But that sideways-on view of the capacity will be very different from mine: I will see it as a presumptively strong capacity, period, taking the effect of my exhortation for granted; I will see it from within an exhortative perspective.

An analogy with the perception of color may help to explain the idea. When I say on the basis of my own observation that an object has a certain color—say, that it is red—I rely on how it looks to my eye. I assume without thinking that if it looks red to my eye, and things are intuitively normal, then it is red: I would presumably identify such a working assumption if asked to explain why I relied on observation. But despite the truth of that assumption, how the object presents to me within my perception is just in this way: as red. It looks like a red object to me. It does not look like an object that looks red under normal conditions to a normal observer (such as me). The redness shows up for me directly from within my perceptual perspective.

Someone who does not see the object may be able to judge from an external perspective, say on the basis of my words, that the object is red because it shows up for me in that way. And this is true even of the color-blind individual who learns about how red objects show up for those who can see redness. But while that person would understand what redness is, they would not grasp the color in the primary way; their grasp would be possible only because others like me understand colors in that different manner: in that sense, it would be a parasitic rather than a canonical form of understanding.

Something parallel will hold of the humanoids on our account of how exhortation works for them. To me as an exhorter, the capacity of the person I address will present in a way that presupposes my exhortative presence and power. If asked to explain why they can tell the truth, I would probably respond that they are sensitive to the value of truth-telling and, on reflection, I might identify my unthinking assumption that exhortation would sensitize them further and strengthen that capacity. But how their capacity presents to me while I am exhorting them is just in the simple way I express in the words: 'you can!' In other words it will look like the capacity of an agent to tell the truth, period, not like the capacity of an agent-who-is-exhorted-to-tell-the-truth to tell the truth. A third person may only be able to judge in this detached way that the person can tell the truth in virtue of being exhorted. But like the color-blind person's grasp of redness, their understanding of the capacity I ascribe will be parasitic on the understanding of those like me who know what it is to exhort.

The analogy with color is useful in emphasizing the epistemic importance of the exhortative perspective. But it is important to note that unlike the color case, that perspective is epistemically important because of its pragmatic importance in scaffolding the very capacity it targets. We human beings, and presumably the humanoids also, will take objects to remain red even when there is no one to whom they look red. But the humanoids, by the story told, will take the sort of capacity ascribed in exhortation to depend for its resilience against disruption, and for the probability of its exercise, on the exhortation being in place: specifically, on the influential role that the exhortation plays in rousing the agent to pay attention to the relevant values. Looks reveal colors, as we think of them, but the exhortation within which capacities are registered by humanoids may itself be essential for those capacities to remain intact; the exhortation helps to reinforce the very capacities it reveals.[13]

The exhorter will recognize that there are a variety of disruptive influences that may prompt the agent to free ride; otherwise, they would not have any reason to worry about whether they will comply. But at the same time they will recognize that by exhorting them, they can rouse them to withstand those pressures; otherwise, they would not have any motive to rely on exhortation to allay their worry. From within their standpoint, the agent will present to the exhorter as someone possessed of a valuational control that is effective over a range of such disruptive pressures.[14]

One final observation before moving on. We saw earlier that the active attempt to discipline others that is constituted by exhortation is grounded in the way in which the humanoids are going to be passively disciplined by the manifest expectations of others and by the cost of not meeting those expectations. But once the practice of exhortation gets to be established, as is likely in the presence of a relevant motive and means, there is another mode of influence that the humanoids may exercise that is neither fully passive, nor fully active. This, in a familiar metaphor, is virtual or standby exhortation.

Suppose that I am manifestly expecting something of an agent—say, that they should tell the truth—but decline to exhort them for an incidental but salient reason: say, because I think exhortation is unnecessary or because I would find it embarrassing in the circumstances. In such a case we might expect the agent to be sensitized and scaffolded by my observed presence and my presumptive

---

[13] Thus, the possibility ascribed in the 'you can' is token-reflexive in the sense in which indexicals and demonstratives are usually taken to be token-reflexive. It is a possibility registered in the utterance of the 'you can', but a possibility that is identified in part by reference to that very utterance itself. In that respect, it resembles an indexical assertion such as 'I am tall'. The state of affairs registered in this utterance is identified in part by reference to that utterance itself: specifically, by reference to the speaker.

[14] How will the capacities ascribed in exhortation be constituted, from within the naturalistic perspective of physics and related sciences? As colors are allegedly constituted by spectral reflectances, to recall a point from Chapter 1, so they will presumably be constituted by the physical configurations of agents who are suitably exposed to exhortation.

disposition, and even to be sensitized and scaffolded as effectively as if I had resorted to active exhortation.

6.2.5 When exhortation is inappropriate

We are able at this point to begin to explore how the exhortative stance that the humanoids are likely to take toward one another connects with the practice of holding someone responsible for certain deeds. But before doing that, it will be useful to notice that there are conditions that will presumably make exhortation inappropriate among the humanoids. This is important, because it turns out that they mirror conditions that are taken to be necessary in human practice for taking someone to be blameworthy.

One condition for taking someone ex post to be blameworthy for enacting an option Y rather than X is, first, that Y-ing counts as undesirable by the standards of the person blaming and, second, that it counts as undesirable—directly or indirectly—by the standards of the party blamed. In parallel to the first element in this condition, there is going to be no sense in one humanoid's exhorting another to do something X rather than Y if they themselves do not take X to be the desirable option in the choice. Why try to get another to act in a way that offends against your own standards? And in parallel to the second element, there will be no point in their exhorting another to do X rather than Y if the other's standards do not make X-ing directly or at least indirectly desirable. Why would you exhort another to take an option when there is nothing in the other's psychology that might make them susceptible to that exhortation?

Another condition necessary for finding someone blameworthy for an action introduces three elements: rationality, knowledge, and voluntariness. According to this condition, it is inappropriate in human practice to take someone to be blameworthy for taking an option Y rather than X if they made that choice under circumstances where their capacity for rational choice, their knowledge of what the option involved, or their voluntariness in the choice was compromised. A deficit on any of those fronts would count as a plausible obstacle and a blame-lifting excuse for what the agent did: a full, final and fitting excuse, assuming that the deficit was sufficiently radical.

As it is in the human practice of assigning responsibility to someone ex post for doing Y rather than X, so it will be in the humanoid practice of exhorting the agent ex ante to do X rather than Y. It will not make sense for anyone, human or humanoid, to exhort another to choose the option X in such a situation, if they take the agent to suffer an unremovable obstacle—the counterpart of a full, final, and fitting excuse—to rational, knowing, or voluntary choice.

Consider the rationality element. If one humanoid exhorts another to do X rather than Y, they must assume that the other is in a position to act rationally according to their beliefs and desires—they are not disabled or blocked in any way—and that they are not in the grip of compulsive or obsessive desires, or of paranoid beliefs or *idées fixes*, that might push them irresistibly to go the Y route.

Again, going to the knowledge requirement, it will not make sense for the humanoid to exhort another to do X if that individual is ignorant of relevant facts: if they do not know the demands of the norm, for example, or are mistaken about where it applies. Of course, it may be that by exhorting the agent to abide by the norm, they can remedy such ignorance, alerting the agent to something that they had ignored or overlooked. But if the ignorance does not lend itself to being dispelled in that way, then its presence will undermine the point of the exhortation.

Finally, to move to the voluntariness element, the humanoid agent will hardly exhort another to X if the apparent cost to the other of acting as they are exhorted to act will make that action intuitively unacceptable in comparison with one or more alternatives; we may assume that X-ing does not have an intrinsic appeal that might eclipse that prospective cost. By our earlier account, the cost will be unacceptable if no humanoid agent could reasonably be expected to assume it: if, in other words, it would require a rare form of heroism for someone to take on that cost. Like irrationality and ignorance, involuntariness will figure as a block that makes exhortation inappropriate. The cost that would inhibit exhortation may be a personal loss, a coercive threat, or even the fact that acting on the exhortation would mean breaching a weightier obligation.

The third condition required in human practice for someone to count as blameworthy for doing Y rather than X is that they could have done X. They were not hampered by excusing factors, as the second condition requires, and neither were they blocked by any in an open range of potentially disrupting influences: while such disrupters may well have been present, the agent, if truly blameworthy, had the power to resist them. A counterpart of this condition too will inhibit the humanoids from exhorting an agent to do X rather than Y. What would be the point of exhorting someone to X, when it is assumed that they are unable to counter the sorts of disrupting, non-excusing influences to which they will inevitably be subject? The valuational control ascribed in exhortation must be potentially effective against such a range of disruptive pressures; it must promise to enable them to do that which they are exhorted to do, even when such obstructive influences are present,.

This means that when I, as a humanoid, exhort someone to do X rather than Y, say to tell the truth rather than lying, I must assume that the person shares in the valuation of truth-telling, is not prevented by any excusing obstacle from telling the truth, and is capable of resisting the effect of any influences that are likely to compromise their truth-telling disposition. If I assume that those conditions are fulfilled, why do I think that still, there is reason to exhort the person? Presumably, because I assume, no doubt as an unthinking default, that the exhortation may be necessary to enable them actually to resist—or at least probably and resiliently to resist—the disrupting influences that may get in the way of their truth-telling.

6.2.6 When the exhortation fails: a constraint on how to respond

We can now take our genealogy further by considering how I or any other humanoid will respond to someone's failure to be moved by an exhortation. Suppose that I exhort another humanoid, whether actively or in a standby fashion, to comply with a beneficial norm to which we are both manifestly committed: I say, to take the active case, that they should and can tell the truth. Suppose that there seems to have been nothing inappropriate about the exhortation. And suppose that despite my exhorting them to conform, the other actually goes on to tell a lie and offend against the norm. What am I likely to think?

I might be able in retrospect to see that actually the exhortation was clearly inappropriate, because the agent clearly failed to meet one of the conditions required for exhortability. But what if I cannot see any reason to think that the exhortation was out of order? Suppose that, for all I can register in considering their circumstances, there was no condition that would have put them beyond the reach of exhortation. What am I to conclude in such a case?

Like other humanoids, I will naturally assume that an appropriate form of exhortation will empower any individual exhorted, increasing the resilience of their disposition to conform with the norm at issue, or the likelihood of their doing so. That assumption will be grounded, by the account so far, in the role of commissive practices within our humanoid community; in the power that anyone's commitment to a shared norm will put in the hands of others; and in the way another's exhortation can activate that power, awakening or reawakening the other's sensitivity to the considerations supporting their commitment to the norm.

This belief in the general power of exhortation means that however I respond to my addressee's failure to tell the truth, the response will have to be consistent with that belief. The response must not require me to deny that I and others live within a common expectational and commissive forcefield, conducting our lives within the exhortative reach of others. It must allow me to continue to hold that when we operate in full, adult possession of our faculties, we humanoids generally prove responsive to what others manifestly expect of us and to what they may articulate in exhortative demands. We enjoy valuational control: the ability to maximize the expected satisfaction of our values.

This belief in the power of exhortation might allow me in the case of a particular addressee's failure—say, the failure of someone I have known long and well—to think that there must have been something, unbeknownst to me, that went wrong. Despite appearances, I may refuse to believe that this person, whom I have known for many years, would have failed to tell the truth, if all the conditions for exhortability were really satisfied: if they had maintained their commitment to truth-telling; if they were not excused by any lack of rationality, knowledge, or voluntariness; and if they were capable of resisting any non-excusing disruptive influences. But while I might refuse to think that someone was exhortable in a particular case, I and other humanoids could not adopt it as a default response with anyone who fails to act as it seems they were appropriately exhorted to act.

If I and the humanoids in general were to adopt such a default response, that would put the belief in the power of exhortation beyond the reach of empirical testing or support. It would imply that in any circumstances where someone acts against how they were exhorted to act, and where the conditions of exhortability were apparently satisfied, still one or another condition must actually have been breached. The agent must have changed commitments, so that response might go, must have been disabled by some excusing factor, or must have lacked the ability to counter disrupting influences. The response would turn the belief in the power of exhortation into a matter of blind faith, denying it any possibility of being empirically tested and vindicated.

6.2.7 When exhortation fails: the should-and-could-have response

We may conclude from these observations that the humanoids would generally spurn any response to someone's failure to act on an appropriate exhortation, that effectively jeopardized the general belief in the power of exhortation. But what alternative would be available to them? What alternative response might I make to the addressee who fails to act on my exhortation to tell the truth?

By assumption, the agent met the three conditions for exhortability: they were committed to the value of truth-telling; were unaffected by an excusing failure of rationality, knowledge, or voluntariness; and had the capacity to overcome any non-excusing, disruptive hurdles that stood in their way. I cannot think that either of the first two conditions was unsatisfied, since that would mean that they were not exhortable after all. The only view I can take is that while they had the capacity to resist disruptive influences, which exhortability presupposes, they did not exercise it fully or properly.

If I endorse that view of the agent, as I must, then I will reaffirm the exhortation rather than retracting it. I will think that it was appropriate on my part to have said, 'You should and can tell the truth', and that they enjoyed the valuational control ascribed and scaffolded in that act of exhortation. Giving expression to the thought I will presumably say: 'You should and could have told the truth'. Those words will express ex post the attitude expressed ex ante by 'you should and can'. The message will be the same, only the temporal standpoint different.

If I say that they should and could have told the truth, believing that the conditions for exhortability were fulfilled, then I will have to hold that the offender's failure was due to the influence of some disruptive factor, and this, despite the fact that they had the power to resist such influences and exercise their valuational control. They had the capacity to deal with temptations, as I must think, even temptations to which a glitch of functioning or a mishap of circumstance made them unusually vulnerable, but they failed to exercise that capacity effectively.

If I take a view of broadly this kind with the addressee, then I will identify with myself in the role of an ex-ante exhorter, maintaining that perspective and insisting on the level of control that I registered when I said, 'You should and can tell the truth'. I will insist ex post, 'You should and could have told the truth'. Those words will not serve to recall, wistfully as it were, that something was possible then that is not possible now. They will give expression to a belief in the valuational control of the agent, buttressed by my awakening or reawakening them to the values underlying their commitment to truth-telling.

Thus, when I say to the offender, 'You should and could have told the truth', I will see them as I saw them from the exhortative standpoint: that is, as someone with the valuational control ascribed in appropriate exhortation. Sure, they failed to tell the truth as a result of some disrupter that got in the way: perhaps a disrupter like the laziness or akrasia, the irresolution or caprice that we humans invoke in explaining similar failures without excusing them. But they failed to exercise the capacity, which I rightly ascribed to them in exhortation, to counter the effect of such a disrupter and tell the truth; they told a lie, despite having an exhortatively enhanced capacity to do otherwise.[15]

So much for the content of the should-and-could-have remark. But what about the motivation for making it? Where I will have expected 'You should and can tell the truth' to scaffold the agent's capacity to live up to that norm, and will have said it out of that evocative desire, I can hardly think that 'You should and could have told the truth' will have the same effect. It will certainly identify truth-telling as a value but it can hardly get the addressee, as if in an instance of backwards causation, to have told the truth in the past. So what might be the point of making this ex-post pronouncement?

The primary point to the response, presumably manifest to all, will be to identify the agent's failure to live up to the norm, and to present the offense as one that the agent committed in the presence of the sort of control ascribed in the exhortation. We saw earlier that in exhorting a person to tell the truth or abide by any norm, I presuppose and rely on the exhortative power I thereby deploy—I act as a would-be influencer—and in saying 'you can', I ascribe a capacity that is properly

---

[15] Note that the capacity ascribed, on this account, requires the agent to have been both responsive and exposed to exhortation, and responsive and exposed to the demands of the values or reasons invoked. This marks a distinction between the view taken here and the more standard view that equates the agent's fitness to be held responsible for a given action with their having been responsive to the relevant values or reasons. The exposure element in the condition is required to make sense of the claim that the agent could have done otherwise: that they had that sort of control over how to act.

discernible for me only from within that engaged, empowering perspective. When I insist after the failure that the agent could have told the truth, I imaginatively identify with my earlier, exhortative self, simulating the perspective of an influencer, and reaffirm ex post the presence of the capacity I earlier ascribed. I identify the failure as one that occurred in the presence of that sort of capacity to tell the truth. To borrow and rework a legal term, I thereby indict the agent for the offense.

In virtue of indicting the agent in this sense—in virtue of identifying the lie as an offence that the agent committed, despite being able to control for telling the truth—the should-and-could-have response may be expected to prompt them to admit the failure and indeed to apologize for it: to express regret for the way in which they let me and others down. Such an admission and apology would presumably help to restore relationships of reliance with those, including myself, whom the agent let down, as the indictment registers. And that restoration of relationships would presumably be welcome to all of us, since it would hold out the prospect for each of the benefits that everyone's compliance with shared norms ensures.

But if indicting the agent is the primary and manifest point in the should-and-could-have response, it is important to notice that the response is also likely to have a secondary rationale, albeit one that the humanoids may not always register. It will communicate to the agent, and perhaps to others, that in my view they belonged at the time of action to the exhortative fold—they were within exhortative reach—and that there was nothing inappropriate about my having sought as an influencer to get them to tell the truth. And that message will be important insofar as I assume, as I normally will, that the agent has not changed their nature and that, when circumstances are appropriate, they remain firmly within that fold, susceptible like the rest of us to the effects of exhortation.

This means that there is a difference, but not a deep difference, between the rationale for ex-ante exhortation and the rationale for ex-post indictment. The should-and-can exhortation and the should-and-could-have indictment will each serve the goal of marking truth-telling as an appropriate standard—the 'should' sends the same message in both cases—but will serve distinct action-related aims. The aim in the *can* case will be to try to elicit performance and reinforce the capacity to live up to it: that is, to empower the agent. The aim in the *could-have* case will be to cast the agent as someone who despite their failure can still be activated by exhortation to register and respond to the relevant norm and value. The indictment will send the message that the offender remains within the exhortative fold, where that message may be expected to motivate them to do better in the future.

The humanoids may not actively register that the indictment of an offender like the person in our example can serve this motivational role. But consciously or not, they are likely to act as if they took it to play that role. This appears in the fact that they would surely lose their interest in the practice of indictment if it became obvious that it had no motivational effect: if it clearly failed to increase the likelihood that indicted offenders would mend their ways.[16]

By this account, the desire in the you-could-have indictment, like the desire in the you-can exhortation, has a motivational rationale, noticed or unnoticed. The could-have remark will invest the person with an exhortation-responsive status in the hope of getting them to embrace that status and to live up to what it requires in future interactions. Where the you-can remark is designed to exhort them on a particular occasion, the you-could-have remark is designed in the wake of a failure on that occasion to exhort them to do better in the future: to alert them to suitable values and to prime them for suitable action.

6.2.8 Extending the should-and-could-have response

Once we see why I will likely respond in this way to another's failure to comply with a shared norm, when I myself exhorted them to comply, it should be clear that I will have a similar motive to respond in that way even if it was someone else who did the exhorting, whether their exhortation took an active or a standby form.

If I think that the other's exhortation was appropriate, I will be able to identify imaginatively with them in that exhortation and, simulating their perspective, I will be able to see the agent at the time of action as having had the capacity ascribed in the you-can way: I will be positioned to indict them for their offense. And, assuming that the agent did not change for the worse in the meantime, I will be able to do something on which I can rely, consciously or not, to motivate them to do better in the future; I will be able to play the role of a future-oriented influencer.

But does some humanoid—myself or another—have to serve as an external exhorter if it is to be appropriate to respond in the should-and-could-have manner to an individual's failure to abide by a norm? No, for if the agent plays exhorter to themselves, then no external exhorter needs to have been present at the time of action.

While exhortation, as we have described it, is a social practice that presupposes a society in which the members make commitments to shared norms, it is manifestly possible that the practice will be interiorized by any humanoid. An individual will be able to exhort themselves actively to conform to a relevant norm by playing the part of another agent in their own psychology, sensitizing themselves to the values supporting conformity and thereby scaffolding their capacity to conform. The humanoids will have a motive to practice self-exhortation insofar as it promises to

---

[16] Peter Strawson (1962, 25) makes a similar observation about human blaming practices: 'when certain of our beliefs about the efficacy of some of these practices turn out to be false, then we may have good reason for dropping or modifying those practices'. For an insightful interpretation that makes good sense of this concession, see (McGeer 2014).

improve their performance, and this interiorization of the social practice will offer them a means of doing so.

When I assume that another humanoid individual is an active self-exhorter, playing the part of an exhortative influencer with themselves, then that will give me ground for responding to their failure to live up to a shared norm of truth-telling in the should-and-could-have manner. I will be able to see the agent as someone who was on the verge of complying with the norm; to identify with that self-exhortation imaginatively, simulating their influencer view of themselves; and to represent them therefore as an agent who enjoyed an exhortatively empowered capacity to conform in the failed past. In short, I will be able to indict them as I might have indicted them had I been the one to do the exhorting.

Thus, assuming they have not changed character, I will be able to play the role of a future-oriented influencer, consciously or unconsciously presenting them as someone who can bring themselves to comply with the norm on later occasions. I will have the same basis for thinking here, as in other cases, that that individual should and could have told the truth. Doing so will manifestly invest the person with the status of someone exposed and responsive to exhortation, call them back to the truth-telling ideal, and help to motivate them on that basis to comply with the norm.

But this observation only applies on the assumption that the agent was actively exhorting themselves to live up to the norm involved. What if they were not engaged in such active self-exhortation? Does that mean that I will not be able to identify with them imaginatively and, ascribing the capacity that they would have seen in themselves, say that they could have complied with the norms? No, it does not.

As another's exhortation may have a standby or virtual character, so self-exhortation may also have a standby form. We illustrated standby exhortation by the case where an independent observer says nothing to someone who faces a difficult choice like that between telling the truth and telling a lie, but is manifestly aware of the options that the person faces, and is manifestly disposed to exhort them actively, should that seem to be desirable and feasible—should a red flag go up. Active exhortation works, as we know, by sensitizing the agent to relevant values, making them aware of those values and exposing them to their energizing effect. But the mere presence of that sort of silent observer ought to have the same effect, alerting the agent to the values at issue in their choice, and awakening or re-awakening them to the appeal of those values. It ought to constitute a virtual form of exhortation, even if the observer says nothing; the observer will be there on standby, manifestly ready to play an active part should there be a need and an opportunity to do so.

As we saw, it will certainly be possible for a humanoid agent to exhort themselves actively to live up to a norm like truth-telling: to get themselves to do so, as we might put it, by focusing on the energizing values at issue and by insisting evocatively with themselves that they can respond appropriately: 'I can and will tell the truth'. But even if such an individual does not exhort themselves actively on this pattern, they will be manifestly positioned to do so, should that be needed and—as it always will be—possible. They will count as virtual or standby self-exhorters.

Spelling this out a little, each of the humanoids will be pledged by assumption to the norm at issue in any decision, and responsive to the values that support compliance. Thus, they are almost certain to notice, if on this or that occasion a temptation threatens to lead them astray: it will raise a red flag, and alert them to the values that the temptation puts at risk. But being alerted to those values will be equivalent to being exhorted to live up to what they require; it will have the same effect, perhaps in muted vein, of active exhortation by another or by themselves. That means that with any shared norm like that of truth-telling each of the humanoids will be permanently on standby, occupying the role of a virtual self-exhorter. Whether they like it or not, they will be an inhibiting presence in their own lives, ready to nudge themselves to do better at any point where they are in danger of failing.

Absent positive evidence to the contrary, then, each humanoid will count by default as an agent who self-exhorts in at least a virtual manner. They may only rarely resort to an active, self-exhorting effort to comply with a shared norm like truth-telling. But they will be alert to the occasions when lying is a temptation—this will raise a red flag—and they will be prompted by any flag of that kind to think again. Even as they immerse themselves in practical decision-making, they will remain a silent self-observer, whose inhibiting presence is likely to prime resistance to such a temptation; whether they like it or not, they will be dragooned by their nature into playing a virtual self-exhortative role.

These observations mean that I as a humanoid will be entitled to indict anyone who offends without excuse against shared norms and values: that is, to respond to them in the should-and-could-have manner. Even if I had not exhorted them to comply, and even if no one else had exhorted them to do so, I can identify with that individual as a virtual or active exhorter to themselves. I can simulate their position as a self-exhorter and treat them as both responsive and exposed to exhortation. I can take the perspective of an ex-ante exhorter and, ascribing the valuational control that is implied in exhorting anyone, I can hold ex post that they acted contrary to their values in the presence of such control.

6.2.9 Blameworthiness and blame

We saw earlier that in human practice one person takes another to be blameworthy when they take them to have performed a suitably undesirable action, to have done so in a rational, knowing, and willing way, and to have acted in the presence of a capacity to have done otherwise, overcoming a range of non-excusing disrupters. We are now in a position to see that when the humanoids react in the should-and-could-have manner to someone's failure to comply with a shared norm—when they indict them for the action taken—then they will see the agent in something close to this manner.

Taking up the first condition on the human practice of blaming, if I as a humanoid say that an offender should have told the truth, that implies that in virtue of a shared norm to which they are committed, they acted in a suitably undesirable way. By the stipulation that no excusing obstacle was present, to turn to the second condition, my saying this also implies that they acted in a rational, knowing, and willing manner: they were not affected by an excusing obstacle that might have stopped them from telling the truth and inhibited ex-ante exhortation. And my insistence that they could have told the truth implies that they were possessed of an ability to resist any non-excusing hurdles that might have stood in their way—the ability to resist temptations that an ex-ante exhorter would have recognized—but failed to exercise it effectively.

This shows that the response that the humanoids will generally make with someone who offends against a shared norm amounts to taking them to be blameworthy, as we analyzed that notion in the first section. It represents them as having rationally, knowingly, and voluntarily done something undesirable in the presence of a capacity not to have offended in that way. But not only does our account of the humanoid response of indictment amount to taking the agent to be blameworthy for what they did. It appeals also on three other, related counts. First, as promised earlier, it explains why blaming someone involves more than taking or believing them to be blameworthy; second, it makes sense of why the practice of blaming should require the blamer to satisfy various conditions of standing; and, third, it avoids the hard problem of responsibility, as we described it in the first section. We look now at these three points in turn.

We have emphasized that when I as a humanoid respond to an offender in the manner described, I will take them to be blameworthy for what they did. While that is certainly true, however, it understates the lesson supported. For what I do in making that response—in indicting them for the offense, as we put it—plausibly amounts not just to believing them blameworthy, but to actually blaming them.

When I indict another humanoid for what they did that, I accuse them of having done something undesirable, without any excuse, and despite having the capacity to have done something else. This, intuitively, is not just to hold them blameworthy, but actually to blame them. What will it be for me to believe that the person is blameworthy for an offense, then, yet not actually indict or blame them? Plausibly, it will be to believe that it would be appropriate for someone, or at least someone with an appropriate standing, to blame them in the sense explained. I might believe that this is appropriate while choosing not to blame the person myself, whether because of wanting to keep my distance, because of looking to form a different sort of relationship with the person, because of having forgiven them for the offense insofar as it was directed against me or mine, or perhaps, to anticipate the next point, because of not having the standing required for blaming them.

The second count on which the story about humanoid indictment should appeal is that it enables us to see why someone must satisfy various conditions of standing if they are to be entitled to blame a particular offender. It will be intuitively obvious among the humanoids, as it is obvious among our own kind, that my exhorting another to do something that is desirable by shared standards would be out of place—it would manifest assumptions that do not fit with our relationship—under a variety of conditions. But if those conditions make ex-ante exhortation inappropriate, of course, then presumably they will make ex-post indictment inappropriate too. And it turns out that the sorts of conditions that have this status among the humanoids correspond very nicely with those that are taken in human practice to be conditions required for someone to have the standing to blame an individual.

Exhorting someone to be prudent in looking after their future would certainly be out of place if I were not invested in their life as a family member or close friend. Exhorting someone to do something I manifestly failed to do myself would be out of place on grounds that the other might well ask: who are you to tell me how to behave? Again, exhorting the person to perform this or that action would be out of place if I occupied an official role—say, that of therapist—that intuitively ruled out such exhortation. Those conditions would make it equally inappropriate to indict an offender ex post. And it is very striking that the examples given correspond perfectly with standard exemplars of conditions for the standing to blame. They rule against blaming someone in a meddlesome, hypocritical, or unprofessional manner.

A third reason for the appeal of identifying humanoid indictment with human blaming is that it does not raise the hard problem of responsibility that plagues standard, naturalistic theories of blaming. The problem, as we saw, affects attempts to explain the capacity to have done otherwise that is ascribed in blaming an agent for what they did. Let this capacity be taken, to cite a standard approach, as a general capacity to act well in the appropriate way—a capacity that would have been on display in lots of nearby scenarios—that just happened to be disrupted in the actual circumstances. On this account, we may certainly denounce the action taken as undesirable. But why should we want to censure the agent, given that their capacity to have done well was actually impeded? Wouldn't it be more appropriate to compliment them on the fact that while they offended, at least the offense was out of character?

This problem evaporates on our account of humanoid indictment. When I exhort someone appropriately to comply with a shared norm—or identify with the agent's own exhortation or the exhortation of another—I ascribe a capacity, reinforced by that very ascription, to resist an open range of potential, non-excusing disrupters. If the person then fails to act as exhorted, I must take them at one and the same time to have had the capacity to comply with the norm and yet not to have actually complied. And that means that my indictment of the offense is bound to have a censorious character: 'You ought to have complied, you were able to comply, and still you failed'.

Expanding a little on this theme, assume that like us, the humanoids will be prone to experiencing the emotions of anger and its relatives. In that case it is very likely that I as a humanoid will co-opt anger in response to my frustration with the agent whom I indict and blame in such a manner: in other words, that I will ratify or endorse a reactive attitude of resentment or indignation at the offender's failure (Strawson 1962; Wallace 1996). Taking an exhortative stance toward the other, I will have held out proactive hopes of success. And so, it will make perfect sense for me, when those hopes are dashed, to feel a reactive form of anger (McGeer 2013).

While humanoid indictment and blaming will naturally connect with such emotions, however, it is important to distinguish it from punishment of any kind, in particular the punishment that might be imposed by law. Like forms of blame, standard varieties of punishment presuppose blameworthiness; it is that observation that lies behind the claim that ideally punishment serves the function of expressing blame (Feinberg 1965). Punishment might make an appearance among the humanoids, if only to bolster the effect of exhorting an offender to avoid in the future a sort of action for which they are currently censured. But the materials marshaled in this genealogy do not provide any ground for thinking that it is robustly likely to appear.

These observations about the merits of identifying humanoid indictment with human blame open up issues to do with free will, and we turn to these in the final section. Before considering those questions, however, it may be useful to look briefly at how this account of how the humanoids will blame those who offend against their shared norms can generalize to an explanation of why they would develop comprehensive practices of responsibility, akin to those that prevail among our own kind. The generalization should help to boost the idea that as it is with the humanoids so it may be with us.[17]

6.2.10 Responsibility more generally

The account we have given of blame among the humanoids is restricted on a number of fronts. It focuses on holding agents responsible for failures but not successes; on holding agents responsible only on the basis of shared, collectively beneficial norms; and on holding only other agents responsible, and then only individual rather than corporate agents. The account generalizes insofar as it can make sense of why the humanoids would praise as well as blame; why they would

---

[17] I do nothing to compare the claims of the account in relation to other views of responsibility. For a useful collection of papers representing other approaches, see (Coates and Tognazzini 2013).

praise or blame on grounds other than those deriving from widely shared norms; and why they would do this with themselves as well as others, and with corporate as well as individual agents.

Taking up the first point, the account of blame among the humanoids, makes it easy to explain why they should often praise as well as blame, commend as well as censure. In censuring another for doing something undesirable by shared standards or values, the humanoids will represent the action as a failure on the offender's part to exercise their exhortatively empowered capacity to control for the satisfaction of those standards; specifically, to control for that satisfaction even in face of non-excusing disrupters that push them in other directions. That suggests, plausibly, that the humanoids will represent the agent's action in a parallel fashion when it is desirable by shared standards or values, and that this will prompt them to commend.

They will see the desirable action, on this suggestion, not as a failure by the agent to exercise their valuational control, but as a successful display of just the same sort of control. The recognition of the controlling capacity in this case will not lead them to think that the agent could have done otherwise but rather to hold that it was not a lucky accident that they acted as they did. They would have acted in a way that satisfied their values, so the idea goes, even if certain salient costs or difficulties or some other obstacles were greater.[18]

To take up the second point, the account may extend from the responsibility incurred by the humanoids under shared, beneficial norms and values to the responsibility they will incur on other grounds too. It will make sense of why they might hold one another responsible to epistemic as well as practical values, for example, invoking these to censure or commend another's transitions in reasoning: say, to censure them for affirming the consequent or for succumbing to the gambler's fallacy. And it will make sense of why they might hold one another responsible to the more partisan commitments they will inevitably make and to the more restricted values supporting them. Thus, within a family, a network of friends, or even a gang of thieves, they will hold one another responsible for abiding by the background commitments, active or virtual, that the members of such a group will have made to one another.

Expanding further on this point, the account would make good sense too of why the humanoids might hold one another responsible to norms that one or another values only in an indirect rather than a direct manner, to recall a distinction from the first section. Assuming their own norms are egalitarian, they may well

---

[18] This construal treats praise and blame as being on a par in that respect. It diverges from the view under which praising someone for acting well may mean just admiring them for being that sort of agent, while blaming them for acting badly means holding them responsible for what they did and need not have done. On that alternative way of understanding praise, it may be sensible to praise someone for an action even while holding that, intuitively, they were psychologically unable to do anything else; on this possibility, see (Wolf 1990).

censure someone who holds by racist norms for acting in a racist way, to return to that example, when the other holds by deeper norms or values—perhaps just the epistemic ideal of treating likes alike—that they may invoke to censure the other's embrace of racist norms and the racist actions that those norms prompt.

The third advantage mentioned earlier is that the account can also make sense of why the humanoids would extend censure and commendation to themselves as well as other individual agents, and to agents of a corporate kind as well as to individuals.

Holding themselves responsible will make sense in any creatures like the humanoids that can practice self-exhortation and judge their actions as they judge the actions of others. This exercise may involve holding themselves responsible to shared, beneficial norms or to quite partial commitments made to others. But it may involve holding themselves responsible to a purely personal self-commitment: say, the resolution to adopt and stick by a certain diet. And it may involve holding themselves responsible to epistemic values, as in castigating or congratulating themselves for how they reasoned their way to this or that conclusion.

The account would also make sense of why the humanoids are liable to hold corporate bodies as well as individual agents responsible for what they do. Suppose a group of individual humans or humanoids pledge to act with one another, under the direction of a personally or procedurally authorized voice, in reliably pursuing common goals according to common judgments. Those individuals will act jointly so as to constitute a corporate agent, by our account of agency: they will be organized so as to be able to pursue their goals across different situations, whether by this or that member or sub-agency; they will operate, in human examples, like a corporation or church or voluntary association.

It is intuitively important that such bodies, whether in human or humanoid society, should be fit to be held responsible under shared norms and laws, since otherwise individuals may be able to hide from censure behind the corporate veil, arguing that they were individually blameless (Pettit 2007c; List and Pettit 2011). Our account explains why the humanoids will likely take such bodies, if they emerge in this society, to be fit to be held responsible for the things they do. It will make perfect sense for them to exhort such a body to comply with certain standards. And so it will make sense for them to hold that body responsible for their success or failure in living up to such standards.[19]

---

[19] This observation is consistent with thinking that the internal dynamics of a corporation—the relationship between creditors, shareholders, and management—may limit the range of values to which it can prove answerable; such a body may have valuational control over whether or not to obey the law without having control over whether or not to respond to the sorts of considerations that might move a virtuous individual or group (Pettit 2023b, Ch. 6). The observation would seem to extend also to the unincorporated group of jointly acting individuals—say, those on a beach who might save a swimmer in difficulty; plausibly, such a group can be exhorted ex ante to organize a rescue and be held responsible ex post for not having done so.

6.3 From responsibility to free will

6.3.1 The ought-implies-can assumption

One of the main reasons why we human beings believe in free will is that we take it to be a power or capacity that must be present in anyone, including ourselves, whom we hold responsible for the things they do under suitable conditions. The general presumption is that in the sense associated with obligation, 'ought' implies 'can', so that if it is said that someone ought to have done something, as praise or blame implies, then it must be that in some sense they could have performed the action. The action was up to them, under their control. And what free will consists in is the capacity that is exercised in such control.

Many philosophers have held that free will in this sense is incompatible with the naturalistic view of the world under which every event materializes under a regime of natural cause and chance. This incompatibilism has led some to be non-naturalists, holding that free will represents a force in the world that is not recognized in natural science. Non-naturalism raises a host of problems, however, since it is hard to see how the forces tracked in natural science could operate normally in the presence of such a power. That has led other incompatibilists to embrace a hard naturalism according to which natural science is reliable and the idea of free will is misconceived: it is a fiction or an illusion (Harris 2010; Sapolsky 2023).

Compatibilists hold, in opposition to both of these views, that it is possible to make sense of the free will presupposed by the ought-can connection within a naturalistic view of the world and we shall see that such a compatibilism is implied by the account of responsibility supported for the humanoids by our genealogy. Compatibilism endorses naturalism but naturalism of a soft rather than a hard variety, arguing that natural science and free will, despite appearances, are compatible with each other. Compatibilists are often somewhat revisionary, casting free will as something less than it is often taken to be, but the ideal is to be able to defend a version of soft naturalism that minimizes the need to revise the received concept of free will.

As we shall see, the account of free will supported by our genealogy has a good claim to satisfy this desideratum. It equates free will among the humanoids with the fitness to be held responsible that they will routinely ascribe to themselves and one another. And it turns out that free will in that sense offers a naturalistically intelligible, conceptually faithful model of free will, as it is generally understood among humans.[20]

---

[20] For a useful overview of different recent approaches to free will, ranging from compatibilist approaches to those like non-naturalism and hard naturalism that assert an incompatibility between free will and natural science, see (Kane 2011). As noted later, compatibilism comes in many different forms. For two quite different but significant versions see, for example, (Dennett 1984) and (List 2019).

While the ought-can connection is widely endorsed, it has been treated very differently in two contrasting approaches to free will, both often cast in a compatibilist form. The more traditional approach focuses on the 'can' in the formula that links it with 'ought'; looks for an independent specification of the capacity involved: in effect, an account of freewill; and then goes on to the issue of whether it supports the 'ought': whether it is enough to make sense of the practice of holding responsible. The other approach, championed by Peter Strawson (1962) in his classic paper, *Freedom and Resentment*, focuses instead on the 'ought' and, assuming that the practice of holding responsible is both inescapable and irreproachable, seeks to elaborate the capacity—presumptively, the free will—that it presupposes.[21]

We have been documenting the practice of holding responsible that would likely emerge among the humanoids, being grounded in their capacity for commitment, and the exhortation it licenses. We now go on to look at how this would entitle them to ascribe a capacity that deserves to be characterized in our terms as free will. In following this genealogical line of thinking, we will be adopting a version of the second, ought-first strategy. Starting from a practice of holding responsible that we take to be intelligibly present among the humanoids, we ask after the sort of capacity it presupposes and look at how far this is a capacity that we can identify as free will.

6.3.2 Ought-first and can-first approaches to free will

Any approach to free will which begins from the practice of holding someone responsible presupposes a set of standards or values to which the agent is held responsible and identifies free will with a capacity in the agent to live up to their values, regardless of the presence of various obstacles. This need not commit the approach to any particular view of the values to which the agent should be held responsible in any context. In the humanoid, and indeed the human case, they can be practical or epistemic values, for example; and if practical, they can be identified with the values, personal or shared, that underlie the explicit or tacit commitments agents make in a range of domains. Those commitments may emerge in personal, perhaps idiosyncratic resolutions, in the ad hoc reliance of the members of a gang on one another, in people's presumed endorsement of conventional standards, in their attachment to socially entrenched norms, or in their advocacy of moral ideals in common with other individuals.

In taking free will as that capacity, whatever it is, that makes people fit to be held responsible, the ought-first approach has some significant implications. Thus, in identifying the role of free will it focuses on cases where the demands of the

---

[21] The can-first approach to free will may also be motivated on grounds only contingently connected with the ought-can linkage. It may seem to be supported, for example, by the phenomenology of free choice and the lesson it allegedly teaches about the autonomy of the agent in relation to natural influences on what they do.

agent's values are at issue; if it allows a role for free will in other cases, it can do so only by postulating that were such values engaged there, the agent would be able to live up to them. And the capacity with which it identifies free will in any relevant case is one that may come in degrees, licensing the description of an agent as weak or strong of will. This is to say that on an ought-first way of thinking, free will is likely to be equated with what we know colloquially as willpower. We return to that thought at the end of the section.

By contrast with the ought-first line, the can-first approach tends to cast free will as something that is equally at issue in every choice, no matter how unconnected with the agent's values. Thus, for Hume (1993, S 8.1) it is manifested in the fact that 'if we choose to remain at rest, we may; if we choose to move, we also may'; what we do, he says, depends on 'the determinations of the will'. Moreover, can-first approaches also take the capacity to choose an option to be the same sort of capacity, regardless of the evaluative significance of the option. And they tend to think of free will as something an agent has fully or lacks completely; it leaves little room for talk of the strength or weakness of an agent's will.

As this sketch of the difference between the views indicates, the ought-first approach makes the task of vindicating free will rather easier than the can-first. It needs to establish just that an agent has the ability to act on their values in face of countervailing influences while the alternative, as it is often understood, needs to establish that the agent has the ability to act on their will in face of a more open range of obstacles that might be thought to get in their way. To believe in an ought-first version of free will is to expect the agent to be able to stand by their values and counter a restricted range of countervailing influences; to believe in a can-first version is to expect them to be able to stand with their will, period. Thus, the can-first approach is more likely to generate the thought that free will requires a capacity of an essentially non-natural kind.

Despite this difference, however, both views can claim to be conceptually or analytically acceptable, to return to a point made about philosophical theory in the first chapter. They count as conceptual deservers of the free will name insofar as they each satisfy a significant bunch of the assumptions we ordinarily make about free will. But they identify quite different theoretical deservers, differing about the worldly referent that the concept should be taken to designate: differing about which would best explain the presumptive importance of free will (Pettit 2020). While they may offer equally acceptable, nominal definitions of free will, in other words—distinct articulations of how we think of free will—they conflict sharply in its real definition: in the account of what in the world constitutes free will.

6.3.3 What it takes for a capacity to constitute free will

We may begin with a formula that registers standard assumptions about what free will requires—this among humanoids, presumptively, as well as humans—regardless of whether it is interpreted in the can-first or ought-first manner. Unless a theory makes these assumptions plausible, it can scarcely count as a theory of free will; the capacity that it elucidates will not be a conceptual deserver of the name.

The formula goes like this:

1. An agent enjoys free will in deciding between the options in a choice *insofar as*
2. it is possible for them to realize any of those options,
3. they are at the causal source of whatever option is realized,
4. and they control for whether or not to realize the option
5. regardless of non-excusing, disruptive influences on the choice.

There are a number of observations we should make about this formula, since it is meant to be acceptable within any theory of free will, can-first or ought-first. One feature worth remarking is that while the formula gives us conditions that should suffice for the presence of free will, the use of 'insofar as' rather than a plain 'if' allows that free will may come in degrees. This is important since an ought-first view of free will, as we noted, may allow it to come in degrees. But the 'insofar as' clause does not require that it come in degrees and does not rule out a can-first reading of the capacity.[22]

The three clauses immediately following the first hold respectively that the options in the choice each represent a possibility that the agent may realize or not; that the agent should be the causal source—the author, as it is often put—of the possibility they actually realize; and that they should give rise to that action, not contingently, but in the manner of a controller. It is an important feature of the formula that it keeps all three in the picture: possibility, causality, and control. Rival theories of free will usually have something to say about each, although they differ sharply, of course, in what they say.

The fifth clause in the formula, to note a final interesting feature, marks the connection of free will with issues about compatibilism and incompatibilism that are addressed in almost every theory. According to this condition, free will requires the agent to have control over the natural, non-excusing causes and chances that may affect a choice. Could such control be realized in a naturalistic world, as in a soft-naturalist picture? Or does it entail that free will would have to be a power unknown to natural science, as non-naturalists and hard naturalists would agree? Every standard theory provides an answer to those questions.

---

[22] Why 'insofar as', however, rather than 'just insofar as'? Why the counterpart of an 'if' rather than the counterpart of an 'if and only if'? Most theories will support the stronger claim—including that which is sketched here—but the formula is designed to leave that open.

With this formula in hand, we can now proceed to look at the candidate for free will among the humanoids that our story about responsibility suggests and to explore how far it offers an attractive view. The candidate capacity is that which makes an agent fit to be held responsible in value-engaging choices: fit to be blamed, as it may be, or fit to be praised. We can now take the clauses one by one and identify the ways in which that candidate may meet each. The upshot is a view of humanoid free will—and, potentially, of human free will—that satisfies the various conditions and consequently has enormous appeal.

6.3.3.1 An agent enjoys free will in deciding between the options in a choice
Our theory of responsibility among the humanoids suggests, as mentioned, that a natural candidate for the role of free will—the role defined by the conditions in our free will formula—is the capacity that is postulated in treating someone as fit to be held responsible. This is the capacity in a humanoid agent to control for the expected realization of their values in the absence of obstacles that are recognized as excusing. This capacity will make someone fit to be held responsible for whether or not they do something when their values are engaged—whether or not they tell the truth—and will consist in the valuational control the agent enjoys in virtue of being responsive and exposed to exhortation.

If this power were only present in virtue of the agent's exposure to the exhortation of another, however, then the bearer of free will would strictly be, not the agent as such, but the agent-in-the-presence-of-their-exhorter: a dyad rather than a monad. The first clause in the formula may be taken to rule this out insofar as it focuses on the single agent as the bearer of free will. And that tells us how we should take the power that makes humanoids fit to be held responsible for living up to the demands of some value—say, once again, the value of telling the truth—when we identify free will with that power. We should take it to be the power the humanoids each have in virtue of being responsive and exposed to self-exhortation: the capacity they enjoy qua self-empowering subjects that makes them fit to be held responsible.

According to this first clause, the target of explication in the formula is the nature of the free will that an agent may enjoy in making a choice. This is consistent with thinking that it is primarily involved, as on an ought-first approach, in value-engaging choices—that is, choices where the agent's values are relevant and there are no excusing obstacles in play—and only secondarily involved in others. As already noted, free will is going to be involved in other choices insofar as the valuational control with which it is identified among the humanoids implies that no matter how value-neutral the actual options in any choice, the agent would be able to control for the satisfaction of their values, should their values be brought into play.

But though the range of free will is not greatly restricted by the focus on choices where issues of responsibility arise, that focus is still significant. It marks off the free will that is elucidated in ought-first approaches like that to which we are directed in the case of the humanoids from can-first competitors. On those rival views, free will is engaged on the same pattern in any choice, even one where there is no issue about responsibility to certain values. It will be engaged, for example, in deciding whether to reach for the packet of soap on the right or the packet on the left, whether to wave at a friend or call out a greeting, whether to wear this or that item of clothing: it will be engaged, as it is sometimes said, in picking as well as choosing (Ullman-Margalit and Morgenbesser 1977).

6.3.3.2 It is possible for the agent to realize any of those options
This clause is going to be interpreted differently, like the first, depending on whether free will is conceived in the can-first or ought-first way. If it is taken in the can-first manner, then the possibility invoked is going to be univocal across the different options that the agent may take. This will be so, for example, if free will is taken to consist in a non-natural power of thwarting the forces of natural cause and chance, overriding what naturalistic history and law would otherwise have put in place. And it will equally be so, if free will is taken to consist in some naturalistic counterpart, whatever that might be, of such a power. According to any such can-first theory, the sense in which it is possible to do X or do Y in a choice—to remain at rest or to move, in Hume's example—is the same in each case: it is symmetrical across the options in the choice.

Things are going to be different on any ought-first view, giving free will an asymmetrical character (Wolf 1990). On such a view free will is going to be engaged primarily in choices where the agent's values are engaged and where only one option promises to deliver satisfaction of the relevant values; we may set aside the case where a number of options tie in this regard. In a choice of that kind, it will be one thing to say that it is possible for the agent to live up to the demand of their values and choose the favored option; it will be quite another to say that it is possible for them to fail in this regard by choosing another option instead. Suppose the choice is between telling the truth and lying, and that truth-telling is a shared norm and value. It will be one thing to say that it is possible for the agent to tell the truth and another to say that it is possible for them to lie. This is because of a background assumption that while telling the truth may be difficult in view of free riding and other temptations, failing to tell the truth will face no such obstacles.

On the account of fitness to be held responsible developed in our genealogy, it will be possible for the humanoid agent to tell the truth insofar as they are responsive and exposed to self-exhortation in support of truth-telling. They will be responsive to such exhortation insofar as they are self-exhortable, enjoying the resources required for exhortation to be successful. And they will be exposed to exhortation insofar as they actually self-exhort. But self-exhorting need not mean actively sensitizing themselves to the value of truth-telling and actively scaffolding their capacity to respond. As we know, it may simply mean being on standby to do this if a red flag should go up: if, for example, it is clear to them that they might succumb to the temptation to lie.

It will be possible for the agent to tell the truth, by this account, regardless of the disruptive, non-excusing obstacles that may stand in their way. Assuming the absence of excusing obstacles, and the normal operation of the world, their responsiveness and exposure to self-exhortation will ensure that even if they lie in their actual circumstances, it will remain the case that they could have told the truth in the sense of 'you could have' that corresponds to the exhortative 'you can'.

The sense in which it will be possible for the agent to lie is quite different, by this story, from the sense in which it is possible for them to tell the truth. Lying will be possible for them in the sense that it will be consistent with the absence of excusing obstacles and the agent's responsiveness and exposure to self-exhortation. Those conditions may make it possible in the exhortation-related sense for the agent to tell the truth, but it will not make truth-telling inevitable. And so, by implication, it will remain possible for the agent to lie, albeit in a much weaker sense of possibility.[23]

6.3.3.3 The agent is at the causal source of whatever option is realized

It is not enough according to this condition that the action should be caused by a state within the agent, even an attitudinal state like a desire; it must be the product in some sense of the agent themselves: it must be an action that the agent authors or owns, as it is often put. The kettle may be said to boil the water in the sense that it is something within the kettle—say, the heat of the element—that does that work. But that is hardly all that is involved when an agent decides to change the world in this or that respect. If it were, it would make the agent the arena where the action is caused, contrary to this third requirement, not in any sense its author.

The association between an agent's doing something of their own free will and being the author or owner of the action is marked in many different theories. It is often stipulated in the spirit of this idea that the sense in which the agent is the cause of the action is sui generis: that agent-causation—sometimes agent-causation in a sense that is alien to natural science (Chisholm 1982)—is not reducible to event-causation (see too Steward 2012). But even those who are willing to think of causation as fundamentally a relation between events are likely to hold that there is something special about how an agent relates to their actions, or at least to those actions that are properly the product of their free will.

Thus, Harry Frankfurt (1971; 1988) emphasizes that the agent who counts as the author of an action must identify with that state within them—the profile of their beliefs and desires—that gives rise to an action, and this identification must play an effective role. Frankfurt suggests that the unwilling addict is an exemplar of

---

[23] This observation opens up interesting issues about the semantics of such diverse possibility assignments, but we ignore these here.

someone who does not identify in this way with the desire that leads them to give in to the addiction; such an agent may be the arena where the action materializes but they are not properly its author. But the willing addict is not much better off. For while this agent may claim to identify with their addictive desire, the identification plays no role: the addictive desire would still operate, even if the agent ceased to identify with it. And so this individual too will be the arena of action, not the author at the action's source.

Frankfurt (1988, 18) admits that the notion of authorship, and of the identification that it seems to require, is 'analytically puzzling'. In an earlier response (Frankfurt 1971), he proposed that what it means for an agent to identify with the desire that moves them at the ground-level of action is that they desire at a higher level that that desire should indeed move them, and that they would not be moved by the ground-level desire if it did not conform to the higher-order desire (Dworkin 1970; 1988). The problem with that suggestion as an analysis of the authorship associated with free will is that the higher-order desire may itself have a pathological character of a kind with addiction; it may be the product of childhood indoctrination or whatever (Watson 1975). If addiction at the one level can deprive an agent of the authorship of their action, surely indoctrination at a higher level can do so too.[24]

It is a striking feature of this attempt to vindicate the authorship idea—and of others in the same mold—that it is grounded in a can-first approach to free will. On the sort of ought-first approach supported in the genealogy, however, the authorship issue does not pose a particular problem. Insofar as an agent is fit to be held responsible for an action—by any plausible analysis of such fitness—it is natural to think that they are its author. Thus, the fact that they are responsible for the action, by the account defended here, means that they chose it in the absence of excusing obstacles and in presence of a power derived from their responsiveness and exposure to self-exhortation. That feature of the action would naturally lead us to think of the agent as its author, not just an arena where other forces are at work.

One final observation: that an agent is the author of an action in this sense— that they are fit on this front to be held responsible for it—has to be consistent with their failing to live up to their values in what they do. Thus, authorship, if we may continue to use that term, comes in two varieties. In one, it consists in the agent's having the standing ability to live up to their values, whether or not they actually manage to do so; in the other, it consists in exercising that ability and realizing the ideal. In this respect, authorship is like the Kantian idea of autonomy, as we shall see in the next chapter, for it too can count as an ability that

---

[24] This problem may be postponed, of course, by requiring that the agent identify with the higher-order desire too. But the same sort of problem will arise if that identification is analyzed in terms of conformity with the desire at a higher order still to be moved by that higher-order desire.

agents possess on a relatively enduring basis or as an achievement that they may not always bring off.[25]

6.3.3.4 The agent controls for whether or not to realize the option

It might be possible for an agent to be in some sense at the causal source of an action without having control over it. The agent will have control over the action insofar as they choose it with a view to realizing a certain desired feature or effect; they control for the realization of that result in their choice of action. Control in this sense is exemplified even in a mechanical system like the heating-cooling system in a building: it controls for keeping the ambient temperature within a certain range.

Non-naturalistic theories, whether of a can-first or ought-first variety, will take control of this kind to require a force unfamiliar to natural science, while naturalistic theories will try to make sense of it without resorting to such an extreme. None of these theories, however, requires control to be successful. An agent may enjoy control in a choice without succeeding in realizing the effect for which they control. Control implies merely the robust possibility of success: in the free will case, the distinctive sort of possibility that would license holding the agent responsible for what they did.

Can-first theories that take free will to be compatible with the natural order of cause or chance can assume a number of forms. The most traditional, however, holds that the agent will be in control of the action they causally generate insofar as it is the case, all going well, that something like the following is true in a choice between X and Y: if they were to wish or choose or try to do X, they would do X, and if they were to wish or choose or try to do Y, they would do Y. The idea is that they will be able in that case to control for fulfilling their wish, realizing their choice, or succeeding in what they try to do.

This conditional account of free will is subject to a range of problems (Maier 2022). The main one is that it may apply to an agent in a given choice without that agent's enjoying anything like control over what option to take and so, intuitively, without their enjoying free will. The analysis invokes a mental act like wishing or choosing or trying or whatever and the problem is that while it may be true that the agent would take one or another option depending on what mental act was in place, they might have no control whatsoever over that act itself. Suppose that someone is agoraphobic and cannot bear to leave their home and enter a public space. It may be true of them, consistently with that agoraphobia, that if they were to wish or choose or try to go outdoors, they would, and that if they were to wish or choose or try to stay indoors they would. But it is not true of them, because of the agoraphobia, that they could wish or choose or try to go outdoors: they would be

---

[25] The same applies to the notion of orthonomy that is proposed as an alternative to autonomy in (Pettit and Smith 1996).

incapable of adopting that initiative. In other words, it is not true of them that they have control over what to do in the choice and that they enjoy free will in selecting their preferred option.[26]

The sort of ought-first approach supported for the humanoids in our genealogy does much better than that sort of alternative in making sense of the control condition. The individual who is fit to be held responsible for living up to their values must control, as we saw, for the satisfaction of the relevant values in any choice: they must enjoy valuational control. All going well, it must be that if their values require that they take X in a given choice, they will recognize and respond to that demand, and that if the values require that they take Y, they will recognize and respond to that demand instead. On our story, that will be true of the humanoids insofar as they are responsive and exposed to self-exhortation in the name of those values.

It might be thought that this view is subject to a difficulty analogous to that which arises for a naturalistic, conditional account. It might seem to require that the agent did indeed exhort themselves to live up to their values, raising the question as to whether they enjoyed control over the exhortative act itself. But by our account the agent need not have exhorted themselves actively to satisfy the demand of their values. They will be fit to be held responsible under that account, and they will enjoy the control required for free will, insofar as they self-exhort in a virtual or standby sense. What is essential in other words is merely that they meet a certain specification on their make-up: that they are committed to relevant standards or values and are disposed, should a red flag go up—should they recognize the possibility of failing to act on those values—to resort to active self-exhortation.

Notwithstanding this observation, it may seem that a regress problem arises in the case where the agent does resort to active self-exhortation. For in that case, the question will still arise as to whether the agent enjoys free will in that act of self-exhortation. But there is a ready answer available to that question. The agent will self-exhort as a matter of free will insofar as they are responsive and exposed to the effect of an exhortation to self-exhort in that way: insofar as they have relevant sort of control over the self-exhortation. And that does not open up a regress, since the self-exhortation required to ensure control at that level—or, as it may be, at any prior level—may have a purely virtual or standby character.

---

[26] G. E. Moore (1911, Ch. 6) is famous for defending this sort of conditional account but, as we saw, David Hume (1993, S 8.1) had defended the analysis earlier, arguing that free will appears in the fact that 'if we choose to remain at rest, we may; if we choose to move, we also may'. It may be suggested, of course, that the mental act itself can be controlled by the agent in virtue of a higher-level mental act of wishing or choosing or trying to perform the prior mental act. But the same problem will arise at that higher level—is the agent able to make that higher-level wish or choice or attempt?—and if a similar solution is invoked there, an indefinite regress will loom. For an overview of this and related problems, see (Berofsky 2005).

6.3.3.5 This control obtains regardless of non-excusing, disruptive influences on the choice

By all accounts, naturalistic or otherwise, the actions that agents generate, like any other events in the world, take place under the influence of natural cause and chance. That raises a sharp question about this final condition in our specification of the requirements of free will. If free will requires the agent to be in control of what they do, regardless of the natural influences that may shape their action—apart, of course, from familiar excusing obstacles—then that may suggest that free will requires a power to neutralize such influences. That belief has led hard naturalists to think that free will is an illusion and non-naturalists to celebrate it as a special, even spooky power. Happily, the responsibility-based approach that our genealogy supports can explain why the final condition can be satisfied by the humanoids in a world where natural cause and chance prevail.

The key to the explanation is that, as we saw, the humanoids will resort to exhortation—as indeed human beings will resort to it—only when no excusing or other factors threaten to make it ineffective. Moreover, they will resort to such exhortation, say to tell the truth, only because of expecting it to serve a useful role: in effect, because of taking the addressee to be exhortable to the point where exhortation can help get them to tell the truth. But suppose they realize, perhaps because of being naturalists, that there may be non-excusing natural factors in play that will incline the agent to lie. While these will materialize at the neural level in one or another variety of forms, they may correspond to factors like those that operate under conditions that we human beings name as laziness or akrasia, irresolution or caprice.

Will the recognition of such potential hurdles inhibit humanoid exhortation, as the recognition of radically excusing obstacles would do? Not on the story we told. The humanoids will take exhortation to presuppose and reinforce a power—a power reflected in the evocative *you-can*—of overcoming such hurdles. Indeed, the point of the exhortation will presumably be to get the subject over those obstacles with the help of the sensitization and scaffolding it provides.

This is to say that in exhorting an agent to a course of action like truth-telling, the humanoids will take it to be possible for the agent to tell the truth robustly over variations on their circumstances in which such natural obstacles come into play. But as the humanoids will take their exhortation of an individual to put the recommended action under the agent's control, prompting them to pay greater attention to the values in play, so they will take the self-exhortation of that individual—whether in an active or standby form—to have the same effect.

The humanoids will maintain this view of the individual even in the wake of a failure to act as exhorted. They will identify with the self-exhortative stance of the agent and hold that despite their failure, that responsiveness and exposure to exhortation would have given the agent the ability to live up to their values. They may not have manifested that ability in what they did but they certainly made their choice in its presence.

How will they explain the failure of the individual to manifest the ability with which they credit that agent? Presumably by reference to temptations associated with a temporary impulse, a passing whim, a moment of irresolution, or whatever. Thus, if they hold nevertheless that the agent had the ability ascribed—and that it was appropriate for the agent to exhortatively ascribe that ability to themselves—they must hold that that ability remained intact. They will think that the power the agent enjoyed in virtue of their self-exhortation, active or virtual, was not neutralized by the presence of such a natural, non-excusing influence.

This will not commit the humanoids to a rejection of the naturalistic view that whatever happens in the world is a function of the sorts of forces identified in natural science. Consistently with holding that an individual is sensitive to self-exhortation, the humanoids may think that what gives the agent that sensitivity or power is the scientifically intelligible way they are organized at levels—neural, chemical, physical, or whatever—that are explored in natural science. And they may think that the sensitization provided by the agent's active or virtual self-exhortation to live up to their values helps to consolidate and perhaps increase that power, having an appropriate effect at such lower levels of organization. On this picture, self-exhortation is constituted ultimately by a lower-level factor—a neural catalyst, as it were—and ensures that that factor is in play within the natural framework from which the action emerges.

Assume, on an image already introduced in the second chapter, that the world displays different levels of organization, with higher levels being grounded in lower: this, in the sense that the lower, physical level determines what happens at the chemical, the chemical (and so, physical) what happens at the biological, the biological (and so, physical and chemical) what happens at the psychological, and so on. And allow that a higher-level factor will have programmed for an effect at the same level, first, if its actual lower-level realizer led to the appearance of a lower-level realizer of that effect and, second, if this would have been true, at least in general, of any lower-level realizer that happened to be in place. All that need be true for the humanoid picture to be appropriate is that a self-sensitizing sensitivity to certain values on the part of an individual generally programs for their living up to those values in how they act on this or that occasion.[27]

We noted earlier in this section that the ought-first approach can identify free will, not with a capacity to resist any influences from the natural world, but only those that threaten their valuational control: their fidelity to the values they endorse. It is totally consistent with a naturalistic view of the world, deterministic or indeterministic, to think that humanoids and humans may be so physically organized—this, by virtue of nature, nurture, and habit—that their value commitments generally overcome the various influences that might push them in a different direction: they generally program for fidelity to those values.

---

[27] On this picture of the programming relationship between different levels of causal explanation, see (Jackson, Pettit, and Smith 2004, Pt. 1) and (Pettit 2017).

6.3.4 The upshot of the account

These observations argue strongly in favor of holding that the humanoids—and by analogy humans—will enjoy free will in a sense that meets all five conditions in our formula, and do so in a way that is compatible with naturalistic assumptions. They will each enjoy free will in choices where excuses are absent and their values are engaged. In such a choice it will be possible for them to realize the option that their values support but, this not being guaranteed, it will also be possible for them not to realize that option. They will count as the author or source of whatever they do insofar as they are fit to be held responsible for it. And they will exercise that authorship as an agent who enjoys the capacity, however defeasible, to control for the realization of their values. This valuational control will enable them to resist the sorts of non-excusing lures or pressures—the temptations—that might lead them astray. But being supported by their own physical nature and organization, it will not give them anything like a non-natural power of overcoming natural law and history.

That means that their fitness to be held responsible which we documented in the second section—or, if you like, the control capacity that makes for such fitness—is both a conceptual and a theoretical deserver of the free-will name. It is a conceptual deserver insofar as it makes all the clauses in our formula true and a theoretical deserver insofar as it explains in a parsimonious, naturalistic manner why free will, so construed, would be taken to be important by the humanoids, and indeed by us; its importance shows up in the fact that the presence of free will when an agent makes a certain choice explains why they are fit to be held responsible for what they choose.

In introducing the distinction between ought-first and can-first approaches to free will, we mentioned that ought-first approaches tend to identify free will with what is often cast as willpower. The upshot of the approach developed in our genealogy can be summed up nicely in the idea that the humanoids will enjoy, and ascribe to themselves, precisely this sort of capacity. Their willpower will be potentially if not actually relevant in every choice; it will be possible for them to exercise it or fail to exercise it; its successful exercise will make them the causal source of the consequent action; it will give them a significant, if defeasible degree of control over what they do in the absence of excusing obstacles; and it will do this, regardless of a variety of non-excusing factors that may stand in the way of its successful exercise.

6.3.5 Freewill as willpower

The conception of free will as willpower has some distinctive features that are worth marking and that may help in some part to explain why it should have special importance among the humanoids.

A first feature is that it identifies free will with a capacity that is distinctive of humanoids, and presumably of humans, marking them off from other animals. We may prize giving animals a high degree of freedom, as in the freedom of the wild, but there is little or no tradition of ascribing free will in that sense to them. This is entirely intelligible, since the willpower that constitutes free will requires valuing, exhorting, and ascribing responsibility, and such practices are lacking in other species, even species that are genetically close to humans and indeed humanoids.

But while the account licenses the ascription of free will only to humanoid and human agents, to go to a second feature, it does not restrict it to individuals. A well-organized group of individuals, in particular a group that is collectively committed to certain standards, will not just be fit to be exhorted to comply with those standards and to be held responsible to them. It will also exercise standby self-exhortation insofar as members are required or entitled under its rules of operation to draw attention to any red flag—any danger of failing to stick by its ideals—and positioned to sensitize the group to its received values, scaffolding its capacity to perform up to par. Perhaps the best way of underlining the naturalistic character of free will, on the account suggested by our genealogy, is to recognize that it may be present in the corporate entities that humanoids form as well as in humanoid individuals: depending on how well they are organized they may display a greater or less degree of willpower in relation to their values.[28]

A third feature of humanoid free will, unsurprising in willpower, is that it may come in different degrees of strength. Value-sensitive, self-sensitizing agents may differ both in their sensitivity or exhortability and in the capacity to sharpen that sensitivity when exhorting themselves to be true to those values. This variation corresponds to that which is acknowledged among human beings when we think that someone may be relatively weak or strong of will: in a familiar reworking of ancient Greek terms, they may be more or less *akratic* or *enkratic*.

Given this possibility of variation, individuals are liable to differ in how far they enjoy willpower and free will: in the extent to which they are physically organized by nature, nurture, and habit so as to enjoy valuational control over what they do. Every functioning humanoid, and presumably every human being, will enjoy a sufficient degree of willpower to give them a place in the exhortative community, and to make them fit to be held responsible. But by grace of their genes, their upbringing, or their habits, they may vary considerably in how far they display willpower and enjoy free will.

A fourth feature of the conception of free will as willpower is that it will be possible for the humanoids, as it is for humans, to develop greater strength of will with practice, or to become weaker of will with a lack of practice. Sensitivity and

---

[28] On the conception of corporate agency that would keep this possibility open, see (List and Pettit 2011). Christian List (2019) holds the same view on this issue, but views free will in a can-first way and differs on a range of related questions.

sensitization will presumably improve or decline, depending on the level of exhortation to which an individual is exposed and on the degree of effort they make in exhorting themselves. It implies that making a choice will often constitute a struggle, in which the agent tries to get themselves to act in a manner they value and to resist the temptation to do otherwise: they try to get themselves to mobilize their power of will.

A fifth related feature of the equation of free will with willpower is that it makes sense of the agonistic phenomenology of free will, as that is familiar among humans. We may expect decision-making among humanoids to involve the same sort of struggle that human beings undergo as they exhort themselves to live up to their values, conscious of the pressure exerted by more contingent but sometimes more forceful desires. It explains why in many cases the spirit is willing, as the metaphor has it, but the flesh is weak.

6.3.6 The social embedding of free will

These considerations suggest that humanoid free will, as explained in the genealogy, may offer a good model for human free will. But it is worth emphasizing in conclusion that, on that model, free will is socially grounded in a way that is not often recognized. It evolves on a practice-dependent basis, presupposing for its appearance that agents have learned to commit to certain values in tandem with others and have developed habits of exhorting one another—and themselves—to live up to those values, coming to ascribe responsibility for doing so. And as it is practice-dependently realized, so free will is practice-dependently recognized on the picture emerging from our genealogy. It is only from within the practices of exhortation and holding responsible that people's capacities to live up to their values get to be seen from the appropriate you-can or you-could, I-can or I-could, perspective. Again, none of this is surprising as we begin to recognize that free will in that sense amounts to nothing more or less than willpower.

Despite this practice-dependence, the view supported by the genealogy is compatibilist, as we have already emphasized, since it does not presuppose a non-naturalistic world. The capacities ascribed in ex-ante exhortation and its ex-post counterpart, the ascription of responsibility, may be grounded in the causal or chancy processes that natural science reveals. They may come to exist in virtue of an arrangement of those processes within humans and humanoids that makes them susceptible to exhortation and generally responsive to its sensitizing, scaffolding effects.

But it is one thing to say, in this compatibilist spirit, that the property of free will is constituted of natural materials and that its workings are compatible with all that natural science is likely to reveal about the world. It is quite another, as we mentioned in Chapter 1, to hold that the concept as distinct from the property lends itself to a similar compatibilist account. To say that it does would be to say that the concepts employed in natural science include the concept of free will or that they can serve to define a translational equivalent of that concept. And that is extremely unlikely to be the case. Natural science may be able to explain how the make-up and interactions of humans and humanoids will lead them to recognize the presence of free will in one another or in themselves. But that is not a reason why it should itself make use of the concept in explaining how the world operates.

An analogy with indexical thinking can help to elucidate this possibility, as we also noted in Chapter 1. Natural science has no use for concepts like *now* and *here* and *I*—essential though they may be in ordinary thinking (Lewis 1979a; Perry 1979)—as it views the world in a wholly non-indexical manner. But it can still make sense of how individuals with language and thought may rely on their identity or location—more generally, on their perspective—to introduce such indexical concepts, giving the concepts a distinctive role in the explanation of their own responses. Similarly, natural science may have no use for the concept of free will or willpower, or indeed for related concepts like those of commitment and value, exhortation and responsibility. But it may still be able to make sense of how humans or humanoids can give such concepts an important role within their perspective on themselves and one another, introducing them in a way that relies on the inclinations and sensibilities induced by their social practices.[29]

We saw earlier in the chapter that the humanoids would likely build on their access to normative and evaluative practices and concepts by developing a practice of holding others, and holding themselves, responsible to the values they endorse. As we have seen in this last section, the practice makes room for identifying a capacity they will each have, and ascribe to themselves and one another, as participants within that practice. With all of these elements of our genealogy in place, we are in a position to explain why the humanoids will be robustly likely to go further still, developing a practice in which they come to constitute and see themselves as persons, and to develop a distinctive sense of their personal identity. We turn to that topic in the next chapter.

---

[29] Insofar as the concepts can only be mastered by someone with those responses, they are responsive-dependent in the sense of being response-dependently mastered (Jackson and Pettit 2002; Pettit 2004b, Pt 1). But they are not response-dependent in the more common sense that Mark Johnston (1989) gave the term. On that account, a response-dependent concept like that of being red is better cast as response-dispositional (Johnston 1993). It presents redness as a disposition to elicit the relevant response—a disposition to look red to normal observers—rather than presenting redness as a categorical property that is properly discernible only by those who experience color sensations.

7
Personhood and self-identity

We looked in Chapter 5 at how language would enable the humanoids to make commitments, satisfying their desire to establish their reliability with others and to enjoy mutual reliance in their relationships. And we saw that making commitments would involve their speaking, not just for themselves, but speaking for others too, and that it would enable them to think in evaluative terms, and to recognize the shared value of upholding social norms and complying with them.

With these observations in place, we went on to argue in the previous chapter that commissive creatures of a humanoid kind will develop the practice of holding one another, and themselves, responsible for their actions. By making commitments, they will each expose themselves to a power of active or virtual exhortation by another. And the attitude adopted in this ex-ante exhortation of an individual allows those who identify with it ex post to hold that agent responsible for what they did. But as making commitments to others prompts the idea of making a commitment to themselves—forming a resolution—so exhorting others and holding them responsible will lead each to exhort and hold themselves responsible too. And, as we went on to argue, the control that self-exhortation, active or virtual, will give the humanoids constitutes a capacity that deserves to count as free will.

The profile of humanoids that emerges in this genealogy converges closely with the profile that we present to one another, and to ourselves, as human beings. Like the humanoids, we human beings are psychologically able to make judgments, reason about things, and bring reasoned judgments to bear on perception, developing a capacity we described as percipience. And like the humanoids we are capable of the social relationships established in practices of commitment and responsibility. But one of the distinctive things about human beings, at least as we think about ourselves, is that we treat one another and ourselves as persons and that we each embrace our identity over time as one and the same person. The aim of this chapter is to show that the humanoids will develop a capacity to constitute and relate as persons in just that sense.

The notion of personhood has figured prominently in Western philosophy and common thought, and we look in the first section of the chapter at the elements associated with personhood in the tradition, focusing on what makes a person the same self over time. This discussion involves more intellectual history than the discussion of earlier practices and capacities because the history is needed to uphold the claims made in characterization of persons: they are not so prominent in common thought as the claims made in the earlier cases. In the second section of the chapter, we develop an account of the practices of humanoids that will plausibly lead them to operate and conceive of themselves as persons in a way that explains the elements associated with the idea. And then in the third section, we look at where this conception of personhood will lead them—and perhaps lead us—in thinking about the self-identity of a person over time.

It may seem surprising to associate personhood with a practice or set of practices, taking it to involve an associated capacity or skill. The puzzle will resolve itself in the second section, with an account of why the humanoids will develop a conception of personhood and rely on it in characterizing themselves. The idea developed there is that there is a practice that used to be described in an old English term as personating; that the humanoids will be robustly likely to engage in this practice; and that being a person—or at least being a fully functioning person—consists in having and exercising the capacity to personate in that manner. As will be apparent, the capacity for personation is grounded in the capacities for commitment and holding responsible that we have already explored. It relates to those more basic capacities in much the way that the capacity for percipience relates to the more basic capacities for judgment and reasoning.

7.1 The idea of person and self

7.1.1 The elements of personhood

There are a range of assumptions about persons that are made in common thought—or at least consistent with common thought—and reflected in different philosophical theories. A theory will pass as a plausible theory of personhood only so long as it satisfies most, if not all, of them.

It is a presupposition shared on all sides, that persons are a sub-category of agents, in the sense of agency introduced in Chapter 2, and that like other agents they endure over time. With that in place, the assumptions upheld in philosophical and common thought fall into five broad categories. The first of these focuses on the capacities that personal as distinct from other agents may be expected to display. The next three identify different aspects of the normative status that personal agents and only personal agents allegedly enjoy. The first of these three normative assumptions is that only personal agents will have duties for which they can be held responsible; the second that they enjoy a dignity and a claim to being treated accordingly that distinguishes them from other agents; and the third that personhood will necessarily commit agents to a distinctive ideal of performance. And the fifth assumption, to which we will devote particular attention, is that personal agents enjoy a distinctive from of self-identity over time.

We look in this section at each of those elements in the received conception of personhood, as we may describe it. We do so by examining the ways in which they have been given prominence in the canonical, Western literature. Section 2 will be devoted to showing why their practices would lead humanoids to count as persons, and indeed to see themselves as persons, in this conception. And section 3 will go on to explain the ways in which they would consequently enjoy, and take themselves to enjoy, self-identity over time.

7.1.2 The capacities of persons

Boethius, a Roman senator and writer of the sixth century CE, offered a famous definition of persons that highlighted a capacity that he took to distinguish them from other agents. Often cast as the last of the ancient and the first of the medieval philosophers, he defined a person as: *individua substantia rationabilis naturae*. And, adopted by Thomas Aquinas, this came to represent the most commonly shared view of personhood, at least until the Reformation in the 1500s.

The Boethian definition casts the person as an individual entity, *individua substantia*, of a reasoning or ratiocinative nature: *rationabilis naturae*. The account says little or nothing about exactly what the capacity to reason involves but we can plausibly take it to encompass the range of intellectual capacities that mark human beings off from other animals. As we shall see, many writers in the modern and contemporary traditions have come to link personhood with other features as well but the idea that persons—or at least normally functioning persons—have to possess various intellectual capacities has remained a common assumption down to the present day.

That assumption is already present in the seventeenth-century writer John Locke, whose writing on personhood has been extraordinarily influential. While associating further features with personhood, as we shall see, he casts a person as 'a thinking intelligent Being, that has reason and reflection' (Locke 1975, 2.27.11). And that assumption is also endorsed by Immanuel Kant, writing a century later: 'non-rational beings', he tells us, are 'called *things*, whereas rational beings are called *persons*' (Kant 2012, 40). As his other writing makes clear, rationality for Kant does not mean rationality in the sense in which non-human animals may display it but rather, as in Boethius and Locke, something like the power of reasoning.

Unlike Boethius, Locke and Kant pass quickly over the characterization of personal capacities to focus on the normative features of agents; we shall look shortly at the features they highlight. In this relative neglect of the pre-normative characterization of persons, they are followed by most contemporary writers. But one prominent exception is Daniel Dennett (1979, Ch. 14), who offers a fairly rich account of the conditions of personhood, as he calls them. He takes the capacities of persons to include rationality or reasoning, 'self-consciousness of one sort or another', the ability to interact with others in the mutual ascription of attitudes, and the capacity to communicate in language.

7.1.3 First normative assumption: the responsibility of persons

Apart from assumptions based on the nature of persons, Locke introduced a normative idea that we also commonly make about persons. This appears in a comment to the effect that 'Person' is 'a forensic term, appropriating actions and their merit' (1975, 2.27.28). Elaborating on this feature, Locke explains that 'personality extends itself beyond present existence to what is past' and, as a result, 'owns and imputes to itself past actions, just upon the same ground and for the same reason as it does the present'.[1] He grounds the linkage between being a person and being responsible in the fact that a person, having 'reason and reflection', 'can consider itself as itself, the same thinking thing in different times and places'; not only does it endure over time, as everyone takes for granted, it sees itself as enduring in that way. We will return later in the section to this emphasis on the person's capacity to self-identify over time.

Locke's description of 'person' as a forensic term shows that he gives central importance to the widely accepted assumption that only persons can ascribe responsibility to other agents, or indeed to themselves, and that only persons are fit to be held responsible—at least in the absence of excusing obstacles—for the things they do. They are the sorts of agents, unlike other animals, that can participate in the practice of ascribing responsibility, as we described it in the last chapter, including the practice in which they ascribe responsibility to themselves.

Most of us endorse this connection between responsibility and personhood, despite the variety of human traditions. We may expect that non-human animals will behave on a certain pattern, and we may try to train them into doing so. But we will not hold them to those expectations in the way in which we hold human persons to expectations. We may reward them for meeting the expectations or penalize them for not doing so. But we will not do this in the manner in which we commend or condemn other human beings—in effect, persons—when we treat them as properly responsible.

The responsibility assumption that we make about persons in common thought raises a nice question about incorporated groups insofar as they constitute agents in their own right (List and Pettit 2011). If such groups are fit to be held responsible, as we argued in the last chapter, does that mean that they count as persons in their own right? We will consider this issue in the second section when we consider how far personhood would come to be realized among the humanoids of our genealogy.

---

[1] Associating being held to account with reward and punishment, he takes this concern with responsibility to be 'founded' in the conscious agent's prudent concern that they be happy in the future as well as in the present. A 'concern for happiness', he says, is 'the unavoidable concomitant of consciousness' and 'that which is conscious of pleasure and pain' must desire—presumably, regardless of time—'that that self that is conscious should be happy' (Locke 1975, 2.27.28).

7.1.4 Second normative assumption: the dignity of persons

There is one assumption that is generally made in ordinary language and thought to which Locke does not pay attention, at least in his discussion of what makes an agent a person. This is the assumption that persons have a distinctive moral status or dignity and impose unique claims on how they may be permissibly treated. Since only persons can be subject to such claims, incurring responsibilities or obligations, the idea is that the moral status of persons imposes strict limits on how they may treat one another.

This idea is found in religious traditions that make persons special, distinguishing the ways in which it is permissible to treat them from, for example, the ways in which it is permissible to treat other animals. But perhaps its most forceful expression over the history of philosophy is in Kant.

For Kant (2012, 40–41), as for Boethius and Locke, persons are characterized by the power of reasoning. But the explanation for why reasoning agents are persons, he suggests, is the moral status that this confers: 'rational beings are called persons', he says, 'because their nature already marks them out as ends in themselves'. They are 'entities whose existence in itself is an end, an end such that no other end can be put in its place, for which they would do service merely as means'. In this, as we saw, persons contrast with mere things: 'non-rational beings', that 'have only a relative worth, as means'.

As Locke thinks that the metaphysical character of persons over time makes them fit to be held responsible, whether by themselves or others, Kant thinks that the metaphysical character of persons as reasoning agents—and ultimately as agents that determine how to act in practical reasoning—gives them a distinctive form of dignity. And as Locke makes the responsibility connection central to his conception of persons—this, insofar as 'person' is a forensic term—so Kant makes the dignity connection central to his way of thinking.

'What refers to general human inclinations and needs has a market price', Kant (2012, 46–47) says, 'but what constitutes the condition under which alone something can be an end in itself does not merely have a relative worth, i.e. a price, but an inner worth, i.e. dignity.' His idea, roughly, is that while we give an instrumental value to things in seeing them as means to satisfy certain desires, we must give a distinct, non-instrumental value to ourselves—and, by parity, to others like ourselves—insofar as we reason or deliberate about what to do and what to desire. In that sense we ourselves, and all others like us—all persons—have an inner worth and should never treat ourselves or others as mere means. We should each embrace the categorical imperative: 'So act that you use humanity, in your own person as well as in the person of any other, always at the same time as an end, never merely as a means' (Kant 2012, 41).[2]

---

[2] It is worth noting that in taking this view, Kant shows that he endorses the responsibility as well as the dignity assumption about persons. After all, he has to take persons to be capable of assuming

The connection between being a person and having a distinctive moral status or dignity is preserved among many contemporary philosophers who associate themselves with Kant.[3] Pre-eminent among these is John Rawls. While he breaks with Kant in not seeking a metaphysically grounded conception of the person, he follows him in presenting a remarkably similar conception of the person as the one that moral and political philosophy, or at least a broadly liberal and democratic philosophy, ought to assume. As Rawls (2001, 19) puts it in one statement of his view, 'the conception of the person is not taken from metaphysics or the philosophy of mind, or from psychology', although it must be 'compatible with (one or more) such philosophical or psychological conceptions (so far as they are sound)'. His conception of the person is rather 'normative and political' in character.

The Rawlsian idea seems to be that whatever the grounding reason, persons have a moral status that entitles them to be taken, as they are taken in the theory that he himself espouses, as commanding a certain form of treatment. They ought to be treated by others, and should realize that they ought to be treated, 'as self-authenticating sources of valid claims' (Rawls 2001, 23). This is close to the Kantian idea, since the claims of persons will be self-authenticating insofar as they are claims that persons have, in Kant's phrase, as ends in themselves, not on any other basis.

In assuming that persons have this dignity or status, Rawls has to assume, like Kant, that they have the capacity to grant one another this status. And so, he has to endorse something close to the responsibility assumption that persons can assume responsibility for giving one another this status, honoring the claims that go with it. This is what he does, in effect, when he takes persons to have two moral powers, as he describes them: 'a capacity for a sense of justice and for a conception of the good' (Rawls 1993, 19).

7.1.5 Third normative assumption: the ideal of personhood

As Kant is one of the first to emphasize the dignity of the person, so he is also one of the first to emphasize that there is an ideal built into the very notion of personhood. This is an ideal, as he thinks of it, that any person must countenance, if they are true to their nature as persons or rational beings. He calls it, autonomy: the government of the self by the self.

---

responsibility and incurring obligations, if he is to argue that their moral status obliges them to treat themselves and others in accordance with the categorical imperative.

[3] This is a broad church, encompassing, for example, Christine Korsgaard (1996), Barbara Herman (1993), and Onora O'Neill (2013).

For Kant, as we have seen, persons must assign a non-instrumental value to themselves—and, by parity, to others like them—insofar as they reason or deliberate about what to do. In acting on the basis of deliberation, as he thinks of the exercise, they are not the playthings of their inclinations, as animals may be. Rather, they decide on the basis of considerations that move them in the manner of reasons, about what inclinations to satisfy—if indeed they choose to satisfy any pre-existing inclinations—and what to frustrate. And, in acting on reasons in this way, they implicitly endorse general maxims about how to behave. In acting out of a concern for honesty in this or that situation, for example, they endorse the maxim: act as honesty requires in such and such a situation.

A maxim like this is general insofar as it identifies reasons relevant for anyone and offers an injunction that applies to all. That implies, in Kant's terms, that it has the form of a general law.[4] And so he holds that deliberation amounts to self-legislation—laying down a law for yourself—and that acting out of deliberation means acting in accordance with self-dictated laws. This power of self-determination means that the agent is autonomous in at least the etymological sense: that they are a self or *autos* that acts on their own law or *nomos*. In Kant's (2012, 56) terms, it implies that the will constitutes a capacity to act 'independently of alien causes determining it', and that it enjoys a 'negative' form of freedom.

Autonomy in this negative sense belongs to all persons. 'Autonomy of the will is the characteristic of the will by which it is a law to itself', he says, and a person will enjoy it regardless of the things they choose: 'independently of any characteristic of the objects of willing' (Kant 2012, 51). It is this autonomy, indeed, that is at the source of the dignity of a person. In acting on reasons, the person's will determines the value to put on other things so that, as he holds, it must itself have an independent value: 'the legislation that determines all worth must itself have a dignity, i.e. unconditional, incomparable worth' (Kant 2012, 47).

But this negative idea of autonomy leads us naturally to 'a positive concept of freedom', which he characterizes as 'richer and more fruitful'. On this positive way of thinking, it is not enough for freedom that the person should give themselves the laws on which to act: it is also required that those laws meet a further condition. If the person is to treat others as ends in themselves, not as mere means, then they must be willing for the laws on which they act to be laws on which people in general should act. And it is only if they satisfy that condition that they will be autonomous in a positive sense. 'The principle of autonomy is thus: not to choose in any other way than that the maxims of one's choice are also comprised as universal law in the same willing' (Kant 2012, 51).

His conception of persons as rational beings who reason their way to action leads Kant, in this way, to link personhood with an inbuilt goal. Being an agent

---

[4] Strictly, as Richard Hare (1952) emphasized, it entails only that it is a universal principle, where such a principle may be quite specific in its application conditions, not intuitively like a general law.

who deliberates in the manner of a person means being someone for whom it is inevitably an ideal that they should achieve such autonomy, acting only on maxims that they can treat as general laws that apply to all. Not all persons will achieve this goal, of course—some will languish in heteronomy, as he says—but it will be a significant failure on their part that they fall short of autonomy proper.[5]

Harry Frankfurt (1988) is another thinker who endorses the idea that if an agent—in particular, a human being—is to count properly or fully as a person, they have to meet a certain ideal. Let them fail to meet that ideal and they will be mere wantons, as he puts it. Linking personhood with free will, he holds in line with the view ascribed to him in the last chapter, that while the person must act out of desires, as any intentional agent is bound to do, they should ideally act only on desires with which they identify. Their actions should be the product only of desires that enjoy that sort of *imprimatur*.

Frankfurt's inbuilt ideal clearly has much in common with Kant's autonomy and indeed he gives it the same name (see also Dworkin 1988). But there is a third group of authors who take quite a different ideal to be built into the notion of personhood. They are often known as narrative theorists and the ideal they hail is that persons should be able at any point to tell a coherent story about who they are in life: where they come from, where they stand now, and where they are going.

In the version that concerns us, the narrativity claim has an ethical cast. It holds, in the words of a prominent critic, Galen Strawson (2010, 775), that 'a richly narrative outlook on one's life is essential to living well, to true or full personhood'. In adopting a narrative outlook one 'sees or lives or experiences one's life as a narrative or story of some sort, or at least as a collection of stories'. This claim is put forward generally as a claim about an ideal—the self-narrativity ideal, as we may call it—that is built into the notion of being a person. That the ideal is inbuilt in this way may be defended on the ground that people tend to construct self-narratives anyhow and that they should do so in a fulsome manner. Or it may be defended on the ground that the sort of self-consciousness over time that every person enjoys will inevitably orient them toward the ideal of having a self-narrative.

The narrativity claim, which currently enjoys widespread support, may originate in recent times with Alasdair MacIntyre (1987, 219) for whom 'the only criteria for success or failure in a human life as a whole are the criteria for success or failure in a narrated or to-be-narrated quest'. The point of view he defends is also found in Charles Taylor (1989, 47), for whom a 'basic condition of making sense of ourselves is that we grasp our lives in a narrative'.[6]

---

[5] Christine Korsgaard (2009, 26) formulates the idea very nicely: 'A good person is someone who is good at being a person.'
[6] The theme has been taken up with enthusiasm by a range of recent philosophers, perhaps most prominently by Marya Schechtman (1997; 2014). Galen Strawson (2008, Ch. 7; 2010) presents a very good overview of writing on narrativity, albeit from a highly critical point of view.

Like the claims made by Kant and Frankfurt, the narrativity claim also casts personhood, not just as a condition that certain agents have by nature—first or second nature—but as an ideal to which persons are invariably oriented. Indeed it takes the ideal to be one that enjoys widespread acceptance. Few of us write autobiographies but the idea is that any serious person will be able to speak for who they are, explaining why their lives are not just a fragmented sequence of discrete episodes.

7.1.6 The self-identity of persons over time

While philosophical and common ways of thinking emphasize the features of personhood that we have been charting, they have long shared another characteristic too; as we shall see, this appeared at its clearest, and perhaps at its earliest, in Locke. It consists in a focus on the issue, as we may call it, of self-identity over time. What makes a person the same person at a later time as at an earlier? What means that however they differ in other respects, they remain the same self?

Before we look at how this problem gets to figure in philosophical theory, however, it may be useful to look at a feature of persons that makes it salient. Like all agents, as we shall see, persons form beliefs about themselves, picking out their selves in a special surefire way. But unlike other agents, they identify themselves—they identify their selves—with figures in the public world, bearing names and properties and relationships that situate them among their fellows. They do this, for example, in acknowledging that they, identified in the special surefire way, are responsible for something that a publicly identified person did: they just are that person. Since persons continually alter their public profiles, taking on new initiatives, developing new properties, and forming new relationships, that raises a natural question. What ensures that a person remains the same self as this public profile changes?

7.1.6.1 Surefire self-reference in regular agents

Every agent—and so every person—will have a way of referring to themselves that is surefire in a double sense. First, an agent cannot misidentify another entity for who they are; they cannot get their own identity wrong. And second, they cannot be mistaken about the existence of the entity in question; there is bound to be an agent there to answer to their identification. They are guarded on the first count against error through misidentification and on the second, as we may put it, against error through non-identification (Evans 1982).

The first observation, that an agent cannot misidentify who they are, reflects the fact that no agent identifies itself under an aspect or a description that might not actually apply. I do not connect with myself in forming beliefs about me in virtue of seeing myself as someone raised in Ireland or as being a philosopher, or as living in Australia, or as someone of whom all those things are true. I connect with myself in forming beliefs about me independently of any such description, so that I would still refer to the same agent—to me—even if every such belief I held were false. I connect with the self of whom I hold those beliefs in something like the way I connect with a certain object demonstratively identified—that thing there—for in that case too I would still refer to the salient object even if all the beliefs I formed about it turned out to be false. Being equipped with language, I will be able to connect with myself in that surefire manner in using the indexical 'I' or 'me' to pick out that self.

The second observation about the surefire feature of self-reference comes out in a contrast with this demonstrative identification of a perceived object. It is always possible that the entity I try to pick out in speaking of that thing there does not exist: that I am deceived by a trick of light or whatever. In that case, the belief I allege and seek to convey in saying, 'That entity has such and such features', fails to materialize, since the referential presupposition it makes—that there is something there—is not satisfied. It may not misidentify that entity, but it fails in a deeper way still: it does not identify an entity at all. That sort of failure clearly cannot occur when an agent identifies itself, say by the use of the first-person indexical if the agent has language. The assumption that the agent is there to do the identification ensures that it is there to be identified.

In order to support these observations, consider our simple robot that seeks to put certain bottles and glasses into an upright position, acting for that end on the basis of beliefs about where exactly they lie, and how its own behavior is progressing: how near its motion has taken it to an object, how far its levers have raised it at any moment, and so on. And now think about the robot's belief that an object on its side lies in this or that direction, that it is at such and such a distance or that it is near enough to lift. Each belief of this kind predicates a relationship between itself and that glass or bottle: that the object lies in a certain direction from *its position*; that it lies at such and such a distance *from it*; that the object is near enough *to it* to lift. In every such case, the robot forms beliefs that refer to itself and, as a little reflection reveals, it forms beliefs that refer to itself in the surefire way we characterized earlier.

In holding such a belief, the robot does not identify itself as a referent of the belief by any feature, or under any aspect, as it may identify the glass or bottle that also figures as a referent. Suppose it takes that object to be near enough to be lifted: that is, near enough to itself to be lifted. It might be mistaken about whether the object is indeed near enough to lift but the error in such a belief would have to come about through misidentifying that object or misattributing the relationship of being near enough, not through its misidentifying itself as the subject to which the object is near. And as it cannot fail to relate to itself through misidentifying itself, so of course it cannot fail to relate to itself as a result of there being nothing there to identify. By assumption, it will be there to ensure that as no error of misidentification is possible, so no error of non-identification is possible either.[7]

Every agent must clearly be able to refer to itself, forming beliefs about itself, in this basic aspect-free manner, though only linguistically equipped creatures will be able to use the first-person indexical in this role. Even the simple robot must have a sense of itself as the reference point needed in acting on the spatial environment. And a biological agent will rely on this basic sense of itself in other relations too. In fearing a painful prospect, it will fear *its* suffering pain; in remembering a certain experience, it will remember *its* having that experience; and in planning to do something, it will make a plan in which *it* takes that action. In all such contexts, it itself will be the basic point of reference: the agent that such states and acts engage and move.

7.1.6.2 Surefire self-reference in persons

By our earlier characterization, those agents who constitute persons must not only have beliefs about themselves that self-refer in the surefire, aspect-free manner. Because of being persons, they will have to recognize that they will be seen by other persons as reasoning or relating to them in a certain way, as being fit to be held responsible for certain actions, as enjoying dignity and making corresponding claims, and as manifestly expected to live up to one or another ideal. Each will have to believe of the indexically identified self that they—in their own words, that I— engage with other persons, owe those persons this or that duty, have certain claims against them, and will be expected by them to live up to a suitable personal ideal. Each will have to equate the egocentrically identified 'I' with an allocentrically identified person in the world; each will have to see themselves within a public, interpersonal frame as well as in a private, intrapersonal space.

This dual location of the person in private and public space naturally gives rise to an issue about self-identity. For as a person thinks about themselves in the public world, registering the changes in what was or is or will be true of them in the domains illustrated—true of me, as each will think—then a natural question that will arise for each is this: What is it across those shifts in how I stand or might stand in the public world—what is it, for example, across the changes that materialize between childhood and old age—that makes me me? What is it about me, identified egocentrically in the indexical 'I', that remains the same across the changing public profiles I assume over time?

This problem will not arise for agents other than humans or, as we shall see, humanoids: other, in effect, than persons. It is true that some other animals such as the great apes pass mirror recognition tests, as they are often called. In these tests, the subject is marked on the forehead or ear in a way that is only visible to them in a mirror (Gallup 1970). Then they are tested to see whether they touch that mark

---

[7] On related issues, see (Lewis 1979a) and (Perry 1979). Both emphasize the need for an agent to engage itself in belief—and other attitudes—in a manner that precludes misidentification.

reliably when—and only when—they see themselves in a mirror. If they do display such a sensitivity to how they appear in the mirror, then obviously they do self-ascribe that mark: they think a thought naturally expressed in a sentence: 'That's me, the one with the facial mark'. And that suggests a capacity for self-identification in two spaces of the kind we have been linking with personhood.

But this does not mean that such animals count as persons. To rework an idea introduced earlier, such an animal is unlikely to conceptualize itself in a way that is independent of stimulus—in effect, independent of the mirror presentation—and to treat the mark on its forehead as a contingent feature that it did not previously have or may not have in the future (Camp 2009). For all the evidence provided by the satisfaction of the test, the animal may only have a stimulus-dependent conception of itself: a conception that enables it to form allocentric beliefs about itself only when it sees itself in the mirror (Boyle 2018). It need not be able to maintain a focus on its continuing self as it registers or imagines the different profiles it might assume in the public space that is shared with others.

7.1.6.3 The self-identity issue in the tradition

Boethius says nothing about the self-identification of persons. This is in marked contrast to Locke and to the many writers, including contemporary authors, whom he influenced (Gordon-Roth 2020). When Locke takes the person to be 'a thinking intelligent Being that has reason and reflection', he immediately adds: 'and can consider itself as itself, the same thinking thing in different times and places' (Locke 1975, 2.27.11). This sort of move is repeated in Dennett (1979, 178) when he counts among the capacities distinctive of persons a 'self-consciousness of one sort or another'. But Locke's influence runs even deeper in other recent authors who have tended to concentrate exclusively on his account of self-identification over time.

Assuming that every person enjoys consciousness, Locke suggests that it enables self-identification over time insofar as 'this consciousness can be extended backwards to any past Action or Thought', testifying to 'the Identity of that Person' (Locke 1975, 2.27.11). Indeed, he seems to treat this consciousness, not just as testifying to what individuates the person over time, but as constituting it. 'Wherever a man finds what he calls himself, there, I think, another may say is the same person' (Locke 1975, 2.27.28).

In making self-identification over time constitutive rather than just indicative of personal identity, Locke introduces a notion of the self, familiar in common thought and talk, to the discussion. He describes the person self-identified over time—the person cross-temporally individuated on the basis of consciousness—as the self, using the term as the name of a continuing entity. And he takes that entity to be nothing more or less than the person. '"Person", he says, 'is the name for this self' (2.27.28). He holds that what makes someone the same person or self through the changes that time inevitably brings is consciousness: 'the self is not determined 'by identity or diversity of substance, which it cannot be sure of, but only by identity of consciousness' (2.27.25).

Locke's account of persons opens up a question as to whether a person or self might survive a change of body, with the re-embodied person having the required consciousness of being one and the same with a person previously embodied elsewhere. He himself argues for a positive answer. Thus, he says in a famous passage: 'should the soul of a prince, carrying with it the consciousness of the prince's past life, enter and inform the body of a cobbler, as soon as deserted by his own soul, everyone sees he would be the same person with the prince' (Locke 1975, 2.27.17).

This idea that personal identity over time might survive bodily transfer has given rise to an intense tradition of discussion in recent times of whether indeed that is so: whether I myself—whether my *self*—might survive a change of body. Peter Strawson (1959) argued, famously, that the notion of a person is that of an entity that has various mental properties like those mentioned by Locke and Dennett and others but that also has the material properties associated with a body. This has led some to defend animalism, the thesis that the animal or organism that constitutes a person must remain continuously in place if the person is to continue in existence (Blatti 2020). Others, however, have taken the Lockean view that so long as continuity of consciousness, or some similar psychological relationship, connects a person at one time to a person at another, they will be temporal stages of one and the same person.

In holding by this view, Locke (1975, 2.27.29) himself thought that the person or self could be identified with the soul. Taking 'the soul of a man for an immaterial substance, independent from matter,' he says, 'there can, from the nature of things, be no absurdity at all to suppose that the same soul may at different times be united to different bodies, and with them make up for that time one man.' Many contemporary authors think, like Locke, that the person or self might survive various counterfactual changes of body but few, if any, think that it is therefore non-material.

They may hold that although the person or self is not identical with the body in which it is realized at any time, still it is constituted by that body and could not exist apart from a body to constitute it (Johnston 1987; 1992). The idea, roughly, is that just as the speech that you attend survives in the recording that you make of it—you hear that same presentation when you listen later to the recording—so the person or self that is realized now in this body may later be present in another. An imaginary case in which it would be present in another is provided by teletransportation: an imagined process in which the person moves from place A to place B by having their body replicated, atom for atom, at B, where the original body at A is destroyed in the process of replication.[8]

---

[8] For a view that the self need be neither a continuing substance of the kind that Locke seems to assume, nor something whose identity over time is constituted by physical or psychological connections, see for example (Madell 2015).

Locke's discussion not only opened up the issue about the relationship between the person or self and the body, which has been the focus of much contemporary writing. He also opened up the question of whether talk of the person and the self can come apart. Locke himself, as we saw, took the person and self to be one and the same: in this usage, the substantive self is just the person as that appears in speaking reflexively of oneself. But the possibility of pulling the self apart from the person has been explored in some contemporary approaches.

Thus, Derek Parfit (1984) argues that the self that is identified in one period of a person's life may not be identical with their self in another. An individual at one time may be the same person as that individual at another time: say, by virtue of continuing psychological relationships. But consistently with being the same person, they may be different selves over different periods, where being the self in a given period will be determined by how dense are the intertemporal connections: how closely, for example, are the intentions at an earlier moment reflected in the actions at a later, or the memories at a later moment related to the experiences at an earlier.[9]

As every theory of the person must give an intuitive account of the nature of the person, so every theory must say something about the self that is linked with personhood in common usage, and its identity over time. We shall look at why the humanoids will constitute and conceive of themselves as persons in the second section, and then devote the final section to how consequently they will think about the issue of self-identity over time.

7.2 Personation and personhood

We looked in the last section at a range of assumptions that are often made about persons and that are reflected in various philosophical theories. We did so in order to get a sense of what it will take for an agent to count as a person; presumably, any candidate worthy of the name of person should satisfy at least a cluster of the assumptions we spelled out. Certainly, no agent can count as a person unless they display a distinctive set of capacities. And their claim to count as a person will be boosted, to say the least, if they are fit to be held responsible, can claim a special dignity and status, are naturally oriented toward a certain ideal, and enjoy a distinctive self-identity over time.

---

[9] Galen Strawson (2009, 6) offers a different account of why person and self may come apart, although one we will not explore here: 'Sometimes "I" is used with the intention to refer to a human being considered as a whole, sometimes it's used with the intention to refer to a self—two things that have quite different identity conditions.' The disjuncture between person and self, on this version, springs from the fact that the self is revealed in a particular mode of self-experience, while the person or human being is not.

In this section and the next we look again at the social practices detailed in our genealogy over the last two chapters and argue that under those practices the humanoids will count as persons and come to think of one another, and of themselves, as persons. The idea is that they will satisfy and endorse a conception of themselves under which they satisfy a bunch of the assumptions that entitle them, in established ways of thinking, to count as persons. We look in this section at how the humanoids will satisfy the assumption that they can reason, and also satisfy the three normative assumptions associated with responsibility, dignity and the ideal built into personhood. And then, in the final section, we will explore the ways in which they will display the self-identity over time that we expect in persons.

7.2.1 Converse and commitment: a review

The main aspect of the social life of humanoids, as it has emerged so far, is that they are conversive and commissive agents. They are capable of converse with one another, communicating what they hold about the world and indeed themselves. And they can do this, under a practice that requires them in general to prove reliable: this, on pain of not being able to rely on others or, when they wish it, to secure others' reliance on them. Insofar as they follow that practice, they will not just reveal how they see things, but ratify those claims as well; they will be truthful about how things present and careful about ensuring that that presentation is accurate. They may occasionally be deceptive, no doubt, but it will make sense for them to attempt deception only in exceptional cases where they can hope to escape the costs of detection and retaliation, or where the rewards on offer promise to outweigh such costs.

Not only will the humanoids have the capacity to converse in this sense; being anxious to share in the information that others have, they will also be ready to converse, even at the price of giving up information at their disposal in exchange. Moreover, being anxious to establish their reputation for reliability, and to open up mutually beneficial relationships with others, they will be ready in particular to reveal and ratify information about their own attitudes and dispositions, about their beliefs, their preferences, and their intentions.

They might be able to convey this information about themselves in the standard mode of converse, by reporting on their attitudes. But in this communication about themselves, they can go one better, proving commissive as well as conversive. They can avow such attitudes, communicating them in a way that shuts down the possibility of excusing a failure to act on those attitudes by appeal to a misleading-mind excuse. And they can make pledges about their robust preferences and about their intentions, shutting down appeal to either a misleading-mind or a changed-mind excuse in the event of failing to live up to their words.

By means of such commitments the humanoids will make it especially expensive for them to prove unreliable and that will give more credibility to what they communicate about themselves than a self-report would do. And as they commit to certain preferences, intentions, and policies, they will treat the desiderata that support these behaviors as values: desiderata that make those courses of action robustly and not just contingently attractive.

The sorts of commitment that have these effects, as we saw, need not involve active promises or anything of the kind; they may materialize in a virtual or standby way. This will happen when the humanoids are committed by virtue of acquiescing in the manifest expectations that others form about them, whether on the basis of the social norms they share with others generally or of the more specific relationships they have with family, friends, and other acquaintances. Let them not demur at those attitudinal expectations and ascriptions—let them not demur, presumptively, in a willing or voluntary manner—and they will be taken to be committed by them. Willy-nilly, then, they will each find themselves signed up to a broad range of commitments to others, some to others in general, some to those with whom they have special relationships.

Thus, the humanoids will live in a dense, commissive field or space. Without saying a word, they will be spoken for in a commissive manner. And without saying a word, they will be beholden as well as bespoken. They will exist, not like independent, interacting particles, but like waves that depend for their existence on a common field. Einstein's image in which all the bodies in space contribute to a unified gravitational field offers a better analogue for their social world than Newton's image of distinct, gravitationally attractive bodies, occupying empty space.

7.2.2 Commitment and self-representation

Let a humanoid commit to a set of attitudes, actively or in a standby way, and in the standby case by acquiescence in the manifest expectations of others or in the ascription of a would-be spokesperson. In any such case the individual will represent themselves to others in the society as being of a kind to which such commitments testify. They will make a claim, in effect, to being an agent of such and such a character, setting aside the possibility of excusing any failure to live up to the representation by appeal to a misleading-mind excuse or, where appropriate, the excuse of a changed mind.

The commitments that the humanoids make or accept in these ways will convey an image of the individual that applies on a range of different fronts, not merely in this or that isolated respect. The image will give a picture, not just of what the individual is disposed to do about one or another issue, but of who as a whole they are: of the sort of character that they constitute. There is bound to be a common character, answering to shared norms and values, that they will each project to others. And in each case this will be embedded in a distinct, individualized character that they will present, in varying degrees of detail, to those with whom they are more intimately engaged.

Because it is commissive in character, this representation of themselves that the humanoids will thereby underwrite, will have the status of an authorized self-portrait. They will not just report about what others may expect of them, leaving open the later possibility of excusing error by recourse to a misleading-mind or changed-mind excuse. They will manifestly bet on themselves to live up to those expectations. In effect, they will say to one another: this is who I am, this is who you can rely on me to be.

In this commissive network of relationships, the humanoids will generally have to be sincere; as in the human case, deception will work only to the extent that it is relatively rare. And insofar as they commit sincerely to one another they will commit equally to themselves: they would hardly be sincere if they were not personally resolved to live up to their commitments. This being so, they will invite themselves as well as others to rely on them to enact the self-representation they project. And, of course, they will be able to flesh out that self-representation in making commitments to themselves alone, as in resolving to follow certain personal plans. The self-representation they authorize for themselves will give them a sense of who they are, or at least aspire to be, constituting a personal, guiding ideal.

7.2.3 From self-representation to personhood

The linkage between such self-representation and personhood is marked in the curiously ignored etymology of the word 'person', and in the curiously neglected comments of Thomas Hobbes on what personhood involves (Pettit 2008a, Ch. 4). The etymology of 'person', as Hobbes (1994b, 16.3) himself notes, is from the Latin 'persona', which referred in classical times to a theatrical mask through (*per-*) which an actor would speak or sound (*sonare*). The mask would indicate, like demeanor and dress, the character in the play that they were playing; a mask depicting Jupiter, for example, would indicate that they were playing the part of that god. If we think of the *persona*, not as the mask itself, but as the character it represents, then we may readily see why the Latin word would assume the meaning of the English word 'persona'. The actor might be said in that sense to portray the *persona* of Jupiter, or indeed to represent his person.

Hobbes uses the verb 'personate', which was in relatively common usage at the time, to characterize the activity in which a person offers a representation of themselves to others: potentially, and ideally, a truthful and careful self-representation. Personation contrasts nicely with impersonation. To impersonate someone is to pretend to be that person—an individual identified for the audience under some independent aspect—and to purport deceptively to self-represent that person. To personate is to purport without pretense to represent yourself. But as you may impersonate someone in a way that reflects their character accurately or inaccurately, so you may personate yourself accurately or inaccurately. And in each case you may succeed or fail accidentally or intentionally: you may happen to misrepresent an impersonated other or you may do so for strategic reasons; and you may happen to misrepresent yourself or you may do so out of a wish to win esteem or out of your role as a spy. We may generally assume, however, that insofar as it materializes in commitments, an individual's self-representation with others will generally have to be accurate.

These remarks open up the possibility, embraced by Hobbes (1994, Ch. 16), that we should take the concept of personhood to be closely related to that of self-representation or personation. He is not absolutely clear on the point but the natural way to go in elaborating the possibility would be to say that a person is an agent who can personate. Personhood will be associated, in other words, with the capacity to personate or self-represent.

But a capacity in what precise degree? Think of the joke that goes: 'Can you play the piano? I don't know, I've never tried.' This indicates that the 'can' in 'can personate' is ambiguous. The resolution of that ambiguity was salient in the case of the capacities discussed so far but it calls in this case for some comment.

There are three ways, at least, in which it may be ambiguous to say that a person is an agent who can personate. In a strong construal, it means that the agent is disposed to personate, given the opportunity and motive to do so: they have been inducted in commissive practices and can personate in roughly the sense in which the competent pianist can play the piano. In a weaker sense, it means that the agent is disposed with training to become disposed in that strong sense to personate: this, in the manner of the novice who is ready to take piano lessons. And in the weakest construal of all, it means just that it is consistent with the nature of the species to which the agent belongs—however undeveloped or demented they may be—that they should have that disposition in the weaker sense.

Consistently with associating personhood with personation, it is possible to take any of these options. We may take it here, as Hobbes seems to take it, in the strong sense in which being a person means being primed to personate: being ready to do so, should it be possible and attractive. In this sense, it is only functioning persons, as distinct from the undeveloped baby or the demented adult, who display personhood proper.

This focus on the functioning person does not set the personation approach aside among other theories. Many of the views we looked at earlier do something similar, taking a person to be an agent who can reason to conclusions, for example assume responsibility for their acts or construct a narrative about themselves. Any approach that equates the person with a suitably functioning person, of course, may license a use of the term 'person' for agents who do not fully function in that way, whether for reasons of immaturity or the lack of presupposed capacities. We return to that point a little later.

7.2.4 Personation, social and mental

How attractive is the linkage between personhood and personation? We shall turn later to explore how far it would enable us to vindicate the assumptions listed in the last section. But we can say for the moment that from the viewpoint of our genealogy, it is very attractive indeed. It clearly enables us to argue that the humanoids are bound to count as persons and to be positioned to introduce the concept of a person to distinguish themselves from other animals. Let the person be equated with an authoritatively self-representing agent and each and every humanoid must manifestly enjoy the status of a person within a community of persons: it will be ensured by the commitments that they actively or virtually underwrite.

The reference to community is important, for there can be no possibility of personating without other persons with whom to personate, as there can be no possibility of commitment without others with whom to learn what it is to make commitments. On the genealogy presented, the humanoids will each attain the status of persons simultaneously with others doing so and will not be able to form the concept of a person except in the context of commissive interactions and relationships with those others.

While personation is primarily a social activity, however, it need not be exclusively social in character. We saw that with the practice and concept of commitment in place, the humanoids will be able to make commitments to themselves, some affecting others and some being purely personal in reach. As commitment may be self-directed—and indeed, as ascribing responsibility may be self-directed—so may personation be directed also at the self.

The humanoids will depend on their social experience and interaction to learn what it is to personate, and what it is to count as a person. But they will be able to rely on that practice and concept in thinking about themselves as well as in thinking about others, or about how others think of them. They will be able to represent themselves to themselves in a commissive mode. And self-representing or personating in that mode, they will be able to hold themselves to the persona projected. They will have an exhortative power of getting themselves to live up to that image, by the argument of the last chapter, and they will be disposed to hold themselves responsible for doing so.

David Velleman (2020, 65) also links a person's self-representation to others with their self-presentation to themselves: that is, with their efforts at identifying 'a stable and coherent set of motives' to ascribe to themselves. Thus, he seems to strike the same note when he says that the personhood of agents is tied up with their 'socially recognized status as self-presenting creatures' (Velleman 2020, 12).

But where he takes an agent's self-presentation to themselves to be basic, and their self-presentation to others to be derived, our emerging account of the humanoids suggests that things are the other way around. The activity in which humanoids present themselves to themselves in a commissive mode is dependent on the social activity of presenting themselves commissively to others; it is only because of learning the inter-personal practice that they will be able to interiorize the activity and conduct it in the intrapersonal sphere.

A person may often be deceptive in representing themselves to others, and may even be systematically deceptive in this exercise. While purporting without pretense to represent themselves, not to impersonate another independently identified individual, they may still intentionally misrepresent themselves. Indeed, they may even maintain long-term misrepresentation on this front, like a professional spy, or misrepresent themselves in different personas, as in assuming multiple internet identities. But whatever misrepresentation they practice in relation to others, there must be some image in which they truthfully—though not perhaps carefully and competently—self-represent to themselves. While social self-representation is prior in one sense of priority, then, there is another sense in which priority goes to this presentation of themselves to themselves.

Having set out the personation theory of personhood, as we may call it, and having seen that the humanoids of our genealogy will count as persons under this theory, it is time to test the theory against the assumptions considered in the first section. But before conducting that test, we should note that the theory allows us to recognize corporate as well as natural persons, and indeed that the corporate person played a particularly important role in Hobbes's thinking.

7.2.5 Corporate personhood

To associate personhood with self-representation in the commissive sense, as we saw, is to take a person to be an agent who can speak for themselves, assuming the authority to put aside one or both of two self-reporter excuses—the misleading-mind and the changed-mind excuses—in communicating their attitudes. The person on this account has the status of being a spokesperson for themselves, not just a self-reporter.

Hobbes introduces the idea that the person is a self-representer or self-spokesperson in the course of pursuing his real goal: a theory of group or corporate agency that could apply to the state. The corporate agent is a multitude of individuals, by his account, who are unified by a voice—in the paradigm case, the voice of an individual—that they each pledge to follow. The result of that joint commitment by members is that the attitudes the voice communicates in their name, and the actions that it directs individuals to take in enacting those attitudes, count as the attitudes and actions of a single agent. The voice that is authorized to lead them in that way may be commissioned to determine their attitudes and actions 'without stint', as in his image of a political sovereign, or it may be given a more limited authority, as in the chief executive of a commercial or other sort of group (Hobbes 1994b, 16.14).

In presenting this view of corporate agency, Hobbes sets up a parallel between the way an authorized individual in the paradigm case may speak for a group of other individuals and the way a human agent may speak for themselves as an individual. Indeed, he even says that what it is to be a person is to play spokesperson— that is our word, not his—either for oneself or for others: 'A person, is he, whose words or actions are considered, either as his own, or as representing the words or actions of another man, or of any other thing to whom they are attributed' (Hobbes 1994b, 16.1). But he immediately distinguishes the cases: 'When they are considered as his own, then is he called a natural person; and when they are considered as representing the words and actions of another, then is he a feigned or artificial person' (16.2).

In the case where the representative acts or speaks in the name of other natural persons, Hobbes says that they must have their 'words and actions owned by those whom they represent' (16.4); they act or speak with 'authority' or 'commission' or 'license', so that the represented person is really the 'author' of what is said or done. The same lesson applies to the natural person. When he 'beareth his own natural person' (19.4), acting or speaking in his own name, that individual will own what is said or done in the sense of authorizing it. He will treat it as said or done with his own *imprimatur* or authority, 'there being no author but himself' (16.8).

By this account, a person is strictly a personator, whether they be a personator in relation to themselves or to others. But Hobbes is also happy to apply the word to the individual or the group that is personated: if you like, to the personatee.[10] In treating such groups as persons, Hobbes was picking up a tradition with a medieval origin. The notion that a group could be a person came to life with the appearance in the high Middle Ages of groups like trade-related guilds, monastic orders, and independent towns. The notion of the legal person, as we would describe it, evolved to characterize these bodies in familiar terms. They were legal persons insofar as, like natural persons, they entered into relations of a broadly commissive kind. They bought and sold and owned property, they incurred contractual obligations and held others to such obligations, and they brought judicial charges and were exposed to charges brought by others. They operated in commissive space,

---

[10] He does this, for example, when he says: 'a person . . . is he that is represented, as often as he is represented'(Hobbes 1994b, 42.3). This leads him to take incorporated, agential groups as persons: 'when represented by an individual', he says, the 'multitude are united by covenants into one person civil' (Hobbes 1994a, 20.1). But he is particularly ready to describe a group as a person when they together generate the voice that speaks for them: say, as in his mistaken idea, by majority voting; see (Pettit 2008a, Ch. 5).

albeit a legally restricted space, relating to one another and to natural persons on the basis of mutual commitments and self-representations.

It became common in medieval legal theory to recognize, not just an individual human being, but also a corporate entity as a person. Pope Innocent IV cast such a body as a *persona ficta* in a missive of 1246 (Eschmann 1946). He wanted to emphasize that though a corporate body is a person—this was a surprising concession on his part—it does not have a soul and cannot therefore be excommunicated. But consistently with the group agent not having a soul, Innocent's idea could be taken, and was taken, in two distinct ways. Philosophers and theologians generally regarded it as a fictive or unreal person, those in legal and judicial circles deemed it a real person, albeit of an artificial kind (Canning 1980; Kantorowicz 1997).

Hobbes brought the legal way of thinking into philosophy, defining a person as an entity that could play what he took to be a characteristic role. He defined that role, not in straightforwardly legal terms, but at the more abstract level of commitment and personation. Where medieval thinkers had come to regard corporate bodies as legal persons by analogy with natural persons, he used the notion of the legal person, already well established in his time, to characterize the natural person.

This observation raises a question, of course, as to whether the linkage between personhood and personation requires us to regard incorporated bodies as persons. And the answer, clearly, is that it does (List and Pettit 2011, Ch. 8). This picks up a way of speaking that still has currency in law, although it is frequently contested by those who wrongly assume that this gives corporate agents the moral status of individual persons. We will return to that issue and criticize that assumption shortly.

Putting aside the discussion of corporate persons, at least for the moment, we should now look at how plausible the personation theory of personhood is. This is important since the theory will allow us to cast the humanoids as persons only to the extent that it meets the conditions, as we saw in the first section, that are associated with personhood. Does it satisfy, however loosely, the sorts of assumptions that are present in common thinking and reflected in a variety of theories? Does it fit with characterizing persons as reasoning agents who are fit to be held responsible for what they do, enjoy a corresponding dignity or status, and are naturally oriented to an inbuilt ideal? And does it make good sense of the special sort of self-identity that persons enjoy over time? We postpone the issue about self-identity to next section and look here at the issues about reasoning, responsibility, dignity and the ideal of personhood.

7.2.6 Testing the theory: reasoning

We know that rationality but not the power of reasoning is required for agency. In order for any system, mechanical, biological, or social, to constitute an agent it must act reliably for certain goals in accordance with reliably formed representations of its world. This appears in the fact that reliable performance is an instance of executive rationality, and the reliable formation of representations an instance of cognitive rationality. The power of reasoning is not required for agency, as we know. But is it required for personhood, assuming that a person is just an agent who can personate?

An agent will have the power of reasoning, by our account in Chapter 3, insofar as they can act intentionally in researching and reflecting on evidence about a certain issue, can judge whether the evidence supports one or another judgment, and can choose to form a judgment that enjoys support, drawing it as a conclusion. Whatever the issue addressed, a successful reasoned judgment will always prompt the formation of a belief and, if the issue bears on the desiderata of different sorts of alternatives, will also prompt the formation of a desire: in one sort of case, an intention; in another, a preference. Does personation require the exercise of reasoning, then, whether in an active or virtual mode?

It surely does. The personating agent will often have to make a choice, now in this situation or relationship, now in that, as to what attitudes to avow and what intentions to pledge; or, equivalently, they will have to make a choice as to whether or not to demur at the expectations of others and at the ascription of corresponding commitments. But that choice will require them to act intentionally in resolving connected issues, finding reasons to support this or that commitment. This requirement will be reinforced by the fact that in this or that instance they will have to be equipped to assure others about their avowals and pledges, making clear the reasons that explain and justify the choices they make in the course of personation.

This is to say that the standard assumption that a person must be an agent with the capacity to reason—or reason and reflect, in Locke's terminology—is borne out under the view that a person is an agent who can personate. As we saw, Daniel Dennett (1979, Ch. 14) adds that not only must persons be rational and able to reason, they must also be conscious, have a capacity to communicate in language and be able to ascribe attitudes to one another. Consciousness and the ability to communicate in language are required under our account of reasoning, so those requirements do not count as additional. And the ability to ascribe attitudes to one another—in Dennett's, terms to adopt the intentional stance on one another—is central to the personating picture of persons.

7.2.7 Testing the theory: responsibility

The second of our four assumptions about persons—the first of our three normative assumptions—is that they are able to ascribe responsibility to one another, and to themselves, and that under the usual conditions they are fit to be held responsible. Are personating subjects likely to satisfy this responsibility assumption? And will the humanoids count in that respect, therefore, as persons? Again, the answer is clearly, yes.

By our account, fitness for responsibility is brought onstream among the humanoids insofar as they make commitments to one another; expose themselves to being exhorted by others, or indeed by themselves, to exercise the capacities presupposed; and thereby make themselves available for ex post commendation or blame. Thus, the humanoids may blame others for not living up to their commitments—in particular, the commitments supported by shared norms and values—and of course they may blame themselves for such failures. Indeed, they may also blame themselves for not living up to commitments they make with themselves—resolutions, for example—even when those commitments have no impact on the fortunes of others.

These considerations demonstrate that the humanoids, being of a commissive nature, will satisfy the responsibility assumption as well as that of reasoning. As their commitments, active and virtual, ensure that they personate, so they ensure by the same stroke that they will have the concept of responsibility at their disposal, that they will be able to ascribe responsibility to one another and to themselves, and that they will have the capacity to live up to their responsibilities. By making commitments, they will put themselves within reach of social and self-exhortation, and they will have to acknowledge responsibility for failing to act as they might have been appropriately exhorted to act.

It is worth mentioning in connection with responsibility that the identification of the person with a personating subject may also explain why the idea of shame would gain a hold among humanoids, as it has a hold among us human beings. Insofar as I am conscious of not living up to how I present myself to myself and to others, it is understandable, not just that I should hold myself responsible for the failure in a particular action, but that I should feel what we naturally describe as shame, recognizing that I as a person have proved not to be what I purported to be; shame in this sense is focused on the self, where guilt is focused on the action performed.

The identification of a person with a self-personating or self-representing subject may not only make room for shame but also help to explain why the notion of shame may assume a second form in humanoid experience, as it assumes a second form among humans. Where the first is agential shame of the kind illustrated, this second is what we might describe as bodily shame. Agential shame is that which the humanoids will feel when they fail to live up to the persona that they invite others, or indeed themselves, to rely on: when they fail to exercise their presumptive power of personation. Bodily shame is that which they are likely to feel when they relate to others in a way that does not allow them to personate: when they relate in a domain where they lack a power of personation altogether.

Bodily shame is what Adam and Eve are said in the book of Genesis to have felt in their nakedness (Velleman 2001). It is a form of shame in which the person is presented, not in an image that falls short of the persona they projected, but in a posture that rules out personation altogether. In this exposure, they are seen and flinch from being seen, as a body that digests and defecates, burps and farts, and behaves in patterns beyond the reach of personating control. It is a sense of shame at being presented below the level of the personating self, as distinct from a sense of shame at not proving to be the person projected at the level of personation.

7.2.8 Testing the theory: dignity

But will personating subjects have any claim to the sort of dignity or worth that Kant and others assign to persons, or at least to natural rather than corporate persons? Will the humanoids be positioned to recognize the difference stressed by Kant between persons and things or indeed persons and other animals?[11] We make some brief remarks here in defense of an affirmative answer.

The humanoids relate as personating agents insofar as they make commitments to one another, whether in committing to shared, collectively beneficial norms or committing in the course of forming or maintaining more partial relationships. This means that each will invite others to rely on them, setting aside misleading-mind and changed-mind excuses for ever letting those others down. But this means in turn that they will authorize one another to complain about any failure and censure them for the commissive breach involved. They will thereby put a certain power in one another's hands, denying themselves any means of self-defense: this, at any rate, if they wish to maintain their status in the community.

The powers that the humanoids will thereby confer on one another amount to rights: the right to rely on them to live up to any commitment they make and the right to demand an apology for any offense. The rights they confer correlate with duties to others that they will be required to acknowledge: the duty to make only commitments they intend to keep and to live up to whatever commitments they make. Both the rights and the duties will be categorical in character, even though they need not be absolute: there may be circumstances where a red flag indicates that they are trumped. They will be categorical insofar as they will bind the humanoids as members of their community, not dependently on the purposes, selfish or impartial, that they may have.

The humanoids will enjoy a recognized status in their society insofar as they can claim rights against one another and acknowledge duties that they owe. They will each have the general rights supported by shared norms—for example, negative rights against deception and aggression—as well as the particular rights that they enjoy in virtue of more specific commitments. And they will have those rights in

---

[11] For an attempt to extend Kantian theory to non-human animals, however, see (Korsgaard 2018).

virtue of their personating nature and not because—or at least not just because—satisfying the rights leads to an independently valuable outcome. Their status as rights-holders of this kind will ensure that they can enjoy and claim the dignity associated traditionally with personhood.

The case for their dignity as persons goes through quite smoothly, then, if we take the humanoids to be agents who can personate in the strong sense of being disposed or ready, given opportunity and motive, to personate. This contrasts with the weaker sense in which a child can personate in virtue of being disposed to develop that disposition, and the weaker sense still in which any human or humanoid agent can personate despite being so undeveloped or demented not to have even the disposition of the child. But it is common to think that those who are not adult or able-minded in those senses will still enjoy the dignity of persons. So, does that thought carry over to our humanoids? Or does it raise a difficulty for the personation theory?

If it is a difficulty for the theory, as we mentioned earlier, then it is equally a difficulty for most other theories as well. But in any case, it need not be a major obstacle. Consistently with thinking that natural, personating individuals have dignity as such, and owe one another an associated form of treatment, the humanoids will be able to recognize, as we humans generally recognize, that individuals in those other categories have a corresponding dignity. They will have this dignity in virtue of their trajectory of development, as in the case of children, or in virtue of their common humanoid nature, as in the case of those who are not able-minded by any plausible metric. It will presumably demand that even if they do not enjoy all the rights due to functioning persons, they should have rights that come as close as possible, consistently with their less than fully functioning status.

7.2.9 An aside: dignity and corporate persons

There is more to say about dignity, but it would take us too far afield. Before leaving the topic, however, we should address a question raised by the prospect that the humanoids may incorporate as group agents. The question is whether, as personating agents, such bodies would enjoy the same sort of dignity as natural, personating agents: whether they would be likely to attract the same sorts of rights in a community of members who personate with one another.

Incorporated groups can reason their way to conclusions about theoretical and practical issues, replacing the 'I' of personal reasoning by the 'we' of corporate reasoning. And, as we saw, such bodies can ascribe or be ascribed responsibility because of how they relate commissively with one another and with individual agents (Pettit 2007c; List and Pettit 2011). But it would be highly counterintuitive to think that among humanoids—and by extension among human beings—they can claim the same dignity as individual, personating agents. So, could the humanoids deny corporate bodies that sort of dignity on the personation approach?

Incorporated groups, whether humanoid or human, are created by individuals who rally behind a guiding voice in order to act as a single agent, presumably in the exercise of a right to incorporate that they have as individuals within the community. That voice may be the voice of a natural person who is put in charge or a voice that is generated by suitable procedures like those that operate in corporate bodies like commercial firms or voluntary associations. Once in existence, that body will have to be granted some rights in its corporate name: say, as an association, or corporation, or church. It could not operate as a personating body in the community without some rights in each category. But still, the fact that it will gain some rights as a body does not mean that it should have the rights and the dignity of natural persons.

Assume that the members of a community who personate with one another each enjoy the same rights under their commissive practices, and that this, by any plausible metric of value, is how things ought to be: the ground of those rights, after all—the capacity of members for personation—will be the same in each case. Assume in addition that any rights given to a corporate body in its own name will imply corresponding rights for its members, entitling them to enjoy the benefits of the group's exercise of its rights. It follows that the rights given to such a body ought not to ensure rights for their members of such a kind that others cannot exercise the same rights at the same time; they ought not to mean, for example, that others cannot incorporate with the same ease, for example, and gain access to parallel rights.

This means that the ground on which incorporated bodies may be given rights does not entail, whether among humanoids or humans, that they have the dignity of natural persons. Corporate persons ought to be given only such rights as are consistent with equal rights for all individuals in the community, whether or not they belong to such bodies. Thus, it is essentially the dignity of individuals that determines how corporate bodies are likely to be treated in a relevant community, and that indicates how they ought to be treated, under any plausible metric of value.[12]

7.2.10 Testing the theory: the ideal of personhood

For Kant, as we saw, being a person means being oriented essentially toward the ideal of autonomy in his richer sense of the term: the ideal of self-legislating on the

---

[12] This discussion of corporate rights will only make sense, plausibly, if we take the community in which the humanoids relate as equals to constitute a whole society, not just a subgroup of those at the same level in an unequal society; corporate bodies are likely to come into their own only under an encompassing regime of laws or at least norms (Pettit 2023b). In this consideration of corporate bodies, then, we have to rely heavily on an assumption of society-wide equality that we generally endorse only for the sake of simplicity.

basis of maxims that you can endorse as laws that apply to others in general, not just to yourself. And we saw that for Frankfurt being a person means being directed necessarily toward a similar ideal. In his case it is the ideal of acting only on ground-level desires that, at a higher level, you identify with as a person.

On the personation theory of personhood, there is also an ideal to which the person is going to be naturally directed: an ideal such that it is intuitively a failure on the part of any humanoid not to live up to it, or at least not generally to live up to it. Assuming that a humanoid individual is bound to make or endorse a range of commitments, that ideal involves two distinct pro tanto requirements: first, that they should subscribe only to commitments of the kind they are capable of discharging; and second, that they should discharge any commitments to which they do subscribe.

It is more or less inevitable that any humanoid individual will make commitments, as they learn what relationships involve and are inducted into a society with shared norms and values. It would be a betrayal of the practice of commitment, and ultimately the practice of personation, to be careless about the commitments they underwrite to the point where they cannot hope to keep them, or to be less than conscientious about keeping the commitments they actually undertake. While any agent who can personate in the strong sense will count as a person, the person who fails on such fronts will intuitively fail to act in accordance with their personating nature. They will flout the commissive practices by grace of which they count as a person in the first place.

While the ideal involved here is different from both Kant's and Frankfurt's, it still gives intuitive content to the assumption that being a person essentially involves a challenge: that operating badly as a person means not living fully up to what personhood requires of an agent. But does this mean that the agent who is careless about the commitments they make, or unconscientious about keeping their commitments, fails in a corresponding sense to be a person? Not necessarily. The defective heart is still a heart, the run-down car still a car. And in the same way the person who fails to live up to the personating ideal of personhood will still be a person.

Apart from Kant's and Frankfurt's ideals, we also mentioned a third view under which personhood involves an inbuilt ideal. This is the narrativity view, on which full or true personhood requires the person to be able to tell and live by a story about where they are coming from, so to speak, and where they are going. Self-narration may or may not be inevitable in some measure among persons: the theories differ on that question. The essential claim is that whether or not it is relatively inevitable, the construction of a guiding narrative of one's life is required for being a properly functioning person.

It would be nice if the personation theory could vindicate or explain away the appeal of the narrativity view, which surely has some resonance in common ways of thinking. And, as it turns out, the theory can do something close. Without vindicating or explaining away the narrativity ideal, it does something in between: it gives a non-debunking explanation as to why it should be appealing to endorse the ideal.

On our account of commitment, the humanoid agent who makes or goes along with a commitment, whether it be an avowal or a pledge, bets on themselves to live up to it, claiming an authority to speak for themselves rather than just reporting on themselves. In each commitment, they put their good name on the line, abjuring access to one or both self-reporter excuses, and inviting others to rely on them to perform as advertised: they say, in effect, 'This is who you can rely on me to be.'

We might well describe the persona that the personating agent projects in this way as a narrative. And to the extent that that is so, the humanoid individual will indeed construct and be guided by a narrative of their self. But on the personation theory, they will construct this narrative, not in an intentional effort at self-examination or self-direction, but as a byproduct of what personation involves. To underwrite commitments is to subscribe to an image of the self, and to the story that spells out that image, but the image and the story will emerge as a side-effect of those commitments, not as something at which the committing subject aims.

As a byproduct of commitments, the narrative will generally be unforeseen and unintended. It will be there in the avowals and pledges, active and virtual, personal and shared, that the humanoid person underwrites. But the person will not script that story consciously or carefully. They will not create it in the manner of a novelist or biographer and may not have a ready sense of the elements it contains.

While the commissive pattern involved in personation supports a narrative of this kind, of course, the narrative may change at various points over the course of a person's life. It makes perfect sense for someone to alter their commitments, disowning avowals or pledges they underwrote in the past, whether with others generally or with particular individuals, or even with themselves in purely personal resolutions. And as the pattern of someone's commitments shifts in this way, so of course will the persona they project and the narrative it supports. Narrativity theorists do not deny the possibility of such development, of course. But it is an advantage in the commissive counterpart to the theory that it makes the prospect of such variation almost inevitable.

7.2.11 Conclusion

In ascribing personhood to our humanoids, the personation theory of personhood stands up very well to the tests generated by four assumptions we naturally make about persons. It explains why as persons they should be expected to be able to reason and exercise related capacities; why they should be fit to be held responsible for how they behave; why they should be able to enjoy and claim rights that give them dignity; and why they should be oriented toward an ideal built into the very idea of personhood. But how will the humanoids fare in living up to the assumption that if they are persons, they must constitute a self and enjoy a distinctive sort of self-identity over time? We turn to that important issue in the final section.

7.3 Persons and their selves

On our ordinary habits of thought, and on most philosophical theories, only persons can self-identify over time. They will refer to themselves from within two perspectives: first, in the aspect-free manner in which even a non-personal agent must have beliefs about itself; and two, in the aspect-bound manner in which they pick themselves out as the bearers of certain features, in particular the features associated with personal status. This dual perspective on themselves, together with the manifest fact that they may change significantly in their public profile, highlights the issue of what gives them unity and identity across those changes, in their private profile: in the profile revealed in referring to themselves via the indexical 'I'. What makes it the case from the point of view of each, that I am I? What ensures the identity of myself—my self—over time?[13]

We turn now to exploring this notion of the self and of the identity of the self, to see how far it would apply to the humanoids, and by analogy to humans. We pursue that task by looking in turn at the metaphysics, the epistemology and, in a broad sense, the ethics of the self, as the self might be conceptualized for and by the humanoids. But before we do that, it is essential to distinguish some different ways in which the self is likely to be understood among them.

7.3.1 The self, abstract, authorized, and imposed

The notion of the self is introduced, as we have just noted, by the way in which personating agents identify themselves, as presented in a private perspective, across alterations that materialize in the public. But there are distinct senses in which such talk immediately directs us to something that we might reasonably call the self.

One self that will be present for every humanoid, as for every human, is the agent that is present for them in an aspect-free manner, being implicated in their every attitude and action. It is the self for which they feel fear, whatever they are afraid of; the self at the origin of every memory, whatever the nature of what is remembered; the self that they mobilize to act, no matter what they decide to do. Even the robot of our early example has beliefs about this entity, as when it forms the

---

[13] For an illuminating discussion of the themes of this section in relation to Kant and others, see (Longuenesse 2017).

aspect-free belief about itself that an object is near enough—that is, near enough to *it*—to make lifting possible. But it is only for a person that this self comes into view as that which makes them the same entity across actual and possible variations in their public profile. This is the self considered in abstraction from whatever form the agent assumes, whatever action they take, in the public forum, and we describe it as the abstract self.

But by our account, humanoid persons do not assume just any form, and do not do just anything, in their public role. The thing that distinguishes them as persons is that they project an image of themselves, a persona, that they invite others, and indeed themselves, to rely on. This means that there is another plausible referent for the notion of the self as it applies to them. It may refer, as each will think in their own case, not to me as the enactor in abstraction from whatever I enact—not to the abstract self—but to the enactor considered in the persona I assume and authorize: to the enactor in that more concretely specified identity and self.

On this account, the abstract and the authorized selves are each constituted by the agent involved and differ only in how they are conceived. The abstract self is that agent considered in an active role, independently of what they enact. The authorized self is that agent considered more specifically in a personating role: in the role of an agent who enacts a given persona, holding out an image of themselves to which they are broadly faithful. Where the abstract self will have no features associated with what the agent undertakes—no character, so to speak—the personating agent will have the character that the agent assumes and projects in inviting others to rely on their implementing that persona and in embracing it as an image of what they can expect of themselves. In assuming and embracing that character, every humanoid agent will shape their behavior in the highly specific fashion that speaks for who they aspire—and in the normal case, manage—to be.[14]

But the distinction between the abstract and the authorized self directs us to a third sense that may be given to the self of a personating, humanoid agent. This self is constituted by the character that others may ascribe to them—and perhaps assign as a matter manifest among those in one or another group—without the license that authorization would provide. It is the character that is filled out in third-person gossip about the agent, whether the gossip be hostile or friendly. The driving motive behind such gossip will not be to confirm the persona that the agent endorses—in that sense it will be unauthorized—but to paint a picture of them, out of distinct motives: say, that of engaging the interest of a particular audience, holding up the person for criticism or admiration, and perhaps making the gossiper themselves look good.

---

[14] This supports a claim that David Velleman makes on a phenomenological basis. Attracted to the view that agency inevitably involves some self-narration—we may interpret this as unintentional self-narration—he insists that the self projected by a self-narrator, 'is not just an idle fiction, a useful abstraction for interpreting his behavior. It—or, more precisely, his representation of it—is a determinant of the very behavior that it's useful for interpreting' (Velleman 2020, 289).

Like human beings, the humanoids will have a motive and a means of practicing gossip, and each must be aware that they will attract an unauthorized image—a shared, manifest image—within this or that community of peers: perhaps a welcome image in one group, perhaps an unwelcome one in another. Thus, each will be aware that even as they enact an authorized persona in their behavior, so they are bound to be taken to enact an unauthorized counterpart that is imposed on them in this or that circle of observers and commentators.

The inescapability of this imposed self is nicely captured by Jorge Luis Borges (1962, 246-47) in a short essay, entitled 'Borges and I'. Seeing himself cast as a result of his publicity in a *persona* that is created by others as much as by himself, he comments: 'The other one, the one called Borges, is the one things happen to.' While this Borges is beyond his control, it is not a figure he resents. 'It would be an exaggeration', he reports, 'to say that ours is a hostile relationship; I live, let myself go on living, so that Borges may contrive his literature, and this literature justifies me.'

Where Borges displays an amused indifference to his imposed self, the protagonist in Jean Paul Sartre's (1948) essay 'Portrait of the Antisemite' represents someone who relishes it. This young man, unsure of his identity, is taken by the hostess at a party to be hostile to Jews, as he discovers to his surprise, and finds that the image impresses acquaintances and prompts them to make allowances for his attitudes. Enjoying that recognition, then, he comes to cherish the image in which he finds himself cast. He will do this, Sartre suggests, not because the image appeals independently, but because it makes him into a somebody: it gives him bearings by which to navigate, and rescues him from a sea of existentialist indecision.

Taking account of this third possibility, we can distinguish between three ways in which we might take the self of a humanoid person. This may be identified with the self that the person realizes in abstraction from what they do, or with the self that they realize in authorizing a persona, or finally with the self—strictly the selves—that they are taken by others in this or that group to realize. With these distinctions in place, we may now turn to a consideration of the metaphysics, the epistemology, and the ethics of each type of self, abstract, authorized or imposed, among humanoids and potentially among humans.

Before turning to that task, however, it may be useful to note a complication that we will be putting aside in the following discussion. This is the possibility that not only may a person, humanoid or human, have to live with more than one imposed self—this insofar as different characters may be imposed on the person by different individuals or groups—a given individual may also have a number of abstract or authorized selves. The individual will have different abstract selves if they display a multiple personality syndrome, as it is often called. And they will have different authorized selves if they sincerely and effectively project a different persona—and if this is possible, embrace that persona in their own mental life—across disjoint communities to which they belong. There are interesting issues raised by these possibilities, but we shall ignore them here.

7.3.2 The abstract self: metaphysics

There can hardly be any doubt but that the humanoids will have an enduring self in each of these senses. But while the self in each sense will constitute a reality, the existence conditions of those selves are going to be quite different.

Thus, starting with the abstract self, it is by virtue of being agents who operate in a public as well as a private sphere that the humanoids will each have a self in this sense. That self will constitute the identity of the agent—will make them the same agent—over the different public actions and projects they may undertake. This self is the I, as each of them will say and think, who had the experiences I remember, the I who will undertake the actions I plan, the I whose pain or pleasure I anticipate in fear or excitement, and the I who continues to support the standing attitudes—the beliefs, policies, or values—that nothing has caused me to drop. This self is the I who will survive through any changes over time in those experiences and plans, those anticipations and attitudes.

But what is this I, this self, that can continue the same over time, independently of the character of the agent's experiences or plans, anticipations, or attitudes? What is this self that constitutes a constant point of reference even across protean mutations in the content of the agent's concerns?

The only possible answer runs on the following lines. This self will be a constant point of reference, as we noted, insofar as the person's experiences now explain their memories later, their plans now explain their actions later, and certain expectations for later explain their anxiety or excitement now. And that means that it will come into existence when the mental states, events, and acts that characterize the agent at any moment—the states, events, and acts that explain how the agent performs—connect causally in a certain way with those that characterize the agent later. It means, in short, that this self will be constituted by a causal stream that reaches back into the past and, all going well, will reach forward into the future.

The material that flows in this temporal stream will encompass the memories and perceptions, the plans and actions, the occasional feelings and the standing attitudes that will characterize any humanoid or presumably human agent. The elements in the stream must be connected so that the agent can generally explain why at any moment they are having a certain memory, why they are following a certain plan or taking a particular action, why they feel fear or excitement at a certain prospect, or just why they are maintaining certain attitudes. It is this capacity, and the awareness it presupposes, that will enable them to think of their evolving mental states and acts as their own mental states and acts, not as episodes they observe on an internal, introspective screen.[15]

These observations give us an account of the existence conditions for a humanoid agent to instantiate the abstract self. That self will continue to exist, unifying the agent over time, insofar as a suitably constituted, suitably connected causal stream operates within the agent in generating their performance at any moment. One benefit of this metaphysical account of the abstract self is that it enables us to address some of the questions that have been raised in the literature about the self of humans.[16]

First of all, the account suggests that animalists are mistaken when they suggest that an agent can retain their self in this sense only insofar as they continue to have the same organic body. If the causal stream required for the continuity of the self over time can be maintained without such organic continuity, then presumably the self can be maintained as well. This need not suggest, of course, that we have to think of the humanoid self as an immaterial soul, in the fashion of Locke, since the continuity of the causal stream may be physically or materially sustained, without organic continuity. That will be true, for example, if a process like the teletransportation envisaged by philosophers can keep the causal stream intact while undermining organic unity: while causing the person's body at the starting point of the process to be destroyed, even as the stream is enabled to continue in the body provided at the terminus.

This observation offers a line on other questions that are also familiar from the literature, although raised about humans, not humanoids. If a person undergoes fission at a certain point, do the two or more persons that diverge from that point on each count as a distinct person with a self that reaches back before the fission? Yes, contrary to the line taken by Derek Parfit (1984), they will. Each will be a distinct person with their own distinct causal stream and their own distinct self, although those different persons and selves—those different continuants over time—will share certain elements in their respective streams over the period before the fission took place (Lewis 1976).[17]

Moving from fission to fusion, could two persons survive fusion with one another, so that from the moment when they merge, the agent will have a causal history with conflicting elements that may point them on competing paths? Surely not. There will be no suitably unified causal stream to constitute that person and

---

[15] It is hard to see any readily accessible, independent means of characterizing the right way for the elements to be causally connected in order to have this effect. The claim here is only that there must be some independently characterizable network of connections that would do the job: nothing else, or at least nothing else of a broadly naturalistic kind, would serve.

[16] For a useful presentation of different viewpoints, in dialogue form, see (Perry 2008).

[17] Following this line means that we can avoid taking Parfit's view that since I before the fission will care about each of the persons after the fission, and since I cannot be the same person with each—this, by contrast with Lewis's way of thinking—what matters to me as I look to the future cannot be my identity with either of the future persons; what matters must be the closeness of my connection with each of them.

that self. How could one and the same self at a later time access in first-person memory the potentially competing experiences of the earlier selves? And how could that later self enact the potentially competing intentions of those earlier selves?

7.3.3 The abstract self: epistemology

This is enough on the metaphysics of the abstract self. What is there to be said about the epistemology to which that self will lend itself among humanoids and, as we may assume, among humans?

We know from earlier discussion that a person, humanoid or human, will relate to their abstract self in an aspect-free manner and that the self they connect with in that way is unmissable. They may form false beliefs about that self—even the robot may be wrong about how near it is to an object on the table—but those beliefs must be false in virtue of misattributing a property or relationship, not in virtue of correctly attributing such a feature to the wrong entity (Evans 1982).

This observation about the unmissable nature of the abstract self looks like an epistemological victory. But the victory is Pyrrhic. For while the person cannot misidentify their abstract self, that victory is ensured only by the fact that they do not take that self under any aspect. It does not exist for them, as I do not exist for me, as the bearer of any particular feature; the nature of this self is inherently elusive. Hume (1978, I.6.3) gives striking expression to this view that there is nothing to learn or know about this self: 'when I enter most intimately into what I call *myself*, I always stumble on some particular perception or other, of heat or cold, light or shade, love or hatred, pain or pleasure. I never can catch *myself* at any time without a perception, and never can observe anything but the perception.'

The aspect-free nature of the abstract self might be taken to explain the long tradition of taking the self to be more like an ever-changing process—a locus where things come and go—rather than a substantive entity: a 'no-thing' in Sartre's (1957; 1958) verbal play. But though it is constituted by a causal stream, persons will each have to conceptualize themselves as a continuing entity answering to the referring term 'I' and retaining its identity over time. Georg Lichtenberg, an eighteenth-century author, argued that Descartes's *Cogito ergo sum*—'I think, therefore I am'—conveys nothing more than *Cogitatur, ergo id est*: 'there is thought, so there is something'. As Bernard Williams (1978) observes, the continuing 'I' entails a lesson that goes missing in Lichtenberg's rewriting: namely, the something that thinks and exists, unlike the occurrent thought, has a potential to endure.[18]

---

[18] The rewriting, as Williams says, also overlooks the general fact that it is only because of the continuing identity of a reasoner that the premises endorsed in any argument give that person ground to endorse and believe the conclusion. That the premises are endorsed, but at no particular locus, does not support the derivation of the conclusion at any individual locus.

The epistemological relationship between a humanoid or human person and their abstract self may be compared usefully to the relationship that a viewer will have to the standpoint from which a landscape picture is painted or a photograph taken. That standpoint will not feature in the picture or photograph itself—it will not be something the viewer sees—but it will be there to be detected in the angle of the drawing or the shot: in how various landmarks are depicted as near or far from that standpoint, below or above it, to the left or to the right. Even if the viewer does not focus on that standpoint, they will be aware of it out of the corner of the eye. In the same way, the active self that persons must presuppose in every memory or intention will be there to be seen out of the corner of their eye. It will not be known by acquaintance or description, in an old binary, but in a third fashion: in apperception, as we might put it, re-using a term from Kant.

The presence of the abstract self in the life of the individual person is reflected in the way the self of a corporate agent must be present in the awareness of those who decide or act for that agent and, even more strikingly, in those who reason in its name about what to think on one or another issue (Pettit 2018b). Such active group members must take the corporate body's standpoint as their own. They must validate only group judgments that are endorsed under received protocols, derive conclusions in the group's name only on the basis of those judgments, and act for the group only according to authorized means in pursuit of authorized ends. As they do this, they may immerse themselves in those activities, identifying unthinkingly with the group: letting the corporate body be instantiated, as it were, within themselves. And as they relate to the body that they serve in that way—a body that may cease to be an object of explicit attention—so will persons relate to the abstract selves that they serve in their individual thought and action.

7.3.4 The abstract self: ethics

What, finally, about the ethics of the abstract self? Will that self elicit the concern and care of the agent in a special degree? Will it be natural to think that humanoid persons should identify prudentially with this self and treat it as making different claims on them at any moment from the claims that other persons make?

In view of the divergence over time in the attitudes that the abstract self may assume and enact, Derek Parfit (1973; 1984) suggests that being prudently concerned with that self into the far future may make little sense. A person's ideas and interests may diverge as sharply from their own in that future as they diverge from those of other persons in the present. So why should they worry in particular about that person—that abstract self—long downstream from where they are now?[19]

---

[19] Parfit's line on this issue is connected with his view that the person who is later subject to fission cannot be the same person as each of the post-fission persons. Since he believes that that person will

Parfit's line of thought is hardly intuitive. The abstract self is the self for which any person will fear when they are afraid of dying, even dying a good time from now. It is the self with which they identify as a child when they fantasize about the great deeds they will perform as a grown-up. And it is the self that they charge with responsibility when they commit to others over the long haul, even when they make a commitment to someone 'til death us do part'.

The person cannot but care for themselves and in that sense care for their abstract self, because doing so is part and parcel of agency itself. It is a sort of concern that even the non-personal agent—or at least the animate agent that is capable of feeling—cannot but experience for themselves. There is no reason why an agent with a sense of the future might not feel this concern over long reaches of time. No matter how far into the future, their existence at that time means that their abstract self—the self implicated in their every memory and intention—must figure as an object of natural concern.

Is this sort of self-concern unfetching, as Parfit's critique of prudence suggests it might be? Surely not. You will not care about yourself in this sense—you will not care about your abstract self—because it is you. On the contrary, we might say, that agent and that self will count as you because you relate to it in the caring way. The concern involved is constitutive of who you are over time, not merely indicative or diagnostic of where in time you are to be found. It constitutes the innocent sort of self-love—*l'amour de soi*—that Rousseau thought no animal or human could possibly lack: this, by contrast with *l'amour propre,* a malignant form of self-love that he associated with humans in particular (Dent 1988).

Might this innocent self-love carry over from individual to corporate persons? More specifically, might individuals come to identify in this affective way with a group agent for which they act, finding a joy in its prospects or successes akin to the joy they may find in their own? Our human experience suggests that they surely might undergo this sort of transference, investing in a corporate body and finding satisfaction or frustration in how it performs. By some accounts, for example, the idea of corporate personhood was cherished in the Middle Ages for the sense of immortality that it gave to the members of guilds and orders and towns and, at the limit, to the members of the corporate church: the mystical body of Christ, as it came to conceptualized (Kantorowicz 1997).[20]

---

care about each of those persons, he concludes that it is not personal identity that explains their care but rather, presumably, the psychological connection they enjoy with each. But if connection is the basis of such care, it begins to seem irrational for someone to be concerned much about an agentially continuous person in the future who has few connections with them.

[20] Despite Mark Johnston's (2010) interesting argument to the contrary, however, this sort of effect, could hardly enable people in any literal sense to survive their individual demise: and this, even if it is extended to humanity as a whole, and intensified to the point of nearly silencing personal self-concern.

7.3.5 The authorized self: metaphysics

While the humanoid practice of personation enables us to take the view just outlined on the metaphysics, epistemology, and ethics of the abstract self, it has a much more direct impact on those issues as they arise for the authorized self. This is the self that I am taken to instantiate, as any of the humanoids will be able to think, insofar as the ways in which I commit to others—and, as it will be, to myself—make it the case that I hold up a persona, an image of myself, in which I invest. I will invest in this persona to the extent that I treat the image as one on which others, and I myself, can safely rely; as an image indeed on which I invite such reliance, sidelining self-reporter excuses for any failure to live up to the image and exposing myself to being blamed for a failure.

The metaphysics of this authorized self may seem to raise few problems under the genealogy presented here. Like the abstract counterpart, this self will be identical with the agent picked out in an aspect-free way under the guise of the 'I'. But it will be that agent considered in the role characteristic of persons: that of personating in a commissive manner. Presented in this way, each humanoid will be able to think of the me they take to survive through change and time as one and the same self only to the extent that they sustain the relevant personating project.

But this observation does raise a tricky issue. When will an agent count as sustaining this project? When will it be the case, as they and others may think, that despite various changes in their circumstances, relationships, and commitments, this indeed is the same personating agent? When will they be able to see the agent under this profile as one and the same over time?

Every personating agent will be a personator insofar as they conduct the social and mental activity of authorizing a representation of themselves. But at any time every such agent will also be a personatee, where their identity in this character is associated with the particular self-image that they project. The main question to consider, then, is this. Should the humanoids take the survival of the personator to be enough to ensure the continuing identity of the authorized self? Or does that continuing identity require the persona projected as well as the personating agent to remain unchanged?

Taking the survival of the authorized self to require constancy in the personatee would raise difficult problems, since it might require us to take the counterintuitive line that any change of commitment on the agent's part will make them into a different self: after all, even a single shift of this kind would seem to change the personatee. This difficulty argues for requiring the continuing identity of the authorized self to depend on the survival of the personator rather than on constancy in the personatee. But this line will be plausible only if we distinguish between changes in the personatee—that is, changes in how the agent personates—that the personator constitutionally introduces, as we might put it, and changes that the personator does not author in that way.

Think of the different ways in which a polity may change its way of doing business: say, its electoral system or the relationship it allows between legislature and judiciary. Such a change will be constitutionally authored if it occurs under a procedure—say, a suitably organized referendum—that the constitution recognizes. It will be extra-constitutionally introduced if it occurs in a manner that the constitution does not allow: say, as a result of a violent revolution or in the peaceful manner in which the United States changed its constitution in 1787.

We may take a personating agent to change the content of the persona they project in a constitutionally authored manner if they do so under the active or standby control of reasoned judgment. They will change in this way if they give up a belief they previously held in view of new evidence that counts against it; if they give up on a policy or plan because of registering previously unnoticed costs; if they change their mind about the pleasure or pain that some anticipated event promises and cease to feel fear or excitement at the prospect; or if an unhappy experience prompts them to drop someone as a friend. As such changes will not affect their identity as an abstract self, so we may hold that neither will they affect the agent's identity as an authorized self. In altering in these ways, the person will project a changed image of themselves, to be sure, but they will do this as part of their personating project. These are changes for which they can assume responsibility, confident that they will not be blamed for changing the pattern in which they personate.

But personating agents like the humanoids will be subject to extra-constitutional as well as constitutional changes: that is, changes that come upon them like shocks to the system rather than evolving under the active or standby control of reasoned judgment. Such shocks may come about through transformative experiences that leave the agent disposed to personate in a novel pattern, where the novelty comes upon them without their imprimatur, as it were: this might be the shock of falling in love, or undergoing a religious conversion, or just having a baby (Paul 2014).

Such shocks may also materialize, we may assume, as a result of longer-term shifts of habit and feeling in response to deep changes of circumstance. An example might be the traumatic impact of fighting in a war or being exposed to the threat of violence or spending time in prison. Oscar Wilde sums up the likely effect of such an experience—likely among humanoids as well as humans—in *The Ballad of Reading Gaol*:

> 'The vilest deeds like poison weeds
> Bloom well in prison-air:
> It is only what is good in Man
> That wastes and withers there'.

Returning now to the issue of when we may take a person to remain the same self, in the authorized sense of self, it seems plausible to hold that they will remain suitably the same so long as the changes in the persona that they project are of the constitutional kind that allows them to assume responsibility for the alterations. The self that they see as answering to the 'I', when that is used to refer to them in their personating character, will survive through such endogenously authored changes. It will be replaced by a different self—they will become a different person, as they themselves may say—only when they undergo exogenous shocks that introduce a rupture in their personating relationship with others, and indeed with themselves.

On this picture, the person need not have as many distinct selves over time as Derek Parfit (1984) envisages. He takes it that a given, psychologically continuous person should be ascribed different selves insofar as their psychological continuity over different stretches of their lifetime varies in density. Each densely connected stretch corresponds, on this way of thinking, to a distinct self and the person over time can be equated with a string of such selves. On the view adopted here, the authorized self that each humanoid person holds up as a model of who they are will remain the same self over constitutionally licensed shifts from one period to another: say, from adolescence to early adulthood to later life. If we are to go along with Parfit and carve up the person into different temporally bounded selves, then we will do so only to the extent that the bounds between selves are created by extra-constitutional shocks that may leave the person bewildered about how they have changed.

7.3.6 The authorized self: epistemology

So much for the metaphysics of the authorized self. What now to say about the epistemology and ethics of this self?

The epistemology of the authorized self is rather more straightforward than that of the abstract. This is primarily because this self is constructed by the person and, as a construct, might reasonably be expected to lie within their cognitive reach: the person will presumably have a maker's knowledge of that which they create. But it turns out that this form of knowledge is not guaranteed to be readily accessible.[21]

There are a number of connected reasons why this is so, all of them implied in the contrast we drew between personation and narration. The persona that is projected in the commitments of the individual is a byproduct of commitment, not something intentionally put together. It is the product, moreover, of a range of distinct commitments, not of a single, master commitment. And among the commitments that generate the persona, many will arise from passive acquiescence in the expectations of others, or the silent authorization of a would-be spokesperson, rather than from the person's own active authorship.

---

[21] For an account of the difficulty of self-knowledge on a variety of fronts, including that which is relevant here, see (Cassam 2016).

These observations mean that a person need not be fully aware of all the sides to the self they invite others, and indeed themselves, to rely upon. And they may recognize only after the event that they had moved on at one or another point in their lives and had effectively changed the character they previously assumed and sought to realize. Despite their role in constructing the authorized self, their knowledge of this self may be quite inadequate and may only develop in response to serious effort on their part.

With the authorized self, then, it will make perfect sense to endorse the age-old mantra: 'know yourself'. This will make no sense whatsoever with the abstract self, as indeed we have seen. But with the authorized self it will prescribe a form of knowledge that ought to be appealing in light of the ideal built into the very idea of personation. The exercise of living up to the persona that a person has invited others, and indeed themselves, to rely on—the realization of the personating ideal—will lie within reach only to the extent that the person has a good sense of the persona that they may be taken to have authorized.

7.3.7 The authorized self: ethics

What now about the ethics of the authorized self? Given that this self is the character that the person is committed to realize, it is a self that they ought to care about under any shared norms and values that we might plausibly imagine among humanoids or humans.

One way of not caring about that self would be to refuse to make serious commitments, choosing instead to live under the ebb and flow of opinion and inclination, in the manner of what Harry Frankfurt (1988) calls wantons. This, however, would be to give up altogether on the project of acting as a person and would scarcely be feasible. Another way of not caring would be to make commitments, social and personal, but to fail systematically to live up to them, at least when doing so is costly. This looks equally infeasible, however, since the person could hardly expect the social- or self-forgiveness that would enable them, despite their failures, to continue to make commitments to others or to themselves.

Polonius is a figure of fun in Shakespeare's *Hamlet*, but he strikes the right note on this particular topic. This appears when he gives advice to his son, Laertes, who is about to depart for university.

> 'This, above all: to thine own self be true,
> And it must follow, as the night the day,
> Thou canst not then be false to any man'.

It would make no sense to advise someone to be true to their abstract self, caring about it in that sense since, as we saw, they can do no other. But the advice makes perfect sense, under the personation theory, with the authorized self. And it also makes sense on that theory—assuming, as among the humanoids, a commitment to shared norms—to say, as Polonius does, that being true to that self will mean doing well by others; after all, it means upholding any norm-based commitments made to them.[22]

We noted that the epistemology of the authorized self explains why we might endorse the mantra: 'know yourself'. This observation about the ethics of that self explains why other equally old mantras may also make sense with the authorized self, where they would make no sense with the abstract. These will include 'be yourself' and 'love yourself', for example. The first is an injunction to live up to the self that is authorized, the second an exhortation to savor and embrace that self, taking care to serve that persona faithfully.

The fact that mantras of these kinds have long been endorsed among our human kind suggests that we and our ancestors have always had a richer sense of what the self is than that which is reflected in the currently fashionable focus on the abstract self. It is a welcome lesson of our genealogy of the humanoids that such a richer sense of the self is bound to emerge among them in virtue of their practices of commitment and personation. In this respect, as in others, the discussion of the humanoids may deliver a useful understanding of our human kind as well.

7.3.8 The imposed self: metaphysics, epistemology, and ethics

We come finally to the sort of self that is going to be imposed on someone by this or that individual or group. Like the self that the agent personates—and unlike the abstract self—this self will have a content or character. But it will be a character that they have not invited anyone, least of all themselves, to rely on. There may be many such selves imposed on a person, of course, where each reflects the views adopted in one or another group—or indeed, at the limit, by one or another individual—but we may speak for convenience as if there were only one.

The metaphysics of the imposed self is straightforward. That self will come into existence as the construct of commentators on the person to whom it is ascribed. Unlike the self that that person constructs for themselves in personation, however, this will not be a byproduct of activities pursued on distinct grounds—in the personation case, commissive activities—but a construct pursued for its own sake, even if the pursuit involves insinuation and innuendo as often as it does straightforward characterization.

---

[22] As noted earlier, we may assume that the commitments undertaken by the humanoids, in view of their shared norms and values, will generally be welcome to others; they will not include a commitment, for example, to exacting revenge for any hurt imposed by another. But it is worth noting that the ideal of displaying and living up to an authorized persona is wholly structural; it is consistent with authorizing a nasty self.

What now of the epistemology of this self? Well, an individual person, humanoid or human, may be aware that in adopting different attitudes, and taking various actions, they will invite the interpretation of various others. Sometimes they may have no idea what that interpretation is likely to be and what imposed self they will be taken to serve. At other times, however, and independently of how welcome or unwelcome it is, they may have a relatively good hunch about this: the party politician, for example, will be generally well aware of the figure they cut among the party faithful as well as the figure they cut among the opposition.

No matter how strong their hunch in such a case, however, no one will have personal resources sufficient to enable them to be sure about exactly what capacities and goals are attributed to them by others. Whether friendly or unfriendly, gossip that bears on a given individual will only exist among third parties as they comment to one another about that person. Assuming that the humanoids resemble humans, no one will gossip to a particular person about their character. And so, short of controlling a network of spies, the person will always operate with a degree of uncertainty about how they are construed in the larger world.

What is there to say, finally, about the ethics of the imposed self? Will it make sense for the humanoids, or indeed for humans, to care for that self? The question is not whether there is reason, when someone has evidence, to welcome the imputation of a positive character or to bemoan the imputation of a negative; clearly, the answer there is, yes. And again, the question is not whether someone ought to check on the views of others about how they are viewed—say, on how far they are trusted—when they are left in doubt by the feedback of interlocutors to their commitments; here too the answer is clearly, yes. The question rather is whether there is reason for an individual to desire to shape the imposed, un-personated self in an appealing mold, acting on that desire—if this is feasible—by filtering or massaging the information available about them.

There will certainly be reason for someone, humanoid or human, to form and act on such a desire when they suffer stereotyping or defamation of a kind that may undermine their personation in relation to others, and even in relation to themselves (Langton 2009). The misrepresentation may be so destructive, after all, that it becomes impossible for the person to give credible authority to the personated image of themselves. At that limit, the person committed to personation should do all they can to fight the self that is imposed on them. But short of such a limit, there are many reasons why they should try to set aside the desire to shape this self: many reasons why they should not give that desire the status of a personal value.

One is that indulging that concern may distract them from focusing on something intuitively much more important: the self that they forge for others and for themselves in personation. A second is that it may be impossible for them to tell if that concern is satisfied: the epistemic elusiveness of the imposed self means that trying to see if it is in an appealing shape may be as fruitless as trying to paint a picture of someone in the dark. And a third consideration is that it is a desire that they will need to keep hidden from others, which may be difficult, if they are not to frustrate it. 'The general axiom in this domain', as Jon Elster (1983, 66) says, 'is that nothing is so unimpressive as behaviour designed to impress.'

A final reason why a humanoid or human individual should want to set aside a desire to shape the imputed self is that it is an inherently insatiable concern: it can drive an individual to seek, not just to do well by local standards, but to outscore all others, and by as much as possible. As Rousseau (2020, 232) argued, 'the first feeling excited by this comparison is the desire to be first'. It is this love of being first, this love of pre-eminence, that Rousseau castigated as *l'amour propre*, as distinct from the innocent *l'amour de soi*. Seeing such self-love as a quest for supremacy, Kant (2006, 167) also condemned it, finding it present in 'the manias for honor, dominance, and possession': in these manias, he said, 'the human being becomes the dupe'.

We noted in the Introduction to this book that as language has the effect of enhancing the capacities of those who employ it, according to Hobbes, so it can have the effect of diminishing their performance in other ways. One of the ways in which it does so on his account anticipates Rousseau's warnings about *amour propre* and marks a nice note on which to end the current discussion. Being enabled by language to compare themselves with others, Hobbes (1998b, 5.5) says, 'men compete for honour and dignity'. And the result is dire, as he puts it with characteristic brio: 'every man thinking well of himself, and hating to see the same in others, they must needs provoke one another by words, and other signs of contempt and hatred, which are incident to all comparison' (Hobbes 1994a, 14.4).

Conclusion: toward ethics and politics

The genealogy pursued in the book directs us to two distinct ways in which the advent of language and converse would make humanoids special among other animals. In giving them access to judgment, reasoning, and percipience it would enable them to make up their own minds, think for themselves, and act for their chosen goals. And in giving them access to common norms and values, shared and personal standards of evaluation, and the status and relationships of persons, it would enable them to evolve a community in which they can each establish their own identity and way of life.

Their exposure to one another in converse would enable them, in other words, to come into their own and achieve the highest potential of the nature they share with us human beings. It will be useful, in concluding our story, to look at the precise features of their relationships with one another and the society they maintain that makes it possible for the humanoids to achieve this level of fulfillment. Doing so may teach lessons that carry over to our own kind.

Repurposing the genealogy

The focus of the genealogy developed in preceding chapters is on explaining how language and converse will prompt the emergence of distinctively human capacities among humanoid counterparts, living under conditions of relative equality. Such equality was presupposed in our account of how an economy of esteem will discipline the practices of judgment, reasoning, and percipience among the humanoids, and our story about the appearance of reciprocal practices of commitment to common norms, a related pattern of shared valuing, and the practice of holding one another responsible for breaches. There would hardly be a robust prospect of such developments in the absence of this equality.

We assumed throughout the genealogy that the humanoids live in conditions of society-wide and even world-wide equality. But we argued that while this made the genealogy relatively straightforward, it could still hold a lesson even for human beings living in hierarchical conditions, so long as they grew up within relatively egalitarian subgroups: so long as they enjoyed at least a culturally restricted version of the equality assumed. Even under such limited conditions of equality, the humanoids could come to understand and meet the expectations governing the relevant interpersonal practices and learn how to interiorize the practices intrapersonally.

This line of thought suggests that humanoids, and by analogy humans, will come into their own, mastering the capacities that converse enables, under conditions of relative equality, and only under such conditions. But however we specify the equality required for humanoid and human flourishing, it is clearly going to be more effective, the wider it extends. The individuals who learn the mastery of appropriate practices within the conversive circle of a dominated subgroup will hardly be able to display it in a wider context where they have to defer to those superior in power; they may even develop habits of submission and self-censorship, ingratiation and self-abasement, that are inimical to conversive practice. Nor are those superior in power going to escape conversively distorting influences: they can hardly be suitably disciplined, after all, by interaction with individuals they look down on.

If it is better that equality be wider rather than narrower, then the society of the humanoids takes on a different complexion from that which we have given it up to this point. It no longer figures just as a simple, counterfactual scenario that serves as a useful heuristic in thinking about the likely effects of converse on the make-up of humans. It now presents as a conversive community that will enable the humanoids to respond as well as possible to those effects, avoiding the influence of the power imbalances that hierarchy would introduce. That society will enable the humanoids to make the most of their nature and to flourish in its exercise, as they sort out their own minds in judgment and reasoning and form the mutually commissive and responsible connections of persons.

If the society-wide egalitarian conditions of our genealogy do enable the humanoids to develop their capacities to the fullest extent possible, making the most of their nature, then it is worth exploring the aspects of that society that make it so special. We know that it is a society whose members deal with one another under the conversive practices documented, thereby making it possible for each to develop the potential inherent in their nature. But how to characterize it in more familiar normative terms?

The society must give each a relative equality with others, as we have assumed. But what precise form of equality is required? And what are the other features of the society that make it special? We shall argue that the equality required is a form of relational equality, as it is often called, and that there are two other aspects of the society that are crucial to its appeal. One is that the members will command one another's respect under a plausible, conversive construal of that idea. And the other is that the social order they sustain will guard each against the dominating power of others, ensuring their freedom in the traditional republican sense. We shall look at each of these claims in what follows, concentrating mainly on the humanoids.

If our argument is sound, then relational equality, conversive respect, and freedom as non-domination are ideals that enable the humanoids to come into their own, achieving the best level of functioning that their make-up allows. And if such ideals have that compelling role in the humanoid case, the analogy with humans suggests that they may play a similar role for our own kind. They will count as ideals grounded in our very being: the conversive nature that we share with humanoids. And while they may assume culturally variant forms, they must have an irresistible, species-wide claim on our allegiance: they will identify aspects of our life with one another that are crucial for human flourishing.[1]

Equality

Conversable persons

If their conditions are suitably egalitarian, we can expect from the genealogy that the humanoids will interact as equals in the exercise of their processing and relational capacities. They will be able to provide information for one another carefully and truthfully, relying on common sources of evidence; will be able to explain the assertions and judgments they make by citing evidential facts as reasons they can each generally take to be supportive; and will be able to exercise and share such reasoned judgments on a range of issues, including questions that they percipiently probe in perception, learning to acknowledge that anyone's perception may lead them astray.

According to the genealogy, their egalitarian conditions will also enable the humanoids to make commitments to one another, including commitments to abide by common, collectively beneficial norms, and to form and express their shared or personal valuations, as they commit to corresponding desires. Making commitments of such kinds, they will also be able to hold one another responsible for how far they live up to them, acknowledging in everyone the valuational control over choice—the willpower or free will—that this presupposes. And on the basis of all those developments, they will each be able to commit to a representation of who they are—a persona—and to acknowledge such personation on the part of others.

We saw in the discussion of humanoid personhood that by participating in such conversive practices the humanoids will learn that they can claim rights to the forms of treatment supported by the practices, and by associated norms, and must acknowledge corresponding duties to satisfy the rights of others. And living under such a regime of reciprocally recognized rights and duties, they will enjoy the status and dignity of persons. They will give one another's conversable status a

---

[1] Elizabeth Anscombe (1958, 18) once wrote that for a proper understanding of ethics we need 'an account of human nature' and 'above all of human flourishing'. Our genealogy has provided us with such an account for humanoids and potentially for humans, and the discussion that follows may be seen as a sketch of ideals that answer well to their common nature, enabling them to flourish: to realize that nature fully.

robustly demanding role, privileging it as a reason that carries categorical, inherently motivating force, not a force that is dependent on whether acting as it requires is otherwise for the best in personal or impersonal terms. That the humanoids take another's status to impose a categorical demand on how the humanoids treat one another does not mean, of course, that the demand is absolute, holding come what may. Consistently with taking another's rights to make such a categorical demand, as we saw earlier, the humanoids may be willing to override such a right when a red flag goes up: say, when treating someone as a conversable person would threaten the death of another.

The role of equality

When the humanoids grant one another these conversively generated rights, they treat one another as conversable persons: that is, as persons who understand and act on their rights and duties under conversive practices. But why assume that the humanoids are likely to treat one another in this way—likely to live up to the demands manifestly supported by one another's status—only if there is a relative equality between them? Why take equality to be essential to the development of conversive practices and of the norms supporting such practices?

There are two considerations that support that assumption. The first is that there is no obvious reason why the humanoids would develop society-wide conversive practices of judgment and reasoning, valuation and responsibility, if there were not such a degree of equality between them. Suppose the society was hierarchically structured with those in stronger groups being able to maltreat those beneath them. In that case, the humanoids might each develop conversive practices within their own group, and recognize one another's conversive rights as members. But why would the stronger tie themselves to such practices and rights in dealing with the weaker, especially in any case where the returns from denying such rights—say, from relying on intimidation rather than persuasion to get their own way—promise to be very beneficial?

But suppose, despite this inequality of power, that society-wide practices did happen to get established among the humanoids. The second consideration that argues for the necessity of equality is that such practices would be unlikely to survive any significant inequality. A significant inequality within any relationship would obviously enable the stronger to do better in many circumstances by ignoring the rights of the weaker rather than by satisfying them: again, for example, by relying on intimidation rather than persuasion to get their own way. Since this possibility would be salient to the weaker, they would have a general reason to play safe, making sure to keep the powerful sweet rather than asserting their own rights. And since that would be salient in turn to the powerful, it would deprive them of any reason to expect the powerless to treat them reciprocally as conversable persons: say, to report even unwelcome truths, to insist on their own claims under shared norms, or to hold the stronger responsible for any offense. That being so, the interaction between the stronger and the weaker would likely enter a downward spiral, and rapidly cease to be conversive.[2]

Why would a suitable degree of equality among the humanoids, and the emergence of shared norms, guard against this collapse? By enabling victims to respond negatively to any breach of their rights by another—to shun or sanction the other—and to reduce or remove the temptation for the other not to satisfy their rights as conversable persons. As participants in conversive exchange, even would-be offenders will generally recognize the rights of others and be motivated to satisfy them. But none will be guaranteed in this or that instance to resist conflicting desires and temptations. By allowing would-be victims, or indeed other members of the society, to penalize any such offence, the equality between the humanoids would reduce or neutralize the temptation for would-be offenders to ignore a victim's rights. Thus, generalizing across the society, the equality would help to ensure that the humanoids will recognize and satisfy one another's rights robustly over the presence of conflicting desires or temptations.

Relational equality

For all that we assume in the genealogy, there may be differences of resources and power among the humanoids: differences, for example, in their economic wealth or cultural influence. But whatever form those differences take, they must allow even those with fewer resources to relate as conversable persons to those with more, asserting their own rights under conversive practices and holding others responsible to their correlated duties. There may be factors like self-doubt or timidity that reduce the ability of some to stand up to others in that way. But there should be nothing about the differences of resources and power between them that would rationally induce such submission: nothing, for example, that would give the weaker good prudential reason to watch what they say in speaking for themselves, and to be cautious about the expectations to which they hold others.

What will matter among the humanoids, by this account, is a species of relational equality, as it has come to be called (Anderson 1999; Scheffler 2003). It must be the case that however unequal they are in wealth and influence and the like, the humanoids must be equal enough in their relationships to ensure that they can and do treat one another as conversable persons, asserting their rights under shared norms, and calling others to their duties. They must share equally

---

[2] Arguably, this is related to the lesson taught by Hegel's (2019) dialectic of master and slave in *The Phenomenology of Spirit*. An earlier reflection on the problem of despot and subject is Xenophon's (2006) *Hiero the Tyrant*; my thanks to Melissa Lane for drawing my attention to this.

in the enjoyment of conversive access to one another and in the ability to exercise conversive power.

How far will that equality in conversive access and power be achievable without a high degree of equality in economic and cultural resources? That is an empirical issue that we can put aside here. The important point is that whatever the distribution of such resources among the humanoids, it must not jeopardize their equality in the enjoyment of conversive relationships with one another.

Respect

The notion of recognitional respect

Let us suppose that the humanoids enjoy relational equality in this sense, and that they treat one another as conversable persons, each recognizing and satisfying the rights of others under conversive practices. If they treat one another in that way, then on a plausible interpretation of the idea, they will establish a regime of mutual respect. And the ideal of mutual respect, interpreted in that conversive manner, imposes substantive constraints on how the humanoids will conduct themselves.

The general notion of respect targeted here is that which we invoke in human practice when we say of functioning persons that they ought to respect one another as equals. The targeted notion contrasts on the one side with respect in the sense of esteem or appraisal, as in talk of giving someone respect for their scientific or athletic achievements (Darwall 1977). And it contrasts on the other with respect in the sense of the reverence—and the associated level of care—that we expect functioning persons to give to someone who is insufficiently adult or able-minded to function in the same way.[3] Respect in this sense amounts to recognition, in Axel Honneth's (1996) preferred term, and we may describe it when ambiguity threatens as recognitional respect.

There is good reason to hold that when the humanoids treat one another as conversable subjects, they will establish a regime of mutual recognitional respect. Treating someone as a conversable person fits with the connotations of giving them respect in that sense, holding up respect as an important ideal. In matching ordinary connotations, to invoke an idea mentioned earlier, treating someone as a conversable person is a conceptual deserver of the name of respect, and in

---

[3] Consistently with limiting the constituency of respect to adult and able-minded persons, we might hold that if there is any doubt on the matter, the humanoids should assume by way of default that someone is adult and able-minded. And we might hold, in addition, that they should treat those who are clearly not in that category in a manner—say, a caring and reverential manner—that approximates respect in the closest way that is feasible in their case. Should they respect non-human animals? Yes, we may say, in the sense of giving them a degree of reverence and care that is adjusted to their capacities and sensibilities.

making sense of why such respect is important, it counts as a theoretical deserver too (Pettit 2020). The lesson is that in the society where humanoids realize their potential fully—a society marked by a conversive form of relational equality—they will respect one another as equals in a compelling sense of that ideal.

The connotations of respect

The notion of respecting people as equals has three general connotations. To give individuals such respect means, first, to take them to be equally worthy of respect—equally with oneself and with one another—in virtue of a common nature; second, to treat them as equals on the basis of that commonality, robustly over conflicting impulses and desires; and third, to treat them as equals on a wide front and in a weighty degree. Treating someone as a conversable person in the way in which the humanoids treat one another supports these three connotations, identifying a conceptually appropriate referent for the idea of respect; and since that treatment has substantive implications for how to relate to such a person, it identifies a referent that is theoretically appropriate as well.

The most basic connotation of recognitional respect is that all functioning persons are equally worthy of enjoying it: they have a commonality of nature that supports the case for respecting them in the same measure. This connotation is often taken to raise a problem for the analysis of respect, since the differences between human or indeed humanoid individuals may seem to leave no room for such a commonality (Carter 2011). Happily, however, that problem vanishes if respecting people is equated with treating them as conversable persons. By definition, functioning persons, human or humanoid, are equally capable of understanding and fulfilling conversive requirements, and in that sense equally conversable. Persons are likely to differ, of course, in intelligence and education, in curiosity and confidence, and this divergence will show up in the quality of their conversive contributions. But no matter what those differences are, humanoid persons by the account on offer—and human persons by analogy—will count as equally conversable and may be said on that basis to be equally worthy of respect.

According to the second connotation, treating another as someone worthy of recognitional respect would deserve to be treated will not count as giving them respect unless the treatment is delivered robustly in recognition of their status, and not because it furthers some other project, whether of a prudential or indeed benevolent kind. Treating someone as a conversable person in the way the humanoids treat one another fits this robustness requirement nicely. As we saw, it means treating one another conversively, not just because that happens to be independently appealing, but because they each have the categorical status of a conversable person, as that is defined and reinforced under shared norms. It means treating one another conversively in a manner that is robust over variations in how far alternative modes of treatment prove attractive.

But when the humanoids treat one another as conversable persons, that will count as giving one another recognitional respect only if it means satisfying a third connotation as well. This connotation requires that anything deserving to be taken as recognitional respect, must impose a requirement that is both wide and weighty: it must bear on different domains of interaction, and constrain those interactions to a significant degree. Treating one another as conversable persons will count among the humanoids as giving one another recognitional respect only if it meets this requirement as well, imposing weighty demands that are relevant both when they relate as interlocutors but also when they do not. The treatment they give one another, however, turns out to exemplify recognitional respect on this front too.

The demands of conversability: within converse

In their communicative interactions, the humanoids will treat one another as conversable, by the account developed in our genealogy, insofar as they live up to the expectations shared among practitioners in converse. They will speak truthfully and carefully in judging and reasoning; commit themselves conscientiously and live up to their commitments; hold others responsible for actions over which they have valuational control; and enact the persona projected in their commitments, giving others the confidence to rely on this being a faithful image of who they are. In acting robustly on these conversive patterns they will treat one another as conversable persons.

Enjoying a relative equality of power, and supporting a regime of shared, collectively beneficial norms, the humanoids will hold one another to the expectations that they form on these fronts, shunning or sanctioning those who fail without good excuse to meet them. They will respond in this way to anyone who offers another misleading or careless information, for example, misleads others in sophistical reasoning, makes reckless commitments or breaks commitments already made, or holds another responsible without good ground. And they will respond in a similar way to anyone who coerces another by communicating a threat: an intention to impose some cost or penalty should the addressee not act as directed.

By robustly upholding these patterns of conversive interaction, intuitively, the humanoids will give one another respect as equals within the domain of communicative interactions. It is hard to see how any more could be demanded of mutually respectful interlocutors. But the idea of respecting others as equals, as we understand it generally, also makes weighty demands on a wider front: that is, beyond the domain where people are in active communication. A crucial question, then, is whether treating others as conversable persons will support such requirements.

The demands of conversability: outside converse

Treating one another as conversable will make suitably weighty demands on how they relate to one another in the absence of converse if two conditions hold. First, it requires them each to ratify a predisposition to robustly treat one another as conversable should conversive exchange become possible. And second, ratifying this predisposition imposes quite weighty demands on how they deal with one another: it rules out a range of intuitively disrespectful treatments.

There is good reason why their conversive practices would require the humanoids to ratify a predisposition of this kind, whether in an active or virtual way, in relation to others with whom they are not actively communicating. If they did not at least virtually ratify a predisposition to treat such an individual robustly as a conversable person in the event of an active exchange, then they could hardly expect that person to be open to conversive interaction. It would be hazardous for the other to make a conversive overture to them—or to treat an overture of the other seriously—in the absence of such ratification. Notwithstanding the norms in place, this would expose them to the dangers of being shunned or communicatively duped: say by being misinformed in judgment, misled in reasoning, let down in commitment, or coerced by threat.

How weighty are the demands of this requirement? How many forms of behavior would be excluded by ratifying a predisposition to treat others robustly as conversable persons in the event of conversive exchange, abjuring the resort in such exchange to deception, sophistry, infidelity, coercion, or whatever? In other words, how many forms of behavior would lead other humanoids to doubt the presence of that predisposition in one of their number and to shrink from exposing themselves to converse?

There are many modes of activity that will not be excluded on this count, such as joking or teasing or caviling with someone, lapsing into long periods of silence, or just hanging out together. When one party acts in that way towards another, they will not thereby raise any doubts about whether they are predisposed to treat the other as a conversable interlocutor; acting in such ways in no way suggests that they do not acquiesce in the assumption, presumptively manifest under their shared norms, that they are predisposed to be congenial partners in converse. In that sense, activities of the kind envisaged are pro-conversive.

But while there are many pro-conversive activities that the humanoids might conduct in the course of living together, there are other forms of behavior that are anti-conversive in character and that they must actively or virtually renounce. These are activities that would rationally undermine another's assumption that they are predisposed to treat them as a conversable interlocutor. The activities advertise an attitude toward the person that is inconsistent with privileging their conversability and acknowledging the rights they would have in communicative exchange.

Any form of interference in which one party deprives another of control in the exercise of certain unobjectionable choices—more later on how to identify these—will be anti-conversive in this sense. In such interference, the perpetrator may seek to deprive the other of control by preventing them from choosing certain options, by imposing likely costs on certain of their options, or by taking steps to ensure that they do not perceive or understand the options properly. No humanoid could expect someone who dealt with them in such a manner to be open to treating them as a conversable person within a conversive interaction. It would be reckless of them to form and act on such an expectation, exposing themselves to dangers like those of deception, coercion, and the like.

But there are also other forms of treatment that are out of line on this count. Assuming that humanoids resemble humans in their psychology, no one who hopes for converse with others can shun or ostracize them, for example, mock or humiliate them, or cast them in a negative stereotype, gendered, racist, or whatever. No one, as we might put it, can depersonalize another in these ways without taking the prospect of converse off the agenda. Depersonalization is worthy of mention on its own account—otherwise it might be overlooked—although, strictly, it can be taken as a form of interference; after all, it will tend to put various options out of the reach of the depersonalized agent.

In indicating the sorts of collectively beneficial norms that the humanoids are likely to evolve, we resorted earlier to examples like norms against deception, violence, fraudulence, and the like, as well as norms against infidelity and theft, if conventions of commitment and property have emerged. The recognition that certain patterns of behavior are anti-conversive in the sense explained, suggests that the common feature of the most likely norms will be to restrict any anti-conversive behavior in the pairwise interactions of humanoids. No doubt there will be other norms too, as we indicated, such as fair-play norms in pursuing a collective good and norms that dictate pro-conversive behavior in relationships like that of friendship. But the core norms are likely to be designed to eliminate or minimize anti-conversive activities.

These observations help to establish that when the humanoids treat one another as conversable, as their practices require, the treatment they deliver is one of mutual recognitional respect. If the humanoids are enabled to make the most of their nature in the society we imagined—if they flourish and come into their own under those conditions—that is because they live within relationships of conversive respect. Understood in that sense, respect may assume somewhat different specifications in different cultures, but it must still count as a universally compelling value for those of a humanoid—or, by analogy, a human—kind.

Freedom

We have seen that the social world in which the humanoids thrive, as borne out in our genealogy, is one where equality in a certain relational sense prevails among them and they give one another respect in a demanding conversive sense: they treat one another as conversable. But viewing that society as a whole, is there any salient feature that marks it off as a milieu that is fitted to enable the humanoids to flourish? Yes, there is. It consists in the way in which the society ensures the freedom of its members.

Two conceptions of freedom

Before making a connection with freedom, it is important to distinguish between two particularly salient understandings of the ideal.[4] One is the classical conception of freedom, which goes back to the Roman republic, according to which a person will enjoy freedom in a particular choice to the extent that they are not subject to any other's will in the exercise of that choice; they are themselves in charge of how they act. On this view, which became strongly if not uniquely associated with the long tradition of republican thought, the person will be unfree if there is another who has the power of interfering in that choice, even if that agent happens not to exercise their will in actual interference. In that case the person may manage to act as they wish, but they will be dependent for being able to do that on the will of the other: they will be able to act as they wish only, in effect, because they have the other's permission to do so.

On the most salient alternative to this way of thinking about freedom, which was embraced by classical liberals in the early nineteenth century, a person will be free in the exercise of a choice just insofar as they are not actually interfered with in choosing: just insofar as no other imposes their will on how the person is to choose. On this conception of freedom, to go to the crucial case, the person will be free in the choice insofar as they manage to act according to their own wishes, even if someone else has the power of interfering in that choice, should they want to do so: even if it is just a lucky accident that the other does not exercise their power of interference against them. It does not matter that the person is dependent on the goodwill of that other for being able to act as they wish and that it is the other's will that is ultimately in charge. What matters on this view is simply that those who might interfere grant them the latitude or license to act on their own desires.

Thus, take the choice facing an agent of whether or not to speak on some matter: say, whether or not to speak out against the government. On the classical liberal view, someone will enjoy freedom in such a choice just in case no one interferes in their decision: no one removes or penalizes one of the options, for example, and no one manipulates their perception or understanding of the options. On the republican view, however, that will not be enough to ensure the freedom of

---

[4] Here I draw on my own work and the work of others in broadly the neo-republican network of thinkers. See (Lovett and Pettit 2009) and (Lovett and Sellers 2024) for an overview. For early contributions on the republican conception of freedom, see (Pettit 1997) and (Skinner 1998).

the choice. For, while the person escapes actual interference of such a kind, there may be someone, such as their employer, who could interfere effectively in their choice, if they so wished. And if the person makes the choice in the presence of such a power, then they speak as they wish only thanks to the forbearance of that individual: in effect, only by grace of their permission.[5]

The notion of freedom that derives from the Roman republic is reasonably cast as non-domination. The Romans took even the slave of a kindly master or *dominus*—one who lets them act as they wish—to be unfree insofar as they are subject to *dominatio*, as it was known. Someone subject to another in that measure—or in a measure that approximates it—may enjoy the absence of the other's interference in one or another choice but the non-interference they enjoy will not be secure: it will materialize or fail to materialize, depending on the goodwill of the other. Where the republican view equates freedom with non-domination, the opposed classical liberal conception takes someone's freedom in a choice to require only non-interference, regardless of whether their enjoyment of non-interference is secure: regardless of whether it depends on the will of another remaining benign.[6]

Because of their different views on freedom in choice, adherents of the rival schools of thought differ also in how far they give importance to the notion of a free person. According to republicans, someone will be a free person to the extent that they are suitably secured against the interference of others—this, by a contextually appropriate standard—in making choices that by common consent are unobjectionable: these are usually identified as the basic liberties. According to liberals, a person is free just to the extent that they manage to escape the interference of others in such choices.[7] On the first approach, being a free person is a salient, ideal status for everyone in a society; on the second, it is a benefit that comes in degrees and that people may enjoy at different levels within any society.

That someone is a free person in the republican sense does not mean that they will never suffer interference in their basic liberties; it is always possible, regardless of the security and protection in place, that another may occasionally offend against them. The person will retain the status of a free person, however, to the

---

[5] Will the contrast between the two approaches vanish if the classical liberal requirement is taken to be that the non-interference someone enjoys is likely or probable? No, because it might be probable in view of the goodwill of powerful others; it might be probable without being protected and secure in the way that non-domination requires.

[6] Classical liberals, like neo-liberals today, take freedom as non-interference—as republicans, like neo-republicans, take freedom as non-domination—to be the unique or supreme value relevant in politics. But taken on its own their ideal, unlike the republican alternative, argues for a very minimal state. And so many left-of-center liberals—liberals in the current American sense—insist on the importance of other values as well, in particular values of distributive equality or justice. See for example (Rawls 1993; 2001).

[7] Or perhaps in choices of any kind, as Hobbes suggests in an early defense of something like freedom as non-interference (Skinner 2008; Pettit 2012). While he still uses the notion of a 'free-man', a counterpart of the Roman idea of a *liber*, he defines it as a category that comes in degrees: 'a free-man is he that in those things which by his strength and wit he is able to do is not hindered to do what he has a will to' (Hobbes 1994b, 21.2).

extent that the offender will be denounced—and, if found, penalized—and the victim vindicated, under the system in place. That they are a free person will mean that they can exercise their basic liberties robustly over variations, not just in what they wish to do, but also in what others may wish them to do.

We may now return to the normative implications of the genealogy of humanoid practices and capacities. What we shall see is that the society-wide equality that enables the humanoids to live in mutual respect also grounds a dispensation in which they enjoy freedom as non-domination, albeit one that calls for further institutional development. The lesson is that an arrangement that answers in a uniquely appropriate way to the conversable nature of the humanoids will support, not only ideals of relational equality and conversive respect, but also a distinctively republican ideal of freedom.

Robustness, dispositions, and constraints

We have emphasized in our discussion so far that the humanoids must treat one another as conversable persons on a robustly demanding basis: that is, more or less regardless of the countervailing desires that urge them to offend. And, as that discussion has made clear, there are two factors needed to ensure this robust treatment of one another.

The first is the motive that each will have as a party to conversive exchange to abide by the practices of such exchange to which they are committed, and by the associated norms that support pro-conversive activities. This motivation will presumably lead them to recognize the demands of those norms as categorical duties, and to give a similar status to the corresponding rights, motivating them to act accordingly. The fact that another is a conversable person will give them categorical reason to treat them accordingly, albeit a reason that may occasionally raise a red flag and turn out to be outweighed by a rival consideration. The reason will have a cognitive and affective hold on them that is independent of whether acting on it serves some distinct purpose or project.

But, as we emphasized earlier, there is also a second factor that is needed to ensure that the treatment the humanoids give one another is robust over the presence of countervailing desires or temptations. This is the constraining factor that their relative equality of power makes possible insofar as it enables any of them to respond negatively to an offender, countering the temptations that might lead some to defect from treating others as conversable persons. More specifically, it is the factor that comes into play when common norms do not just establish their demands, outlawing anti-conversive behavior, but also enable the humanoids to hold offenders accountable for neglecting those demands, helping thereby to support general compliance.

The first, motivating factor leads the humanoids to recognize one another's rights seriously, and to be led as a result to satisfy them robustly. The second, constraining factor reinforces that motivation, guarding individuals from the disruptive effect of countervailing desires. It means that even if they have more resources than others, still they are unlikely to be tempted to abuse the power their greater wealth or influence gives them; abuse will trigger the resistance of others that common norms would license and relational equality would make effective.

Could the constraining factor ensure the compliance even of humanoids, if there are some, who do not subscribe to the norms in the sense of recognizing and being moved by their demands? Could it work on its own just by holding out the prospect of a penalty—say, disesteem—for anyone who fails to comply with a norm?

It may be logically possible that in the absence of an independent motive to comply with common norms, the regulative threat of being penalized for any failure would force the humanoids to comply and to satisfy one another's rights. But, however possible in principle, this is unlikely to work in practice. There are bound to be occasions on which a would-be offender will find that they can escape detection and avoid being held to account. And their behavior on such occasions would tend to undermine any norms that might have been established.

Freedom under norms

The upshot of this line of thought is that the humanoids will give one another recognitional respect, robustly satisfying the rights of others, to the extent that they are both motivated and constrained by common norms to act as those rights require. But that means, as we are now in a position to see, that they are going to count in republican terms as free persons in relation to one another.

They will become free persons insofar as their shared norms do two jobs. First, the norms define the unobjectionable choices that humanoids may make as they wish: the choices that are available to them as rights under those norms. And second, the norms defend the humanoids' exercise of those choices, enforcing the duties of others to honor their rights; they will do this by rendering offenders accountable for how they act.

Taking up the first of these jobs, their common norms are bound to identify the activities humanoids may conduct without breaching any norm. The norms will define things they may or may not do, depending on their wishes, consistently with complying with the norms: the things they may or may not do without exposure to the complaints of others. These choices will be unobjectionable by common consent: they will count, in republican terms, as basic or fundamental liberties.

But the norms will serve to defend as well as to define those basic liberties, assuming that the humanoids enjoy enough relational equality to be able to assert their rights under the norms and call others to their duties. For they will expose any offenders to the prospect—the unwelcome penalty, as it is bound to be—of being held accountable or responsible for breaching the relevant norms and thereby interfering with the basic liberties of others. And they will do this against the background of an equality that would enable them to impose such a penalty effectively. As the norms will give the humanoids a sense of the option space in which they can expect to be able to choose as they wish, so too they will secure that space for them, putting penalties in place that we might expect to deter would-be offenders. As they will establish the rights of each in the domain of action, in other words, so they will enforce the duties of others to honor those rights.

Under this regime of common norms, each of the humanoids will be manifestly secured against the interference of others in the exercise of their basic liberties; and this, in the broad sense in which interference includes depersonalization. They will enjoy the secure status of free persons vis-à-vis one another, they will enjoy that security equally with each other and, assuming that the discipline of accountability is effectively deterrent, they will enjoy it at an intuitively adequate level.

Thus, they will be able, in an old republican image, to walk tall and speak boldly, without any need to fawn or toady or ingratiate themselves with others. They will pass the eyeball test of being able to look one another in the eye without any reason for fear or deference, or at least any reason that derives from the other's special power of interference in their lives. Like human beings, of course, they may bind themselves to others as lovers or friends, comrades or colleagues. But they will do so from the position of strength that they will enjoy as free persons. Enjoying 'independency upon the will of another', as a seventeenth-century republican described freedom (Sidney 1990, 17), they will allow another agent authority and influence in their lives only by granting it in the manner of a free, unforced gift.

Upshot

The observations we have made so far suggest that the conditions that would enable the humanoids to develop their processing and relational capacities to the fullest, as the genealogy shows, are conditions of relational equality, conversive respect, and freedom as non-domination for all. Those ideals are not ethnocentric or sectarian values but ideals for humanoids in general. They are ideals that the humanoids need to implement in their individual relationships and their social organization if they are to achieve the best that their nature makes possible: if in that sense, they are to flourish.

Does this lesson carry over to our own kind? Arguably, it does. For if we human beings are conversable persons like the humanoids, then equally it will follow that the ideal prerequisite for our flourishing is that we relate to one another as equals, enjoying mutual respect and freedom as non-domination, and that we induct our children from generation to generation into just such a world.

But this lesson needs to be developed and detailed in a way that takes account of the less than ideal conditions in which most of us live and the myriad other differences between our world and that of the humanoids. There are many societies in our world, not just one. Those societies will offer culturally diverse interpretations of ideals like those of relational equality, conversive respect, and republican freedom. They will raise problems for how people, individually and collectively, ought to behave across as well as within their boundaries, especially when there is a conflict over global resources. And of course the societies will often be so large in population and territory, and subject to such technological and economic change, that they will have to reinforce a regime of norms in a legal system, thereby bringing the coercive, territorial polity or state into existence (Pettit 2023b).

The task of this book has been to make the case for a view of human beings as conversive, conversable creatures, building on the analogy with our humanoid counterparts. And the task of this Conclusion has been to indicate the close tie between that picture of human nature—that philosophical anthropology—and the vindication of certain ideals of equality, respect, and freedom. But the job of developing a moral and political philosophy that works out the implications of those ideals for how we shape our lives and our institutions lies well beyond the remit of the book. My hope is that it will provide something like a metaphysical foundation for that normative enterprise.

In using the genealogy to direct attention to ideals that must be inherently compelling for humanoids and humans, we break with one aspect of the Hobbesian approach discussed in the Introduction. He argued in the human case, as we have argued in the humanoid, that it is the use of language in converse that accounts for abilities like those tracked in the last six chapters. But his view was that while language gives human beings novel and exciting capacities, it also leads to a desire for eminence—*amour propre*, as Rousseau would have called it—and to an endless competition for positional advantage, and ultimately to 'a war of all against all'.

It is the specter of such competition, Hobbes maintained, that should lead people to embrace any political regime, however coercive, that they can use their capacities to invent or that they are lucky enough to have inherited. On this view, no interpersonal ideals can gain a grip on human beings—certainly none can guide their behavior—independently of collective subjection to a deeply coercive state. We take a more optimistic line, arguing that the conversive nature of humanoids and humans should make ideals of equality, respect, and freedom appealing in their own right, not just as byproducts of a harsh political settlement.

Adopting such an optimistic attitude is wholly consistent, of course, with agreeing with Hobbes that the capacities that language and converse make possible may be used, and have been used, for ill as well as good. The break with Hobbes comes in suggesting that the perverse use of those capacities is not quite as inescapable as he takes it to be and that it does not necessitate the recourse that he advocates to an absolutist state. The arc of human progress bends, however uncertainly and however distantly, toward a brighter future: a world in which equality, respect, and freedom prosper and prevail. Or so at any rate we may hope.

In summary: a philosophical anthropology

A summary of the long argument of this book would be useful and in this final section I try to provide something close. Rather than retrace the six steps taken in our narrative of humanoid practices and capacities, I offer a brisk summary of the lessons it supports for the corresponding human practices and capacities if, as I think, there are indeed lessons to be drawn. The summary is mainly designed as a reminder of the terrain covered, however, and may not offer an independently accessible overview of the territory.

In this presentation of the lessons of the genealogy, I concentrate on the themes of Chapters 2 to 7—and briefly, the Conclusion—ignoring the preliminaries addressed in the first chapter and also ignoring the lines defended in the sections I cast as interludes: those discussing the rule-following problem, the relation of belief to credence and the role of rules in reasoning. Apart from being selective in the range of material covered, the presentation is also selective in the way it covers that material, setting aside a variety of implications and qualifications that bulk large in the text. Thus, alas, it can serve only imperfectly as a summary of the lines supported in the book.

In this summary, we set aside the narrative about the humanoids, concentrating on what it suggests about the capacities of human beings associated with judgment, reasoning, and percipience, normativity, responsibility, and personhood. Kicking away the ladder that the genealogy provides, it looks at how human beings present from within the perspective that it motivates. It offers a brisk sketch of the philosophical anthropology that the book is designed to support—readers may differ on how strong they take the support to be—emphasizing the dependence of our human capacities on participation in the conversive practices that language makes possible.

This anthropology is not just of theoretical interest, for the society-first image that it presents of the human mind and soul also has practical implications. It supports a particular view of how to conceive of traditional ideals of equality, respect, and freedom, and of why those ideals should be given a central place in shaping human relationships and institutions. The Conclusion to the book focused on those implications, connecting our philosophical anthropology to core issues in ethics and politics, and we return to them briefly at the end of this overview.

Judgment

Like other animals, we routinely update our beliefs in automatic adjustment to inputs from the world around us. But we go one better as a result of learning to make assertions and exchange information with one another. In order to answer one another's questions, we intentionally seek out and pay attention to how things present—to the evidence, though we may not conceptualize it as such—and, if the evidence allows, we can choose in response to make assertions that are designed to elicit corresponding beliefs in our audience. Thus, I may take advantage of a better viewing point and, assuming intentional control of what to look for, assert in response to a question about a distant animal: 'That's a zebra, not a lion'.

We must each make our assertions carefully and truthfully if we are to have any hope of building a reputation for reliability and achieving reciprocity with others. And in doing this, we ratify or authorize the beliefs that correspond to the assertions we make. In this assertoric exercise, then, we can give information to others, and elicit reliable beliefs on the matters addressed.

But in the course of answering questions from others we are also likely to inform ourselves, since we may not yet have formed beliefs on the relevant matters. I may have barely noticed the animal in the distance, and may give myself information when I determine that it is a zebra. And even if I had already formed that belief in automatic, perhaps subliminal adjustment to perception, I may do myself a distinct service when I check intentionally on the evidence, and find that I am able to ratify a belief that I already held.

In making a careful, truthful assertion we can be said to make a judgment, where judging is distinguished from assertion in not necessarily being public. As an assertion will ratify the corresponding belief, so a judgment, even one that is made only privately, will have the same ratifying effect. Thus, the ability to make assertions brings in its train the ability to make judgments, including judgments that we keep to ourselves, and to form or at least ratify beliefs on questions where the evidence supports answers. And of course we may interiorize this ability fully, relying on it to address questions that we raise for ourselves. Even if no one raises the question, I may ask myself about the animal in the distance and rely on scrutinizing the evidence to judge that it is a zebra.

As we make judgments on factual or theoretical matters, so we can make judgments on the presence or absence of attractive properties—desiderata—in the options and other alternatives we can articulate: for example, in the proposal to hunt the zebra. And in virtue of those practical judgments we can form final desires—intentions or policies—about which option to take in a certain choice as well as qualified desires—preferences—about how to rank various alternatives, assuming their desiderative profile remains in place. Moreover, we can form intentions or policies—plans—that bear on future times and fix in advance what else we can seek to do at those times.

In raising and answering questions in the inner forum we assume a degree of control over our mental lives, making it possible if we decide that the evidence allows, to form judgments and ratify beliefs on an open and potentially important range of issues, practical as well as theoretical. We act intentionally when we enter informational exchange with others, taking charge of what we assert to others and what of course we accept among their assertions. And we bring the same sort of intentional control to the formation of our minds when we raise and answer questions for ourselves. We go beyond the sub-personal control associated with the automatic adjustment to inputs. We establish a society within, on the model of the society without, and debate with ourselves about how to make up our minds. We begin, in short, to think.

Reasoning

Making judgments implies only that we begin to think, however, not that we think in the fullest possible manner. For in raising and answering questions for ourselves we may operate like *savants* who can raise and answer esoteric questions without any sense of how they do it. We human beings generally take thinking to a further stage when we gain access to the concept of evidence and learn to cite the evidence we register in any instance as something that supports our judgment and belief: something, if you like, from which we can reason to such a conclusion. Like the capacity for judgment that it presupposes, this capacity to reason is indebted to developments that language makes possible; it is only in the space of words that our thought can assume an active, personally controlled form.

All creatures that count as agents must be rational in the sense of being reliably, if unthinkingly disposed to form and unform beliefs in response to evidence, to avoid blatant inconsistencies or fill salient gaps in their beliefs, and to act in pursuit of desired goals on the basis of their beliefs. But their rationality may materialize on the basis of their organization—it may be the work of their evolutionary design—and will typically show up in sub-personal adjustments that are beyond their intentional control and beneath the reach of their awareness. Agents of any kind may unthinkingly move from evidence that p to the belief that p, from the belief that p and the belief that if p, q to the belief that q, and so on. But they need not do so out of a recognition that the former in each case provides a reason for believing the latter, or out of a desire to let such reasons shape their beliefs; they need not do so by means of reasoning.

Reasoning, like judgment, begins with assertion. Seeking to maintain a reputation for being careful and truthful informants, we human beings will want to explain any assertion that another doubts—say, my assertion that that animal is a zebra—in the hope of reinforcing our claim. This will require us to look again and attend to what prompted the assertion: say, as I might realize, the striped coat of the zebra. I may then assert that the animal is striped, expecting my interlocutor to take that as an explanation. Or, seeking to be explicit, I may use a sentence in quotation marks—'the animal has a striped coat'—to name the state of affairs that prompted the original claim. The sentence in quotes will serve as a name insofar as it is not itself an assertion, although in this case the state of affairs named is assumed to obtain as a fact, since otherwise it could not have served as a prompt.

Explaining a claim will reinforce it, however, only if the interlocutor accepts the state of affairs that we name as the prompt for the claim and only if they are prompted by it in the same way. Taking one another to respond to a common, normally accessible world and to do so normally in the same way, we will generally expect the explanation to have such a reinforcing effect. If that expectation fails, however, we are likely to assume that something is interfering on one or the other side—or indeed on both, though that possibility can be set aside for convenience—whether by blocking access to the world or by distorting how it presents. And we will often find such a disrupting factor at work. I may discount the testimony of someone who disagrees in the zebra case—indeed, I may persuade them and others that I am right—by pointing out that they are not near enough to see the animal's coat, that the sun is getting in their eyes, or that by independent tests they are only partially sighted.

Since it will be manifest to all that an explanation of a claim will reinforce it only for subjects who can properly access and process the prompt cited—only for subjects in normal, disrupter-free circumstances—we are bound to assume that those conditions are fulfilled when we offer the explanation of a claim out of a wish to reinforce it. But that means that we will cite the explanatory state of affairs—in my case, the fact that the animal has a striped coat—not just as a prompt that happens to have had a moving effect on us but as one that we expect to have such an effect on anyone who is functioning normally: that is, anyone whose performance is not disrupted. We will be able to take that state of affairs as evidence for the claim: as a state of affairs that justifies the claim in the sense of prompting any properly functioning individual to accept it.

Trying to reinforce a claim on this pattern involves getting others to recognize that the evidential state of affairs not only elicits acceptance of the claim but that it does so in virtue of justifying it: in virtue of being fit to elicit acceptance among any normally functioning human beings. And, by ordinary connotations of term, that constitutes reasoning from the evidence to the claim as from a premise or set of premises to a conclusion.

Reasoning with others in that way not only helps us to justify or perhaps fail to justify—to confirm or infirm—things we already assert or accept. It also helps us to figure out whether things we already accept can justify accepting further claims, providing answers to currently open questions. And it enables us to conduct that exercise suppositionally, exploring what would follow if things were or were not actually thus and so. Moreover, it secures those benefits regardless of whether the premises are linked to the conclusion probabilistically or decisively and regardless of whether they are theoretical or practical: they will be practical if they bear on the attractive properties of behavioral alternatives and support an associated preference or intention.

Like the practice of judgment, the practice of reasoning with others can be interiorized by any of us in virtue of our capacity to relate to ourselves as speaker to interlocutor, simulating the social practice within the mind. And we have every motive to do this, as the exercise will benefit us in the same way as its social counterpart. It enables us to check on how far our judgments on one or another issue are justified; to see whether things we accept offer premises for further conclusions; and to perform these exercises, if useful, in a merely suppositional manner. In conducting such exercises we achieve only a degree of intentional, personal control over our mental life—this, because we cannot escape reliance on our sub-personal processing—but a higher degree than that that which would be accessible on the basis of judgment alone. The exercise enables us to think on a broader front and at a greater depth.

One further observation. The language required to enable judgment and reasoning to get off the ground may operate on the basis of convention alone, with the significance of words and of how words combine with one another being determined in the same way for all. But the uses to which language can be put amplify and transform once reasoning is in place. For the manifest presence of reasoning among their audience enables speakers to rely on context, and on shared assumptions about context, to help their hearers to construe messages conveyed in unconventional forms of speech: for example, in figurative forms like metaphor and metonymy, and in the indirect idioms linked with irony, insinuation, and the like. As language enables active, personally controlled thinking to make an appearance, so thinking allows language to break free of conventional shackles.

Percipience

Like other animals, we rely on perception to give us direct, causally transmitted information about the things that register on our sensory channels—these can differ enormously across species—and about the classes into which they fall: the properties and relations they display. And as we and other animals perceive things to be, so we generally believe them to be, letting our actions be guided accordingly. For other animals as for us, some of those similarity classes will stand out by nature, some by conditioning or training. For them as for us, those things and their properties and relations will pass in and out of attention within a larger perceptual field, depending on what is currently of interest and importance. And for them as for us, the perceptual process may mislead—the stick in water may look bent, the stationary train seem to move—and, once this failure is registered, the process will cease to enjoy a directive role in relation to belief and action.

But this continuity with other animals is broken with the advent of language and more specifically with the appearance among our kind of the judgment and reasoning that language enables. We may only rarely bring active judgment or reasoning to bear on how we perceive things to be, but judgment and reasoning may come in a virtual as well as an active form. I will make a virtual judgment that something is the case when I let the judgment form more or less habitually or spontaneously but remain on standby, ready to resort to active judgment, should the belief look unlikely, should it prompt an implausible action, should someone question it, or whatever: for short, should it raise a red flag. I will reason virtually when I let some evidence elicit a conclusion in the same unthinking manner but remain on standby, poised to resort to active reasoning, should something about the conclusion raise a red flag.

Insofar as our perceptions materialize in the presence or precincts of reasoned judgments, active or virtual, we will enjoy percipience, to recruit that word to a novel usage. Percipience enables us as perceivers, first, to register a richer range of properties and relations, conceptualizing them in a novel way; second, to assume personal, intentional control over our exercise of attention, letting it be directed by the wish to find answers to various questions; and third, to recognize that things are not always as they appear to be and that appearance and reality may come apart.

Taking up the first aspect of this percipient empowerment, we learn from being cued to the perceptual use of various terms to detect the corresponding similarity classes, and to perceive things as satisfying the corresponding properties and relations. We learn to perceive instances of finely distinguished plants and animals, of pieces of furniture and types of games, of artistic and architectural styles, and of the bone fractures that show up in medical scans, registering those properties with the immediacy with which we register colors and sounds and shapes. Moreover, we are not aware of perceived properties in their perceived profile only: we are aware of them as properties that can obtain beyond the here and now, even in the realms of non-actual possibility. Thanks to our capacity for judgment and reason, indeed, we can even form higher-level beliefs about them, as in holding of two or more properties that they do or do not generally get to be co-instantiated. We can conceive of them in a stimulus-independent rather than just a stimulus-dependent manner.

The second aspect of our percipience shows up in the fact that while all perception is attentional, we human beings enjoy a distinctive form of personal control over the exercise of attention. We don't just let our attention shift under sub-personal, sensory prompts, primed by random prompts or idle scanning. And we don't just let it shift as a sub-personally activated means of seeking intentionally to achieve a distinct goal: this, in the way the cat's attention moves as it seeks to locate the mouse that is hiding in a cluster of bushes. We are aware that our attention must move in order to answer certain questions—for example, the question about the identity of the animal in the distance—and we can intentionally recruit perceptual attention in the exercise of seeking an answer to such a question.

Perhaps the most striking aspect of our percipient empowerment, however, shows up on a third front, in the contrast between how we deny certain perceptions a role in the formation of our beliefs and decisions and how other animals do so. The puppy may learn that there is not another dog in the mirror but what happens, on the most parsimonious account, is simply that it ceases to believe that there is a dog there. We may also learn to neglect misleading impressions in that unthinking manner but, negotiating perceptual divergence with one another, we often do something more. We come to judge and believe in this or that instance that something that appears to be so is not actually so. We don't just cease to believe that things are thus and so: say, that there is a dog in the mirror; we come to believe that things are not thus and so: that the image in the mirror is not a dog. In other words, we come to perceive the world in light of a recognition that as things appear to be in perception, they may not be in fact; we come to distinguish appearance from reality.

In enabling us to transform perception in these ways, the percipience that language makes possible does us a great service. It enables us to enrich the content of our perception, to regulate what we attend to within perception, and to recognize that to be perceived is not necessarily to be. This last insight licenses us to attend to how things appear independently of whether they are that way, savoring looks and sounds, tastes and smells and textures. And in doing that it opens the way to craft and art. But the insight also licenses us to ask about how things are independently of how they appear, letting us wonder about the hidden structure of things. And in doing that it opens the way, for good or ill, to all forms of speculation, from the mythological to the scientific.

The capacity to judge and reason enables us to know what we believe, since it gives us the ability to conceptualize the propositions involved in the role of content. And making us aware that our beliefs differ from those of others, and may therefore be incorrect, the capacity also alerts us to the fact that it is belief-states within ourselves that give us our take on the world. Our ability to judge and reason ensures consciousness-in-belief, on the first count—awareness of the belief content—consciousness-of-belief on the second: awareness of the belief state.

Such consciousness has a purely cognitive character, reflecting the cognitive character of beliefs themselves; there is nothing it feels like to instantiate such a state consciously. But perceptions have a sensory character insofar as they give us access to properties that the senses mediate. And that raises a question as to whether perception is different, and as to whether percipience plays a role in making it different. Do we enjoy a form of consciousness-in-perception or consciousness-of-perception that means that there is something it feels like to perceive things: a form of consciousness, in current terminology, that is phenomenal in character? And if so, does percipience play a role in making it possible?

We percipient subjects can certainly enjoy consciousness-in-perception and do so in a phenomenal sense. Our perceptual activity provides us with a perceptual field of sensory properties—colors and sounds and the like—that we bring into focus when we exercise attention and judge things to be thus and so by perceiving them to be thus and so at this or that point. We achieve consciousness-in-perception when we become aware of those contents, registering things in the sensory processing of color and sound, taste, smell, and texture. And that gives us an awareness of the felt, phenomenal character of perceived contents, unlike our awareness of the contents of our beliefs.

But while percipience will give the contents of perception a richly patterned, intentionally controlled profile—while it will enhance our consciousness-in-perception—it is not strictly required for such consciousness. Non-percipient animals also perceive their world in sensory materials and can bring the contents of their perceptions into attentional focus, letting how they perceive things to be in that sensory mode to ground how they believe them to be. And that will enable them on similar grounds to enjoy a form, indeed a phenomenal form, of consciousness-in-perception.

As we percipient subjects can enjoy such consciousness-in-perception, however, so we can enjoy consciousness-of-perception. Recognizing that perceptually grounded judgments and beliefs differ across persons, and are sometimes wrong, we must see that how we perceive things to be is sometimes wrong and that is only in virtue of potentially misleading subjective states that things present perceptually as thus and so. Is our consciousness of such states likely to be phenomenal in character? Yes, to the extent that becoming aware of the states means rehearsing them to ourselves, savoring them for what they reveal: this, as in becoming aware of the look of something red as a red look, or the smell of something sweet as a sweet smell, and so on.

But while we percipient subjects can enjoy such consciousness-of-perception, non-percipient animals cannot match us on this front. Not being moved by differences with others to revise perceptually grounded beliefs, they will not have reason to recognize that how the world presents is a function of their subjective, potentially misleading states of perception. They are likely to be immersed in that world, unable to recognize that how things perceptually appear to be is not how they are. No matter how rich their *Umwelt,* and no matter how significant their consciousness-in-perception, their world may lock them in, denying them the capacity to recognize the part their own perceptual states play in making that world visible, audible, and tangible, as well as making it available to taste and to smell.

The upshot is that the percipience we enjoy—the capacity to bring judgment and reasoning to bear on perception—has a complex connection with perceptual consciousness. In virtue of enriching what and how we can perceive, it enhances our consciousness-in-perception but is not essential to it; non-percipient animals also enjoy such consciousness. But in virtue of enabling us to recognize the possibility of perceptual error, it is essential to consciousness-of-perception; this is a form of consciousness that parsimony suggests is unavailable to other animals.

Normativity

As other animals evolve patterns of reciprocal cooperation of the tit-for-tat variety, so we human beings do so too. Spurred by the need to have a good reputation in those respects with others, we will adjust our behavior to our mutual benefit in a number of interactions: in speaking carefully and truthfully, for example, in avoiding violence and fraudulence, and in respecting conventions like those of privacy, queueing, and ownership. Insofar as we do this in any community—or at least in any community of relative equals, be that a whole society or a subgroup within a hierarchical society—we will establish a general regularity there; this regularity will be manifestly recognized by all of us within the community; and, giving it the status of a social norm, we will naturally invoke it in instructing our young, in correcting would-be or actual offenders, and in reminding ourselves about what others expect of us.

Such social norms support prudential advice of the form: you should conform to this regularity if you are to look after your own interests. But to the extent that the norms are collectively beneficial, each of us will internalize them in the sense of wanting everyone to conform. And insofar as that internalization is itself manifest to all, it will allow us, drawing on the resources of a common language, to invoke it in instruction or correction in the name of all. In demanding conformity from someone—even from ourselves—we will be able to speak for others without fear of contradiction or objection: we can present the demand as a commandment of the community. Moreover, it will be manifest to all that anyone can speak in that way without fear of objection, and as a result it will be equally manifest that, not being disposed to object to such a spokesperson, we count as jointly sponsoring the shared norms to which we are individually subject.

When social norms gain this status, they enable us to present the demand for conformity, not as a conditional prudential recommendation, but as a demand of a categorical, if not absolute, kind. The demand will be categorical if it is not conditional on its promoting a certain goal; it calls for conformity, period, not just conformity if it advances our interests, for example, or is for the best overall. But despite being categorical, the demand need not be absolute; there may circumstances where a red flag goes up and indicates a need to think again: say, circumstances in which conforming with the demand would impose enormous costs or require breaching a more important demand.

For all we have seen, however, these injunctively demanding norms, and the demands they enable us to make of others—and by interiorization of ourselves—need not be backed by value judgments. But it turns out that our access to language ensures that we will have the means required for giving them that support, taking us deep into normative space.

Language serves us in this way by giving us the practice and concept of commitment. Committing to an attitude—a belief, a preference, an intention, or whatever—contrasts with reporting its presence. Where the report can often be plausibly excused—that is, explained in a reputation-saving way—on the grounds that the agent was misled about their own mind or even that they changed their mind since making the report, the commitment cannot be so easily excused. And to the extent that it cannot, it is more costly and therefore more credible than a report: not having access to the misleading-mind or changed-mind claim, the agent will be limited in how far they can get off the hook for having failed to live up to a commitment.

We speakers can foreclose the misleading-mind excuse with any attitude by avowing it rather than reporting it: say, by communicating the belief that p by saying that p, or the desire to X by saying that X-ing would be fair or fun or whatever. Communicating the attitude on the basis of such evidence about the world, we will be unable to excuse a later failure to display it by reference to the misleading character of the evidence about our mind: we did not consult such evidence and cannot claim to have been misled by it.

We can go beyond avowal in the case of certain attitudes—preference, intentions, policies—by foreclosing the changed-mind as well as the misleading-mind excuse: that is, by pledging the attitude rather than just avowing it. We can do this insofar as we make it clear to our audience that they can rely on our not changing our mind; we make it clear that we are pledging an intention to meet them somewhere by insisting that we will be there: they can depend on it, as we may add. Pledging locks us into the attitude communicated more firmly than avowal, although it will not remove every possibility of explaining a failure in a reputation-saving way. It may foreclose excuses that cite a misleading or changed mind, but it cannot foreclose excuses that are beyond agential control: obstacles to performance like a broken leg or a bout of amnesia.

As with judging and reasoning, we may commit ourselves in these ways, not by saying anything, but by preserving our silence in face of the manifest expectations of others that we will not fail, and that if we fail we will not appeal to a misleading-mind or changed-mind excuse. Those expectations may materialize on the basis of our performance generally or in virtue of our not demurring at someone's making the commitment in a context where they are assumed to speak for others, including ourselves. Acquiescing in such expectations—going along without protest—can commit us virtually insofar as we could protest should we not want to go along, yet we do not do so: we could say 'Nay', or at least indicate a reluctance to go along, but we make neither of those responses.

Let us return now to collectively beneficial, categorically demanding norms. It should be clear that we will be committed to such norms by acquiescing in the manifest expectation that we will conform to them and will uphold them as co-sponsors, without appealing to misleading-mind or changed-mind excuses for failing on either count. Our silence will constitute a virtual pledge to an intention or policy of complying with the norms, and sponsoring or upholding them.

With commitment in place, we can make sense of valuing. Pledging ourselves to intend to do something, or to hold by a corresponding policy, will put us frequently in a position where we are torn between two desires: the committed desire on the one side, the experienced desire on the other. But in such a case it will generally count as a failure if we act on the experienced desire rather than the committed, for that will undermine the aspiration and assurance conveyed in the commitment. These observations mean that committing to an intention or policy for taking an option X or promoting a prospect, P, can be equated with valuing X or P. This is because being committed to the desire for something meets a range of conditions that we associate with valuing it. To take the two conditions highlighted, valuing something may routinely conflict with actually desiring it and acting on the desire rather than the valuation will count as a failure: it will mean giving into a temptation.

When we pledge ourselves to an intention or policy in this way, valuing the target sought, we will do so because of the desiderata we see in that target. Those desiderata must make the intended or planned option or prospect robustly appealing in order to support our valuing it. Insofar as they do that—insofar as they elicit robust preferences within us—they will count as our values: as properties that explain our particular valuing of this or that option or prospect. Some desiderata may appear as values in virtue of playing this role, but others may assume a valued status in virtue of a more active embrace: a pledge to robustly prefer that they be realized.

In the sense in which valuing something means committing to a desire for it, we human beings may value certain things on a purely sectarian basis, relying on partisan desiderata or values in pledging the relevant desire. We may value things, for example, insofar as they suit the needs of our family, for example, answer to the wishes of our friends, or enable our country to fare better than others. And equally we may value things insofar as they advance our own interests; indeed, we may even commit to others to be self-interested—or at least not to be self-sacrificial—in how we behave in certain contexts.

But we human beings can value things also on a relatively impartial basis. We certainly do so when we are pledged, however virtually, to an intention or policy of upholding and complying with our community's categorical norms, however large or small that community may be. The robustly preferred desiderata supporting such a commitment or valuation are the collective benefits that the norms promise to deliver: say, the benefit of being able to rely on the truth-telling or non-violence or general cooperation of others and the status that goes with being manifestly able to rely on such treatment. In this case, as in others, those desiderata will count as the values that underlie the intentions or policies to which we pledge ourselves.

Aware of the values that underpin our commitment to supporting basic communal norms, we can also develop the practice of valuing in other impartial realms. We can argue for the value of having novel, beneficial norms in place within our community in addition to those already established, or for getting them into place more widely. We can argue for the value of getting rid of social norms that are harmful for some in the community or in the wider world, not collectively beneficial. And we can argue on similar impartial grounds for people's acting in this or that ideal manner—and of course for our personally acting in that manner—outside norm-governed domains: say, in helping to meet the needs of the poor elsewhere. We can take up such initiatives as moral advocates for a better world, as of course we can sponsor recommendations on the basis of more partial values for achieving certain ideals for our family or friends or just indeed for ourselves.

The social practice of supporting partial or impartial patterns of behavior, and actively or virtually committing to a desire for such modes of acting is capable like judgment or reasoning of being interiorized in a purely mental form. Commitment is a social act but having learned what it involves in the social sphere we can interiorize it in a self-commitment too: say, in pledging to ourselves an intention to stick by a certain diet, to look after our friends, or even to honor impartial norms or ideals. This sort of resolution counts as a commitment insofar as it sets aside misleading-mind and changed-mind excuses when we let ourselves down; it forces us to reprimand ourselves for such a failure rather than trying to excuse it to ourselves in that manner. The possibility of self-commitment means that as we value things in the interpersonal sphere, so we may value them in the intrapersonal too: we may value them in the society that we each enjoy within ourselves.

Responsibility

When someone offends without any recognized, full excuse against a norm or ideal that we endorse, and that we think that they endorse, we will not only disvalue the act they took; assuming that it would not be meddlesome or hypocritical or inappropriate on our part to do so, we will also blame or censure them for what they did. We will take them to have done something they should not have done, by the norm or ideal involved, in the presence of an ability to have done something else instead, and this, despite countervailing, non-excusing influences such as those we associate with being lazy or irresolute or weak of will.

What entitles us to ascribe such a capacity to one another, and to ourselves: such fitness to be held responsible? We ascribe that fitness whenever we censure someone for an offense, as in the case envisaged, or whenever indeed we commend them for having avoided such an offense and lived up to relevant values. Or at least we do so in the absence of recognized, excusing obstacles that lie beyond the agent's control: to take the simplest case, obstacles recognized as full excuses. But how do we human beings come to assume and ascribe the control over our actions that such responsibility presupposes?

To address the question, it will be useful to back up a little, looking at how we are likely to view one another in advance of action as well as in its wake. It turns out that how we view another ex post when we condemn or commend an action is a close reflection of how we view another ex ante when we hold out an expectation of how they will behave.

When we commit to shared norms of the kind envisaged earlier, betting on ourselves to uphold and comply with them, we must assume that there are desiderata or values enough supporting the norms to make us confident that we will not fail: confident enough indeed to foreclose misleading-mind and changed-mind excuses for any failure. We must assume, further, that our rational agency is not compromised, that we are not lacking in relevant knowledge of what is at stake, and that acting on those values would not expose us to unacceptable costs, making the choice involuntary; a failure on any front would constitute an excusing obstacle. And finally, we must assume that we are able to control for the expected satisfaction of our values, adjusting reliably in different circumstances so as to make that result more likely: we are able to control for that result in the sense in which the heating-cooling system controls for keeping the ambient temperature within a certain range.

The valuational control that we assume in making such commitments, whether in active or in virtual mode, is bound to be reinforced by the manifest expectations of others that we will live up to them. Those expectations impose a discipline on each of us, since not satisfying them—not living up to our commitments and values—will mean suffering a serious reputational cost. In any community where we enjoy relative equality, and commit ourselves to shared norms, this expectational discipline will create an encompassing forcefield within which we will each be quite heavily constrained. For simplicity of presentation, it may be assumed here that that community involves a whole society and is not restricted to this or that subgroup of citizens.

We generally rely on one another to display valuational control, and satisfy our expectations, when it comes to abiding by shared norms. But in various cases we may have cause to worry that someone is liable to breach a norm, say in telling a lie or resorting to violence. Our worry in such a case may derive from a concern that the person will hurt me or mine, or that they will undermine their own reputational prospects, or just that they will breach an accepted norm. The fact that we assume that they are sensitive to the values associated with the norm, however, means that in response to our worry we may seek to reinforce that sensitivity, thereby increasing the likelihood of their conforming or at least making their disposition to conform more resilient.

We can reinforce another's sensitivity by reminding them of the values at stake in the decision, where these may range from a concern for their own welfare, a concern for not hurting us or any others, or a concern about breaching a norm and jeopardizing its benefits. By doing this, we can ensure that they become aware of those values, which they may have ignored or neglected. And apart from making them epistemically aware of the desiderata at issue, we can also energize the person's response, awakening or reawakening them to the appeal and relevance of those values. Sensitive though they may already be to the values, we can sensitize them further. And we can thereby scaffold their performance, increasing the probability or resilience of their conformity.

I will do this actively in a given instance by saying to the individual 'you should and can tell the truth', assuming that that is the norm at issue. I will do it virtually or on a standby basis if I am manifestly present and manifestly disposed to make such a remark, should there be need and opportunity to voice it. My presence will help to remind them of the relevant values in just the same way as the active intervention and help to prime them to act as the relevant norm requires. It will make sense indeed for the person themselves to interiorize such exhortation and exhort themselves actively to tell the truth: that is, to rehearse the values at stake to try to get themselves to tell the truth.

The 'should' in the 'should-and-can' formula directs the person to the norm and the values at stake, which I may or may not spell out in greater detail. The 'can' does not ascribe an independent ability that is unaffected by the ascription. It is used evocatively, in an attempt to rouse the person to action—to scaffold their disposition to conform—by sensitizing them to the values implicitly or explicitly invoked. Whether communicated actively or even in a virtual way, the effect will be exhortative: it will communicate the presence of a capacity that it itself helps to reinforce.

Thus, the capacity registered by the exhorting subject is a capacity empowered by that very exhortation. But in actually exhorting someone to tell the truth, I will not see that capacity as one I empower. Putting my empowering into the background—letting it determine the standpoint or perspective from which I view the agent—I will see it simply as a power, period. I may see the red color of an object in virtue of the object's looking red to me, a normally functioning observer, but I will see it simply as red, not as being disposed to look red to a normal observer. Similarly I may register the person's capacity to tell the truth in virtue of my empowering them to do so, but I will register it simply as their ability to tell the truth, not as their being empowered by me to do so. Still, the ability I ascribe may be greater than the ability that the agent would have had in the absence of exhortation: it may be more likely to be exercised or may endure more resiliently.

This sketch of how we tend to see one another, and indeed ourselves, prior to action puts us in a position to return to how we are likely to see one another or ourselves in the wake of action: how we are likely to view our valuational offences or successes. We focus for simplicity on the case of offenses.

How will I likely respond if it turns out that the person I exhorted to tell the truth turns out to lie? I may discover that there was a failure of rationality or knowledge or voluntariness—a factor recognized as an excusing obstacle—that undercut the exhortation and judge that they could not have told the truth. But absent any evidence of that sort of factor, I will tend to stand by my original exhortation, taking it to have been appropriate and to have scaffolded the agent's capacity to conform.

In doing that I will identify ex post with the ex-ante exhortation, simulating the earlier standpoint. As I said beforehand 'you should and can tell the truth', so I will later reaffirm the claim, saying 'you could and should have told the truth'.

This remark will count as an indictment, as we might say. It will signal by the 'should' that the agent was in breach of the truth-telling norm and value, contrary to an active or virtual commitment. And it will signal by the 'could' that they breached the norm in the presence of a capacity for valuational control: specifically, the capacity as it presented to me in my ex-ante exhortation.

No doubt there was some factor at work, some natural chance or cause—some glitch or mishap—that led the offender astray: the sort of factor we associate with non-excusing conditions like laziness or irresolution or weakness of will. But despite the influence exerted by such a factor I will continue to think that despite the lie it led them to tell, still the offender could have told the truth.

In other words, I will take them to have had the degree of control ascribed in the ex-ante exhortative stance that I simulate and stand by. And from within that stance it will be clear that they could indeed have done that. After all, in exhorting them earlier to tell the truth I will have assumed that there were factors in play that might lead them to lie. Otherwise, why would I have bothered to exhort them? And equally I will have assumed that the empowered capacity I registered was enough to overcome any such factor. Otherwise why would I have thought there was any point in exhorting them? Thus, in seeing them ex-post as I saw them in the ex-ante exhortative stance, I will judge that they could have told the truth, despite any of the countervailing, non-excusing factors that may have led them to lie.

This is to say that in such a case I will blame them for having lied. I will take them to have breached a shared norm, without any obstacle recognized as an excusing condition, in the presence of a capacity to have done otherwise. Indeed I may blame them even if it was not I but another who exhorted them. I will do so if I simulate and stand by the other's exhortative stance and see them ex post as they would have presented to that exhorter ex ante.

I may blame them, indeed, even if there was no one there to exhort them. For I may reasonably assume that they were there to exhort themselves, and I may identify with their exhortative stance, ascribing the capacity to have told the truth that they would have seen in themselves. I may blame them on this basis, if the self-exhortation was active: if they tried to get themselves to tell the truth, as we say, in spite of the temptation to lie. But, more important, I will be entitled to blame them on this basis, even if they did not go through any such active exercise. It will be manifest to me and others that insofar as they really embraced the norm of truth-telling, they would have been alerted to any sign that they might defect—a countervailing temptation would have raised a red flag—and they would have been awakened or reawakened to the presence and appeal of the values that support telling the truth. It will be manifest, in other words, that they would have exhorted themselves virtually, if not actively, to tell the truth.

If this line of thought is sound, then there is nothing problematic about why we human beings hold another responsible for a failure to abide by a shared norm or indeed for a success in doing so. Blame will be appropriate insofar as the agent offended against the norm in the presence of a capacity for valuational control. And praise will be appropriate insofar as they complied with the norm in the exercise of a capacity for valuational control and not, for example, by a lucky break.

The account of how we are positioned to hold others responsible for their actions is readily extended to explain how we also hold ourselves responsible. This will make sense insofar as we can interiorize the social practice and relate to ourselves as an engaged interlocutor. Moreover, the account can be extended to make sense of how we may blame ourselves or one another beyond the domain of shared norms for breaching any commitment we made to another in a restricted group or indeed for any commitment we made to ourselves as in the resolution to keep a diet. Wherever it would have made sense ex ante to exhort an agent to take a certain action, there it will also make sense to hold them responsible ex post for not having done so.

Our fitness to be held responsible, as that is ensured by exhortation, gives us a plausible candidate for free will. Absent recognized excusing obstacles, someone will exercise free will in a choice, plausibly, insofar as it is possible for them to choose any of the options on offer; they as an agent are at the causal origin of their choice, not just a state within them; and they are in control of whether or not to choose the option taken, regardless of countervailing, non-excusing influences. Fitness to be held responsible does well in meeting those conditions.

It will be possible for an agent to choose an evaluatively supported option in any choice if they have a self-exhortatively empowered capacity to do so; and it will be possible for them to choose a rival option by which they are tempted in view of the defeasibility of any such capacity. They will be at the causal origin of the action in virtue of being fit to be held responsible for acting on their values or failing to do so. They will be in control of whether or not to realize that action insofar as they control, albeit defeasibly, for the satisfaction of their values. And they will enjoy that control regardless of the non-excusing influences that they may have to resist or neutralize.

This view of free will gives it characteristics that are more often associated with what we describe as willpower. Like willpower, it is essentially tied to the agent's ability to track their values in action; it applies only indirectly to value-neutral choices insofar as it would come into play if values were relevant. Like willpower, it comes in degrees, since an agent may enjoy it at one or another degree of probable exercise, and with one another measure of resilience. And like willpower, it is capable of strengthening with regular exercise and of weakening in the absence of exercise.

One of the main attractions of this view is that it makes free will perfectly naturalistic. For we human beings may have this or that degree of willpower just in virtue of how we are constituted at physical, chemical, biological, and neurological levels, and of how our organization at those levels is responsive to exhortative inputs: that is, to those inputs as they materialize at such lower levels. We will enjoy willpower to the extent that our sensitivity to the values we recognize, and our sensitization to those values in self-exhortation, program for actions that will realize the values. No matter how that sensitivity-cum-sensitization is realized at lower levels, the realizing state will tend to give rise to behavior that answers to those values.

Personhood

We adult, relatively able-minded human beings treat ourselves and one another as persons in a distinctive sense of the word. We use the term to apply to human beings who are undeveloped or demented with a view to emphasizing their moral status. But we recognize across a variety of theoretical and other perspectives that the notion of the functioning person is used paradigmatically of human beings who satisfy conditions associated mainly with competent adults.

There are a number of conditions highlighted in most of those perspectives, though they are often ranked in different ways. They include the basic assumption that persons in the relevant sense are agents with a variety of capacities, in particular the capacity to reason with themselves and others. They include three assumptions of a more normative kind: that persons can hold themselves and one another responsible for what they do; that they enjoy an inherent dignity and a claim to being treated accordingly by one another; and that there is an ideal of performance that they should satisfy if they are to measure up to what is expected of them as persons. And they include an assumption that persons conceive of themselves, regardless of changes in their public profile, as retaining their self-identity through the flux of those changes.

Theories of personhood can be assessed for how far they vindicate those assumptions and make personhood into a category deserving of the importance we generally give to the idea. Perhaps the most general and persuasive account relates personhood to personation, in an old sense of that term. To personate is to represent yourself in a certain character to others, and indeed to yourself, and to claim a special authority for the representation you underwrite. It is to make commitments, and assume responsibility for honoring them, on such a wide front that they project a relatively full persona. In effect, it is to invite others, or indeed yourself, to rely on your displaying that character or persona in how you act.

Personation is the counterpart of impersonation. In impersonation, we purport deceptively to self-represent a distinct, independently identified agent: we pretend to be that person; in personation we purport honestly or without pretense to self-represent ourselves. But impersonation, despite the pretense involved, may be an accurate or inaccurate representation of the targeted individual. And, similarly, personation, despite the absence of pretense, may be an accurate or inaccurate representation of ourselves. In each case, indeed, the inaccuracy may be accidental or intended; we may deliberately misrepresent an impersonated other and of course we may deliberately misrepresent ourselves, though we can hardly expect to do this systematically.

When you self-represent in the personating mode, you do not just communicate, as if in a report, that this is who you think you are. Inviting others and indeed yourself to rely on the representation offered, you authorize it in the manner of a commitment to enact the persona with which you identify. You bet on yourself to live up to that image, whether in a commitment to others—and assuming sincerity, to yourself as well—or to yourself alone, as in the case of a personal resolution.

But committing to others in that way, whether by way of avowing or pledging attitudes, need not require an act of any kind. As we have seen, it may only require that we acquiesce in the manifest expectations of others that we will live up to those expectations and not try to excuse a failure in ways that a mere report of our attitudes would allow, by appeal to a misleading or a changed mind. Those expectations may materialize just on the basis of how we generally perform or by virtue of someone's making the required commitment in the name of others, ourselves included.

Materializing in those ways, the expectations we commit to satisfying will constitute a dense commissive network in which we are each embedded whether we like it or not. Some of the expectations will constrain us equally, as when they are grounded in norms that bind everyone in the community and are supported by all. Many will differ between individuals, however, reflecting commitments we make to others among our family, friends, colleagues, and the like.

According to the view of personhood that these considerations support, to be a person—a functioning person—is nothing more or less than to have and exercise the capacity to personate; it is to be able to personate in the sense in which the competent pianist is able to play the piano. This conception is unusual insofar as it makes personhood dependent on the enjoyment of a social, indeed a conversive life with other persons. But the conception fits with the earlier claims, according to which judgment, reasoning, and percipience, normativity and responsibility are dependent also on community and converse. And it has the virtue of satisfying in some measure all of the conditions associated with personhood.

As agents, like other animals, we must display rationality in forming and acting on our beliefs, though we may do so only via adjustments that are sub-intentional and subconscious. As personating agents, however, we must also be able to reason, demonstrating to others, where that is necessary, that our commitments are grounded on plausible considerations and that the commitments provide those others with reasons to be able to rely confidently on our living up to them in action. Indeed we must also be able to demonstrate this to ourselves, insofar as we will want to be able to rely on our own fidelity to those commitments and to more personal resolutions. This means in short that we must have capacities associated by the account given earlier, with reasoning.

Moving to the normative conditions on personhood, we as personating agents must also be ready to acknowledge responsibility for the things we do, and accept the ascription of responsibility by others. Fitness to be held responsible is grounded in the commitments we underwrite, whether to others or to ourselves. Those commitments presuppose a modicum of valuational control and open up the possibility of enhancing that control. We will enhance it in self-exhortation, active or standby, of the should-and-can variety. And we will have to acknowledge the should-and-could-have censure that any commissive failure will therefore license.

Again, the fact that we are personating agents has a number of implications bearing on the dignity we claim for ourselves and other persons. In making commitments to one another, denying ourselves recourse to a self-reporter excuse for failure—a misleading or changed mind—we acknowledge the right of others to rely on our fidelity and our right to rely on theirs: this, insofar we each expose ourselves to censure in the event of failure. Otherwise put, we acknowledge important duties that we owe to one another in virtue of personating with them. Those duties will range from the negative duties supported by common norms—not to lie, not to be violent, and the like—to the positive duties supported by more particular relational and contractual commitments. In acknowledging the rights that we each have, and the duties that correspond to those rights, we will recognize and claim the dignity associated with personhood.

Moving to the final normative assumption, we will be required as personating agents to recognize that there is an ideal that is built into personation and personhood. Since personating means committing directly to others and indirectly to yourself, or committing directly to yourself alone, then it will bring onstream a corresponding ideal: to make only commitments that we can live up to in action and to live up to any commitments that we make.

These observations argue forcibly for taking persons to be agents who can and do personate with others and with themselves. But the notion of the person is also taken to engage issues of self-identity that do not arise for other agents. And the personation theory of persons provides a powerful vindication for this idea as well.

All agents, persons included, must form beliefs about their environment that engage themselves in a surefire way. When even a simple robotic agent believes that something it targets is to the right or to the left, for example, at a distance of a meter or a kilometer, it will hold a belief about itself: that the target is to the right or left *of it*, at a meter's or a kilometer's distance *from it*. And in that belief about itself the agent cannot fail to refer to something that is really there, nor can it mistake that agent for someone else. It will be immune to error through non-identification or misidentification; its belief engages itself in a manner that is surefire on both counts.

Unlike other agents, however, we who personate, and thereby count as persons, must also be able to have beliefs about ourselves in the various public profiles we display. And in particular we must have beliefs about ourselves under the character or persona we project, registering how far we succeed or fail in the personation enterprise. We will vary over time in the public aspects of our presence and performance, as our fortunes alter and as we assume new roles, form new relationships, and adjust our commitments to others or to ourselves. And that will mean that for each of us, to put the question in the first person, there will an identity issue. What is it that makes this public person me? What is it that ensures my self-identity over the changes that that person undergoes and inaugurates?

There are three sorts of self that might be invoked in answering this question: the bare or abstract self, the personated or authorized self, and the self that is imposed without authorization by others. And in each case there is an issue about what constitutes the self, how important it is to know this self, and how far it makes sense to care about it especially.

My bare or abstract self is that unique agent whose future memories will reflect how I perceive things to be, whose actions will spring from the intentions I form, and whose experience will determine whether my current anxiety about going to the dentist is warranted. That self, that me, exists just insofar as those attitudes and actions connect with one another in a special way: it is the subject whose experiences determine its memories, whose intentions shapes its actions, and whose anxieties are later assuaged in later experience.

This self of mine is constituted, then, by the intertemporal connection between the attitudes and actions that are ascribed to it. Can I know it? And should I care for it? Well, it is impossible to be deluded about the existence of this self or to pick it out incorrectly but, as Hume observed, it lacks any character that I might detect in introspection and later describe. And while it is a self that I cannot help but care about in the special manner ensured by the intertemporal connections of my states and acts, I do not care about that self because it is me; on the contrary, it is me because I care about it in that special way. The care I have for this self is not selfish or reprehensible: it comes with the territory.

But there is a more specific, authorized aspect under which I will continue over time and display a self. I will remain the same under this aspect insofar as I continue to represent myself either in the same persona or, more likely, in a suitably evolving persona: that is, in a persona whose attitudes emerge, not in erratic jumps that are prompted by random shocks, but under the pressure of evidence and related inputs that provide a reason for updating.

The self in this authorized, personated role is rather different from the self that counts as the continuing bearer of connected attitudes and actions. It is a self to which we give a substantive character as we construct it. But we construct it, not in a self-conscious narrative, but only as a byproduct of the commitments we make to others and ourselves.

We may not know this authorized self as well as we might, since many of our commitments, even ones we make truthfully and carefully, will materialize on a standby basis without our giving them much attention. But it is a self that we ought to care about, if we are to perform well as personating subjects: if we are to be true to the image that we invite others, and indeed ourselves, to rely on. It is with this self that it can make sense to counsel someone to be themselves, to know themselves, and to be true to themselves.

There is also a third, less important aspect under which I may be thought to retain an identity over time and constitute a self. This is the self that is imposed on me by others—it may vary with variation in the group of others involved—as they form and share an image of me without my own authorization. It is a self that is constituted by the opinions of others, a self that it is futile to try to know, and that there is little cause to care about: doing so can generate the desire to stand out among others that is associated with *amour propre*.

Toward ethics and politics

The genealogy is built on the assumption that a relative equality in power is essential among humanoids and humans if the relevant processing and relational practices are to emerge and elicit corresponding capacities. We assumed throughout the genealogy that there is only one humanoid society and that it is characterized by society-wide equality among its members, but argued that the developments that it makes possible might be replicated among humans in a hierarchically structured world, provided that they each enjoyed such equality within one or another subgroup.

We noted in the Conclusion, however, that the society-wide equality postulated among the humanoids would provide a much firmer ground for expecting the emergence of the practices and capacities targeted here; the need of some to defer to others outside their subgroup might inhibit the exercise of certain capacities and even degrade them. Thus, the egalitarian world of the humanoids envisaged in our genealogy is one in which they are most likely to come into their own, developing distinctive practices and capacities to the fullest extent possible, and making the most of their nature.

What are the features of that society, and the relationships between its members, that promise to enable the humanoids to achieve this sort of fulfillment or flourishing? Such features will represent ideals that should have a compelling appeal for the humanoids and, by analogy, for human beings. After all, they will be ideals that are grounded in the needs of the nature that humanoids and human beings share. The argument sketched in the Conclusion is that they are ideals of relational equality, conversive respect, and republican freedom.

Focusing on the human case, the equality required is meant to ensure that people are not intimidated by any others or indifferent to them. They must each worry enough about one another's opinion and esteem to evolve habits of taking due care in every exercise of judgment and reasoning; and they must be willing, without discriminating against any, to commit to others in their society and to hold others to their commitments. The equality required on these counts is relational in character. It is constituted by an equality in the relations between people that requires them to be responsive at a certain level to others in general, not just to those in a favored group. Whatever resource inequalities emerge among them— whatever are allowed by law to emerge—they must not undermine this fundamental equality in their relative power and mutual sensitivity.

Given such relational equality, people will treat one another as conversable persons, taking everyone to understand and live up to the demands of conversive exchange. Treating another in that conversive way can be equated with giving them respect in the recognitional sense in which it makes sense to respect people as equals. It satisfies the connotations of such respect insofar as it is grounded in a conversable nature that humans, like humanoids, share equally in common; it requires a form of equal treatment that is robust over conflicting desires, being triggered by the conversability of others; and, although it is grounded in the needs of conversive practice, it makes wide and weighty demands.

It makes wide demands because it requires, not just that people should recognize one another's rights as interlocutors in active exchange, but also that they should ratify a predisposition to recognize such rights in the event of exchange being accessible; they may ratify it, of course, just by acquiescing in the manifest expectation that they will prove to be amenable partners in such exchange. The demands within converse are clearly weighty, for recognizing the rights of others as interlocutors rules out ostracism, deception, infidelity, coercion, and the like. And they are weighty outside converse, because ratifying a predisposition to recognize such conversive rights rules out hostile behavior involving any forms of interference, broadly understood, in choices that are unobjectionable by common consent. No one could rationally take someone who practices hostile behavior of that kind to be ratifying, or have ratified, a predisposition to treat them as conversable interlocutors.

Like their humanoid counterparts, human beings who live under such an egalitarian, mutually respectful regime will evolve norms against any kind of anticonversive behavior, where that behavior may be taken to include conversive offences of deception, infidelity, and coercion, as well as wider offences of an interfering kind. Such norms will have a striking effect on their lives together insofar as they will define and defend the range of choices that are unobjectionable by common consent. The norms will define the choices as ones that people can make without breaching any norms: the choices that they have the right, under the norms, to make as they wish. And the norms will defend people in the exercise of those choices by making offenders accountable, thereby enforcing the duties of each to honor another's rights.

When a regime of conversive norms has these effects, it will manifestly ensure that each member of the society has a status in which they are secure against the offences of others in the exercise of unobjectionable choices. They will not only tend to escape actual interference by others: they will be protected, indeed protected in a publicly registered manner, against such interference. While offences may still occur when people give into temptation, offenders will be condemned under the norms, and victims will be vindicated. And those offences will tend to be few, since any offenders identified will be subject to the unwelcome, deterrent effect of being held to account.

Under such an ideal regime of norms, people will enjoy the status of free persons in the traditional republican sense. The regime will ensure their freedom insofar as they are able to exercise their unobjectionable choices—their basic liberties under the norms—robustly over variations in what they themselves wish to do and, more important, over variations in what others may wish them to do; they are able to live their lives without exposure to a power of interference on the part of others: without domination or subjection. Their security against interference cannot ever be total, of course, but it will give them freedom as non-domination if it enables them, by local criteria, to walk tall and speak for themselves, in the traditional image of the free person: if it enables them to look others in the eye without good reason for fear or deference.

These observations indicate that if they are to come fully into their own, making the most of their nature, then like the humanoids of our genealogy, human beings must ideally enjoy relational equality, mutual conversive respect, and a regime of republican freedom. The observations make a good case, then, for the species-wide import of those ideals. But of course they merely take us to the borders of normative thought. An ethics or politics that is grounded in those ideals will have to take account of how they apply under non-ideal conditions, how they should be interpreted in different cultures, how they should be implemented in a world of many peoples, and how they should shape the laws and the states that large and dynamic societies are bound to require.

Bibliography

Anderson, E. (1999). "What is the Point of Equality." *Ethics* **109**: 287–337.
Andrews, K. and J. Beck, Eds. (2018). *The Routledge Handbook of the Philosophy of Animal Minds*. London, Routledge.
Anscombe, G. E. M. (1957). *Intention*. Oxford, Blackwell.
Anscombe, G. E. M. (1958). "Modern Moral Philosophy." *Philosophy* **33**(124): 1–19.
Appiah, K. A. (2010). *The Honor Code: How Moral Revolutions Happen*. New York, Notrons.
Arpaly, N. (2015). Huckeberry Finn Revisited: Inverse Akrasia and Moral Ignorance. *The Nature of Moral Responsibility: New Essays*. R. Clarke, M. McKenna, and A. M. Smith. Oxford, Oxford University Press: 141–56.
Aubrey, J. (1994). The Brief Life. *Thomas Hobbes The Elements of Law, Natural and Politic*. J. C. A. Gaskin. Oxford, Oxford University Press: 231–53.
Axelrod, R. (1984). *The Evolution of Cooperation*. New York, Basic Books.
Azzouni, J. (2017). *The Rule-following Paradox and its Implications for Metaphysics*. New York, Springer.
Battistutti, O. C. (2021). *The Savant Syndrome; Intellectual Impairment, Astonishing Condition*. Mexico City, Libro digital, Amazon Kindle.
Beck, J. (2019). "Perception is Analog: The Argument from Weber's Law." *Journal of Philosophy* **116**: 319–49.
Bennett, J. (1964). *Rationality*. London, Routledge, and Kegan Paul.
Bennett, J. (1976). *Linguistic Behaviour*. Cambridge, Cambridge University Press.
Berofsky, B. (2005). Ifs, Cans, and Free Will: The Issues. *The Oxford Handbook of Free Will*. R. Kane. Oxford, Oxford University Press: 181–201.
Berwick, R. C. and N. Chomsky (2016). *Why Only Us? Language and Evolution*. Cambridge, Mass., MIT Press.
Bicchieri, C. (2006). *The Grammar of Society: The Nature and Dynamics of Social Norms*. Cambridge, Cambridge University Press.
Bicchieri, C. (2017). *Norms in the Wild: How to Diagnose, Measure, and Change Social Norms*. Oxford, Oxford University Press.
Birch, J., A. K. Schnell, and N. S. Clayton (2020). "Dimensions of Animal Consciousness." *Trends in Cognitive Science* **24**: 789–801.
Blackburn, S. (1984). "The Individual Strikes Back." *Synthese* **58**: 281–301.
Blatti, S. (2020). Animalism. *Stanford Encyclopedia of Philosophy*. E. N. Zalta.
Block, N. (1981). "Psychologism and Behaviorism." *Philosophical Review* **90**: 5–43.
Block, N. (1997). On a Confusion about a Function of Consciousness. *The Nature of Consciousness: Philosophical Debates*. Ned Block, Owen Flanagan, and a. G. Guezeldere. Cambridge, Mass., M.I.T. Press: 375–416.
Block, N. (2002). Concepts of Consciousness. *Philosophy of Mind: Classic and Contemporary Readings*. D. Chalmers. Oxford, Oxford University Press: 206–18.
Boehm, C. (1999). *Hierarchy in the Forest: The Evolution of Egalitarian Behavior*. Cambridge, Mass., Harvard University Press.
Boghossian, P. (2012a). Blind Rule-Following. *Mind, Meaning and Knowledge: Essays for Crispin Wright*. A. Coliva. Oxford, Oxford University Press: 27–48.
Boghossian, P. (2012b). "What is Inference?" *Philosophical Studies* **169**: 1–18.
Boix, C. and F. Rosenbluth (2014). "Bones of Contention: The Political Economy of Height Inequality." *American Political Science Review* **108**: 1–22.
Borges, J. L. (1962). *Labyrinths: Selected Stories and Other Writings*. New York, New Directions.

Boyle, A. (2018). "Mirror Self-Recognition and Self-Identification." *Philosophy and Phenomenological Research* **97**: 284–303.
Boyle, M. (2009). "Two Kinds of Self-knowledge." *Philosophy and Phenomenological Research* **78**: 133–64.
Braddon-Mitchell, D. and F. Jackson (1996). *Philosophy of Mind and Cognition*. Oxford, Blackwell.
Brandom, R. (1994). *Making it Explicit*. Cambridge, Mass., Harvard University Press.
Brandom, R. (2000). *Articulating Reasons: An Introduction to Inferentialism*. Cambridge, Mass., Harvard University Press.
Bratman, M. (1987). *Intention, Plans, and Practical Reason*. Cambridge, Mass., Harvard University Press.
Bratman, M. (1999). *Faces of Intention: Selected Essays on Intention and Agency*. Cambridge, Cambridge University Press.
Bratman, M. (2000). "Valuing and the Will." *Philosophical Perspectives* **14**: 249–65.
Bratman, M. (2014). *Shared Agency: A Planning Theory of Acting Together*. Oxford, Oxford University Press.
Brennan, G., L. Eriksson, R. E. Goodin, and N. Southwood (2013). *Explaining Norms*. Oxford, Oxford University Press.
Brennan, G. and P. Pettit (2004). *The Economy of Esteem: An Essay on Civil and Political Society*. Oxford, Oxford University Press.
Broome, J. (2013). *Rationality Through Reasoning*. Oxford, Blackwell.
Buchak, L. (2015). *Risk and Rationality*. Oxford, Oxford University Press.
Byrne, A. (2011). "Transparency, Belief, Intention." *Proceedings of the Aristotelian Society* **Supp. Vol. 85**: 201–21.
Camp, E. (2009). "Putting Thoughts to Work: Concepts, Systematicity, and Stimulus-Independence." *Philosophy and Phenomenological Research* **78**: 275–311.
Canning, J. P. (1980). "The Corporation in the Political Thought of the Italians Jurists of the Thirteenth and Fourteenth Century." *History of Political Thought* **1**: 9–32.
Carroll, L. (1895). "What the Tortoise Said to Achilles." *Mind* **4**: 278–80.
Carruthers, P. and P. K. Smith, Eds. (1996). *Theories of Theories of Mind*. Cambridge, Cambridge University Press.
Carter, I. (2011). "Respect and the Basis of Equality." *Ethics* **121**: 538–71.
Cassam, Q. (2016). *Self-knowledge for Humans*. Oxford, Oxford University Press.
Chaitin, G. J. (1975). "Randomness and Mathematical Proof." *Scientific American* **232**, May: 47–52.
Chaitin, G. J. (1988). "Randomness in Arithmetic." *Scientific American* **259**, July: 80–85.
Chalmers, D. (1996). *The Conscious Mind: In Search of a Fundamental Theory*. New York, Oxford University Press.
Cheney, D. L. and R. M. Seyfarth (1985). "Vervet Monkey Alarm Calls: Manipulation through Shared Information." *Behaviour* **94**: 150–66.
Cheney, D. L. and R. M. Seyfarth (1990). *How Monkeys See the World: Inside the Mind of Another Species*. Chicago, Chicago University Press.
Chisholm, R. M. (1982). Human Freedom and the Self. *Free Will*. G. Watson. Oxford, Oxford University Press: 24–35.
Clendinnen, I. (1999). *Reading the Holocaust*. Cambridge, Cambridge University Press.
Coates, J. D. and N. A. Tognazzini (2013). *Blame: Its Nature and its Norms*. Oxford, Oxford University Press.
Coleman, J. (1990). *Foundations of Social Theory*. Cambridge, Mass., Harvard University Press.
Cooter, R. D. (1996). "Decentralized Law for a Complex Economy: The Structural Approach to Adjudicating the New Law Merchant." *University of Pennsylvania Law Review* **144**: 1643–96.
Craig, E. (1990). *Knowledge and the State of Nature*. Oxford, Oxford University Press.
Crispo, E. (2007). "The Baldwin Effect and Genetic Assimilation: Revisiting Two Mechanisms of Evolutionary Change Mediated by Phenotypic Plasticity." *Evolution* **61**: 2469–79.
Darwall, S. (1977). "Two Kinds of Respect." *Ethics* **88**: 36–49.

Davidson, D. (1980). *Essays on Actions and Events*. Oxford, Oxford University Press.
Davidson, D. (1984). *Inquiries into Truth & Interpretation*. Oxford, Oxford University Press.
Deacon, T. (1997). *The Symbolic Species: The Co-evolution of Language and the Human Brain*. London, Penguin.
Dennett, D. (1979). *Brainstorms*. Brighton, Harvester Press.
Dennett, D. (1984). *Elbow Room: The Varieties of Free Will Worth Wanting*. Cambridge, MIT Press.
Dennett, D. (1987). *The Intentional Stance*. Cambridge, Mass., MIT Press.
Dennett, D. (1991). "Real Patterns." *Journal of Philosophy* **88**: 27–51.
Dent, N. J. H. (1988). *Rousseau*. Oxford, Blackwell.
Descartes, R. (1985). *The Philosophical Writings Vol 1*, tr. J. Cottingham, R. Stoothoff, D. Murdoch. Cambridge, Cambridge University Press.
Dietrich, F. and C. List (2013). "A Reason-Based Theory of Rational Choice." *Nous* **47**: 104–34.
Dietrich, F. and C. List (2018). "From Degrees of Belief to Binary Belief: Lessons from Judgment-Aggregation Theory." *Journal of Philosophy* **115**: 225–70.
Dretske, F. (1999). *Knowledge and the Flow of Information*. Stanford, CA, CSLI Publications.
Dretske, F. (2003). "Experience as Representation." *Philosophical Issues* **13**: 67–82.
Dretske, F. (2006). Perception without Awareness. *Perceptual Experience*. T. S. Gendler and J. Hawthorne. Oxford, Oxford University Press: 147–80.
Dummett, M. (1973). *Frege: Philosophy of Language*. London, Duckworth.
Dworkin, G. (1970). "Acting Freely." *Nous* **4**: 367–83.
Dworkin, G. (1988). *The Theory and Practice of Autonomy*. Cambridge, Cambridge University Press.
Elster, J. (1983). *Sour Grapes*. Cambridge, Cambridge University Press.
Elster, J. (1999). *Alchemies of the Mind: Rationality and the Emotions*. Cambridge, Cambridge University Press.
Empson, W. (1949). *Seven Types of Ambiguity*. London, Chatti and Windus.
Enoch, D. (2014). "Authority and Reason-giving." *Philosophy and Phenomenological Research* **89**: 296–332.
Eriksson, L. and A. Hajek (2007). "What are Degrees of Belief?" *Studia Logica* **86**: 183–213.
Eschmann, T. (1946). "Studies on the Notion of Society in St Thomas Aquinas, 1. St Thomas and the Decretal of Innocent IV Romana Ecclesia: Ceterum." *Medieval Studies* **8**: 1–42.
Evans, G. (1982). *The Varieties of Reference*. Oxford, Oxford University Press.
Fehr, E. and S. Gächter (2002). "Altruistic Punishment in Humans." *Nature* **415**: 137–40.
Feinberg, J. (1965). "The Expressive Function of Punishment." *The Monist* **49**: 397–423.
Fine, K. (2012). Guide to Ground. *Metaphysical Grounding: Understanding the Structure of Reality*. F. Correia and B. Schnieder. Cambridge, Cambridge University Press: 37–80.
Fischer, J. M. and M. Ravizza (1991). "Responsibility and Inevitability." *Ethics* **101**: 258–78.
Fischer, J. M. and M. Ravizza (1998). *Responsibility and Control: A Theory of Moral Responsibility*. Cambridge, Cambridge University Press.
Fitch, W. T. (2010). *The Evolution of Language*. Cambridge, Cambridge University Press.
Fodor, J. (1975). *The Language of Thought*. Cambridge, Cambridge University Press.
Fodor, J. (1983). *The Modularity of Mind*. Cambridge, Mass., MIT Press.
Fodor, J. (1990). *A Theory of Content*. Cambridge, Mass., MIT Press.
Frank, R. (1988). *Passions within Reason: The Strategic Role of the Emotions*. New York, W.W.Norton.
Frankfurt, H. (1969). "Alternate Possibilities and Moral Responsibility." *Journal of Philosophy* **66**: 829–39.
Frankfurt, H. (1971). "Freedom of the Will and the Concept of a Person." *Journal of Philosophy* **68**: 5–20.
Frankfurt, H. G. (1988). *The Importance of What We Care About*. Cambridge, Cambridge University Press.
Fricker, M. (2007). *Epistemic Injustice: Power and the Ethics of Knowing*. Oxford, Oxford University Press.

Gallistel, C. R. (2002). Frequency, Contingency and the Information Processing Theory of Conditioning. *Etc. Frequency Processing and Cognition*. P. Sedelmeier and T. Betsch. Oxford, Oxford University Press: 153–71.
Gallup, G. G. (1970). "Chimpanzees: Self-Recognition." *Science* **167 (new series)**: 86–87.
Gardner, J. (2007). *Offences and Defences: Selected Essays in the Philosophy of Criminal Law*. Oxford, Oxford University Press.
Geach, P. (1957). *Mental Acts*. London, Routledge.
Geach, P. (1972). *Logic Matters*. Berkeley, CA, California University Press.
Gibbard, A. (2003). *Thinking How to Live*. Cambridge, Mass., Harvard University Press.
Gibson, J. J. (1979). *The Ecological Approach to Visual Perception*. Boston, Houghton Mifflin.
Gilbert, M. (2015). *Joint Commitment: How We Make the Social World*. Oxford, Oxford University Press.
Gilovich, T., D. Griffin, and D. Kahneman, Eds. (2002). *Heuristics and Biases: The Psychology of Intuitive Judgment*. Cambridge, Cambridge University Press.
Godfrey-Smith, P. (2020). *Metazoa: Animal Life and the Birth of Mind*. New York, Farrar, Straus and Giroux.
Goldberg, S. C. (2015). *Assertion: On the Philosophical Significance of Assertoric Speech*. Oxford, Oxford University Press.
Goldfarb, W. (1985). "Kripke on Wittgenstein on Rules." *Journal of Philosophy* **82**: 471–88.
Goldman, A. (1970). *A Theory of Human Action*. Englewood Cliffs, NJ, Prentice-Hall.
Goodman, N. (1969). *Languages of Art*. London, Oxford University Press.
Gordon-Roth, J. (2020). Locke on Personal Identity. *The Stanford Encyclopedia of Philosophy*. E. N. Zalta.
Grice, H. P. (1957). "Meaning." *Philosophical Review* **66**: 377–88.
Grice, H. P. (1975a). Logic and Conversation. *Syntax and Semantics Vol 3*. P. Cole and J. L. Morgan. New York, Academic Press.
Grice, H. P. (1975b). "Method in Philosophical Psychology." *Proceedings and Addresses of the American Philosophical Association* **68**: 23–53.
Grice, H. P. (1989a). *Studies in the Ways of Words*. Cambridge, Mass., Harvard University Press.
Grice, P. (1989b). *Studies in the Ways of Words*. Cambridge, Mass., Harvard University Press.
Haddock, A. and F. McPherson, Eds. (2009). *Disjunctivism: Perception, Action, Knowledge*. Oxford, Oxford University Press.
Hajek, A. (2008). "Arguments for—or against—Probabilism." *British Journal for the Philosophy of Science* **59**: 793–819.
Hare, R. M. (1952). *The Language of Morals*. Oxford, Oxford University Press.
Harman, G. (1986). *Change in View*. Cambridge, Mass., MIT Press.
Harman, G. (1990). "The Intrinsic Quality of Experience." *Philosophical Perspectives* **4**: 31–52.
Harris, S. (2010). *Free Will*. New York, Free Press.
Hart, H. L. A. (1961). *The Concept of Law*. Oxford, Oxford Unviersity Press.
Hart, H. L. A. (2012). *The Concept of Law, 3rd edition*. Oxford, Oxford University Press.
Hauser, M., N. Chomsky, and T. Fitch (2002). "The Faculty of Language: What is it, Who Has it, and How Does it Evolve?" *Science* **298**: 1569–79.
Hegel, G. W. F. (2019). *The Phenomenology of Spirit*. Cambridge, Cambridge University Press.
Heider, F. and M. Simmel (1944). "An Experimental Study of Apparent Behavior." *American Journal of Psychology* **13**: 243–59.
Herman, B. (1993). *The Practice of Moral Judgment*. Cambridge, Mass, Harvard University Press.
Hewes, G. W. (1973). "Primal Communication and the Gestural Origins of Language." *Current Anthropology* **14**: 3–12.
Heyes, C. (2018). *Cognitive Gadgets: The Cultural Evolution of Thinking*. Cambridge, Mass., Harvard University Press.
Heyes, C. (2023). "Rethinking Norm Psychology." *Perspectives on Psychological Science* **20**: 1–27.
Hobbes, T. (1994a). *Human Nature and De Corpore Politico: The Elements of Law, Natural and Politic*. Oxford, Oxford University Press.
Hobbes, T. (1994b). *Leviathan*. ed E.Curley. Indianapolis, Hackett.

Hobbes, T. (1998a). *Man and Citizen*, ed and tr B. Gert. Indianapolis, Hackett.
Hobbes, T. (1998b). *On the Citizen*, ed. and trnsl. R. Tuck, R. Silverthorne. Cambridge, Cambridge University Press.
Holguín, B. and H. Lederman (2024). "Trying without Fail." *Philosophical Studies* 181: 2577–604.
Holton, R. (2009). *Willing, Wanting, Waiting*. Oxford, Oxford University Press.
Honneth, A. (1996). *The Struggle for Recognition*. Cambridge, Mass, MIT Presss.
Hornsby, J. (1980). *Actions*. London, Routledge.
Hume, D. (1978). *A Treatise of Human Nature*. Oxford, Oxford University Press.
Hume, D. (1993). *An Inquiry Concerning Human Understanding*. Indianapolis, Hackett, ed. Eric Steinberg.
Hurley, S. (1998). *Consciousness in Action*. Cambridge, Mass., Harvard University Press.
Hyman, J. (2006). "Knowledge and Evidence." *Mind* 115: 891–916.
Jackson, F. (1987). *Conditionals*. Oxford, Blackwell.
Jackson, F. (1992). Block's Challenge. *Ontology, Causality, and Mind: Essays on the Philosophy of David Armstrong*. K. Campbell, J. Bacon, and L. Rhinehart. Cambridge, Cambridge University Press: 235–48.
Jackson, F. (1998). *From Metaphysics to Ethics: A Defence of Conceptual Analysis*. Oxford, Oxford University Press.
Jackson, F. and P. Pettit (1990). "Program Explanation: A General Perspective." *Analysis* 50: 107–17; reprinted in F. Jackson, P. Pettit, and M. Smith, 2004, *Mind, Morality and Explanation*. Oxford, Oxford University Press.
Jackson, F. and P. Pettit (1992). "In Defence of Explanatory Ecumenism." *Economics and Philosophy* 8; reprinted in F. Jackson, P. Pettit, and M. Smith, 2004, *Mind, Morality and Explanation*. Oxford, Oxford University Press: 1–21.
Jackson, F. and P. Pettit (1995). "Moral Functionalism and Moral Motivation." *Philosophical Quarterly* 45: 20–40; reprinted in F. Jackson, P. Pettit, and M. Smith, 2004, *Mind, Morality and Explanation*. Oxford, Oxford University Press.
Jackson, F. and P. Pettit (2002). "Response-dependence without Tears." *Philosophical Issues* (supp. to *Nous*) 12: 97–117.
Jackson, F., P. Pettit, and M. Smith (1999). Ethical Particularism and Patterns. *Particularism*. B. Hooker and M. Little: 79–99; reprinted in F. Jackson, P. Pettit, and M. Smith, 2004, *Mind, Morality and Explanation*. Oxford, Oxford University Press.
Jackson, F., P. Pettit, and M. Smith (2004). *Mind, Morality, and Explanation: Selected Collaborations*. Oxford, Oxford University Press.
Jeffrey, R. C. (1983). *The Logic of Decision, 2nd edition*. Chicago, University of Chicago Press.
Johnston, M. (1987). "Human Beings." *Journal of Philosophy* 84: 59–83.
Johnston, M. (1989). "Dispositional Theories of Value." *Proceedings of the Aristotelian Society* Supp. 63: 139–74.
Johnston, M. (1992). "Constitution Is Not Identity." *Mind* 101: 89–106.
Johnston, M. (1993). Objectivity Refigured: Pragmatism with Verificationism. *Reality, Representation and Projection*. J. Haldane and C. Wright. Oxford, Oxford University Press.
Johnston, M. (2004). "The Obscure Object of Hallucination." *Philosophical Studies* 120: 113–83.
Johnston, M. (2010). *Surviving Death*. Princeton, Princeton University Press.
Joshi, H. (2017). "What's the Matter with Huck Finn?" *Philosophical Explorations* 20: 70–87.
Kahneman, D. (2011). *Thinking, Fast and Slow*. New York, Farrar, Straus, and Giroux.
Kahneman, D., P. Slovic, and A. Tversky (1982). *Judgment Under Uncertainty: Heuristics and Biases*. Cambridge, Cambridge University Press.
Kane, R., Ed. (2011). *The Oxford Handbook of Free Will*. Oxford, Oxford University Press.
Kant, I. (1998). *Groundwork of the Metaphysics of Morals*, tr. M. J. Gregor. Cambridge, Cambridge University Press.
Kant, I. (2006). *Anthropology from a Pragmatic Point of View*. Cambridge, Cambridge University Press.
Kant, I. (2012). *Groundwork of the Metaphysics of Morals*. Cambridge, Cambridge University Press.

Kantorowicz, E. H. (1997). *The King's Two Bodies: A Study in Mediaeval Political Theology*. Princeton, N.J., Princeton University Press.
Kind, A. and D. Stoljar (2023). *What is Consciousness? A Debate*. New York, Routledge.
Kipper, J. (2021). "Intuition, Intelligence, Data Compression." *Synthese* **198**: 56469–89.
Klin, A. and W. Jones (2006). "Attributing Social and Physical Meaning to Ambiguous Visual Displays in Individuals with Higher-Functioning Autism Spectrum Disorders." *Brain and Cognition* **61**: 40–53.
Korsgaard, C. (1996). *The Sources of Normativity*. New York, Cambridge University Press.
Korsgaard, C. (2009). *Self-Constitution: Agency, Identity, and Integrity*. Oxford, Oxford University Press.
Korsgaard, C. (2018). *Fellow Creatures: Our Obligations to the Other Animals*. Oxford, Oxford University Press.
Kratzer, A. (2012). *Modals and Conditionals: New and Revised Perspectives*. Oxford, Oxford University Press.
Kripke, S. A. (1982). *Wittgenstein on Rules and Private Language*. Oxford, Blackwell.
Lakoff, G. and M. Johnston (2003). *Metaphors We Live By*. Chicago, University of Chicago Press.
Lalande, K. L. (2017). *Darwin's Unfinished Symphony: How Culture Made the Human Mind*. Princeton, Princeton University Press.
Langton, R. (2007). Disenfranchised Silence. *Common Minds: Themes from the Philosophy of Philip Pettit*. H. G. Brennan, R. E. Goodin, F. C. Jackson, and M. Smith. Oxford, Oxford University Press: 199–214.
Langton, R. (2009). *Sexual Solipsism: Philosophical Essays in Pornography and Objectification*. Oxford, Oxford University Press.
Lederman, H. (2018). Common Knowledge. *Handbook of Social Intentionality*. M. Jankovic and K. Ludwig. London, Routledge: 181–95.
Leitgeb, H. (2015). "Belief and Degrees of Belief: The Humean Thesis on Belief." *Proceedings of the Aristotelian Society* **Supp. Vol. 139**: 143–85.
Leitgeb, H. (2017). *The Stability of Belief: How Rational Belief Coheres with Probability*. New York, Oxford University Press.
Leonard, N. (2023). Epistemological Problems of Testimony. *Stanford Encyclopedia of Philosophy*. E. N. Zalta and U. Nodelman.
Lewis, D. (1969). *Convention*. Cambridge, Mass., Harvard University Press.
Lewis, D. (1976). Survival and Identity. *The Identities of Persons*. A. O. Rorty. Berkeley, CA, University of California Press: 17–40.
Lewis, D. (1979a). "Attitudes de dicto and de se." *Philosophical Review* **88**: 513–43.
Lewis, D. (1979b). "Scorekeeping in a Language Game." *Journal of Philosophical Logic* **8**: 339–59.
Lewis, D. (1983). *Philosophical Papers Vol 1*. Oxford, Oxford University Press.
Lewis, D. (1988). "Desire as Belief." *Mind* **97**: 323–32.
Liebert, H. (2016). *Plutarch's Politics: Between City and Empire*. Cambridge, Cambridge University Press.
List, C. (2019). *Why Free Will is Real*. Cambridge, Mass, Harvard University Press.
List, C. and P. Pettit (2011). *Group Agency: The Possibility, Design and Status of Corporate Agents*. Oxford, Oxford University Press.
Loar, B. (1981). *Mind and Meaning*. Cambridge, Cambridge University Press.
Locke, J. (1975). *An Essay Concerning Human Understanding*. Oxford, Oxford University Press.
Longuenesse, B. (2017). *I, Me, Mine: Back to Kant, and Back Again*. Oxford, Oxford University Press.
Lovejoy, A. O. (1961). *Reflections on Human Nature*. Baltimore, Johns Hopkins Press.
Lovett, F. and P. Pettit (2009). "Neo-Republicanism: A Normative and Institutional Research Program." *Annual Review of Political Science* **12**: 18–29.
Lovett, F. N. and M. N. S. Sellers (2024). *Oxford Handbook of Republicanism*. Oxford, Oxford University Press.
Ludwig, K. (2016). *From Individual to Plural Agency: Collective Action. Vol I*. Oxford, Oxford University Press.

McDowell, J. (1979). "Virtue and Reason." *Monist* **62**: 331–50.
McDowell, J. (1980). Meaning, Communication, and Knowledge. *Philosophical Subjects*. Z. van Straaten. Oxford, Oxford University Press: 117–.
McDowell, J. (1996). *Mind and World*. Cambridge, Mass., Harvard University Press.
MacFarlane, J. (2014). *Assessment Sensitivity: Relative Truth and its Applications*. Oxford, Oxford University Press.
McGeer, V. (1996). "Is 'Self-knowledge' an Empirical Problem? Renegotiating the Space of Philosophical Explanation." *Journal of Philosophy* **93**: 483–515.
McGeer, V. (2003). "The Trouble with Mary." *Pacific Philosophical Quarterly* **84**(4): 384–93.
McGeer, V. (2008). "The Moral Development of First-Person Authority." *European Journal of Philosophy* **16**(1): 81–108.
McGeer, V. (2013). Civilizing Blame. *Blame: Its Nature and Norms*. J. D. Coates and N. A. Tognazzini. Oxford, Oxford University Press: 162–88.
McGeer, V. (2014). P. F. Strawson's Consequentialism. *Oxford Studies in Agency and Responsibility, Volume 2*. D. Shoemaker and N. Tognazzini. Oxford, Oxford University Press: 64–92.
McGeer, V. (2015). "Mind-making Practices: The Social Infrastructure of Self-knowing Agency and Responsibility." *Philosophical Explorations* **18**(2): 259–81.
McGeer, V. (2018). "Scaffolding Agency: A Proleptic Account of the Reactive Attitudes." *European Journal of Philosophy* **27**(2): 1–23.
McGeer, V. and P. Pettit (2002). "The Self-regulating Mind." *Language and Communication* **22**: 281–99.
McGeer, V. and P. Pettit (2015). The Hard Problem of Responsibility. *Oxford Studies in Agency and Responsibility*. D. Shoemaker. Oxford, Oxford University Press. **3**: 160–88.
MacIntyre, A. (1987). *After Virtue*. London, Duckworth.
Madell, G. (2015). *The Essence of the Self: In Defense of the Simple View of Personal Identity*. London, Routledge.
Maier, J. (2022). Abilities. *Stanford Encyclopedia of Philosophy*. E. N. Zalta and U. Nadelman.
Martin, M. (2006). On Being Alienated. *Perceptual Experience*. T. S. Gendler and J. Hawthorne. Oxford, Oxford University Press: 354–410.
Mason, E. (2019). *Ways to be Blameworthy: Rightness, Wrongness, and Responsibility*. Oxford, Oxford University Press.
Maynard Smith, J. and D. Harper (2004). *Animal Signals*. Oxford, Oxford University Press.
Mercier, H. and D. Sperber (2011). "Why Do Humans Reason? Arguments for an Argumentative Theory." *Brain and Behavioral Sciences* **34**: 57–111.
Mercier, H. and D. Sperber (2017). *The Enigma of Reason*. Cambridge, Mass., Harvard University Press.
Merleau-Ponty, M. (1965). *The Phenomenology of Perception*. London, Routledge.
Michel, M. and H. Lau (2021). "Is Blindsight Possible under Signal Detection Theory? Comment on Phillips." *Psychological Review* **128**: 585–91.
Miller, A. (2015). "Blind Rule-Following and the 'Antinomy of Pure Reason.'" *Philosophical Quarterly* **65**: 396–416.
Miller, A. (2018). *The Philosophy of Language*. London, Routledge.
Miller, A. (2024). *Wittgenstein and the Possibility of Meaning: "To Follow a Rule Blindly."* Oxford, Oxford University Press.
Miller, D. T. and D. A. Prentice (1994). "Collective Errors and Errors about the Collective." *Personality and Social Psychology Bulletin* **20**: 541–50.
Miller, D. T. and D. A. Prentice (1996). The Construction of Social Norms and Standards. *Social Psychology: Handbook of Basic Principles*. E. T. Higgins and A. W. Kruglanski. New York, Guilford Press: 799–829.
Millikan, R. (1984). *Language, Thought and Other Biological Categories*. Cambridge, Mass., MIT Press.
Mole, C., D. Smithies and W. Wu, Eds. (2011). *Attention: Philosophical and Psychological Essays*. Oxford, Oxford University Press.
Moore, G. E. (1911). *Ethics*. Oxford, Oxford University Press.

Moore, R. (2016). "Meaning and Ostension in Great Ape Gestural Communication." *Animal Cognition* **19**: 223–31.
Moore, R. (2017). "Gricean Communication and Cognitive Development." *The Philosophical Quarterly* **67**: 303–26.
Moran, R. (1997). "Self-Knowledge: Discovery, Resolution, and Undoing." *European Journal of Philosophy* Vol. **5**: 141–61.
Nagel, T. (1979). *Mortal Questions*. Cambridge, Cambridge University Press.
Neale, S. (1992). "Paul Grice and the Philosophy of Language." *Linguistics and Philosophy* **15**: 509–59.
Nesse, R. M. (2001). Natural Selection and the Capacity for Commitment. *Evolution and the Capacity for Commitment*. R. M. Nesse. New York, Russell Sage: 1–44.
Nietzsche, F. (1997). *On the Genealogy of Morals*. Cambridge, Cambridge University Press.
Nowak, M. (2006). "Five Rules for the Evolution of Cooperation." *Science* **314**: 1560–63.
Nussbaum, M. C. (2011). *Creating Capabilities: The Human Development Approach*. Cambridge, Mass., Harvard University Press.
O'Connor, C. (2019). *The Origins of Unfairness: Social Categories and Cultural Evolution*. Oxford, Oxford University Press.
O'Neill, O. (2013). *Acting on Principle: An Essay on Kantian Ethics* 2nd ed. Cambridge, Cambridge University Press.
Olsaretti, S. (2004). *Liberty, Desert and the Market*. Cambridge, Cambridge University Press.
Origgi, G. (2018). *Reputation: What it Is and Why it Matters*. Princeton, Princeton University Press.
Parfit, D. (1973). Later Selves and Moral Principles. *Philosophy and Personal Relations*. A. Montefiore. London, Routledge: 137–69.
Parfit, D. (1984). *Reasons and Persons*. Oxford, Oxford University Press.
Paul, L. A. (2014). *Transformative Experience*. Oxford, Oxford University Press.
Peacocke, C. (1983). *Sense and Content*. Oxford, Oxford University Press.
Perner, J. (1991). *Understanding the Representational Mind*. Cambridge, Mass., MIT Press.
Perry, J. (1979). "The Essential Indexical." *Nous* **13**: 3–21.
Perry, J., Ed. (2008). *Personal Identity*. Berkeley, CA, University of California Press.
Pettit, P. (1986). "Free Riding and Foul Dealing." *Journal of Philosophy* **83**: 361–79.
Pettit, P. (1990). "*Virtus Normativa*: Rational Choice Perspectives." *Ethics* **100**: 725–55; reprinted in P. Pettit, 2002, *Rules, Reasons, and Norms*. Oxford, Oxford University Press.
Pettit, P. (1991). Decision Theory and Folk Psychology. *Essays in the Foundations of Decision Theory*. M. Bacharach and S. Hurley. Oxford, Blackwell; reprinted in P. Pettit, 2002, *Rules, Reasons, and Norms*. Oxford, Oxford University Press.
Pettit, P. (1993). *The Common Mind: An Essay on Psychology, Society and Politics*, paperback edition 1996, New York, Oxford University Press.
Pettit, P. (1997). *Republicanism: A Theory of Freedom and Government*. Oxford, Oxford University Press.
Pettit, P. (1999). "A Theory of Normal and Ideal Conditions." *Philosophical Studies* **96**: 21–44; reprinted in P. Pettit, 2002, *Rules, Reasons, and Norms*. Oxford, Oxford University Press.
Pettit, P. (2002). *Rules, Reasons, and Norms: Selected Essays*. Oxford, Oxford University Press.
Pettit, P. (2003). "Looks as Powers." *Philosophical Issues* (supp. to *Nous*) **13**: 221–52.
Pettit, P. (2004a). Motion Blindness and the Knowledge Argument. *The Knowledge Argument*. P. Ludlow, Y. Nagasawa, and D. Stoljar. Cambridge, Mass., MIT Press: 105–42.
Pettit, P. (2004b). *Rules, Reasons and Norms: Selected Essays*. Oxford, Oxford University Press.
Pettit, P. (2006). Preference, Deliberation and Satisfaction. *Preferences and Well-being*. S. Olsaretti. Cambridge, Cambridge University Press: 131–53.
Pettit, P. (2007a). Joining the Dots. *Common Minds: Themes from the Philosophy of Philip Pettit*. H. G. Brennan, R. E. Goodin, F. C. Jackson, and M. Smith. Oxford, Oxford University Press: 215–344.
Pettit, P. (2007b). "Rationality, Reasoning and Group Agency." *Dialectica* **61**: 495–519.
Pettit, P. (2007c). "Responsibility Incorporated." *Ethics* **117**: 171–201.

Pettit, P. (2008a). *Made with Words: Hobbes on Language, Mind and Politics*. Princeton, Princeton University Press.
Pettit, P. (2008b). Value-mistaken and Virtue-mistaken Norms. *Political Legitimization without Morality?* J. Kuehnelt. New York, Springer: 139–56.
Pettit, P. (2012). "Freedom in Hobbes's Ontology and Semantics: A Comment on Quentin Skinner." *Journal of the History of Ideas* 73: 111–26.
Pettit, P. (2014). *Just Freedom: A Moral Compass for a Complex World*. New York, W. W. Norton and Co.
Pettit, P. (2015). *The Robust Demands of the Good: Ethics with Attachment, Virtue and Respect*. Oxford, Oxford University Press.
Pettit, P. (2016). "Broome on Reasoning and Rule-following." *Philosophical Studies* 173: 3373–84.
Pettit, P. (2017). The Program Model, Difference-makers, and the Exclusion Problem. *Making a Difference: Essays on the Philosophy of Causation*. H. Beebee, C. Hitchcock, and H. Price. Oxford, Oxford University Press: 232–50.
Pettit, P. (2018a). *The Birth of Ethics: Reconstructing the Role and Nature of Morality*. Oxford, Oxford University Press.
Pettit, P. (2018b). "Consciousness Incorporated." *Journal of Social Philosophy* 49: 12–37.
Pettit, P. (2018c). "Naturalizing Tomasello's History of Morality." *Philosophical Psychology* 31: 722–35.
Pettit, P. (2018d). "Three Mistakes about Doing Good (and Bad)." *Journal of Applied Philosophy* 35: 1–25.
Pettit, P. (2019). "Social Norms and the Internal Point of View." *Oxford Journal of Legal Studies* 39: 229–58.
Pettit, P. (2020). Analyzing Concepts and Allocating Referents. *Conceptual Engineering and Conceptual Ethics*. A. Burgess, H. Cappelen, and D. Plunkett. Oxford, Oxford University Press: 333–57.
Pettit, P. (2023a). A Pragmatic Genealogy of Rule-following. *Neo-Pragmatism in Practice*. J. Gert. Oxford, Oxford University Press: 140–69.
Pettit, P. (2023b). *The State*. Princeton, NJ, Princeton University Press.
Pettit, P. and M. Smith (1990). "Backgrounding Desire." *Philosophical Review* 99: 565–92; reprinted in F. Jackson, P. Pettit, and M. Smith, 2004, *Mind, Morality and Explanation*. Oxford, Oxford University Press.
Pettit, P. and M. Smith (1996). "Freedom in Belief and Desire." *Journal of Philosophy* 93: 429–49; reprinted in F. Jackson, P. Pettit, and M. Smith, 2004, *Mind, Morality and Explanation*. Oxford, Oxford University Press.
Phillips, I. (2016). "Consciousness and Criterion: On Block's Case for Unconscious Seeing." *Philosophy and Phenomenological Research* 93: 419–51.
Phillips, I. (2021). "Scepticism about Unconscious Perception Is the Default Hypothesis." *Journal of Consciousness Studies* 28: 186–205.
Planer, R. J. and K. Sterelny (2021). *From Signals to Symbols: The Evolution of Language*. Cambridge, Mass., MIT Press.
Premack, D. and G. Woodruff (1978). "Does the Chimpanzee Have a Theory of Mind?" *Brain and Behavioral Sciences* 4: 515–26.
Priest, G. (2008). *An Introduction to Non-Classical Logic*. Cambridge, Cambridge University Press.
Queloz, M. (2021). *The Practical Origins of Ideas: Genealogy as Conceptual Reverse-Engineering*. Oxford, Oxford University Press.
Quine, W. V. O. (1970). *Word & Object*. Cambridge, MIT Press.
Quine, W. V. O. and J. S. Ullian (1978). *The Web of Belief*. New York, McGraw-Hill.
Quinn, W. (1993). *Morality and Action*. Cambridge, Cambridge University Press.
Radick, G. (2007). *The Simian Tongue: The Long Debate about Animal Language*. Chicago, University of Chicago Press.
Railton, P. (2014). "Reliance, Trust, and Belief." *Inquiry* 57: 122–50.
Rawls, J. (1993). *Political Liberalism*. New York, Columbia University Press.

Rawls, J. (2001). *Justice as Fairness: A Restatement*. Cambridge, Mass., Harvard University Press.
Renfrew, C. (2007). *Prehistory: The Making of the Human Mind*. New York, Modern Library, Random House,.
Ricoeur, P. (1966). *Freedom and Nature: The Voluntary and the Involuntary*. Evanston, Ill., Northwestern University Press.
Rogers, B. (2017). *Perception: A Very Short Introduction*. Oxford, Oxford University Press.
Rosen, G. (2010). Metaphysical Dependence: Grounding and Reduction. *Modality: Metaphysics, Logic, and Epistemology*. B. Hale and A. Hoffman. New York, Oxford University Press: 109–35.
Rosen, G. (2015). The Alethic Conception of Moral Responsibility. *The Nature of Moral Responsibility: New Essays*. R. Clarke, M. McKenna, and A. M. Smith. New York, Oxford University Press: 65–88.
Rousseau, J. J. (2020). *Emile*. New York, Public Domain Books, Kindle ed.
Ryle, G. (1949). *The Concept of Mind*. Chicago, University of Chicago Press.
Rysiew, P. (2016). *Stanford Encyclopedia of Philosophy*. E. N. Zalta.
Sapolsky, R. M. (2023). *Determined: A Science of Life without Free Will*. New York, Penguin Books.
Sartre, J. P. (1948). *Portrait of the Anti-Semite*. London, Secker and Warburg.
Sartre, J. P. (1957). *The Transcendence of the Ego: An Existentialist Theory of Consciousness*. New York, Farrar, Straus and Giroux.
Sartre, J. P. (1958). *Being and Nothingness*. London, Methuen.
Scanlon, T. M. (1998). *What We Owe To Each Other*. Cambridge, Mass, Harvard University Press.
Scanlon, T. M. (2008). *Moral Dimensions: Permissibility, Meaning, Blame*. Cambridge, Mass, Harvard University Press.
Schechtman, M. (1997). *The Constitution of Selves*. Ithaca, NY, Cornell University Press.
Schechtman, M. (2014). *Staying Alive: Personal Identity, Practical Concerns and the Unity of a Life*. Oxford, Oxford University Press.
Scheffler, S. (2003). "What is Egalitarianism?" *Philosophy and Public Affairs* **31**: 5–39.
Scheffler, S. (2010). *Equality and Tradition: Questions of Value in Moral and Political Theory*. Oxford, Oxford University Press.
Scott, J. C. (2017). *Against the Grain: A Deep History of the Earliest States*. New Haven, Conn, Yale University Press.
Scott-Phillips, T. C. (2015). *Speaking our Minds: Why Human Communication Is Different, and how Language Evolved to Make it Special*. London, Palgrave Macmillan.
Searle, J. (2010). *Making the Social World: The Structure of Human Civilization*. Oxford, Oxford University Press.
Sellars, W. (1997). *Empiricism and the Philosophy of Mind*. Cambridge, Mass., Harvard University Press.
Sen, A. (1983). "Poor, Relatively Speaking." *Oxford Economic Papers* **35**: 153–68.
Sen, A. (1985). *Commodities and Capabilities*. Amsterdam, North-Holland.
Seyfarth, R. M. and D. L. Cheney (1984). "Grooming, Alliances and Reciprocal Altruism in Vervet Monkeys." *Nature* **308**: 541–43.
Shapiro, S. (2011). *Legality*. Cambridge, Mass., Harvard University Press.
Shoemaker, D. (2015). *Responsibility from the Margins*. Oxford, Oxford University Press.
Sidney, A. (1990). *Discourses Concerning Government*. Indianapolis, Liberty Classics.
Siegel, S. (2016). The Contents of Perception. *Stanford Encyclopedia of Philosophy*. E. N. Zalta.
Siegel, S. and A. Byrne (2016). Rich or Thin? *Current Controversies in the Philosophy of Perception*. B. Nanny. London, Routledge: 59–80.
Skinner, Q. (1998). *Liberty Before Liberalism*. Cambridge, Cambridge University Press.
Skinner, Q. (2008). *Hobbes and Republican Liberty*. Cambridge, Cambridge University Press.
Skyrms, B. (2010). *Signals: Evolution, Learning, and Information*. Oxford, Oxford University Press.
Smith, A. M. (2012). "Attributability, Answerability, and Accountability: In Defense of a Unified Account." *Ethics* **122**: 575–89.
Smith, M. (1987). "The Humean Theory of Motivation." *Mind* **96**: 36–61.
Smith, M. (1994). *The Moral Problem*. Oxford, Blackwell.

Smith, M. (2003). Rational Capacities, or: How to Distinguish Recklessness, Weakness and Compulsion. *Weakness of Will and Practical Irrationality*. S. Stroud and C. Tappolet. Oxford, Oxford University Press: 17–38.
Sober, E. and D. S. Wilson (1998). *Unto Others: The Evolution and Psychology of Unselfish Behavior*. Cambridge, Mass., Harvard University Press.
Soteriou, M. (2020). The Disjunctive Theory of Perception. *Stanford Encyclopedia of Philosophy*. E. N. Zalta.
Sperber, D., D. Premack, and A. J. Premack, Eds. (1996). *Causal Cognition: A Multidisciplinary Debate*. Oxford, Oxford University Press.
Sperber, D. and D. Wilson (1986). *Relevance: Communication and Cognition*. Oxford, Blackwell.
Stalnaker, R. (1978). Assertion. Syntax and Semantics. P. Cole. New York, Academic Press 9: 315–23.
Stalnaker, R. C. (1984). *Inquiry*. Cambridge, Mass., MIT Press.
Stanley, J. (2005). *Knowledge and Practical Interests*. Oxford, Oxford University Press.
Sterelny, K. (2012). *The Evolved Apprentice: How Evolution Made Humans Unique*. Cambridge, Mass., MIT Press.
Steward, H. (2012). *A Metaphysics for Freedom*. Oxford, Oxford University Press.
Stoljar, D. (2006). *Ignorance and Imagination: The Epistemic Origin of the Problem of Consciousness*. Oxford, Oxford University Press.
Stoljar, D. (2016). "The Semantics of 'What is is Like' and the Nature of Consciousness." *Mind* 125: 1161–98.
Stoljar, D. (Forthcoming). A Euthyphro Dilemma for Higher-order Theories of Consciousness. *Grounding and Consciousness*. G. Rabin. Oxford, Oxford University Press.
Strawson, G. (2003). "Mental Ballistics: The Involuntariness of Spontaneity." *Proceedings of the Aristotelian Society* 103: 227–56.
Strawson, G. (2008). *Real Materialism and Other Essays*. Oxford, Oxford University Press.
Strawson, G. (2009). *Selves: An Essay in Revisionary Metaphysics*. Oxford, Oxford University Press.
Strawson, G. (2010). "Narrativity and Non-narrativity." *Wiley Interdisciplinary Reviews: Cognitive Science* 6(1): 775–80.
Strawson, G. (2024). *Consciousness and its Place in Nature*. Exeter, Imprint Academic.
Strawson, P. (1962). *Freedom and Resentment and Other Essays*. London, Methuen.
Strawson, P. (1964). "Intention and Convention in Speech Acts." *Philosophical Review* 73: 439–60.
Strawson, P. F. (1959). *Individuals*. London, Methuen.
Swindlehurst, Z. M. (2020). "Blind Rule-following and the Regress of Motivations." *Inquiry* 66(6): 1170–83.
Taylor, C. (1989). *Sources of the Self: The Making of the Modern Identity*. Cambridge, Cambridge University Press.
Tomasello, M. (2009). *Why We Cooperate*. Cambridge, Mass., MIT Press.
Tomasello, M. (2014). *A Natural History of Human Thinking*. Cambridge, Mass., Harvard University Press.
Tomasello, M. (2016). *A Natural History of Human Morality*. Cambridge, Mass., Harvard University Press.
Tomasello, M. (2022). "What Is it Like to Be a Chimpanzee?" *Synthese* 200(2): 1–24.
Tuomela, R. (2007). *The Philosophy of Sociality: The Shared Point of View*. Oxford, Oxford University Press.
Turner, C. R. and L. D. Walmsley (2020). "Preparedness in Cultural Learning." *Synthese* 199(1–2): 81–100.
Ullman-Margalit, E. and S. Morgenbesser (1977). "Picking and Choosing." *Social Research* 44: 757–85.
Velleman, D. (2001). "The Genesis of Shame." *Philosophy and Public Affairs* 30: 27–52.
Velleman, J. D. (2020). *Self to Self: Selected Essays*. Ann Arbor, MI, Michigan Publishing.
Vetter, B. (2022). An Agency-based Epistemology of Modality. *Epistemology of Modality and Philosophical Methodology*. A. J. Vaidya and D. Prelević. London, Routledge: 44–69.

Wallace, R. J. (1996). *Responsibility and the Moral Sentiments*. Cambridge, Mass., Harvard University Press.
Watson, G. (1975). "Free Agency." *Journal of Philosophy* 72: 205–20.
Watson, G. (1996). "Two Faces of Responsibility." *Philosophical Topics* 24: 227–48.
Watzl, S. (2017). *Structuring Mind: The Nature of Attention and How it Shapes Consciousness*. Oxford, Oxford University Press.
Weiskrantz, L. (1986). *Blindsight: A Case Study and Implications*. Oxford, Oxford University Press.
Williams, B. (1978). *Descartes*. Harmondsworth, Penguin.
Williams, B. (1995). *Making Sense of Humanity*. Cambridge, Cambridge University Press.
Williams, B. (2002). *Truth and Truthfulness*. Princeton, Princeton University Press.
Williamson, T. (1996). "Knowing and Asserting." *Philosophical Review* 105: 489–523.
Williamson, T. (2000). *Knowledge and its Limits*. Oxford, Oxford University Press.
Wimmer, H. and J. Perner (1983). "Beliefs about Beliefs: Representation and Constraining Function of Wrong Beliefs in Your Children's Understanding of Deception." *Cognition* 13: 103–28.
Winch, P. (1963). *The Idea of a Social Science and Its Relation to Philosophy*. London, Routledge.
Winters, S., C. Dubuc, and J. P. Higham (2015). "Perspectives: The Looking Time Experimental Paradigm in Studies of Animal Visual Perception and Cognition." *Ethology* 121: 625–40.
Wittgenstein, L. (1958). *Philosophical Investigations*. Oxford, Blackwell.
Wittgenstein, L. (1978). *Remarks on the Foundations of Mathematics*. Oxford, Blackwell.
Wolf, S. (1990). *Freedom within Reason*. Oxford, Oxford University Press.
Wright, C. (1980). *Wittgenstein on the Foundations of Mathematics*. London, Duckworth.
Wright, C. (1992). *Truth and Objectivity*. Cambridge, Mass., Harvard University Press.
Wright, C. (2012). Replies Part I: The Rule-following Considerations and the Normativity of Meaning. *Mind, Meaning and Knowledge: Essays for Crispin Wright*. A. Coliva. Oxford, Oxford University Press: 379–401.
Wu, W. (2023). "We Know What Attention Is!" *Trends in Cognitive Science* 28(4): 304–18.
Xenophon (2006). *Hiero the Tyrant and Other Treatises*. London, Penguin.
Yamamoto, S., T. Humle, and M. Tanaka (2009). "Chimpanzees Help Each Other upon Request." *PLOS One* 4(10): https://doi.org/10.1371/annotation/80db4649-46c1-40af-851b-f01968eec5d7.
Yamamoto, S., T. Humle, and M. Tanaka (2012). "Chimpanzees' Flexible Targeted Helping Based on an Understanding of Conspecifics' Goals." *Proceedings of the National Academy of Sciences* 109: 3588–92.
Yong, E. (2022). *An Immense World: How Animal Senses Reveal the Hidden Realms around Us*. New York, Random House.
Zahavi, A. and A. Zahavi (1999). *The Handicap Principle: A Missing Piece of Darwin's Puzzle*. Oxford, Oxford University Press.
Zarka, Y. C. (1995). *Hobbes et la pensee politique moderne*. Paris, Presses Universitaires de France.
Zawidzki, T. W. (2013). *Mindshaping: A New Framework for Understanding Human Social Cognition*. Cambridge, Mass., MIT Press.

Index

For the benefit of digital users, indexed terms that span two pages (e.g., 52–53) may, on occasion, appear on only one of those pages.

action, -s
  intentional 33–34, 55–57, 97, 102
  undesirable 211–17
activities, pro-conversive 309–10, 313
aesthetics 153–55
agency
  agential skills, teaching 23–24
  basic 50–57
  communicative 24–26
  functionalist model 53–55
  human 50–57
  individual 222
  judgment and 49–92
  perceiving 21–22
  rationality and 94–95
  sharing 22–23
  simple model of 50–53
agents, artificially intelligent xii
akrasia 69n.20, 141, 218, 231, 251
Anscombe, Elizabeth 79, 303n.1
Aquinas, Thomas 259
Aristotle xi–xii
arithmetical practice xiii
assertion, -s
  belief and 68–70
  false 66–67
  judgment and 14, 20, 67–72, 83–86, 104–5, 106, 168, 303, 318
  stakes-sensitivity of 83–86
  truthful 68–73
assumptions
  applicational 37
  causal and factual 109–10
  guiding 38, 66
  normative 258, 279–80
  shared 124, 321
attention 131–66
attitudes, avowing and reporting 183–84
autonomy
  cognitive 77, 117
  epistemic 15
  ideal of 283–84
  thinking and 76–78
avowal 183–89

Ballad of Reading Gaol (poem) 295 *see also* Wilde, Oscar.
belief, -s
  assertion and 68–70
  automatic adjustment of xiv, 318, 319
  belief-to-action condition 95
  binary 87, 89–90, 91–92, 96–98
  common 62–63, 64–65, 110–11, 123–24, 179, 181, 192
  consciousness-in-belief 156, 162, 323
  credence and 82–83, 88–90
  degrees of 81–92
  evidence-to-belief condition 95
  formation of xiv, 1–2, 14, 18, 33–34, 40–42, 52, 58–59, 67, 76, 89–90, 92, 101–6, 108, 146, 157, 158, 160, 265–67, 319, 335
  meta-propositional 98, 100, 102, 119
  ratification of 73–75, 131
  shared 110–11, 124, 194
benefits
  collective 205–6, 219, 327
  valued 221–22
bias, confirmation 112
blame-lifting 215, 227
blameworthiness 209–11, 235–38
blind-sensed subjects 158, 159
blindsight 158
Boethius 259, 261, 268
Borges, Jorge Luis 40n.35, 288
Bratman, Michael 5n.2, 81, 198–99
Broome, John 98–99

capacities
  human-specific 1–4
  processing xiv–xv, 3, 20, 168, 207
  relational xiv, xv, xix–xx, 2, 169, 303, 315
  targeted xiv–xv, 7–9
chimpanzees 25–26, 58
closure 95, 97–98, 116, 121
Cogito ergo sum 291 *see also* Descartes, René.
cognitive autonomy 77, 117
cognitive rationality 52, 94–95, 278–79

354 INDEX

commitment, -s
  making 2, 168, 195–96, 219–20, 233–34, 257, 273, 275, 280, 281, 284, 297, 303, 333, 335
  mutual 168, 276–78
  partial 240
  self-commitment 195–97, 240, 328
  value and 197–206
  virtual 189, 194, 212, 331
communication
  active 308
  advent of 207
  developing xii
  features of 24
  forms and modes of 24–25, 184
  intentional 24
  language of xii, 26
  linguistic 36, 124–25
  nature of 25
  resources of 124
confirmation bias 112
consciousness
  belief, in 156, 162, 323
  feel, with and without 156–57
  perception, in and of 157–58, 159–65
  perceptual and percipient 11–12, 132, 155–66, 324
  phenomenal 157, 157n.14, 163
  self-consciousness 259, 264, 268
  two sorts of 155–56
conventions 171–73
  counterfactual world without 6
  cultural 22
  emergence and evolution of 6–7, 11, 124–25, 204, 310
  function of 4, 6
  genealogy of 30–31
  nature of 6
  property 204
conversability, demands of 308, 309–10
Copernicus, Nicolaus 153
corporate agency 254n.28, 276–77
counterfactual
  capacities xix
  genealogy xvii, 5, 8, 10, 18
  humanoids 167–69
  model 6
  observation 7
  world 6
credences 81, 82–83, 86–87, 88–90, 91, 96–97
cultural development 10, 22–23
curiosity, thinking and 76

decimal system xii–xiii
decision theory 81, 83, 91–92

demystifying effects 6, 12, 15, 18
Dennett, Daniel 21–22, 54, 259, 268, 269, 279
depersonalization 310, 315
Descartes, René xviii–xix, 4, 8, 11–12, 291
desiderata 78–81, 90, 95, 97–98, 116, 121, 122–23, 131, 167, 186–87, 189–90, 193, 195, 198, 200–3, 205, 214, 219, 221–22, 272, 279, 318, 327, 329–30
desire
  addictive 247–48
  avowing 186–88, 189
  compulsive or obsessive 227–28
dignity 281–83
disagreement, reconciliation and 66–67
disciplinary power 220, 221–22
discretion requirement 193–95
divergence, negotiating 111–13, 130, 151, 323
Dretske, Fred 137n.4, 159–60
Dummett, Michael xvii

egalitarian
  conditions 7–8, 302, 303
  societies 204–5, 220n.11
  subgroups 20, 301–2
  world 6
Einstein, Albert ix, 272
Elster, Jon 299–300
epistemic
  autonomy 15
  normativity 168
epistemology 291–92, 296–97, 298–300
equality 303–6
esteem, economy of 19, 20, 60–62, 64, 168, 169–83, 184–85, 204, 301
ethics 292–93, 297–300, 301–16, 337–39
  politics and xix–xx, 19–20, 301–16, 317, 337–39
  self, of the 286, 292, 294, 296, 297–300
evidence
  concept of 51–52, 67, 73–74, 93, 97, 319
  evidence-to-belief condition 95
  identification problem, the 105–8
  investment problem, the 109–11
  misleading 184–85
  relevant 56, 69–70, 75, 93–94, 97, 108, 111–12
  responsiveness to 93
  sufficient 99–100, 150
  suitable 74–75, 81, 214
  testimonial 65n.19
exercise, spheres of 2–3
exhortation
  active 226–27, 234–35, 257
  self-exhortation 233–34, 240, 245, 246–47, 248, 250–52, 254, 257, 332–33, 335

INDEX   355

factual assumption 109–10
Frankfurt, Harry 198–99, 210, 247–48, 264–65, 283–84, 297
freedom 310–15
  conceptions of 311–13
  Freedom and Resentment (paper) 242 *see also* Strawson, Peter.
  norms, under 314–15
  robustness, dispositions, and constraints 313–14
free will 207–56
  constituting 243–52
  ought-first and can-first approach 241–43
  social embedding of 255–56
  willpower, as 253–55
Freud, Sigmund 150

gambler's fallacy 69, 71, 93, 183–84, 239
genealogy
  conventions, of 30–31
  counterfactual xvii, 5, 8, 10, 18
  demystification and 11–15
  extending 72–74
  history and 9–11
  judgment, of 74
  methodology xv–xvii
  morals, of 6–7
  norms, of 173, 176–77, 182
  project 4–18
  repurposing 301–3
genetic assimilation 10, 11n.7, 21n.13, 22–23, 174n.7
goals xii, 18–19, 21–23, 50, 52, 74, 85, 117, 142, 161, 240, 278–79, 299, 301, 319
  common and shared 109–10, 240
gossip 61, 85, 174–75, 287–88, 299
Grice, Paul 24–25, 64

hallucination 137n.4, 139n.5
Hamlet (play) 297–98 *see also* Shakespeare, William.
Hart, Herbert 6–8, 11
Hawking, Stephen xi–xii
hierarchy
  common awareness, of 175
  domination, of 204–5
  societal 19–21, 169, 172, 204–5, 220, 301–2, 304, 325, 337
Hobbes, Thomas xviii–xix, xxi, 4, 8–9, 41, 76, 176, 180, 196–97, 273–74, 276–79, 316
Honneth, Axel 306
humanoids
  character of 18–26
  indictment 237–38
  interaction, context of 19–21
  organisms and agents, as 18–19
  responsibility in 218–40
Hume, David 52–53, 243, 246, 250n.26, 291, 336

imagining 17–18, 49, 164, 172
indexical speech and thought 13–15, 32–33, 58, 256, 266–67, 286
informational exchange 59–60, 64–65
information-sharing 62–63
injunctive demand 170–71, 178, 180, 181, 217
intentional action 33–34, 55–57, 97, 102
interiorization xii, xv, xvii–xix, 4, 8, 49–50, 72, 74, 94, 104, 116–17, 147–48, 167, 181, 233–34, 275–76, 301–2, 318, 321, 325, 328, 330, 332

judging
  believing, as a means to 74–76
  thinking and 72–81
judgment, -s 318–19
  agency and 49–92
  assertion and 14, 20, 67–72, 83–86, 104–5, 106, 168, 303, 318
  practical 78, 81, 102–3, 104, 122–23, 131, 318
  reasoned 93–94, 101–2, 104, 115, 131, 144, 146–47, 158, 167, 257, 279, 295, 303, 322
  reasoning and xii, xiv–xv, 1, 11–12, 94, 130, 131–34, 142–43, 147–48, 150, 152–53, 166, 168, 207, 258, 302, 304, 321, 322, 324, 337–38
  reinforcing 104–14
  rules in 130
  stakes-sensitivity of 83–86

Kant, Immanuel xiv, 182–83, 248–49, 259–65, 281, 283–84, 292, 300
knowledge
  ascription of 4n.1
  concept of 29n.24
  generation of 76
  scientific 166n.18
  self-knowledge 296n.21, 297
Kripke, Saul 35, 36–39, 45

language
  access to xiii–xiv, xx, xxi, 8, 9, 21, 24, 35–36, 48, 93, 106, 146, 150–51, 325
  advent and introduction of xiii–xiv, xv–xvi, xvii, 5, 7–8, 9–10, 23–24, 27, 49, 57, 128, 144–45, 147–48, 167, 174n.7, 207, 301, 322
  communication, capacity for 93, 259, 279
  conversive xvi, 317
  human xiii, xv–xvi, 32, 33–34

language (*cont.*)
  induction in 144
  mastery of 33, 57
  natural xiii, 1, 14, 24–25, 26, 34
  necessity and sufficiency of 33–34
  non-indexical 13–14
  percipience, and eliciting of 167, 207
  practices, language-dependent xviii
  reason, and capacity to 319, 321–22
  science, language of 17
  simple form of 1, 9–10, 27, 33, 35, 48
  verbal xiii
laws 171–73
Lewis, David 6–8, 11, 30–31, 54, 119n.14
linguistic tuning 145–46
Locke, John 259–60, 261, 265, 268–70, 290

MacIntyre, Alasdair 264
Martin, Michael 139n.5
mathematical notation xiii–xiv
memory 49, 68, 77, 93, 97, 105, 136, 286–87, 289–91, 292, 293
metaphysics xvi–xvii, 9, 15–18, 47–48, 135, 288, 289–91, 294–96, 298–300, 316
  demystification and 15–18
mind, human xi–xii, xiv, xviii–xix, 4, 317
modus ponens principle 118–19
Morgenbesser, Sidney xix

Nagel, Thomas 157, 165–66
narrativity claim 264–65
naturalism 11–18, 132–33, 166, 218, 241, 244, 251–54
  non-naturalism 15, 132–33, 218, 241, 244, 249, 251
Newton, Sir Isaac 272
Nietzsche, Friedrich 6–8, 170
non-identification 265, 266–67, 335
normativity xvi, xix, 8, 27, 33–34, 67, 81, 100, 167–206, 317, 325–28
  epistemic 168
  functional 169–70
  injunctive 114, 168, 169–83
  prudential 169–70
  rational 114
  reputational 168
  value and 167–206
norms 171–73
  assumptions, normative 258, 279–80
  case of 192–93
  commitments and 183–97
  freedom under 314–15
  genealogy of 173, 176–77, 182
  information-sharing 62–63

  internalized 178
  moral 203–6
  property, of respect for 204
  shared 194–95, 207, 220–21, 232, 233–34, 235, 238–39, 240, 272–73, 280, 281–82, 284, 297–98, 304–5, 307–8, 309, 314, 325, 329, 332
  social 2, 63, 173–83, 202–6, 207, 218–19, 257, 272, 325, 327–28

ought-first and can-first approaches to free will 241–43

Parfit, Derek 270, 290, 292–93, 296
perception
  attentive 163
  blind 158
  consciousness, perceptual and percipient 11–12, 132, 155–66, 324
  consciousness-in-perception 157–62, 164–66, 323–24
  consciousness-of-perception 157–58, 162–66, 324
  general account of 133–42
  high- and low-level 145
  humanoid 108n.12, 134, 151, 165–66
  non-percipient 161–62, 164–65
  percipience, with 131–66
  presentational, as 133–35
  quasi 158, 162–63
  recruiting 142–43
  veridical 139n.5
percipience xiv–xv, xvi, xix, 1–2, 8, 11–12, 27, 33–34, 131–66, 167–69, 207, 257–58, 301, 317, 321–24
  advent of 142–55
  aesthetics, speculation, and 153–55
  consciousness and 155–66
  perception with 131–66
  perception, non-percipient 161–62, 164–65
  percipient consciousness 11–12, 132, 155–66, 324
persona xv, xviii, 2, 3, 273, 275, 278, 280–81, 285–89, 294–97, 298, 303, 308, 333–34, 336
personation 258, 270–86, 294, 296–300, 303, 333–34, 335–36
  social and mental 275–76
personhood xvi, xix, 8, 12, 27, 33–34, 168–69, 257–300, 303–4, 317, 333–37
  corporate 276–78
  depersonalization 310, 315
  elements of 258–59
  free will and, link between 264
  ideal of 262–65

personation and 270–86
self-identity and 257–300
self-representation and, link between 273–75
persons
  capacities of 259
  conversable 303–4
  corporate 276–78, 281, 282–83, 293
  dignity of 261–62, 282–83
  idea of 258–70
  nature and self-identity of 265–70
  responsibility of 260
  selves, and 286–300
  surefire self-reference in 267–68
phenomenal consciousness 157, 157n.14, 163
philosophical theory 243, 265
pledging 190–92
politics 301–16, 337–39
  ethics and xix–xx, 19–20, 301–16, 317, 337–39
"Portrait of the Antisemite" (essay) 288 *see also* Sartre, Jean-Paul.
probabilities 81, 87, 114
processing capacities xiv–xv, 3, 20, 168, 207
pro-conversive activities and behaviours 309–10, 313
properties, tagging 35–36, 39–40, 42–45

Quinn, Warren 79

rationality
  agency and 94–95
  blind 96, 103
  cognitive 52–53, 94–95, 278–79
  reasoning, and 93–130
Rawls, John 111n.13, 262
reasoned judgment 93–94, 101–2, 104, 115, 131, 144, 146–47, 158, 167, 257, 279, 295, 303, 322
reasoning 319–21
  active 1–2, 101–2, 118–19, 322
  actual-world 99–100
  applicational theory of 127–28
  deductive 102–3, 121, 128
  discussion of 63, 67
  effortless 118–19
  following rules in 125–27
  implementational model of 128–30
  interpretive 120, 123–25
  judgment and xii, xiv–xv, 1, 11–12, 94, 130, 131–34, 142–43, 147–48, 150, 152–53, 166, 168, 207, 258, 302, 304, 321, 322, 324, 337–38
  mental 100–1, 117–18
  parallel 87

practical 114, 120, 122–23, 261
probabilistic 102–3, 120–22
rationality and 94–104
rules of 125–27, 130, 317
social 116–17
social and mental 114–18
theoretical 102–3, 104, 114, 120, 122–23
utility of 100–3
varieties of 120–25
Reformation, the 259
relational capacities xiv, xv, xix–xx, 2, 169, 303, 315
respect 306–10
  connotations of 307–8
  recognitional 306–7
responsibility 238–40, 328–33
  ascription of 279–81
  blaming, practice of 235–38
  colour, analogy with the perception of 224–27
  commitment, control, and discipline 219–20
  exhortation 222–33
  free will and 207–56
  humanoids, in 218–40
  notion of 208–18
  scaffolding 222–24
  sensitization 222–24
  should-and-could-have response, extending 233–35
robots xii, 50–53, 54–55, 67, 96, 103, 105–6, 266–67, 286–87, 291, 335
Roman numerals xii–xiii
Roman republic 311–12
Rousseau, Jean-Jacques xviiin.5, 293, 300, 316
rule-following 36–45, 46–48
  assertion and judgment, signs in 125–26
  basic 94, 127, 129–30
  exercise of 127–28
  problem 146, 317
  reasoning, in 125–27
  signalling, in 126–27
rules
  implementing 38
  judgment, in 130
  reasoning, in 125–27, 130, 317
  role of 125–30
  signalling, of 126

Sartre, Jean-Paul xx, 288, 291
savants 97, 117, 131, 319
Scanlon, Thomas Michael 13
self
  abstract 286–93
  authorized 286–89, 294–98
  imposed 286–89, 298–300

self-commitment 195–97
self-consciousness 259, 264, 268
self-identity 257–300
self-knowledge 296n.21, 297
self-representation xv, 2, 272–76, 277–78
  personhood and, link between 273–75
Sellars, Wilfred 4n.1, 148
Shakespeare, William 297
Siegel, Susanna 148
signalling 28, 29–30, 31, 35, 36, 39–40, 47–48, 57–67, 124–27, 129–30
  asserting and 57–67
  informing and 57–59
  intentional 29–30
  non-intentional 28–29
  rule-following in 127
  rules of 126
  speech and 26–34
sincerity 2–3, 4n.1, 62, 68–69, 74, 116, 185, 195–96, 273, 288–89, 334
Smith, Michael 198–99, 218n.10
social
  capacity 49
  language xviii, 10
  norms 2, 63, 173–83, 202–6, 207, 218–19, 257, 272, 325, 327–28
  practices xvii–xix, xxi, 4, 10, 11–12, 49–50, 74, 116, 233–34, 256, 271, 321, 328, 332
  pressure 193, 194
  reasoning 116–17, 120
  relationships 257
society, hierarchical 19–21, 169, 172, 204–5, 220, 301–2, 304, 325, 337
Socrates 47, 127
soul, human xi–xii, xiv, xix, 4, 269, 278, 290, 317
speculation 153–55
speech
  acts 69, 124, 208
  inner 117
  innovation in 124–25
  ironical modes of 124–25
  making sense of 124–25
  regulative 180
  signalling and 26–34
  thought and, indexical 13–15, 32–33, 58, 256, 266–67, 286
  unconventional forms of 321
stakes-sensitivity 63, 83–86, 121
Stalnaker, Robert 54
Sterelny, Kim 23–24
Strawson, Galen 102n.8, 264, 270n.9
Strawson, Peter 242
subjective probabilities 81
subjects, blind-sensed 158, 159

tagging 35–36, 39–40, 41–45, 46–47, 66–67
targeted capacities xiv–xv
Taylor, Charles 264
thinking
  autonomy and 76–78
  curiosity and 76
  desiderata 78–81
thought, *see* indexical speech and thought.
Tomasello, Michael 22–23, 24
truth telling 4n.1, 64, 216–17, 225, 228–32, 234–35, 246–47, 251, 327, 331
truthful assertions 68–73

value, -s 200–3
  commitment and 197–206
  desiderata and 200–2
  human life, in 198–99
  humanoid concepts of 207
valuing, practice of 199, 207, 327–28
Velleman, David 275–76, 287n.14
voluntariness 55n.8, 214–15n.6, 215, 227–28, 229–30, 330–31

Wilde, Oscar 295
Williams, Bernard 291
Wittgenstein, Ludwig 35, 36–38, 45

Yiddish *modus tollens* xix

Zarka, Yves Charles xviiin.6